NetWare 4 Network Design and Implementation

Dorothy L. Cady

New Riders

New Riders Publishing, Indianapolis, Indiana

NetWare 4 Network Design and Implementation

By Dorothy L. Cady

Published by:
New Riders Publishing
201 West 103rd Street
Indianapolis, IN 46290 USA

Printed in the United States of America 1 2 3 4 5 6 7 8 9 0

CIP data available upon request

Warning and Disclaimer

This book is designed to provide information about NetWare 4 network design and implementation. Every effort has been made to make this book as complete and as accurate as possible, but no warranty or fitness is implied.

The information is provided on an "as is" basis. The author(s) and New Riders Publishing shall have neither liability nor responsibility to any person or entity with respect to any loss or damages arising from the information contained in this book or from the use of the disks or programs that may accompany it.

Publisher Don Fowley
Publishing Manager Emmett Dulaney
Marketing Manager Ray Robinson
Managing Editor Carla Hall

Acquisitions Editor
Mary Foote
Development Editor
Emmett Dulaney
Production Editor
Nancy Albright
Associate Marketing Manager
Tamara Apple
Acquisitions Coordinator
Stacia Mellinger
Publisher's Assistant
Karen Opal
Cover Designer
Karen Ruggles
Book Designer
Gary Adair
Manufacturing Coordinator
Paul Gilchrist
Production Manager
Kelly Dobbs
Production Team Supervisor
Laurie Casey
Graphics Image Specialists
Sonja Hart
Clint Lahnen
Laura Robbins
Craig Small
Todd Wente
Production Analysts
Jason Hand
Bobbi Satterfield
Production Team
Angela Calvert
Kim Cofer
Tricia Flodder
Aleata Howard
Erika Millen
Christine Tyner
Karen Walsh
Indexers
Gina Brown
Jennifer Eberhardt

About the Author

Dorothy L. Cady is a former senior technical writer for Novell, Inc. in Provo, Utah. Ms. Cady started with Novell in 1990 as a team leader for the Software Testing Department's Documentation Testing Team, helping to ensure the quality of the documentation that ships with NetWare 2, 3, and 4, NetWare Lite, and Personal NetWare products.

Ms. Cady is a Certified Novell Instructor (CNI), a Certified Novell Engineer (CNE), a certified Novell Administrator (CNA), and an Enterprise CNE (ECNE).

Ms. Cady is now a freelance writer and instructor with over twenty years experience in the computer industry, both in private and public service. She also is the author of *CNA Study Guide* and *New Riders Guide to NetWare Certification*, as well as co-author of other New Riders books. She is also the author of *Bulletproof Documentation: Creating Quality Through Testing*.

Trademark Acknowledgments

Acknowledgments

The list is long of people who, besides myself, are responsible for the successful completion of many hours of work. I wish to acknowledge all of them by acknowledging all of you who put your faith, as well as your cold, hard cash in all of us. We hope you see this book as an open door of opportunity to your future, and that through your own diligence and motivation, you prove the words of Helen Keller to be ones which apply only in part (the good part, of course) to you:

When one door of happiness closes, another opens; but often we look so long at the closed door that we do not see the one which has been opened for us.

Contents at a Glance

Table of Contents

Introduction

Introduction Introduction Introduction Introduction

NetWare is the world's best-selling network operating system, outpacing most of its competitors by a wide margin. NetWare 4 is the latest version of the NetWare operating system, and it is far more complex and functional than any of its predecessors. NetWare 4 is so much more complex and functional, in fact, that many of today's existing NetWare administrators, computer Information System managers, corporate executives, and other individuals responsible for designing and implementing a NetWare 4 local area network (LAN) or wide area network (WAN) are not sufficiently prepared to take on the full responsibilities of such a job.

The process explained in this book will help you fulfill your responsibility of designing and implementing one or more NetWare 4 networks successfully—whether you are an existing network administrator, a professional consultant, a Novell NetWare reseller, a corporate executive, or other company employee, *NetWare 4 Network Design and Implementation* will help you successfully design and implement NetWare 4 networks.

NetWare 4 Network Design and Implementation explains and simplifies the NetWare network design and implementation process. It also provides a standardized process to follow so that you can successfully analyze a company's need for a NetWare 4 network, design a network to meet that need, plan a strategy for implementation that is appropriate to a particular company, and successfully implement the strategy you planned.

Who Should Read This Book

If you are at all associated with the design and implementation of one or more NetWare 4 networks, *NetWare 4 Network Design and Implementation* is for you. Specifically, you should read this book if you are one (or more) of the following:

- A network consultant responsible for working with one or more companies on the design and implementation of its NetWare 4 network
- An Information Services (IS) manager chosen to spearhead the design and implementation of a company's NetWare 4 network
- A corporate executive assuming the responsibility of updating your company's network through the installation of NetWare 4 and the design and implementation of a related NetWare network
- An authorized Novell NetWare reseller specializing in NetWare 4 and the design and implementation of networks that include the NetWare 4 operating system
- A member of a project team that has been assigned the responsibility of determining whether to update an existing network to NetWare 4, how that task should be accomplished, what the network design should look like, and how and when it will be implemented

In short, if you have *any* responsibility for the design and implementation of a NetWare 4 network in your company, no matter how limited or how extensive that responsibility may be, you can benefit from reading this book. Even if you do not expect to be immediately involved in the design and implementation of a NetWare 4 network, you can still benefit from this book. The information it contains will help you better understand NetWare 4 and the most important aspects of a NetWare 4 network.

For example, after reading *NetWare 4 Network Design and Implementation*, you will understand why time synchronization is important and what your options are for designing and establishing time synchronization on your network. You will also understand how to keep time synchronization costs from escalating out of hand on a WAN by implementing a time synchronization strategy that does not cross the WAN to reach a time source.

After reading this book you will also have a better understanding of not only the process associated with successfully designing and implementing a NetWare 4 network, but also of the important factors of a NetWare 4 network's design, which can make it successful, prepare your network for future growth, or doom the project to failure.

You should also read this book if you are currently a Certified Novell Engineer (CNE) or are enrolled in Novell's CNE program, because taking and passing the related Novell test is a CNE requirement. This book will help you prepare to take and pass the CNE test associated with Novell's NetWare 4 Design and Implementation course. This book provides all the basic information that the related Novell course covers—and much more. In addition to the basics, it provides much of the detailed information you are expected to know already about NetWare 4, and which you must be able to incorporate if you are to design and implement a NetWare 4 network successfully or to pass the CNE test. This one book can save you hours of research through your other Novell course books and Novell's electronic documentation set, because it provides the most important information about NetWare 4 at the time you need it the most.

How This Book Can Help You

The days of being able to buy a new PC, install NetWare on it in just a few hours, and have the network up and running in a day or two are long behind us. NetWare 4 networks can be complex and time-consuming to design and implement. If not correctly designed and implemented, a NetWare 4 network may prove to be unwieldy and unresponsive to users' needs. Correcting the initial design and implementation mistakes and problems may be an option, but doing it right the first time will save time, money, and frustration. *NetWare 4 Network Design and Implementation* can help prepare you to do it right the first time.

If you are a Novell NetWare consultant, you may soon find yourself making the majority of your living by designing and implementing NetWare 4 networks of various sizes. The smaller LANs that use NetWare 4 will be relatively easy to design and implement, once you know all the factors that go into network design and implementation. Larger WANs will become easier to design and implement as well. This book will show you not only what you need to know to design and implement a NetWare 4 network, but can also be a continuing source of reference for you as you help various companies design and implement their networks.

Even if you have responsibility for only one company's NetWare 4 network design and implementation, this book will help you prepare to do the best possible job you can for that company. Learning the information contained within the pages of *NetWare 4 Network Design and Implementation* can save you both time and money as a network user and a network designer. For example, one little trick you will learn in this book about positioning replicas can save you seconds on your login process each time you log in to the network. Knowing this information can, in one year with multiple daily logins, easily save hours you would have otherwise spent sitting idly while you waited for your network login to be completed.

If you are an authorized Novell reseller, you will find this book a source of information to help you answer customer questions such as these:

- Will NetWare 4 let us place replicas of the NDS database on file servers in different countries?
- Does NetWare 4 let us configure our time servers to reduce network traffic across our T1 links?

- Is NetWare 4 truly sufficient for our company, with over 5,000 users and 300 file servers spread across two continents?
- Can NetWare 4 solve our problem of limited communication due to a variety of network operating systems, incompatible hardware, and great distances between company divisions?

If you have been chosen as a member of a company's NetWare 4 network design and implementation team, you also can benefit from reading this book. You will learn the basic process of systems analysis and design, as well as the process that Novell's Consulting Services recommends. After reading this book, you will understand where you fit into the design and implementation process and have a much better idea of what is expected of you during that process. You will also understand how you can contribute to the design and implementation of the NetWare 4 network and where your own individual talents and skills can best be utilized on the team. At the very least, if you are a member of a NetWare 4 network design and implementation team, reading *NetWare 4 Network Design and Implementation* may help answer that one burning question—why in the world did they pick me?

Even if you never want to be a network consultant, hope only to administer—not design and implement—a NetWare 4 network, or just want to pass the Novell NetWare 4 Design and Implementation certification test, this book can help you learn what you need to know. It provides the relevant and important information needed to help you answer the test questions, and it gives you sample questions to help you get an idea of what to expect when you take the actual test. It also provides case histories to help you understand how to apply what the book has taught you.

NetWare 4 Network Design and Implementation provides enough information to give you a good grasp of the NetWare 4 network environment, regardless of how limited or extensive your involvement may be in the design and implementation of one or more NetWare 4 networks. If you want or need to understand why NetWare 4 networks are designed the way they are, how to improve the design of an existing NetWare 4 network, how to design and implement a NetWare 4 network from scratch, or just how to survive your assignment on the NetWare 4 design and implementation team, you should read this book. Who knows? Maybe reading this book will even help you to live long and prosper.

New Riders Publishing

The staff of New Riders Publishing is committed to bringing you the very best in computer reference material. Each New Riders book is the result of months of work by authors and staff who research and refine the information contained within its covers.

As part of this commitment to you, the NRP reader, New Riders invites your input. Please let us know if you enjoy this book, if you have trouble with the information and examples presented, or if you have a suggestion for the next edition.

Please note, though: New Riders staff cannot serve as a technical resource for NetWare or for questions about software- or hardware-related problems. Please refer to the documentation that accompanies NetWare or to the applications' Help systems.

If you have a question or comment about any New Riders book, there are several ways to contact New Riders Publishing. We will respond to as many readers as we can. Your name, address, or phone number will never become part of a mailing list or be used for any purpose other than to help us continue to bring you the best books possible. You can write us at the following address:

New Riders Publishing
Attn: Publisher
201 W. 103rd Street
Indianapolis, IN 46290

If you prefer, you can fax New Riders Publishing at 317-581-4670.

You can also send electronic mail to New Riders at the following Internet address:

`edulaney@newriders.mcp.com`

NRP is an imprint of Macmillan Computer Publishing. To obtain a catalog or information, or to purchase any Macmillan Computer Publishing book, call 800-428-5331.

Thank you for selecting *NetWare 4 Network Design and Implementation*!

Chapter 1

Chapter Chapter Chapter Chapter Chapter Chapter

Understanding the Design and Implementation Process

Do you recall the story of the Tower of Babel? The story basically relates how people believed they could climb to the heavens by building a tall-enough tower. To prevent the people from reaching the heavens, their language was changed from one common language to that of many different dialects. This change prevented the people from successfully communicating the work that needed to be done and the process that needed to be followed; thus, they could not work together to build the tower. Eventually, the tower was abandoned. Although building a successful NetWare 4 network may not be as difficult as building a tower to the heavens, both efforts have one thing in common—a process that, if followed, can lead to success. As long as some people work toward their common goal, some type of tower and some type of network can be built. Neither group of people is likely to reach the heights its goal was designed to reach, however, unless everyone understands the process to be followed.

If you have any responsibility at all for designing and implementing a NetWare 4 network, you stand a better chance of reaching your goal by following a process that has proven itself to be effective in business after business.

That process is taught in Novell's 532 course: NetWare 4 Design and Implementation. The course teaches the system design process developed by Novell's Consulting Services and refined to suit NetWare 4 network design and implementation. The basic process upon which the NetWare 4 design and implementation process was developed has been a standard in the industry for many years and, although known by several names, is commonly referred to as *system design life cycle (SDLC).*

Depending on which author you reference, there are four or five variations of the SDLC that are considered to be industry standard.[1] Each variation is known by a different name, but generally follows the same process to complete the assigned task. Novell's NetWare 4.1 Design and Implementation course manual references four of the standard variations:

- Linear
- Structured
- Incremental
- Modified spiral

Developing an understanding of those variations can be an effective way to begin learning the NetWare 4 network design and implementation process. The four variations of the SDLC discussed in Novell's 532 course manual are explained in this chapter.

As a networking consultant, an Information Services (IS) manager, a corporate executive, an authorized Novell NetWare reseller, a member of a NetWare 4 design and implementation project team, a Certified Novell Engineer (CNE), a Certified Novell Instructor (CNI), or any other individual with responsibility for understanding, participating in, or managing the design and implementation of a NetWare 4 network, you will find the information contained in this chapter to be useful.

If you are an experienced systems analyst or designer, much of this chapter may function as review for you. In that case, you can probably afford to skim this first chapter. If you plan to take the NetWare 4 Design and Implementation certification test, or if you don't have a lot of design experience, you may want to review this chapter more carefully.

The four variations of the SDLC are reasonably representative of the general types of variations of the SDLC. Each of these variations of the SDLC has been consistently and methodically followed throughout the electronic information industry to design, implement, maintain, and revise information systems. Although all four variations of the SDLC are discussed in this chapter, because the NetWare 4 process is a subset of the linear variation, the linear variation of the SDLC is discussed first.

Note

Although the SDLC methods discussed in this chapter were chosen because they are discussed in the 532 course materials, many professionals in the industry have their own variations or interpretations of each of these methods. To provide you with a clear understanding of these four variations used in the industry as a whole, and not just as viewed by Novell's Education division, this chapter was written by using multiple references by different authors who are respected by their industry peers for their systems design knowledge.

The following are the four phases into which the various steps associated with each of the four common variations of the SDLC can be grouped:

- Analysis and specification
- Design

- Implementation
- Maintenance

Understanding the Linear Variation of the SDLC

The linear variation or approach to system design is also commonly referred to as the *waterfall model* and is the best known of the more common variations. Its primary characteristic is that it views development "...as proceeding through successive stages called 'phases,'" in which each phase has as its ending process "...a validation and verification activity whose objective is to eliminate as many problems as possible..." in one phase before beginning the next phase.[2]

For those of you who are familiar with programming processes, the linear approach has been compared to the procedural approach to software programming, because it is often the process followed in the bottom-up approach to design. In the linear approach, system design and development follow a logical step-by-step process (see fig. 1.1), with no step started until its predecessor has been successfully completed.

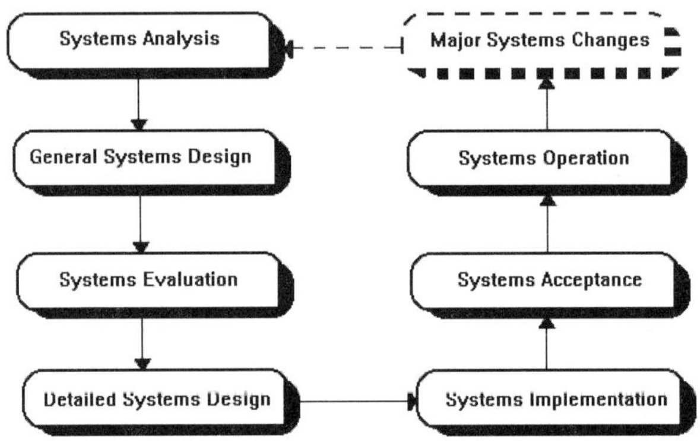

Figure 1.1
Linear approach to system design.

There are eight major processes in the linear approach to system design:[3]

- Systems analysis
- General systems design
- Systems evaluation
- Detailed systems design
- Systems implementation
- Systems acceptance
- Systems operation
- Major systems changes

Each of these phases can be grouped into one of the four procedures common to each SDLC variation. For example, the systems analysis and general systems design phases map into the analysis and specification phase, which is common to each of the four SDLC variations discussed in this chapter. Figure 1.2 shows the relationship of the eight phases in the linear method to the four phases common among the four SDLC variations.

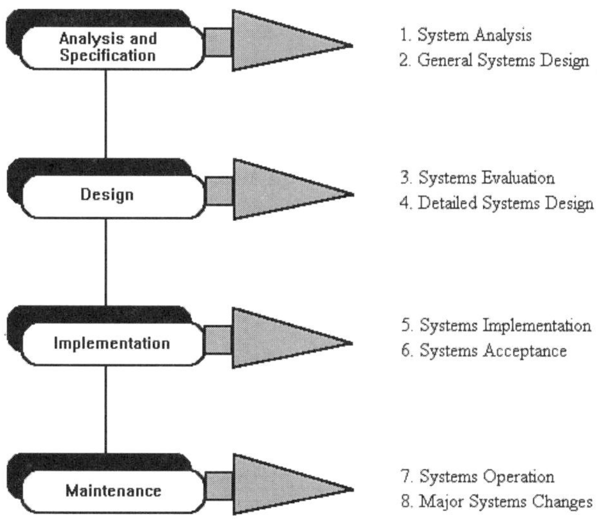

Figure 1.2

Linear variation phases associated with the four common SDLC phases.

Systems Analysis

Determining the problem and defining the user's needs are the primary goals of the systems analysis phase. All relevant information is gathered, and the true problem is clearly defined. The anticipated result of the systems analysis phase is to be prepared to "...attack problems from a broad total-system point of view...."[4] To attack a problem, you must first have a good grasp of what that problem is.

In the waterfall model, this phase is referred to as the *requirements analysis phase* and may be preceded by a feasibility study. The feasibility study is a process used to determine whether the criterion defined for the project can be reasonably fulfilled by designing a new system. Both the economic viability of the proposed project and the likelihood that the ultimate solution will solve the business problem are determined during the feasibility study.

There are major tasks or goals associated with each phase of a project, including system design life cycles. Four tasks that may be readily associated with the systems analysis phase of the SDLC are shown in figure 1.3. Although numbered, these tasks are not always performed in the exact order in which they appear in the list. Sometimes, for example, the company might choose the design and implementation team before a consultant is brought in or an in-house team is put together to identify the problem and design a solution. As a general process, however, the steps as presented are arranged in a reasonably logical order.

The first listed major task of the systems analysis phase is defining the problem. Defining the true problem may not be as easy as it first seems. When asked to define the problem to be solved, many corporate executives are not always sure what the true nature of the problem is. Management may be able to provide you with a relatively close description of the problem, but that description may be colored by a political agenda that may not be readily apparent. In some instances, the problem as defined by management may not be the same as the problem definition offered by others in a company—the group that needs the system, for example.

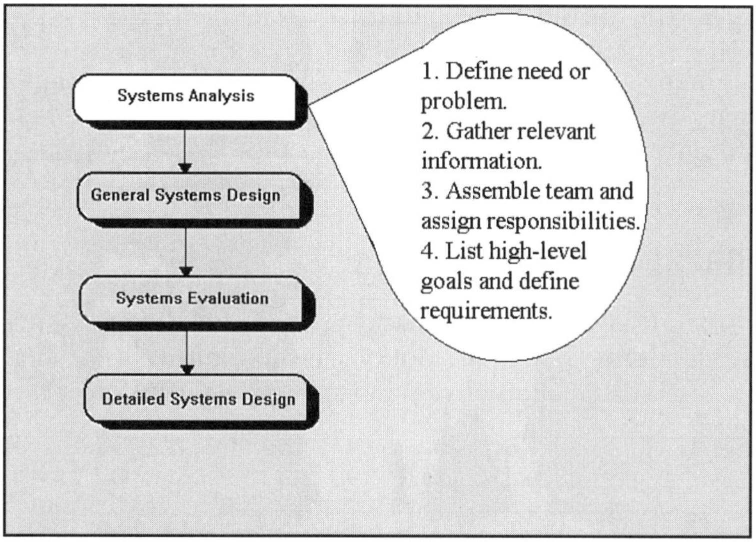

Figure 1.3

Major tasks of the systems analysis phase.

The second task is gathering all relevant information. This responsibility may fall to the consultant or be assigned to one or more of the members of the project team. Generally, a wide variety of information must be gathered in order to be able to see a complete picture of the existing system, as well as to be able to design a more effective system.

When the project team is responsible for designing a NetWare 4 network for example, the variety of information that must be gathered may include such things as a list of existing file servers, the current location of each of those file servers, a list of workstations, the type of workstations and operating systems being used on the network, the topology and geography of the existing network, and so on.

The third task is to assemble the project team and assign responsibilities. As noted earlier, however, the project team may be assembled earlier in this phase. In addition, if the project is limited enough in size, the entire project team may consist of only one individual.

The fourth task is that of listing high-level goals and defining requirements to be met. In the waterfall process model, this fourth task generally results in the output associated with the specification phase. As the result of this phase, a document is often produced that describes the requirements of the new system and the goals the system is to be designed to accomplish. This document is then used as the input to the next phase—general system design.

General System Design

The general system design phase commonly involves three major tasks: identifying potential solutions, evaluating and choosing from the available alternatives, and developing a high-level design system (see fig. 1.4).

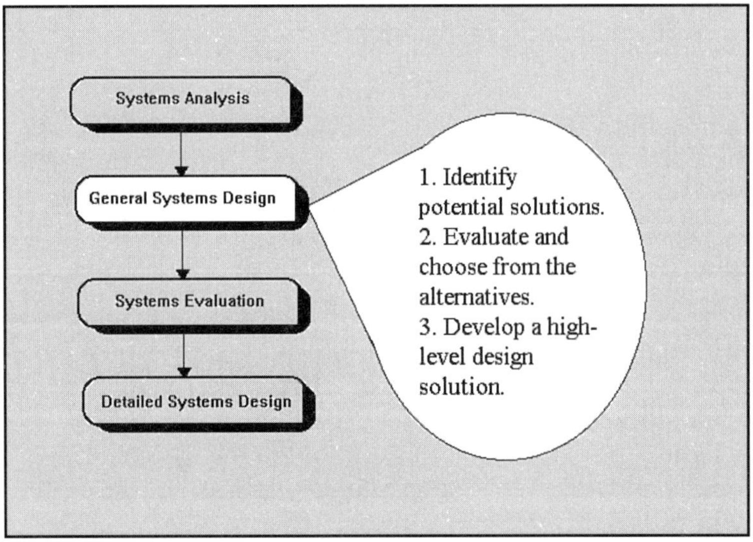

Figure 1.4
Major tasks of the general systems design phase.

The process of identifying potential solutions is generally accomplished after reviewing the output from the previous phase—the requirements document. In addition, the team members may want to review further the original information gathered by or for the team to ensure they thoroughly understand what is expected of the system they will be designing. Team members often must review all available information, discuss ideas for potential solutions, and narrow down the suggestions to the best and most likely solution.

Once the best and most likely solution is chosen, a high-level design that will successfully implement the chosen solution is then developed. At this point, only a general or basic overview of a proposed design is created; the details of the design are not developed.

In comparison to the phases defined in the waterfall process model, the general system design phase is somewhat similar to the early attempts at design in the design phase. In the waterfall process, however, the detailed systems design of the system is actually accomplished in full and includes what is called the *systems evaluation* and *detailed systems design* phases of the linear process.

Systems Evaluation

The systems evaluation phase is one major task: reviewing the proposed system design and evaluating it against the problem definition. The purpose of this phase is to determine whether the basic design of the system will solve the problem for which it was designed. Evaluating the basic system design helps ensure that all potential problem areas have been considered in the basic design.

Detailed Systems Design

Once the basic design has been evaluated, the next phase is to develop the details of the design. For example, the systems evaluation phase may define such general tasks as which departments will be implemented initially, and which ones will be implemented at a later date. The detailed systems design phase may then include a list of which steps are required to implement the system within each department successfully.

This phase may also include the time line for implementation. Once all the relevant tasks are listed, the amount of time to complete each task can then be projected. From those time projections, a detailed schedule for implementation can be produced.

Systems Implementation

This is the phase during which the system design is actually implemented. In some instances, the development of the implementation schedule may be considered the first stage of this phase. In other instances, the development of the implementation schedule may be the last stage of the detailed system design phase.

The actual implementation phase may require only a short period of time (a few days to a few weeks) or may take a much longer amount of time (several weeks to a year or longer). The amount of time required to implement the design is determined by several factors. If the process is being followed to implement a NetWare 4 network design, factors that may affect the time required to implement the new design can include the following:

- The number of file servers to be upgraded or added
- The number of workstations on the network
- Whether the network is strictly localized to a limited geographic area (LAN) or is more widespread, possibly using T1 or slower communication links (WAN)

This phase also generally includes a test implementation. A smaller, more controllable section of the system may be implemented first, to work out any potential problems before implementing the entire system design.

Systems Acceptance

Once the entire design has been implemented, a period of adjustment will be needed. This time frame, like the time frame for implementation, may be short or long. The length of the systems acceptance phase is determined primarily by how successful the implementation was, how effective the design is, and how well everyone was prepared and trained for the changes. Other factors such as the complexity of the design and quantity of changes required can also affect the length of this phase.

In the waterfall process model, this phase is referred to as the *integration and testing phase.* Charette describes this phase as being "...the creation of a fully functioning software system from the software components implemented, and the determination of whether the system satisfies the requirements."[5]

In the linear approach, determining whether the designed system meets the specifications and satisfies the requirements of the system falls into the next phase—systems operation.

Systems Operation

During the systems operation phase, the primary emphasis is to monitor the new system to determine its overall success. This phase also helps those who designed and implemented the system to pinpoint its weaknesses and determine whether to correct those weaknesses or to try to live with them temporarily. Minor corrections to the system may be appropriate. On the other hand, the decision to make all changes during another design and implementation process may be made, in which case, the next phase is implemented.

Major Systems Changes

Change is a constant reality. Sometimes, changes around us have only limited effect on us. At other times, changes around us may force us to make changes as well. When change once again becomes necessary, the last phase of the system design life cycle—major systems changes—must be implemented.

The major systems changes phase, also referred to as the *maintenance phase* in the waterfall process model, often provides the input to begin the entire process over at the first phase—systems analysis. Information about the problems currently encountered within the existing system are sometimes the catalyst for determining when it is time to stop making temporary fixes to the system and redesign and implement another system.

As with all of the approaches to system design, there are some benefits to following the linear approach when designing either an electronic data processing system or a NetWare 4 network. As much as possible, the linear process follows what some people believe to be the ideal approach to system design. As Charette defines it, "Ideally, one ought to define everything that is required before moving on to the next step, to ensure nothing is lost or forgotten."[6] This is the basic idea behind the linear approach to design. In most instances, this approach is successful, and thus it is also commonly followed when developing systems. The linear approach has proven itself reasonably effective in small systems.

Besides its logical step-by-step approach, the linear system also functions to integrate the design process, and it provides a series of points where the team can get back on track if the development process has begun to stray too far from its intended path. Unfortunately, the linear process is not very effective if the design process starts to encounter serious problems. If the chosen design is not suitable, the linear approach is not very flexible. The process may have to begin again from the first phase in order to deal with serious problems.

One other major drawback of the linear process is that it is not very effective when used to design computerized processes. By its nature, the linear approach works better when designing a manual process than it does when attempting to design a computerized process. Does this drawback make the linear approach unsuitable for network design? Not at all. In fact, it may be the drawback that makes the linear approach most effective for network design. Although networks make extensive use of electronic equipment, the design process is ultimately a manual process. Yes, it must take into consideration the hardware and software that make the network fully functional, but its design is still a manual process.

Understanding the Structured Variation of the SDLC

The structured variation of the SDLC, although not the method chosen by Novell's Consulting Services group as the model for the NetWare 4 process, may still be a valid approach to follow when designing and implementing a NetWare 4 network. Unlike the linear approach, the structured approach may at first appear to be rather haphazard and confusing (see fig. 1.5). There is a logical structure and process behind its appearance, however.

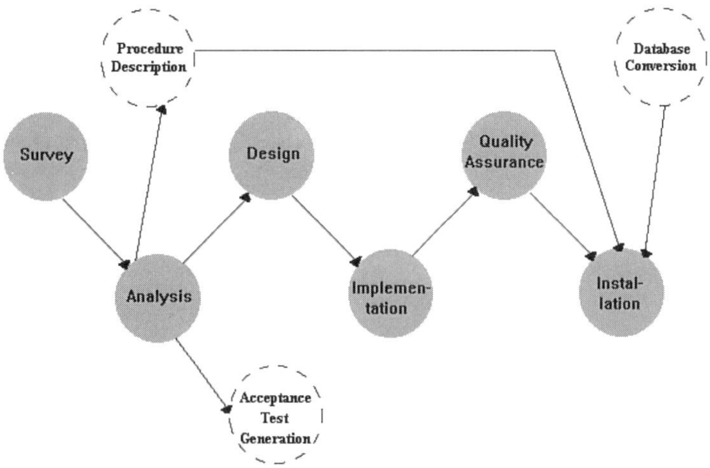

Figure 1.5
Pictorial representation of the structured approach.

The structured variation of the system design life cycle involves nine definable phases (also referred to by Edward Yourdon as the nine activities of the structured life cycle[7]):

- Survey
- Analysis
- Design
- Implementation
- Acceptance test generation
- Quality assurance
- Procedure description
- Database conversion
- Installation

During each phase, a variety of information is generated, referred to as the output of a phase. The output of one phase is often used as the input to another phase. For example, the output of the survey phase is a project charter at a minimum, but it may also include documents such as a preliminary cost/benefit report and a list of project constraints.

In the NetWare 4 process, various types of output documents are often generated as well. For example, the anticipated output of the project approach phase is a type of project charter—a document that defines the scope of the project. A preliminary schedule is also often an output of the project approach phase of the NetWare 4 process.

Although each of the nine phases of the structured life cycle has some type of input and output, only the overall general activities associated with each phase are discussed. Do not lose sight of the fact, however, that input and output documents exist at each phase of the structured life cycle just as they do at several of the phases of each of the variations of the SDLC, including the subset of the linear variation—the NetWare 4 process.

Survey Phase

The survey phase, along with the analysis phase, closely resembles the systems analysis phase of the linear approach. In addition, the survey phase is similar to the goal of gathering company information defined in the project approach phase of the NetWare 4 process.

During the survey phase, the problem is defined, relevant information is gathered, and the information is reviewed and shared in an effort to begin determining the appropriate approach to take in the design of the network. Also during the survey, input is sought and accepted from system users, basic system requirements are presented, and cost and benefit reports may be provided. In addition, a project charter as well as a list of project constraints may be an output of this phase to be used as an input for the next phase.

Another term associated with the survey phase is feasibility study. Yourdon refers to the survey phase as activity 1 of the structured life cycle (SLC), and describes it as follows:

> This activity is also known as the feasibility study or initial business study. Typically, it begins when a user requests that one or more portions of his business be automated. The major purpose of the survey activity is to identify current deficiencies in the user's environment; to establish new goals; to determine whether it is feasible to automate the business, and if so, to suggest some acceptable scenarios; and finally, to prepare a project charter that will be used to guide the remainder of the project.[8]

The feasibility study or initial business study activity as associated with a NetWare 4 network also typically begins with someone in the company (a user) requesting the creation of, or the upgrade to, a NetWare 4 network. Typically, a user becomes disgruntled with the current system or determines that the current system is ineffective, too time-consuming, too costly, or that it simply no longer meets all the company's business needs. The user may then begin to seek alternatives.

In some instances, the user seeks ways to upgrade the current system without completely replacing it. If the current system is a NetWare network, upgrading may merely mean adding a few NetWare 4 file servers and pulling the system together as a whole. If the current system is a manual operation, the user may decide to seek ways to computerize the process. If the current process is computerized but functions are performed primarily on stand-alone computers, the user may decide it is probably time to consider networking those computers.

Regardless of what causes users to decide to upgrade their current systems, the user who ultimately decides to upgrade to NetWare 4 had, at some time, some exposure to the Novell NetWare 4 operating system. Once the decision is made to move a current system to a NetWare 4 network, the survey activity of the structured life cycle begins.

In an electronic data processing (EDP) environment, the first phase (activity) of the SLC is the survey. When designing and implementing a NetWare 4 network, the first phase may also consist of a survey activity, which consists of a series of steps for designing and implementing a NetWare 4 network. The major purpose is the same as well:

- To identify deficiencies in the user's current networking environment
- To establish new network goals commensurate with company goals
- To determine whether it is feasible to update the existing network to NetWare 4
- To suggest possible upgrade scenarios
- To establish a network upgrade project charter that can be followed to guide the remainder of the project

During the survey phase of the system life cycle, "...problems and deficiencies in the user's environment are evaluated, with the assumption that they may provide the justification for developing new approaches."[9] This is also true of the related procedure of a NetWare 4 network design and implementation—gathering company information.

Analysis Phase

The primary purpose of the analysis phase is to review the gathered information in an effort to determine what the new system must accomplish. In the structured life cycle, terms such as "user policy" and "project charter" are used to describe the information or documentation that should be produced as a result of this phase.

When designing a NetWare 4 network, documents that may be produced as a result of the related phase—project approach—may include a list of project team members and their assignments, training required by the project team, a project scope document, and a preliminary schedule encompassing the steps and time required to design the network.

Design Phase

The design phase of the structured approach resembles the general systems design, systems implementation, and systems acceptance phases of the linear approach to the system design life cycle. During the design phase, the structured approach determines a basic design for the system under development. The system is then implemented, and the acceptance or effectiveness of the system is determined.

The design phase of the project life cycle as defined by Yourdon, "...includes a step known as packaging, in which the design is adjusted or modified to take into account the limitations of the computer hardware being used to implement the system."[10] The computer hardware, as well as the computer software must also be taken into account during the design phase of the NetWare 4 process.

For example, the physical location of network file servers affects how you design the NetWare directory tree. If you follow Novell's recommendation for designing the directory tree, you are careful not to create network partitions that encompass geographically dispersed areas (also known as "not spanning the WAN").

Implementation Phase

The implementation phase encompasses what its name implies—implementation of the new system. This is also true for the NetWare 4 process. As with the design phase, the physical location of network file servers also affects the implementation of the design, and thus must also be considered in preparation for the implementation phase.

The actual coding of the software for implementation of an electronic data processing system is the primary function associated with the implementation phase of the structured life cycle. In addition, this phase includes organizing the individual modules of software coding into a logical order so that the system runs smoothly and performs the tasks for which it was designed—the ultimate goal of a system.

Acceptance Test Generation Phase

If the coding is effective, the acceptance test generation phase is easier. During this phase, tests are designed and generated that can be applied against the software code to determine whether the code is meeting the specifications against which it was designed. If the process is followed and all concerned are diligent at their jobs, the acceptance test generation phase results in a series of test cases that prove the design of the system.

In the NetWare 4 process, the comparable phase is the implementation phase, and the comparable step is developing a migration strategy.

When the migration strategy is developed, one of the processes that may occur is defining a pilot department. One or more file servers within a company department may be used as the test site for implementing the network design on a limited basis. The portion of the network thus implemented is used to determine whether the complete implementation is likely to be successful.

Within the pilot department, problems that occur can be resolved, and modifications can be made to the overall network design as needed to accommodate those corrections. The modified and improved network design can then be put into place throughout the company.

Quality Assurance Phase

The quality assurance phase of the structured approach can be compared to the systems operation and major systems changes phases of the linear approach. During the quality assurance phase, the new system is monitored and checked for problems, and solutions to those problems are designed as needed.

This phase is similar to the use of a lab in the implementation phase of the NetWare 4 process. A testing lab is set up to help you find the weaknesses associated with the network design and then work out and test alternatives to those weaknesses.

Procedure Description Phase

This phase of the system life cycle can be seen as implemented in different phases of the NetWare 4 process. During the procedure description phase, a formal description of the manual procedures associated with the new system is created. During the NetWare 4 process, formal procedural documents are also created. The best example of a formal procedural document in the NetWare 4 process is the document containing the naming standards associated with the NetWare directory tree.

Database Conversion Phase

In the database conversion phase, a current database is converted to run with the new system. There is no associated phase in the NetWare 4 process, although the installation of NetWare 4 includes a software program that enables you to use an existing company database as input to the automated creation of network user objects.

Installation Phase

The installation phase of the structured approach overlaps the systems implementation phase of the linear approach. When applied to the design and implementation of a NetWare 4 network, installation generally includes installation of the hardware and software required to implement the design.

In the structured system life cycle as defined by Yourdon, the accepted system design as produced as an output of the quality assurance phase, as well as the output generated by the procedure description and database conversion phases, constitute the inputs for the installation phase. During the installation phase, the accepted system is put in place. "In some cases, however, installation may simply mean an overnight cutover to the new system, with no excitement or fanfare; in other cases, installation may be a gradual process, as one user group after another receives user's manuals, hardware, and training in the use of the new system."[11]

In larger NetWare 4 networks, the installation process may be quite gradual, involving only one department, workgroup, or building at a time. It may also involve training a large number of individuals to help implement the process simultaneously. In smaller networks, installing or implementing one department or workgroup may mean you have installed the entire company.

How you complete the installation process is determined in the implementation phase. The actual installation then merely follows the procedures you outlined during the implementation phase.

Understanding the Incremental Variation of the SDLC

Charette defines the incremental approach to software development as being "...the creation of a software system in small, manageable functional components of the system called increments, where each successive increment is made up of the currently existing system with additional functionality...." The incremental variation of the system design life cycle divides activities into two categories: *phase-dependent,* and *phase-independent* (see fig. 1.6).[12]

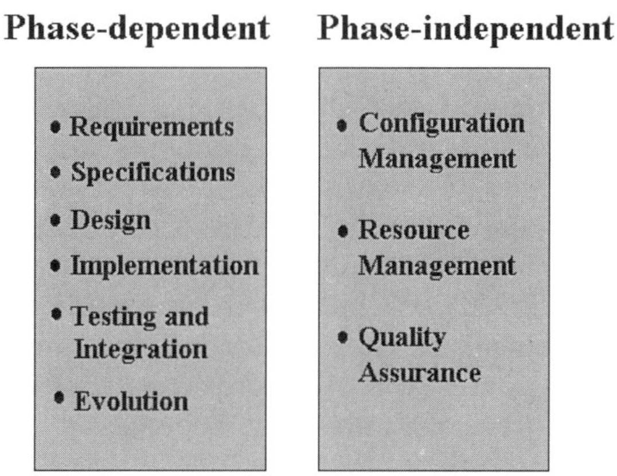

Figure 1.6
System design life cycle incremental approach.

Phase-dependent activities are those that depend on the completion of an earlier activity, or that are required for an upcoming activity. Phase-independent activities can be conducted at different phases in the process without being dependent on the successful completion of other activities. In the incremental approach, the "...system is not viewed as a monolithic entity with a single delivery date, but as an integration of the outputs of successive steps of each iteration. Only at the end is the 'complete system' available, although each increment is a working system in and of itself."[13]

Six phase-dependent activities can be readily identified:

- Requirements
- Specifications
- Design
- Implementation
- Testing and integration
- Evolution

As with other SDLC variations, the first phase of the incremental approach involves defining the problem to be solved and determining what requirements must be met in order to consider the completed project to be a success. The requirements specified in this phase do not need to be exhaustive, particularly the first time they are developed, because in the incremental approach you can modify the requirements as the project evolves. This phase in the incremental variation of the SDLC varies substantially from the linear variation. One of the biggest drawbacks of the linear variation is its lack of flexibility. Once set, the requirements developed while following the linear approach to design cannot easily be modified without setting the entire project back, sometimes requiring the project practically to be started over.

The second phase—specifications—involves analyzing the information that has been gathered, including information learned as the result of analyzing the success or failure of different iterations of this and other phases of the process. Then you can determine what must be done in order to complete the project. The second phase of the incremental approach can be compared to the second phase of the structured life cycle—analysis. The major difference here is that in the incremental variation, if the specifications are not perfect the first time, improvements can be made in the specifications during successive iterations.

The third activity is the design phase. This phase often involves the use of rapid prototyping (developing a quick mock-up of the system so as to determine whether the requirements and design seem reasonable). The purpose of rapid prototyping is to "...buy information in order to provide early warning to the developers and management of possible risks before too much money, and time, is spent on possibly building the wrong system."[14]

The fourth activity—implementation—is basically the same from one SDLC variation to another. The ultimate goal is to put the new system into place. With the incremental variation, implementing the system can be done more slowly, correcting problems and mistakes as needed. The primary difference between the incremental variation and other variations is the level of implementation that is accomplished before problems are encountered. In many of the other variations, the entire system is put in place, then it is watched for problems, and corrections are made if and as needed. In the incremental approach, the current system is put into place, problems are detected, problems are corrected, and the next build is implemented. This process of build, implement, correct, and build again is continuous until a point is reached when the system is considered to be good enough to meet the final specifications.

Testing and integration involves testing the build that has been put into place and integrating it into the environment in which the final product will be used. Testing provides the feedback on the successes and failures associated with each build so that the design and implementation can be improved for the release of the next iteration of the build.

Evolution can be compared to the manage and monitor phase in the NetWare 4 process. The last portion of the manage and monitor phase is recognizing when it may be necessary to scrap or rebuild the current system from the beginning. Evolution is the process of growing the system to accommodate needed change and growth until the cumulative result of the changes and growth is a system that may no longer resemble the system originally put into place.

There are also three phase-independent activities associated with the incremental variation of the SDLC:

- Configuration management
- Resource management
- Quality assurance

The three activities are mostly continuous, and implemented as needed. Managing the configuration of the system and the resources going into its design and implementation may be necessary at any of the phases of the incremental variation, but they are particularly important during the early phase-dependent activities. Quality assurance is also somewhat continuous but is most important when the final design is to be put into place.

The incremental variation of the SDLC can be an effective approach to design. It does not require an extensive or exhaustive list of requirements to be developed before system design begins, because the process itself enables corrections to the list of requirements as the project progresses. In addition, because successive builds of the system can be created, the project itself is flexible enough to deal with change, regardless of the source or cause of the change. Although errors still occur during design and implementation by using the incremental approach, and those errors are likely to be just as costly to correct as they are when other variations to the SDLC are followed, at least the incremental approach makes it easier to make those corrections.

Understanding the Modified Spiral Variation of the SDLC

The fourth common variation of the SDLC processes is the modified spiral variation (see fig. 1.7).[15]

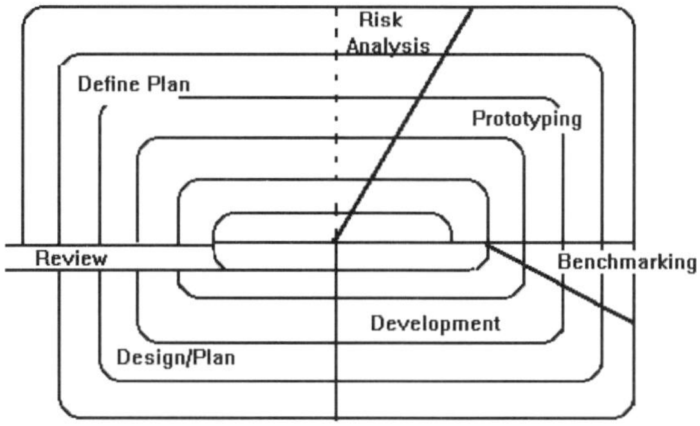

Figure 1.7
System design life cycle modified spiral approach.

The modified spiral variation is "...used in inherently risky, costly, or unstable development efforts (where the requirements change during the life of the project)."[16] As the figure indicates, each phase seems to follow another, but each phase also wraps around other phases. The figure may also give the impression that there is no real starting point, but all projects have a beginning—even if that beginning is not always easy to pinpoint.

The modified spiral variation of the SDLC looks at system design as a continuous process that must accommodate the possibility of constant change. At any given point in the process, it must be possible to modify any aspect of the project, including its requirements, basic design, inputs, outputs, and so on.

Although a deliberate design methodology, the modified spiral approach is also a design methodology of evolution. Companies sometimes begin projects by following another type of design methodology, and, because of unforeseen and unpredictable requirement changes, the process may end up evolving into an uncontrolled spiral with no apparent end to the project in sight. In an environment where the risks are great or development cannot be completely controlled, the spiral variation of design may be the only realistic approach. It can be a successful and controlled approach, despite its outward appearance, if the methodology is understood and closely watched. In addition, some limitations or boundaries must be set to ensure that at least a minimal design is acceptable. Otherwise, the process can continue indefinitely.

The modified spiral approach has seven definable phases, each of which can be performed at varying times in the process, even though the pictorial representation of the modified spiral seems to indicate a definable process:

- Plan definition
- Risk analysis
- Prototyping
- Benchmarking
- Development
- Design/plan
- Review

At some point in time, the project plan must be defined. Goals or project objectives must be established. Alternative approaches for meeting the defined goals or objectives must be reviewed, and constraints must be assessed to guide the final project approach decision.

Once an approach to meeting the defined goals is chosen, some type of risk analysis is needed. Bearing in mind that the modified spiral approach is most suitable in an environment where the project itself is inherently risky, the project approach that sets itself out as being the least risk for the most benefit is likely to be the chosen approach. This does not mean the chosen approach will not still carry major risks, only that the risk seems to be worth the potential result.

One way of controlling the risk associated with the project is the next phase—prototyping. As with the incremental approach to design, prototyping in the modified spiral approach can be an effective way of determining the viability of the chosen design.

"Prototyping has the usual meaning that the system is built quickly, tried out, criticized by the users and changed." Because the "process is repeated until satisfaction is achieved," prototyping seems to fit well into the modified spiral design approach. In fact, prototyping may even help to eliminate the need for lengthy system design. One unorthodox view of prototyping even suggests that prototyping "...eliminates the need for system analysis because you can very quickly put up a sketch of the system and then continually modify it towards a finally acceptable version."[17]

During prototyping, various alternatives for system design may be identified, and the risks associated with each can be resolved as much as possible. Another way to resolve risks is to benchmark each alternative solution. *Benchmarking* is the process of establishing standards against which all testing is done and comparisons are made. Benchmarking different system designs helps determine which of the alternatives carries the least risk while providing the greatest reward. At a minimum, benchmarking provides a set of standards against which all options can be tested, whether or not the level of risk is greater in one alternative than in another.

Once the best alternative system design is chosen, the next phase is to begin developing the design. In the modified spiral variation, development can be successive, verifying the next level in the design process as development progresses.

Once development is underway, determining or planning the next phase is the next step. Unlike the linear variation of the SDLC, project planning in the modified spiral approach is not all done at the beginning. Rather, planning is done as the project progresses, enabling quick direction shifts if needed.

Summary

To determine whether a shift in planning, commitment, project direction, and so on is needed, some type of review is generally conducted. The review process enables all those involved in the design and development to assess whether the project should continue as designed or be modified and then proceed, or even whether the project should be continued at all. This review phase may sometimes be referred to as the *commitment review*.

As noted at the beginning of this chapter, each of the four types of system design life cycles encompasses four major phases: analysis and specification, design, implementation, and maintenance. Novell's NetWare 4 Design and Implementation course manual provides information about these four phases that sets a starting point for understanding the NetWare 4 process. The course manual notes that

> The major difference between the variations of the SDLC is the extent to which each phase occurs linearly or concurrently. For example, one variation suggests that you must perform your project analysis before you begin design, and the other variations indicate that analysis and design can and should overlap to different extents.[18]

In general, each of the four phases has a similar expected outcome or process to be followed, regardless of which type of SDLC is being used. In the analysis and specification phase, the project team must determine what is wrong with the current system (or lack of a system) and what to do about it. During the design phase, the project team creates a broad and general plan for dealing with the problem or accomplishing the goal set during the analysis and specification phase. During the implementation phase, the team creates and tests a pilot or proposed solution, modifying and retesting it as needed until a reasonably effective solution is designed. In the final phase—maintenance—the new process is monitored, corrected on an as-needed basis, and managed for maximum effectiveness.

These four phases deemed common to the different types of system design life cycles are also the four phases upon which Novell's Consulting Services based the design and implementation process it documented for Novell NetWare 4 networks. Understanding the SDLC from which Novell's process was designed is, therefore, a good starting point from which to begin learning the Novell NetWare 4 network design and implementation process—the subject of Chapter 2, "Understanding the NetWare 4 Network Design and Implementation Process," and the subject of the remainder of this book.

Notes

1. Maloy, Paul, Mng. Ed. "Resolving Issues Regarding Course 532," *Novell Education Bulletin.* October, 1995, 31–4.
2. Charette, Robert N. *Applications Strategies for Risk Analysis.* New York: McGraw-Hill Book Company, 1990, 169.
3. *NetWare 4.1 Design and Implementation Instructor's Guide, Beta rev.* Provo: Novell, Inc., 1995, IG 1–6.
4. Davis, William S. *Computers and Business Information Processing.* Massachusetts: Addison-Wesley Publishing Company, 1981, 422.
5. Charette, Robert N. *Applications Strategies for Risk Analysis.* New York: McGraw-Hill Book Company, 1990, 170.
6. Ibid., 171.
7. Yourdon, Edward. *Managing the System Life Cycle.* New York: Yourdon Press, 1982, 45.
8. Ibid., 45.
9. Ibid., 51.
10. Ibid., 45.
11. Ibid., 46.
12. Charette, Robert N. *Applications Strategies for Risk Analysis.* New York: McGraw-Hill Book Company, 1990, 174.
13. Ibid., 175.
14. Ibid., 174.
15. *NetWare 4.1 Design and Implementation Instructor's Guide, Beta rev.* Provo: Novell, Inc., 1995, IG 1–6.
16. Ibid., IG 1–7.
17. Collins, Garfield, and Gillian Blay. *Structured Systems Development Techniques: Strategic Planning to System Testing.* New York: John Wiley & Sons, 1982, 239.
18. *NetWare 4.1 Design and Implementation Instructor's Guide, Beta rev.* Provo: Novell, Inc., 1995, IG 1–8.

Chapter 2

Understanding the NetWare 4 Network Design and Implementation Process

The SDLC was used, at least for reference, by Novell's Consulting Services group when developing their suggested NetWare 4 network design and implementation process. The group found that the modified process it recommends, which it actually considers to be a subset of the SDLC, is better adapted to dealing with the design and implementation of a NetWare 4 network than are most of the original SDLC processes. The Novell design and implementation process does, however, base itself on the linear approach to the system design life cycle.

The NetWare 4 network design and implementation process has several advantages over the original SDLC linear process from which it was developed. The advantages of this customized NetWare 4 network design and implementation process include the following:

- It is designed to help you effectively deal with networking computers, a task that the SDLC process could not have separated out when the process was originally designed.
- It considers and was developed to work with computers running NetWare 4 and all the peculiarities associated with NetWare 4.
- It can help you design a more efficient network, whether that network includes only NetWare 4 file servers or encompasses NetWare 2 and NetWare 3 file servers.
- It helps you choose the best design for your network, whether it is a small LAN or a geographically dispersed WAN.
- It is relatively blind to the operating system, helping you design and implement a NetWare 4 network that includes upgrading other non-NetWare network operating systems to NetWare.

The purpose of this chapter is twofold. The first is to provide you with an understanding of the NetWare design and implementation process as suggested by Novell's Consulting Services group, including the steps involved in each of the phases it defines. The second purpose is to provide you with the information you need to understand the differences between Novell's defined process and the types of SDLC processes previously discussed.

The Four Phases

The Novell NetWare 4 Network design and implementation process consists of four primary phases, as do each of the four types of SDLC processes. Although Novell's NetWare 4 design and implementation process is very similar to the four phases deemed common to the different types of system design life cycles, it is not exactly the same. The most noticeable difference between Novell's four phases and the four phases defined for the SDLC is that two of the four phases are named differently (see fig. 2.1). The phase name changes are not just for the purpose of calling them something different, however. The changes are more for the purpose of giving each phase a name that is more descriptive of its function within the design and implementation process as it has been defined for NetWare 4 networks.

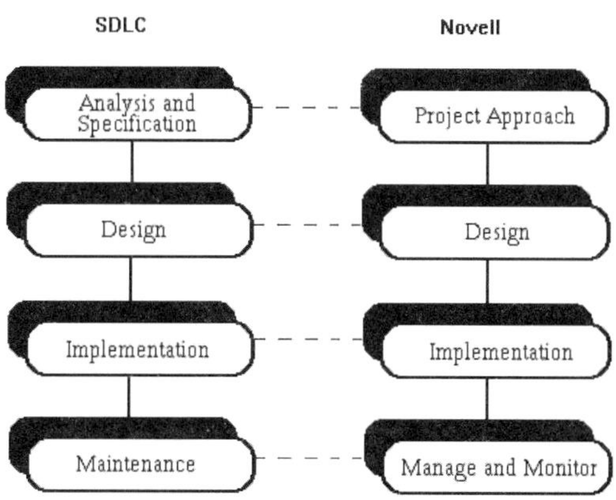

Figure 2.1
SDLC versus Novell design and implementation process.

Note

The Novell NetWare 4.1 Design and Implementation course covers only the first three of these four phases. Novell considers the fourth phase—manage and monitor—to be sufficiently covered in other Novell courses. Consequently, the fourth phase is not discussed in the course, and questions about the details of managing and monitoring NetWare 4 networks are also not included on the CNE version of the NetWare 4.1 Design and Implementation test. The fourth phase is, however, discussed in some detail in this book because consultants, project team members, IS managers, and others involved in the three initial phases of a NetWare 4 network's design and implementation are also likely to be participants in the fourth phase.

The following are the four phases of the Novell NetWare 4 network design and implementation process:[1]

- Project approach
- Design
- Implementation
- Manage and monitor

Other differences exist between the phases of Novell's design and implementation process and the phases of the four SDLC processes. The differences are not as important, however, as developing an understanding of and the capability of successfully following the phases and processes that make up the Novell NetWare 4 design and implementation process. Concentrate your efforts on learning the Novell process rather than on learning the differences between the SDLC and the Novell, even though the differences may become apparent as you learn about the Novell process.

Project Approach Phase

The project approach phase is the first of the four phases in the NetWare 4 design and implementation process. The primary purpose of the project approach phase is to establish the scope of the project. The project approach phase consists of several activities that, like the feasibility study aspect of project development, lead to developing the "...scope and the objectives of a project. Also developed are preliminary cost, benefit, and design presentations. To the level necessary, any required capital budgeting decisions are also made."[2]

In order to complete the project approach phase as defined by Novell's Consulting Services group, one major procedure must be accomplished, consisting of five tasks (see fig. 2.2):

- Establish the project team.
- Collect relevant information.
- Educate the project team.

- Establish the project's scope.
- Develop a preliminary schedule.

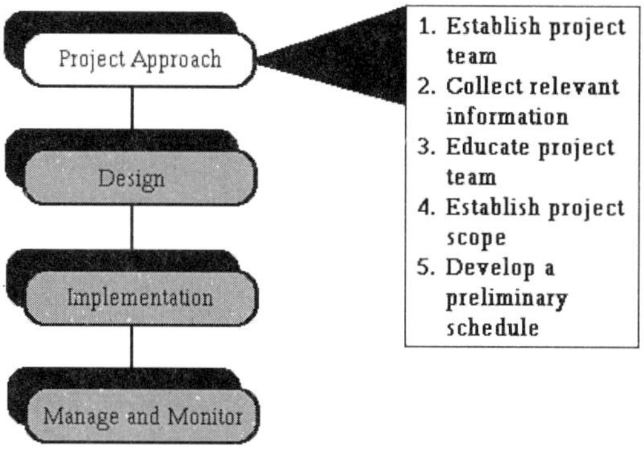

Figure 2.2
Project approach phase procedure and steps.

Of these five, the first three are preliminary to the last two. Once a project team has been assembled, information relevant to the design and implementation of the network has been gathered, and the project team has been educated regarding the project, the team can then complete the next two tasks and thus accomplish the major purpose of the project approach phase—determining the scope of the project and creating a preliminary schedule for designing and implementing the project.

One aspect of the project approach phase of a NetWare 4 network's design and implementation is similar to one area of structured systems development—the feasibility study. During the project approach phase, the project team must make a realistic determination of what can be expected from the resulting network design and implementation. The project team must also make a basic decision as to how the design and implementation of the network will occur before any preliminary schedule can be created. Conducting a structured systems development feasibility study is one approach used in the SDLC process to provide input from which to make the necessary decisions. Although a structured feasibility study is not conducted during the NetWare 4 process, a similar approach is taken to gathering and analyzing the related information. It is useful, therefore, to understand the process associated with conducting a feasibility study.

The structured systems development feasibility study has as its purpose, "...to identify broadly the systems requirements within the application area and to select an appropriate physical solution which meets these requirements."[3] To that end, the feasibility study also has a series of tasks or steps that it logically follows; the following are the primary ones:[4]

1. Determine scope and plan study.
2. Examine existing system.
3. Determine requirements.
4. Evaluate alternative solutions.
5. Plan future phases.
6. Draft and review feasibility report.
7. Seek approval.

You can see that all the steps in the feasibility study do not match all the steps in the project approach phase. In the project approach phase, some of the steps that are completed can better be matched to other phases of project development.

For example, the project approach phase includes gathering and educating a project team. There is no equivalent step in the feasibility study because, as a rule, the team or individual conducting the feasibility study is generally chosen before the feasibility study phase. The process of gathering and educating a team may be performed either early in the development of a project under structured systems development, or it may simply happen as a result of actions taken by various company employees on their own and their company's behalf.

This volunteer-like approach may still be found in use in some companies today. That does not mean, however, that it is an effective approach. Instead, it may be more an indication of how hard it can be to replace old habits with new actions. A planned, coordinated, and logical approach to choosing a project team, such as that defined in the project approach phase of NetWare 4 network design and implementation, is more likely to result in a team with all the skills required to design and implement a NetWare 4 network successfully.

Another advantage to organizing the project team following the approach defined by Novell's Consulting Services group is that this approach "also gives members of the team an idea of their roles throughout the process." In addition, "the company information gathered during this procedure is used throughout the design and implementation process."[5]

Design Phase

The design phase is the second of the four phases in the NetWare 4 design and implementation process. The primary purpose of the design phase is to develop an overall network design that meets the needs of the company, functions efficiently, simplifies access to the network by users, and makes it as easy to administer as possible. The design phase consists of four procedures, two of which may be considered conditional (optional) depending on the needs of the company and its users (see fig. 2.3).

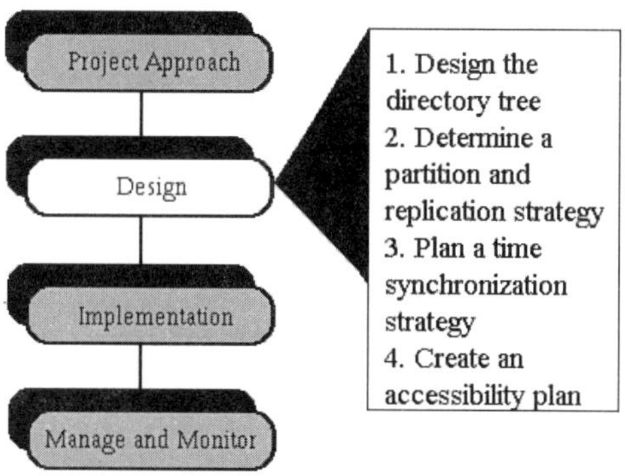

Figure 2.3
Design phase procedures.

Here are the four procedures defined by Novell's Consulting Services group that may be performed during the design phase:[7]

- Design the directory tree.
- Determine a partition and replication strategy.

- Plan a time synchronization strategy.
- Create an accessibility plan.

The design phase of the NetWare 4 design and implementation process includes procedures that are mostly unique to designing a network. Structured systems development techniques and the system design life cycle, therefore, do not contain procedures that are the same as the four procedures for this design phase. The only true similarity between the SDLC and structured systems development and the design phase of the NetWare 4 design and implementation process is that all contain some type of design phase.

For example, there is more than one type of design methodology that can be applied when designing business systems. Two primary design methods have become relatively common. These two design methods are called the *data flow method* and the *data structure method*. The data flow method concentrates on how data moves through the system; the data structure method concerns itself with how the data itself is structured, rather than how it flows.

Although there seems to be no apparent similarity between the design phases of the data flow and the data structure methods of system design and Novell's NetWare 4 network design, one primary similarity does exist. All three design methodologies are concerned with the needs of the user. In the data flow method, analysis centers around various documents, but the ultimate result is a system that fulfills the needs of the final user. This is true in the NetWare 4 network design and implementation process as well.

For example, a payroll processing system can be designed using the data flow methodology. In this methodology, the flow of payroll data through the system is studied. A dictionary of the data (information and other inputs) processed during this procedure is created, and structure charts that define the functional components of the system as well as the relationship between those components are developed. Then some type of general step-by-step description of the procedures necessary to process the incoming payroll information and create the desired output reports (often referred to as *pseudocode*) is developed. Finally, the actual program code needed is written and tested.

In the NetWare 4 process, inputs may include such documents as a company organization chart; a diagram of the network's topology; maps displaying the location of corporate offices, plants, and so on; and a list of all hardware and software resources included on the network. Other information can include details about the flow of work for various departments, workgroups, divisions, and so on in the company. A general description of the company, its history of growth or downsizing, its mission statement, and other information that helps to define the company may also be useful input when designing the network.

For example, the resource list is useful to the project team when deciding where to locate replicas of the NDS database. The resource list provides the team with information about the quantity and current location of various NetWare and non-NetWare file servers. Before the project team can determine where replicas of the NDS database should be placed, they need to know what file servers are available to hold replicas.

Implementation Phase

The implementation phase is the third of the four phases in the NetWare 4 design and implementation process. The primary purpose of the implementation phase is to implement the NetWare 4 network design successfully. The implementation phase consists of three procedures (see fig. 2.4):[6]

- Develop a migration strategy.
- Create an implementation schedule.
- Implement NetWare 4.

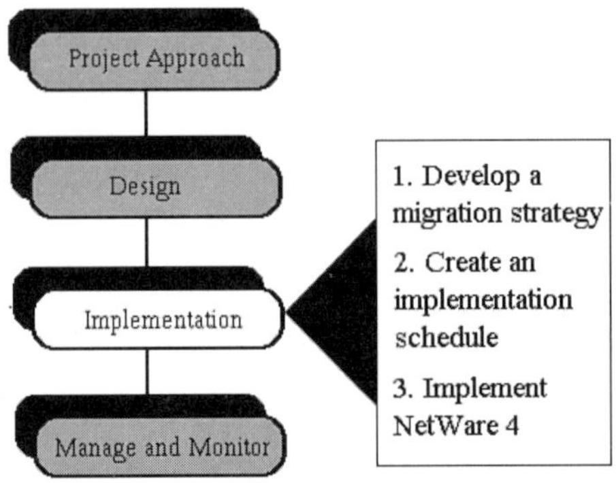

Figure 2.4
Implementation phase procedures.

During the implementation phase, NetWare servers may be migrated from previous versions of NetWare or from other NetWare operating systems to NetWare 4. Whether file servers will be migrated, which file servers will be migrated, when file servers will be migrated, if bindery services will be needed, and a host of other options must be considered when developing a migration strategy. Once those options have been considered and the decisions made, the project team creates an implementation schedule and implements the NetWare 4 network.

Implementation is also a systems development activity although its process includes procedures that vary from those defined in the NetWare 4 design and implementation process. For example, there are two procedures defined in *Computer Control & Audit* as details associated with implementation planning:[7]

- Develop specific plans and schedules for conversion, system test, and user training.
- Review and validate the programming plan and revise as necessary.

In addition to the differences in the steps associated with the procedures, some systems development techniques describe the implementation phase as beginning at an earlier phase in the design and implementation process. For example, Collins and Blay state that the "planning of implementation commences during the feasibility study phase. At that stage, it is necessary to produce an outline plan and for some events...it may then be necessary to plan in detail. The implementation plan is progressively refined during the project as more detailed information becomes available."[8]

During the NetWare 4 process, an approach to migrating the existing network to NetWare 4, or building a NetWare 4 network where none existed before must be developed and documented. Factors such as the current version of workstation software and whether it will have to be updated must be considered. So, too, must variables such as whether current application programs can run in a NetWare 4 environment, who will handle problems with user workstations, whether workstations will be configured for SMS backup, and so on.

Once the project team members are comfortable that they have considered all factors, the team can then develop a time plan for completing the migration and implement the migration strategy. Once the migration strategy is in place, the final phase of the NetWare 4 process—manage and monitor—begins.

Manage and Monitor Phase

The manage and monitor phase is the last of the four phases in the NetWare 4 design and implementation process. The primary purpose of the manage and monitor phase is diagnosing and resolving network problems. The manage and monitor phase consists of two procedures—managing the NetWare 4 network and monitoring the NetWare 4 network[9] (see fig. 2.5).

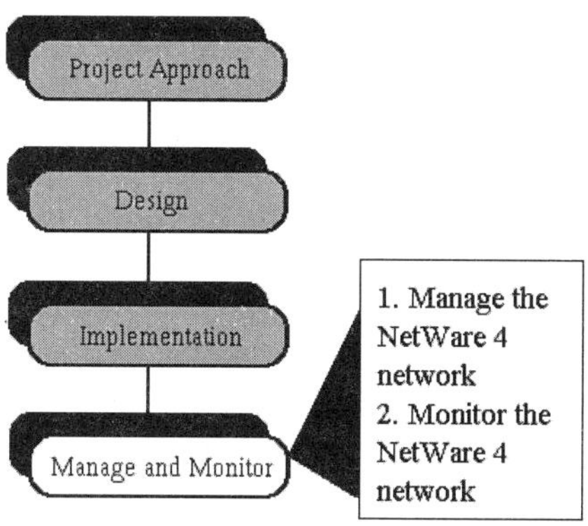

Figure 2.5
Manage and monitor phase procedures.

Managing and monitoring a NetWare 4 network is somewhat different from the equivalent process in the system design life cycle because of the nature of networking itself. With a NetWare 4 network, for example, you must manage and monitor the network operating system software, the network's usage, how accessible the network is for users, and a variety of other issues. When you design and implement a single software program, such as a payroll application, which has been designed and implemented as the result of following one of the system design life cycle processes, generally only the performance of that one system is managed and monitored.

For example, any of the system design life cycle processes may be used to design and implement a new accounts receivable software program. The inputs to the program, who will use the program, how it will be used, and the anticipated outputs are reviewed and analyzed. The phases of the system design life cycle is completed, up to and including the final phase—maintenance—but only for the one program—the accounts receivable software. Although how it interacts with other programs is also a concern, the accounts receivable software is of primary concern.

With a NetWare 4 network, whether it functions properly determines how well everything works, including the accounts receivable software running on one or more of the network file servers. The maintenance phase of the system design life cycle is concerned with how well the individual software runs. The manage and monitor phase of the NetWare 4 network is concerned with the entire network, and is thus more complex and detailed a process than maintaining an accounts receivable or other individual software program.

The persons responsible for managing and monitoring a NetWare 4 network use several software programs to manage and monitor the NetWare 4 network. Some of the application programs provided with the NetWare 4 operating system software and available to those responsible for network monitoring are DSTRACE, DSVIEW, DPING, DSREPAIR, and PARTMGR. Using each of these programs, the network's operation can be monitored and, if necessary, repaired to ensure continued and successful functionality.

Each phase of the NetWare 4 network design and implementation process has several procedures and thus several steps that must be performed in order to ensure the best possible network design and implementation. Understanding the details of each procedure is necessary to be successful at designing and implementing a NetWare 4 network. To help you understand what you need to know about the process, the next section provides more detail about the procedures and tasks associated with each of the NetWare 4 network design and implementation phases.

Understanding the Procedures

As you have seen, each of the four phases of the NetWare 4 network design and implementation process has various procedures associated with it. Those procedures require a variety of tasks to be accomplished in order to complete each procedure. Not every task—not even every procedure—is required for all NetWare 4 networks, however.

Smaller networks (250 or fewer users) that do not span large geographic areas may not require a testing lab to be set up before a pilot program is implemented, for example. In addition, if the smaller network is quite small (50 or fewer users), a pilot program may not even be necessary. With only a few file servers with which to work, you may have no choice but to design the system and implement it without much more testing than verifying that everything is compatible on the first NetWare 4 file server before upgrading or installing any additional NetWare 4 file servers.

Project Approach Phase Procedures

As previously noted, the procedures that must be followed in order to fulfill the primary purpose of the project approach phase include the following:

- Establish the project team.
- Collect relevant information.

- Educate the project team.
- Establish the project's scope.
- Develop a preliminary schedule.

From this phase's first step of establishing the project team to its last step of developing a preliminary schedule, whether each step must be performed depends primarily on the size of the network. For companies where the network itself is relatively small, the project team is likely to consist of one (or perhaps two) individual who is assigned to or volunteers for the project. In this situation, there really is no project team to gather, and thus less formality is required. The steps associated with gathering the project team, therefore, are generally not done.

The NetWare 4 network design and implementation process has been developed to accommodate the design and implementation of all network sizes. Whether you are working with networks ranging from only a couple of NetWare 4 file servers to hundreds of NetWare 4 file servers, you can follow this same process, moving from phase to phase, completing only those steps that apply. When you are done, you will have successfully designed and installed a NetWare 4 network that meets the needs of the company for which it was designed.

There are four tasks that do not have to be completed when working with a relatively small network. The first is organizing the project team.

The second task—educating the project team—is also part of the project approach phase. If you are the individual responsible for designing and implementing the network, you may need to educate yourself. This is not the same, however, as trying to educate an entire project team.

The third and fourth tasks are part of the implementation phase. Before completing a full-scale implementation of a large network, you may want to set up a test lab to verify the network design and success of the implementation process. In addition, you may also want to set up a pilot test, implementing the design on a small scale and verifying that it is functioning as intended before implementing it throughout the company. Setting up a test lab and running a pilot test do not generally have to be completed in a small LAN.

Establishing the Project Team

Establishing the project team means bringing together various individuals to fulfill different roles during the design and implementation of the NetWare 4 network. A variety of roles needs to be filled if the network design and implementation is to be successful (see fig. 2.6).

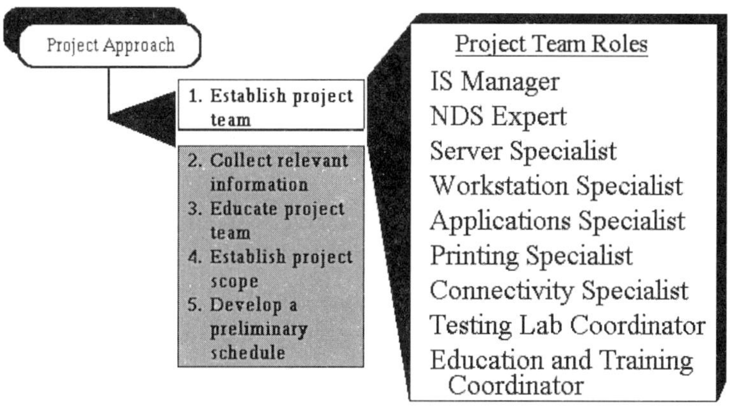

Figure 2.6
Project team roles.

Fulfilling each job function contributes to the success of the design and installation of the NetWare 4 network. To fulfill each function, the project team must understand the responsibilities associated with each job function as described here and on the following pages.

The IS manager role has several job functions, primarily overseeing the entire NetWare 4 design and implementation project. The IS manager must coordinate with all other project team roles, but in particular with the NDS expert. Successful coordination between the IS manager and the NDS expert job functions helps to ensure a smooth transition from the old network (or no network) to the NetWare 4 network.

In addition to the responsibility for coordinating and overseeing the project, the IS manager also functions as the link between upper management and the project team. The IS manager accepts assignments from upper management and passes on needs and requirements to the rest of the project team. In return, the project team can expect the IS manager to relay its concerns and needs to management.

When the team or the project itself requires specific resources, obtaining those resources is also the IS manager's responsibility. Ultimately, the IS manager must be concerned that the network's design and implementation process is as efficient, effective, timely, productive, and seamless as possible.

The NDS expert is primarily responsible for ensuring the design of the directory tree and the security of the network. Because the network is a NetWare 4 network, the NDS expert also often assumes the role of project team leader. The responsibility for the majority of the procedures that are performed during the design phase of the NetWare 4 network design and implementation process falls to the NDS expert.

The NDS expert is also often responsible for choosing other project team members, because of this expert's knowledge of both NetWare 4 and the company's existing network and its network needs. In addition, the communication with various management and company department personnel enables the NDS expert to have a broad picture of the company's networking needs.

The server specialist is primarily responsible for ensuring that the move to a NetWare 4 network does not adversely affect network performance or the stability of the network as a whole. Ensuring that the pilot implementation is successful, and then participating in the plan for upgrade and migration as well as for time synchronization and server placement, are all important responsibilities or concerns of the server specialist.

The server specialist also provides information to other team members regarding server-related issues. For example, the server specialist may take on the responsibility of gathering and then providing to the team a list of servers, applications running on those servers, workstations accessing those servers, and other resource information.

Because of the server specialist's network responsibilities, other concerns can include disk space requirements for file servers, backup of data on network servers, registration of IPX numbers, and standards for such things as protocols and frame types.

Just as the server specialist is primarily responsible for ensuring that the move to a NetWare 4 network does not adversely affect network performance or stability, the workstation specialist is primarily responsible for ensuring that workstations on the network can still access all the resources needed by the user. Two primary issues are key to the workstation specialist. The first is updating workstations to the version of the Requester that is currently compatible with NetWare 4. The second, more applicable to larger networks, is that of automating the upgrade of software on network workstations.

Software upgrades on the workstation may not always be successfully compatible with all the workstations. Compatibility issues, such as insufficient memory on older workstations, have to be considered and planned for by the workstation specialist. Other issues related to workstation software may include configuration file upgrades and consistency, naming conventions as used in client configuration files, compatibility of software and the new client requester, login scripts, bindery services, and traveling users.

By necessity, the workstation specialist has to work closely with at least the server specialist, application specialist, NDS expert, printing specialist, and connectivity specialist. Interaction with the testing lab coordinator, education and training lab coordinator, and NDS expert may also be important.

The application specialist has the responsibility of ensuring that applications are compatible with NetWare 4 and migrating applications to the NetWare 4 network. If users access applications through one or more menus, the application specialist has to be concerned with existing network menus. Because login scripts can be used to set up access to applications, the applications specialist may need to coordinate with the NDS expert to ensure that login scripts are created as needed to accommodate access to applications.

The printing specialist is responsible for ensuring that users can access printers and that printer software, including drivers, is upgraded where needed. Printers that are directly connected to the network must have bindery services provided for them. The printing specialist sees to this.

The connectivity specialist has the responsibility of ensuring that routing, protocols, telecommunications, and any other connectivity issues are dealt with when designing and implementing the network.

Internetwork packet traffic and bandwidth must be considered and planned for in order to ensure efficient and effective network communications. Routing issues, such as whether routers or bridges are used on the network, must be considered as well because the decision can affect the speed of network traffic. As a rule, routers have lower packet-per-second data throughput than bridges, so if routers are the primary connection method, router location can affect the speed of network traffic. If gateways are used on the network to interconnect the NetWare 4 network with other environments, such as a mainframe computer, the connectivity specialist must consider this.

It is the connectivity specialist's responsibility to bring these types of issues to the design team's attention when network design can be positively or negatively influenced by connectivity issues.

The testing lab coordinator's primary concern is that the NetWare operating system functions properly with existing and planned applications. To ensure NetWare 4's proper functioning, the testing lab coordinator sets up an environment that resembles the real network environment and then tests the company's various applications running on the test NetWare 4 network.

Besides ensuring that applications function with NetWare 4, the testing lab coordinator needs to determine whether applications continue to meet minimum requirements for such factors as response time. The testing lab coordinator may set up minimum performance benchmarks, therefore, and test against those benchmarks.

The education and training coordinator has the responsibility of determining what skills the individual project team members need to have and then makes arrangements to provide training, including any resources necessary to provide that training. This coordinator must perform this same function for both users and administrators as well.

By carefully choosing team members to include various individuals with a wide variety of skills on the project team, you help ensure that all important issues are addressed. Even the best team can overlook important issues or not even know that it should be addressing certain issues if it does not have all the relevant information it needs to make appropriate choices. Once the project design team is assembled and responsibilities have been assigned to team members, the information needed to make good decisions must be collected, reviewed, and analyzed by project team members.

Collecting Relevant Information

The project team should have a variety of information available. Any information that may affect the design of the network should be collected, reviewed, and analyzed by the project team to ensure that all factors are considered.

At a minimum, these are the types of information that should be collected and referenced for designing the NetWare 4 network:

- Company history or background overview
- Company organization charts
- Network topology diagrams

- Business and office location maps
- Hardware and software resources
- Workflow information

The company history or background overview documents should help the project team understand the design and function of the company. Understanding what the company wants to accomplish can help the team design the network to meet the company's needs.

Because the lower levels of the directory tree often resemble a company's organization, organization charts are necessary. In addition, a good knowledge of the company's organization helps the team to understand who will be affected by the network.

Issues such as which file servers hold partition replicas are affected by the topology of the network. As an example, writeable replicas should be placed on file servers close to the users who need access to that portion of the NDS database in order to access the network. For the project team to determine which file servers should hold which replicas, the team needs to know the physical layout of the network. The physical layout of the network, in the form of topology diagrams, is important information for the project team.

Maps displaying where users' offices and various network resources are physically located is also important information. By the same token, the project team also needs information about what resources are available on the network. Resource information such as applications, types of computers and their operating systems, backup devices, and so on are all relevant when determining the design of the network.

Designing an efficient and effective network also requires that the project team members have an understanding of how company employees perform their duties. Workflow documents give the project team this type of information.

Educating the Project Team

The project team must be educated about various aspects of the company that will be or are currently affected by the network. As noted earlier, this responsibility falls to the education and training coordinator, and it must be planned for as part of the network design and implementation process.

Although the main responsibility for educating the project team falls to the education and training coordinator, part of the education process is the responsibility of each individual team member. Each team member must read and understand the information that has been gathered. There are additional educational responsibilities that the project team must fulfill as well.

One or more members of the project team must take on the responsibility of ensuring that team members understand NetWare 4 and the implications of installing a new network or migrating their existing network to NetWare 4. Each team member needs to have a basic understanding of networking in general, and of NetWare 4 in particular.

To understand networking in general, team members should have a basic understanding of the following terms and aspects of networking:

- Networking concepts
- Physical transmission characteristics
- Access control methods
- Network architectures
- Network operating systems

Project team members should also have a basic understanding of NetWare 4. Team members should understand the overall concept of NetWare 4, and in particular, should be familiar with NDS.

> **Note** If you want a review of networking basics and NDS, or you will be responsible for educating other project team members, you may find Appendix B and Appendix C of this book to be useful. Appendix B contains a quick introduction to networking, covering the topics included in the previous list, and Appendix C provides a brief overview of NDS.

If more than a basic understanding of networking and NDS is required by one or more project team members, self-study materials, Novell documentation, trade publications, product-related books such as those available from New Riders Publishing, and NetWare courses are all available options for training one or more members of the project team.

Establishing the Project's Scope

What the network design will and will not include, and the expectations that will be fulfilled as a result of completing the network design are the important factors that define the scope of the project. Assessing the company and its needs, as well as determining which factors affect that design so as to set reasonable expectations for the project, are also part of establishing the project's scope.

Developing a Preliminary Schedule

Once reasonable expectations are determined, the time required to complete the design phase of the network design and implementation project can be established. Certain minimum default time requirements can be used to establish a preliminary project schedule.

For example, a network with more than 30 file servers may require the use of configured time sources, rather than the default time configuration. If that is the case, a minimum of one-half day should be included in the preliminary schedule for determining how to best configure time sources for the network.

The number of file servers on the network, the number of replicas needed, whether the network is a *Local Area Network (LAN)*, *Municipal Area Network (MAN)*, or *Wide Area Network (WAN)*, and several other factors contribute to the amount of time required to design the network successfully.

Determining how much time will be needed is the first step. The time frame of the project can be affected by factors such as the number of days in each work week, how many holidays or other nonwork days fall in the time frame, and how many team members are available during the design process.

Design Phase Procedures

The design phase procedures in the NetWare 4 process vary substantially from procedures associated with the SDLC. The general SDLC system design phase commonly involves three major tasks (see fig. 2.7):

- Identify potential solutions.
- Evaluate and choose from potential solutions.
- Develop a high-level design system.

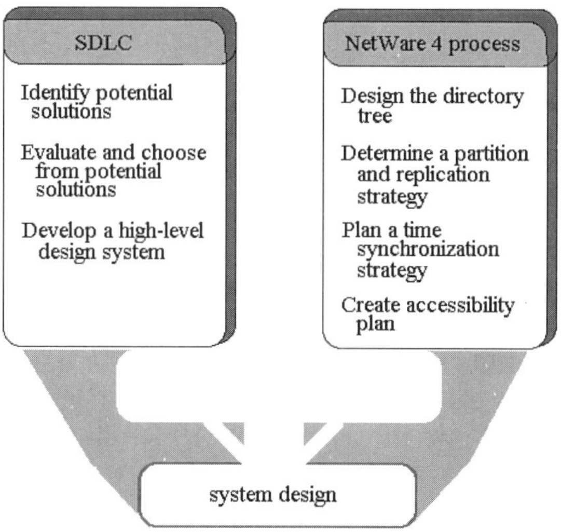

Figure 2.7
SDLC versus NetWare 4 design phase tasks.

Although the end result of the SDLC design phase and the NetWare 4 design phase are the same—a system design—there are four procedures that may be performed during the design phase of the NetWare 4 process, and they are substantially different from the three typical procedures associated with the SDLC design phase:

- Design the directory tree.
- Determine a partition and replication strategy.
- Plan a time synchronization strategy.
- Create an accessibility plan.

Of the four procedures, not all procedures have to be performed under all circumstances. The size of the network and its topology determine which of the four must be done. Regardless of the size of the network, the directory tree must still be designed. In a small network localized within one geographic area, however, the default partition and replication strategy and the default time synchronization strategy are often sufficient. An accessibility plan has to be devised, however, regardless of the size of the network.

Designing the Directory Tree

The most important procedure in the design phase is determining the layout of the directory tree. Unless properly designed, partitioning may be difficult, as well as replication. In addition, a poorly designed tree may make growth difficult and ineffective. Daily network use and management also may be more difficult and complicated than it would otherwise be, both for administrators and users.

Part of designing the directory tree includes establishing standards for naming the various container and leaf objects in the tree. The design should include examples of how the standard is to be implemented for each type of object, as well as information about why the standard was chosen. This information makes it easier to explain the standard to those who will be responsible for following it, and it provides the logic behind the decisions made by the team (see fig. 2.8).

Naming Standards Document

User Objects:

Login (common) name begins with the first six characters of the user's last name, followed by the first character of the user's first name, and the first character of the user's middle name. If no middle name exists, use the first two characters of the user's first name instead.

Example:

Charles J. Smith would be SMITHCJ

Charles Smith would be SMITHCH

Figure 2.8

Sample naming standard for user objects.

One other consideration before designing the tree should be whether any standards are appropriate for assigning both internal and external network *Internet Packet Exchange (IPX)* numbers. If IPX standards are to be implemented, those standards must be set and documented the same as object naming standards, although the logic behind the standard may not have to be documented.

When tree design begins, the upper layer of the NDS directory tree is designed first. In larger networks, the upper layer generally functions best if designed around the geographical layout of the company. In smaller networks, department, division, or workgroup representation in the upper layers of the tree is often satisfactory, particularly if little or no growth is expected.

After the upper layer of the NDS directory tree is designed, the lower layers must be considered. Lower layers should be as extensive as necessary to meet the company's needs, but should be designed with the user's needs in mind. Workgroup, department, division, functionality, and so on can all be reasonable approaches to designing the lower layers of the tree, even in a large network.

Determining a Partition and Replication Strategy

When establishing a strategy for partitioning the NDS directory and then placing replicas, there are two goals to be accomplished. The first is fault tolerance. It is important that no partition of the

NDS directory have only one replica. Multiple replicas on different file servers help to ensure that if the master replica becomes corrupted beyond repair, an alternative copy is available.

Even if the master never becomes corrupted, the location of replicas on various file servers across the network makes it possible to accomplish the second goal—easy network access. For a user to log in to the NetWare 4 network, a writeable replica of the partition containing that user's object must be accessible to the user. The closer the writeable replica is to the actual user, the quicker and more efficient the login process.

One other factor needs to be considered when creating a partition strategy, and in reality, should have been considered when the NDS directory tree was initially designed. No network partition should cross geographic boundaries. Doing so is referred to as "spanning the WAN." Do not span the WAN when partitioning the NDS directory tree.

Planning a Time Synchronization Strategy

All transactions on the network are provided with a time stamp to help NetWare determine the order in which to process requests for services, changes to the NDS database, messaging services, and so on. The NetWare time synchronization strategy affects time stamping. For this reason, time synchronization planning is an important step in the design process.

Certain time synchronization defaults exist when NetWare 4 is installed. If the network is contained within a single location, and the number of file servers and objects is relatively limited, the default time synchronization plan is generally sufficient. With a larger network, some customization of time synchronization may be required. A time synchronization strategy will be necessary, and it is developed as part of the NetWare 4 network design phase.

Creating an Accessibility Plan

One of the important, if not the most important, aspects of a network is the user's capability of accessing and sharing various resources. Designing an accessibility plan is, therefore, also an important procedure of the NetWare 4 design phase.

Creating an accessibility plan involves first determining which resources are needed by which users. Next, the project design team must determine how to group those resources for easy access. Guidelines that specify the decisions made by the project design team then need to be created. This is particularly important in larger networks where the actual network implementation may involve many people. Everyone needs to follow the same approach.

The project team is responsible for including information in the accessibility guidelines that specify how resources are grouped, how access to resources from one container to another are achieved, and so on. For example, the project team may decide to provide Directory Map objects and Alias objects to simplify network data administration and access to physical resources.

Whatever decisions the project team makes regarding user access to network resources, those decisions must be documented in some type of accessibility guidelines document. Those guidelines must be explained and their use must then be taught to those who will implement the network design.

Implementation Phase Procedures

As with structured systems development, the planning of implementation begins early in the design process. The plan itself is refined as the design process proceeds, adding details as required information is provided and needed decisions are made. As with structured system development, the NetWare 4 planning process also consists of a series of procedures that must be completed. In structured system development, the procedures consist of scheduling implementation, converting data, acquiring and training staff, designing the clerical part of the system, producing operations manuals, and converting over to the new system.[10]

The implementation phase procedures for a NetWare 4 network are not quite as complex or lengthy as those defined in the structured system development phase for the development of an EDP system. There are only three procedures in the NetWare 4 implementation phase:

- Develop a migration strategy.
- Create an implementation schedule.
- Implement NetWare 4.

These three procedures also do not include the same types of tasks as the procedures listed for EDP development. This lack of resemblance is due primarily to the fact that the implementation phase for a NetWare 4 network involves a software program (NetWare 4) that has already been designed and tested, long before its implementation by various companies. In the EDP process, the software itself is what is new and different, not just the fact that it is being introduced and implemented as a new software program to the same company that was responsible for its design and development.

Developing a Migration Strategy

When developing the strategy for migrating an existing network or installing a new NetWare 4 network, three network resources must be considered. Those three resources are workstations, file servers, and applications. Several questions must be answered and tasks performed, in order to ensure that all resources are included.

For example, existing DOS workstations must be checked to establish whether the NETX network shell is loaded or older versions of the NetWare DOS Requester (VLM files) are being used. Workstations have to be brought up to the latest versions of the VLM client files to ensure proper network functionality.

The project team also has to determine which Novell tools to use to upgrade existing network file servers. For example, if NetWare 3.1*x* file servers will be upgraded to NetWare 4.1, three options are available. Those options are across-the-wire migration, same-server migration, and in-place upgrade. The decision is likely to depend, at least in part, on whether new hardware will be purchased for the network or only existing hardware will be used. Whatever the decision, the choice must be made during the development of the migration strategy.

The migration strategy may also include setting aside testing time and obtaining equipment to set up a testing lab. This equipment can then be used to determine whether all existing applications will be fully functional in the NetWare 4 environment. This is a particularly important aspect of the migration strategy, because uninterrupted and easy access to existing applications is the primary way network users judge the success or failure of the network's implementation.

Testing applications is important for another reason as well. Some existing applications may not be compatible with NetWare 4 in its fully functional mode. Those applications are likely to be usable, however, if NetWare 4 file servers have bindery services activated in the proper containers. The project team must determine whether bindery services have to be enabled, and if so, where and for how long.

Budgeting for upgraded versions of these applications may also be necessary. Although budgeting is not usually the responsibility of the project team, it is its responsibility to let management know which applications will eventually have to be upgraded.

All these factors must be assessed by the project team before implementing NetWare 4. Considering all relevant factors and planning accordingly helps to ensure a smooth and effective migration to NetWare 4.

Creating an Implementation Schedule

The primary goal of the implementation schedule is to list, organize in a logical order, and prioritize all the tasks that must be completed in order to implement the NetWare 4 network. To accomplish this goal, the project team must first identify each task that must be performed.

Identifying all the tasks related to implementing the NetWare 4 network is probably the most difficult aspect of this procedure. Tasks such as upgrading the workstations, installing NetWare 4 on new hardware, and upgrading NetWare 3 file servers to NetWare 4 are common and easily remembered tasks. Other tasks are not.

For example, if a network running NetWare 3 with dial-up modems from remote sites already exists, remembering to test your remote access program—by actually dialing into the system—for compatibility with NetWare 4 can be difficult. On the other hand, it should be relatively easy to remember to test any applications used regularly on the network.

Some questions the project team can ask to help develop the implementation schedule may include the following:

- What is the maximum length of time this project can take?
- How many individuals will be assigned to the task of implementing the NetWare 4 network?
- In which order do the tasks need to be performed in order to proceed with as few problems as possible?

Once all tasks are identified, a preliminary schedule for implementation can be created. The appearance of the preliminary schedule is up to the project team. One design commonly used in the development of electronic data processing systems is a type of work schedule. On the work schedule, each task is listed and briefly described. A time interval chart is placed across the page. The time intervals for each task are then marked according to when they will be completed.

Novell's NetWare 4 process uses a similar approach. Figure 2.9 provides an example of the type of approach displayed in Novell's NetWare 4.1 Design and Implementation course manual.

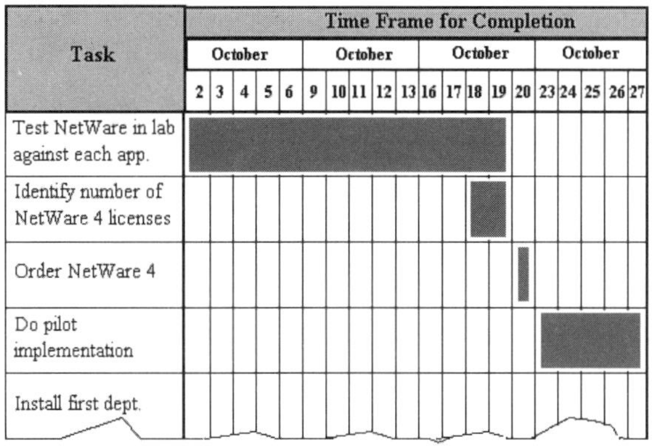

Figure 2.9
Sample implementation schedule.

When there is more than one group in the company responsible for implementing the NetWare 4 network, the project team should coordinate the preliminary and any subsequent versions of the implementation schedule with other groups before settling on a final implementation schedule.

A pilot implementation to test the network in a small, localized, and controlled portion of the company (such as a workgroup or department) is the next step in the creation of the implementation schedule. The pilot test should point out areas where problems are likely to occur and help you come up with solutions that can be implemented throughout the company.

Implementing NetWare 4

After the pilot implementation is successful, the project team and other responsible groups can begin the full implementation of the NetWare 4 network. Full implementation may require that only one aspect of the network is implemented at a time.

For example, the project team may choose to upgrade the company headquarters office and ensure that it is implemented in full before moving on to upgrade another department, division, or area. On the other hand, if sufficient personnel are available to assist with the upgrade, the team may choose to upgrade all sites at one time.

Either approach—or something between—may be acceptable. The project team must choose some approach, however, before implementation can proceed.

Manage and Monitor Phase Procedures

Once the implementation process is complete, the next phase of the NetWare 4 design and implementation process can begin. That phase is the manage and monitor phase.

There are two procedures defined for the manage and monitor phase: managing the NetWare 4 network, and monitoring the NetWare 4 network. These procedures include a variety of tasks, the purpose of which is to ensure that the network meets the needs of the users, fulfills the goals for which it was designed, and functions as efficiently as possible.

Managing NetWare 4

Effectively managing the NetWare 4 network requires that management guidelines first be established. For the most part, network administrators are able to determine what they must do to keep the network functioning properly. These management guidelines give administrators with little or no NetWare 4 experience an idea of where to start.

Network management guidelines may include information about which network utilities are to be used for managing the network. Several management utilities are included with the NetWare 4 operating system software, but the company may also choose to add other utilities.

The following are some of the NetWare 4 utilities that can be used to manage the NetWare 4 network:

- DSREPAIR
- DSTRACE
- PARTMGR

- NetWare Administrator
- NWAdmin
- SERVMAN
- SBACKUP

Guidelines may take into account the use of these utilities. For example, the management guidelines may indicate the use of the SBACKUP or other Storage Management Services (SMS)-compliant utilities to perform regular NDS backups. Network management guidelines may also specify who is responsible for network management, although that decision was probably made by management even before the design team was assembled.

Monitoring NetWare 4

The purpose of monitoring the network as a procedure in the design and implementation process is to determine whether the network as designed and implemented is fulfilling its intended goal. To make that determination, the network must be tracked. A report of the results of the project may also be necessary.

Monitoring the NetWare 4 network also helps in efforts to anticipate network problems. Finding potential problem areas before they become problems helps to keep the network running as smoothly and efficiently as possible.

Network monitoring also includes troubleshooting network problems once they surface. You must determine the source or cause of network problems as soon after they become apparent as possible, then devise an approach to solving those problems.

When network problems are not caught in time, or unforeseen events occur that interrupt or bring down the network, a recovery process must be followed. Before a recovery process can be followed, however, some recovery procedures need to be defined.

There is likely to come a time when no amount of monitoring, troubleshooting, or recovery is sufficient to cause the network to meet the continuing needs of the user. Sometimes, the network design simply outgrows its original design or is overshadowed by changes in technology. Eventually, it may be necessary to determine at what point in time to upgrade the network or replace the current process. Making this determination can be part of the network monitoring task, and is also often the impetus for starting the network design and implementation process over from the beginning.

Summary

Designing and implementing a NetWare 4 network can be a relatively easy process—or a complex and time-consuming one. Two primary factors determine the ease or complexity of the process. The first is the size of the network, and the second is an effective, tested design process.

Small networks are generally easier to design and implement than larger networks. Issues such as time synchronization strategy become a moot point when working with a network that is small enough to accept the default approach to time synchronization.

In addition, not all the procedures in the design and implementation process have to be performed for small, localized networks. For example, the default partitioning and replication strategy may be sufficient for a LAN with only a few file servers.

The time required to plan and implement a small network may be substantially less than that required for a large network. For example, if the network has only one or two sites connected by a WAN, the length of time needed to design custom partitioning, replication, and time synchronization is likely to be closer to one day. A larger network with several sites connected by a WAN may require three to four days to plan for custom partitioning, replication, and time synchronization.

The other primary factor that determines the ease or complexity of the design and implementation of a NetWare 4 network is whether an effective, tested, design and implementation process is available and can be successfully followed. Such a process has been documented by Novell's Consulting Services group in conjunction with various companies who have designed and installed their own NetWare 4 networks. Following the NetWare 4 process makes it easier to design and implement any NetWare 4 network.

Although based on the system design life cycle, the NetWare 4 process is more of a subset of the SDLC. Its four phases—project approach, design, implementation, and manage and monitor—are described and discussed in this chapter to help you understand the basics of the NetWare 4 process. The following chapters explore the details of each of the procedures associated with the four phases of the NetWare 4 network design and implementation process to make it easier for you to complete the process in one or more companies successfully.

Case Study

You have been contacted by the president of Johnson Shoes, Mr. Samuel Johnson, to help upgrade the company's existing network to NetWare 4. During a telephone conversation with Mr. Johnson, you learned that the company's current network administrator has no NetWare 4 experience, but has convinced Mr. Johnson that future expansion plans and wide area networking necessitate a move to NetWare 4. Mr. Johnson has agreed to hire a consultant to oversee the design and implementation of the network, and he is meeting separately with two consultants who have been recommended to him. Mr. Johnson knows very little about NetWare 4 and has never met either of the consultants, including you, so he has asked you to provide him and his staff with an overview of what is involved in designing and implementing a NetWare 4 network.

You agree to meet with Mr. Johnson and his staff. The following overview of the company is faxed to you by the president's assistant, along with a written request to make a presentation two days from now. You will be given ten minutes to make your presentation, which must explain the process you will follow to design and implement a NetWare 4 network for Johnson shoes. Because you are quite familiar with the NetWare 4 network design and implementation process, you need only to familiarize yourself with Johnson Shoes and provide yourself with an outline of the process on note cards to ensure your presentation goes smoothly.

Here is the information you receive:

1. Johnson Shoes is a small business with two retail outlets that sell footwear and accessories, such as purses, shoe polish, shoelaces, socks, and a variety of small items on point-of-sale displays.
2. Johnson Shoes presently has three NetWare 3.11 file servers. One is located in the smaller of the two retail stores on Broadway Avenue in Buffalo, New York. The larger store is located on Fifth Avenue in New York City. The company is planning to open an upscale shoe store on Rodeo drive in Beverly Hills, California, sometime within the next 12 months. It wants to add a third NetWare file server and locate it in the Beverly Hills store so that all three of their retail outlets can be connected to the corporate headquarters in New York.
3. Presently, its two retail stores use their local file servers to track store inventory and sales. They also use a word processing program for creating correspondence. Each file server has a modem connection used for ordering inventory and transmitting sales and inventory information to the headquarters on a daily basis.

Given this information about Johnson Shoes, prepare a bullet list of points you want to cover when explaining the design and implementation process you will follow if chosen as the consultant on this project.

Review Questions

1. The project's scope ____________.
   - A. should be established before choosing team members
   - B. is set after the project team is trained
   - C. cannot be changed once relevant information is collected
   - D. can be changed only after a preliminary schedule is determined

2. During the ____________ phase, the project team must make a realistic determination of what can be expected from the resulting network design and implementation.
   - A. project approach
   - B. design
   - C. implementation
   - D. manage and monitor

3. Gathering and educating the project team is included in the ____________ phase of the NetWare 4 process.
   - A. project approach
   - B. design
   - C. implementation
   - D. manage and monitor

4. Inputs, such as a diagram of the network's topology and a list of resources, are used to ____________.
   - A. choose project team members
   - B. develop a migration strategy
   - C. create the implementation schedule
   - D. design the directory tree structure

5. The project role whose occupant is responsible for providing the team with a list of network file servers and other related resource information is the ____________.

   ○ A. workstation specialist
   ○ B. applications specialist
   ○ C. server specialist
   ○ D. NDS expert

6. The ____________ is ultimately responsible for ensuring that the design of the directory tree and the security of the network are adequate to meet the company's needs.

   ○ A. connectivity specialist
   ○ B. IS manager
   ○ C. server specialist
   ○ D. NDS expert

7. Planning a time synchronization strategy is performed after ____________.

   ○ A. designing the directory tree
   ○ B. determining a partition and replication strategy
   ○ C. creating an accessibility plan
   ○ D. developing a migration strategy

8. The naming standards document is created during which procedure?

   ○ A. Designing the directory tree
   ○ B. Determining a partition and replication strategy
   ○ C. Creating an accessibility plan
   ○ D. Developing a migration strategy

9. Establishing whether the NETX network shell currently exists on network workstations, and then planning to upgrade the network shell to the most recent version of the Requester, is part of ___________.
   - A. planning a time synchronization strategy
   - B. creating an implementation schedule
   - C. developing a migration strategy
   - D. managing and monitoring the network

10. Which of the following statements are true?
    - A. Small networks are generally easier to design and implement than larger networks.
    - B. A time synchronization strategy does not have to be planned in a WAN because the default design is sufficient.
    - C. The NetWare 4 process is operating relatively system-blind.
    - D. A small network can be defined as having fewer than 250 users and not spanning large geographic areas.

Answers

1. B
2. A
3. A
4. D
5. C
6. B
7. B
8. A
9. C
10. A C D

Notes

1. *NetWare 4.1 Design and Implementation Instructor's Guide, Rev. 1.0*. Provo: Novell, Inc., IG 1–15.
2. Mair, William C., Donald R. Wood, and Keagle W. Davis. *Computer Control & Audit*. Florida: The Institute of Internal Auditors, Inc., 214.
3. Collins, Garfield, and Gillian Blay. *Structured Systems Development Techniques: Strategic Planning to System Testing*. New York: John Wiley & Sons, 55.
4. Ibid., 56.
5. *NetWare 4.1 Design and Implementation Instructor's Guide, Rev. 1.0*. Provo: Novell, Inc., IG 1–32.
6. Ibid., IG 1–26.
7. Mair, William C., Donald R. Wood, and Keagle W. Davis. *Computer Control & Audit*. Florida: The Institute of Internal Auditors, Inc., 214.
8. Collins, Garfield, and Gillian Blay. *Structured Systems Development Techniques: Strategic Planning to System Testing*. New York: John Wiley & Sons, 35.
9. *Netware 4.1 Design and Implementation Instructor's Guide, Rev. 1.0*. Provo: Novell, Inc. IG 1–30.
10. Collins, Garfield, and Gillian Blay. *Structured Systems Development Techniques: Strategic Planning to System Testing*. New York: John Wiley & Sons, 35.

Chapter 3

Determining the Design and Implementation Approach

Determining the approach to take in order to design and implement a NetWare 4 network successfully can be a simple process, particularly if the network is relatively small. With small networks, issues such as time synchronization strategy do not have to be addressed beyond a decision to accept the default time synchronization strategy. Larger networks require more design planning and more time to implement.

This chapter includes information on how to accomplish the following:

- Assemble the project team
- Determine the approach to network design

After reading this chapter, you will understand the processes of assembling the project team and establishing how the team will approach the design of the network. You will have a method for determining approximately how complex the network is and how long it will take to design the NetWare 4 network.

Assembling the Project Team

The size of the project team is determined primarily by the size of the company and its proposed or current network. Larger companies are more likely to have more personnel available to participate as project team members than smaller companies. As Chapter 1, "Understanding the Design and Implementation Process," points out, some tasks do not need to be performed when dealing with a relatively small network. For example, if the network and company are small enough, organizing the project team may take no more than a few seconds because only a very limited number of project team members—rarely more than two people—will be available to design and implement the network.

Regardless of the size of the network, almost all the same types of information must be gathered and analyzed and the same types of decisions must be made. The information is collected and analyzed, and the decisions are made based on the collective knowledge and skills of several individuals. Each individual fulfills certain roles and responsibilities on the project design team. If the network and company are small, the information is still needed, thus the roles must still be fulfilled. The difference is the number of people fulfilling those roles.

Regardless of the number of personnel on the project design team, when the design phase of the NetWare 4 process is completed, an effective NetWare 4 network design should also be completed. If the NetWare 4 design procedures were followed, the design will meet the needs of the company for which it was designed, and may continue to do so for a long time to come. The first of the NetWare 4 process design procedures to be accomplished is that of choosing the project's team members.

Project Team Members

As noted in the second chapter, there are several job functions that must be fulfilled in order for the project team to design and install a NetWare 4 network successfully. Recall that those job functions include the following:

- IS manager
- NDS expert
- Server specialist
- Workstation specialist
- Applications specialist
- Printing specialist
- Connectivity specialist
- Testing lab coordinator
- Education and training coordinator

Each project role has assigned responsibilities. Some or all of those project roles may be filled with company personnel who are chosen because of their knowledge and experience with the company or the existing network. Some of those responsibilities may be assigned to a consultant hired from outside the company, a NetWare reseller, or another qualified individual. Regardless of whether the company uses only internal personnel or hires from outside, the design and implementation process is the same. The project team roles that must be fulfilled are also the same.

IS Manager

Someone, regardless of the size of the company or the network, must take responsibility for the design and implementation of the NetWare 4 network. That person is assigned the role title of IS manager by the NetWare 4 process. The IS manager has several responsibilities that coincide with overseeing the entire NetWare 4 design and implementation project, including the following:

- Choosing other project team members
- Coordinating all aspects of the NetWare 4 process with all other project team members (roles)
- Acting as liaison between upper management and the project team
- Obtaining resources needed by the project team
- Assuming responsibility for the majority of the procedures performed during the NetWare 4 network design phase

Ultimately, the IS manager is responsible for ensuring that the design of the directory tree and the security of the network are adequate to meet the company's needs. To fill that responsibility, the IS manager may be expected to provide the project team with answers to some or all of the following questions:

- What is the structure or organization of the company?
- What resources must be managed and made available to the project team so it can fulfill its goal?
- How quickly does management require the network to be designed and implemented?
- What company documents are available to the team?
- How may the flow of work in the company affect the organization's network?

Many of the answers will come from existing company documents. Other questions may require answers directly from management.

NDS Expert

The NDS expert participates in and oversees the design of the directory tree and network security. A properly designed tree makes partitioning, replication, and time synchronization easier to accomplish, and is an important step toward designing and implementing network security. Because the NDS expert has a reasonably thorough understanding of NetWare 4, the NDS expert also often assumes the role of project team leader.

The following are other responsibilities that may be assumed by the NDS expert:

- Choosing other project team members
- Providing a method of communication between company management and various department personnel and the project team
- Guiding network design so it takes into consideration the organizational structure as well as the needs of the company
- Working with the testing lab coordinator to ensure that various aspects of the network design are tested as needed
- Coordinating server, workstation, and application resources with the related project team members

Ultimately, the NDS expert is responsible for ensuring that the directory tree's design and network security meet the company's needs. To fulfill that responsibility, the NDS expert may be expected to provide the project team with answers to some or all of the following questions:

- What are the major divisions of the company?
- What workgroups exist within these major divisions?
- Is the company geographically dispersed, and, if so, how will that dispersion affect network design?
- Does information flow across the WAN, and, if so, how does it flow?
- What major network resources exist and how should they be grouped so as to best make those resources available on the network?
- Should there be only one directory tree, or would more than one directory tree be appropriate for this company?

Some of the answers to these questions will be the result of careful consideration of all information by the NDS expert. Other answers will come from various corporate documents. Still other answers will come only as the result of review and analysis of all relevant information by the project team. For the most part, however, the

NDS expert's input will be invaluable in designing the directory tree and network security.

Server Specialist

The server specialist is primarily responsible for ensuring continued network performance and stability during the design and implementation of the NetWare 4 network. Other responsibilities may include the following:

- ◆ Ensuring the success of the pilot implementation, if one is conducted
- ◆ Providing server-related issues and information to other team members
- ◆ Monitoring disk space requirements for file servers to ensure that the minimum requirements for NetWare 4 are met and provided for
- ◆ Ensuring that all existing file server data is backed up before the implementation of the NetWare 4 network begins
- ◆ Registering all IPX numbers and following standards set by the project team for protocols and frame types

Ultimately, the server specialist is responsible for keeping the existing network functioning effectively during the design and implementation of the new NetWare 4 network, and also making sure that the new network functions as effectively as the old network. To meet that responsibility, the server specialist may be expected to provide the project team with answers to some or all of the following questions:

- ◆ How many servers currently exist on the network?
- ◆ What versions of the NetWare operating system are currently running on those file servers?
- ◆ How many non-NetWare file servers exist on the network, and what network operating systems are they running?
- ◆ Will any of the NetWare 4 file servers provide special services, such as electronic mail or database (not NDS database) services?

- Where are the existing network file servers located?
- Who is presently responsible for administering the network file servers, and will they continue to be responsible for the NetWare 4 file servers?
- What is the hardware configuration of existing network file servers, and will any of the hardware need to be upgraded to accommodate NetWare 4?

The stability of the network as a whole can be positively or adversely affected by the workstations on the network. For example, a workstation running an older version of the Requester, or running the NetWare shell may have intermittent or no success at accessing the network and its resources. Although the problem originates at the workstation, it reflects poorly on the network. The server specialist must, therefore, coordinate with the workstation specialist to ensure that all workstation problems are corrected.

Workstation Specialist

The workstation specialist is primarily responsible for ensuring that workstations on the network can still access all the resources needed by the user. To accomplish this task, the workstation specialist must be particularly concerned about two workstation-related issues:

- That the most current NetWare 4-compatible version of the Requester is running on each workstation
- That the upgrade of software on network workstations is as automated as possible to speed the updating process and reduce potential errors

In addition, the workstation specialist will have to be concerned with the following:

- Compatibility of workstation hardware with the Requester
- Configuration file upgrades and consistency
- Consistent use of naming conventions within client configuration files

- Compatibility of software and the Requester
- Proper functionality of login scripts and bindery services
- Access to the network by traveling users

The workstation specialist cannot accomplish all these tasks alone. At a minimum, the workstation specialist has to work closely with the server specialist, the application specialist, the NDS expert, the printing specialist, the connectivity specialist, the testing lab coordinator, the education and training lab coordinator, and the NDS expert.

While working with other project team members, the workstation specialist will be expected to provide answers to some or all of the following questions:

- What hardware is currently being used for network workstations?
- Does the current workstation hardware have sufficient memory to be upgraded to the Requester?
- How many workstations exist on the network?
- Will workstation configuration files have to be upgraded, and what changes will be required?
- Can workstations be upgraded across the network, or will they have to be done manually?

The workstation specialist must participate as a project team member, always keeping in mind the current configuration of workstations on the network and how users can best continue to access the resources they need, both during and after the design and implementation of the NetWare 4 network.

Application Specialist

The application specialist ensures compatibility between existing applications and NetWare 4. In addition, the application specialist must be concerned with the following:

- Any menus used by network users to access applications
- Any login scripts used to set up access to applications

- Any applications planned for future purchase

Menus, login scripts, and current as well as planned applications must be compatible with NetWare 4. Ensuring their compatibility is the application specialist's responsibility. To fulfill that responsibility, the application specialist will probably have to work closely with the server specialist, the NDS expert, the workstation specialist, and the testing lab coordinator. In addition, the workstation specialist will be expected to provide the team with answers to most if not all of the following questions:

- Which servers presently contain network application programs?
- How will users access those servers once the network is migrated to NetWare 4?
- Are the existing applications compatible with NetWare 4, or must they eventually be upgraded?
- Will bindery services be needed in order to enable users to continue to access applications that are not NetWare 4-compatible, and that cannot be simultaneously upgraded with the network?
- Do sufficient application licenses exist to support the network's users?
- Are there any custom applications on the network that cannot be quickly upgraded to function with NetWare 4?
- Which users access network menus and will the menus they use need to be updated?
- What changes to login scripts will be required to accommodate user access to applications in the NetWare 4 network environment?

Ensuring simple and efficient user access to network applications and applications that are compatible with NetWare 4 are the primary concerns of the application specialist. Answering these questions for the project team should help to ensure the successful transition of network applications from the current network operating system to NetWare 4.

Printing Specialist

The printing specialist ensures that users have easy access to network printers. In addition, the printing specialist must also ensure the following:

- That printer software, including drivers, is upgraded where needed
- That direct-connect printers have bindery services provided for them
- That additional printers are added to the network if needed

The printing specialist must work closely with the applications specialist, the NDS expert, the server specialist, and the connectivity specialist. Close coordination among these team members helps to ensure that network printing services are easy to access, sufficient, and properly enabled and maintained for user access.

In order for these other team members to help the printing specialist fulfill the goal of ensuring that users have easy access to network printers, the printing specialist has to provide answers to some or all of the following questions:

- How many printers currently exist on the network?
- Which of the existing printers need to have their print drivers updated?
- Can rearrangement of any printers during the upgrade provide better printing services?
- Do new printers need to be added to the network?

With answers to these and other questions as they come up, the project team can help the printing specialist ensure that network print services are provided in the new network.

Connectivity Specialist

The connectivity specialist is responsible for ensuring that routing, protocols, telecommunications, and any other connectivity issues are dealt with when designing and implementing the network. The connectivity specialist must consider the following issues:

- Internetwork packet traffic
- Bandwidth
- Use of routers, bridges, and gateways

The connectivity specialist must ensure that these types of issues are considered by the project team when it is designing and planning for the implementation of the NetWare 4 network. To bring connectivity issues to the attention of project team members, the connectivity specialist may have to answer any or all of the following questions:

- Where are the network routers, bridges, and gateways located?
- How fast or slow is each network connection?
- Do remote sites exist and, if so, how often do they dial in to the network?
- How and where is the local network routed?
- What protocols are being used on the network, do they all have to be supported, and will any additional protocols be added?
- Should all remote sites be included in the directory tree, and, if so, what will it cost to include them all?

Answering all necessary questions helps to ensure that connection-related issues are dealt with in the design and implementation of the network—before they become problems.

Testing Lab Coordinator

The testing lab coordinator is primarily responsible for ensuring that the NetWare operating system functions properly with existing and planned applications. To fulfill that responsibility, the testing lab coordinator must do the following:

- Set up a testing lab that represents the various topologies and other conditions of the network.
- Conduct, coordinate, or supervise tests of the company's various applications running on a NetWare 4 network.
- Report testing results to the project team.
- Recommend changes to or replacement of applications that function poorly or not at all on the NetWare 4 network.
- Perform, coordinate, or supervise the testing of modified, upgraded, or new applications.

The testing lab coordinator may also determine whether applications continue to meet minimum performance requirements by periodically testing them after the network has been implemented. The results of such tests may then be turned over to the applications specialist so that corrections or changes can be made.

To ensure that applications function properly on the NetWare 4 network, the testing lab coordinator may need to provide the project team with answers to some or all of the following questions:

- How will the proposed network design and layout be simulated in the testing lab?
- What approach can be taken to simulate routing in the testing lab?
- What configurations for workstations, file servers, and printers will be used in the testing lab?
- Which applications will be tested for NetWare 4 compatibility?

Many of these questions may be answered as the design process itself proceeds. Some may be answered by other team members as they provide information regarding their own areas of responsibility. Regardless of who provides the information, these questions must still be answered in order for the testing lab coordinator to prepare for and then test applications on the network. Then, the testing lab coordinator can fulfill the goal of ensuring that existing and planned applications function properly with the NetWare operating system.

Education and Training Coordinator

The primary responsibility of the education and training coordinator is to determine team member skill levels, then arrange for and provide training to team members as needed. To accomplish this task, the education and training coordinator must do the following:

- Develop a means of assessing current skill levels and training needs.
- Determine which resources are required to provide the necessary training.
- Establish a training center or area, or at least decide where the training will be conducted.
- Obtain any resources needed to provide training.
- Create a training schedule.
- Implement the training schedule.

In addition to training the project team, the education and training coordinator may be called on to train network administrators and users. This will probably not be necessary until the NetWare 4 network is implemented.

Regardless of whether the education and training coordinator has to also train network administrators and users, the project team must at least be trained. To accomplish that task, there are several questions the education and training coordinator needs to answer or have answered. Those questions may include the following:

- What groups and individuals need training?
- What types of training need to be provided?
- Who schedules the training and provides the resources to conduct that training?

- What effect will the update to NetWare 4 have on users, and how much will they need to know about NetWare 4?
- How should training be planned and implemented to increase productivity and workflow in the company, rather than just familiarize users with the network?

Part of the design and implementation process is providing answers to all the questions that need to be answered. Obtaining those answers requires that certain types of information about the company and the network be gathered, analyzed, and shared with the project team. Gathering related business information is, therefore, the next procedure in the design phase of the NetWare 4 process.

Gathering Related Business Information

Each project team role has an associated responsibility of gathering various types of information that the team needs in order to design and implement the NetWare 4 network properly. Although not all these documents may be needed when designing and implementing a small local area network, most of these documents will be valuable when working with larger networks.

Novell's NetWare 4.1 Design and Implementation course provides information on various types of documents that can be useful when designing and implementing a NetWare 4 network:[1]

- Company background information
- Organization chart
- LAN and WAN topology
- Regional/location maps
- Resource list
- Workflow information

There are many ways to obtain this type of information from a company. Because it could be difficult for a single individual to obtain all the needed information, particularly in a large company, many team members are often asked to participate in gathering the necessary information. For example, high-level corporate documents are generally obtained through the IS manager or NDS expert. Documents containing information about the WAN topology and a list of resources may be gathered by the connectivity, workstation, and server specialists. Once obtained, all the information should be shared with other members of the team to help ensure that everyone understands the needs of the company and the resources currently available for designing and implementing the NetWare 4 network.

Company Background Information

Company background information can be provided in a variety of different documents. It may also be delivered to the project team in the form of a verbal presentation when specific company documents are either not available or do not provide all the needed information.

Company documents that might contain the necessary background information include annual reports, corporate newsletters, and letters to stockholders. The company might also have history information or copies of newspaper articles and other items of interest. Items of this nature are often kept by the corporate personnel department or the company library. Local public libraries may also contain this type of information.

If the company is a nonprofit organization, a copy of the company's constitution, by-laws, and rules and regulations may also provide some information that would be helpful in designing the network. For example, the *Constitution, By-laws, Rules & Regulations* booklet for the Lake Havasu Soccer League, Inc., contains information about how students are assigned to teams:

1. Players will be assigned to a team based on school attended and/or geographic area of residence whenever possible, thereby minimizing travel for practices and allowing players to participate with their friends from the school they attend.[2]

This information, in concert with a map of the soccer league offices and the location of each school, can be used to help determine the directory tree design. This information may also be useful in determining partitioning, replication, and time synchronization strategies.

Company background information that might also be useful may include details about such things as the following:

- The company's mission
- The field or product in which the company specializes
- Other companies, divisions, or businesses the company owns or operates
- Future plans for expansion, growth, or acquisition

Any information that may affect the network's design and implementation, and that can be obtained by gathering and reviewing information about the company, its history, and its future plans, can be useful to the project team.

Organization Chart

A company organization chart shows the hierarchy of management in the company. To some extent, the company's organization chart may also represent the physical layout of a company. For example, position titles such as North American Distribution Manager may indicate that a North American distribution center or office exists in the company.

Because people tend to work in groups that are often determined by the management structure that surrounds them, the company's organization may provide insight into the company's existing workgroups. This information can be valuable when designing the lower layers of the directory tree.

Figure 3.1 shows an organization chart for a fictitious company called RMC Education, a provider of business training courses catering mostly to city and state offices in the neighboring cities of Pinetop and Lakeside.

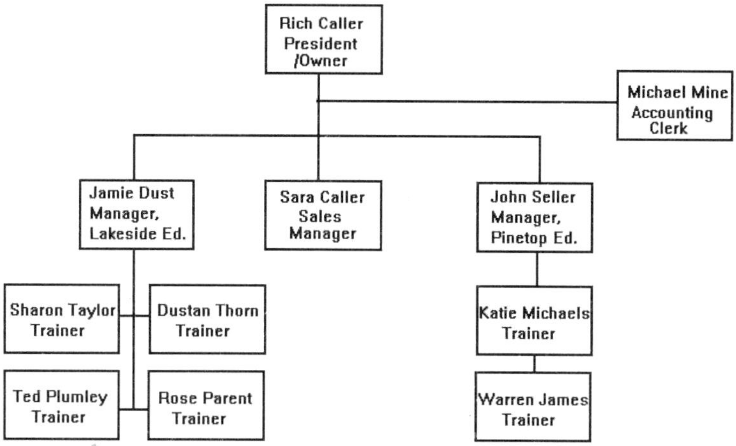

Figure 3.1
Sample organization chart.

LAN and WAN Topology

LAN, WAN, and MAN topology documents are designed to display the layout of the existing network. Although not usually drawn to any realistic scale, their purpose is to show how the network is connected.

Topology documents generally include information such as the name of the city, state, and country in which each portion of the network is located. In addition, the type of communication link between areas (microwave, T1, dedicated leased lines, dial-up lines, ISDN, and so on) is shown.

Other information, such as the number and type of file servers and the number of users at each site, may also be included on the topology document. If a *Public Data Network (PDN)* is used, this information may also be included.

Figure 3.2 shows a sample topology document for the RMC Education company.

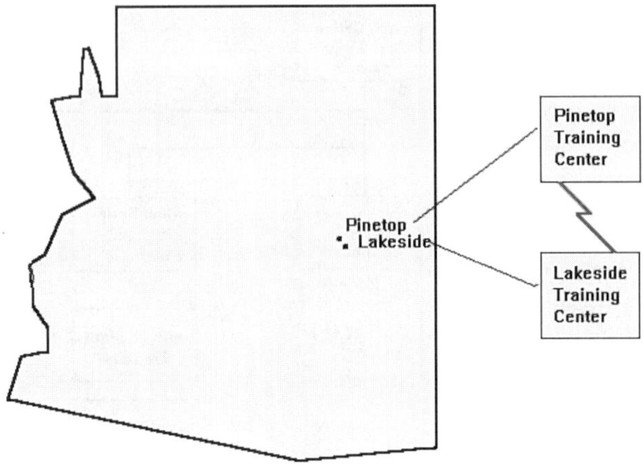

Figure 3.2
Sample topology document.

Regional/Location Maps

When a company has offices in multiple locations, regional and location maps may be of some benefit to the project team. Understanding the physical location of network resources makes designing a more effective directory tree a little easier. The better the design of the directory tree, the easier partitioning and replication will be.

Figure 3.3 shows a regional map for a fictitious company called World Wide Electronics, which manufactures and sells components for the development and repair of various electronic devices, such as televisions, radar equipment, and personal computers. World Wide Electronics sells only to manufacturers and retail companies, not the general public.

Smaller, more localized maps are also often useful when creating the directory tree design. These types of maps often show exactly where network communications exist for a company within a given geographic location. Information such as whether the PDN is used, what speed communication links are used, and where communications begin and terminate in relation to various company offices can also be provided on this type of a map.

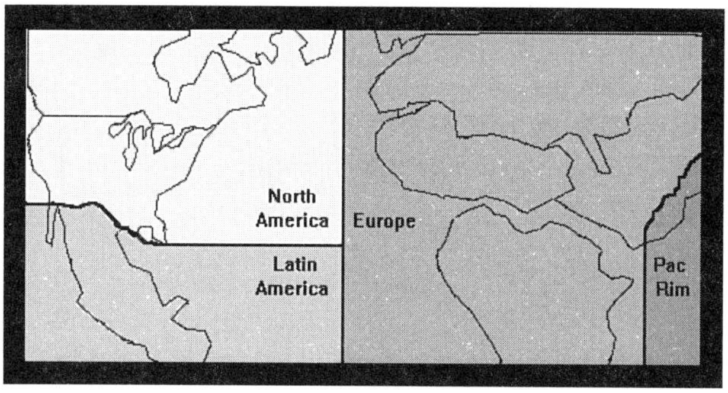

Figure 3.3
Sample regional map.

Resource List

Project teams will also find a resource list to be a valuable document when designing the network. Information such as the number of printers used on the network and their locations can help the printing specialist determine how best to include printer access in the network's design.

Resource lists can be organized by location. This is particularly useful when designing a NetWare 4 WAN for a geographically dispersed company. Regardless of the way the resource list is organized, however, it should include information such as the following:

- Types of existing file servers, workstations, printers, routers, bridges, and so on
- Quantity of each type of existing file server, workstation, printer, router, bridge, and so on
- Description of each type of resource

Figure 3.4 shows a portion of a sample resource list for a company with a WAN.

Figure 3.4

Sample resource list.

List of Resources by City			
Location	Item	Qty.	Additional Information
Springfield	NetWare 4.1 file servers	7	All Compaq 486/66 machines
	DOS Clients	573	50 are Pentiums, balance are 386 clones. 7 have only 4 MB of memory, but all others have at least 8. The pentiums all have 12 MB of memory plus 120 MB hard disks.
	Macintosh	4	All 4 are PowerMacs, used for graphic design work.
Tempe	NetWare 4.1 file servers	3	Older 386 machines with 16 MB of memory and 80 MB in each

Workflow Information

Depending on the size of the company, workflow information may range from one or two pages to several pages of description of the work for which each area of the company is responsible. The purpose of the document containing workflow information remains the same, however: to explain how each area of the company utilizes its current network and related equipment to accomplish its purpose.

For example, a company with a single customer service department may have workflow information such as the following included in the complete workflow document:[3]

> Customer service (CS) is the most important department in the long-term success of the business. The CS department gets great equipment and is well staffed.
>
> High-level technical support creates a lot of traffic on a network as personnel test various configurations. Three superservers are set aside for this department.
>
> These superservers store various technical troubleshooting tools (online docs, service record databases, diagnostic tools, copies of all versions of software that the company supports, and so forth).

All the data stored is immediately available during support hours. One server also acts as a worldwide web site, and so needs to support TCP/IP and must have access to an outside line. A CompuServe forum exists for online support.

The equipment for the customer service includes the following:

- Three superservers
- Two printers (although the department needs various models for testing drivers)
- Three Macintosh computers for testing
- Seven hundred DOS/Windows workstations

This description is obviously for a rather large company, as noted by the fact that this single department has seven hundred DOS/Windows workstations. Even smaller companies need workflow information provided to the project team, however.

For example, most small companies do their own payroll and, although the payroll personnel may also be the accounting and human resource personnel, their workflow still needs to be described. In fact, when several company functions are performed in one area by just a few individuals, workflow information may be even more critical to the project team.

Although background information about the company, organization charts, LAN, MAN, and WAN topology documents, regional and location maps, resource lists, and workflow information are commonly used by the project team, other documents may be useful as well. In addition, other documents may need to be used in place of some of these more common documents, because not all companies have all these documents or may have other documents that must be considered.

As noted earlier, for example, nonprofit companies often have one or more documents that explain the company's constitution, by-laws, and rules and regulations. These documents may also have to be considered by the project team in order to ensure that the network design does not unintentionally violate any rule, regulation, or by-law of the company.

Training the Project Team

As stated earlier, it is the education and training coordinator's responsibility to train the project team—or at least to design and schedule the training and see to it that the training is correctly administered. To accomplish this task, the coordinator must first determine what training the project team requires. Often, attending project team meetings provides the coordinator with enough input to determine the basic needs of each project team member. More research may sometimes be needed, however.

The education and training coordinator can meet separately with project team members to assess their training needs or discuss it as part of one meeting's agenda. Although there may be a variety of needs, the following are two common training needs:

- Developing an understanding of the NetWare 4 design and implementation process, how each team member fits into that process, and what is expected of each team member
- Learning NetWare 4, particularly NDS and other aspects of NetWare 4 that affect the network design and the implementation process

Project team members are likely to be chosen to fulfill different roles because of their existing knowledge of one aspect or another of the network. That does not mean, however, that team members are necessarily familiar with the overall process of designing and implementing a project of any type, including a network. It may fall to the education and training coordinator, therefore, to provide some basic related training.

Most team members do not have to be experienced analysts and designers. Understanding how the project team functions as a whole to design and implement the network, and then understanding where their particular experience and expertise fits into the overall process, will make the entire design and implementation process proceed more smoothly. It is in the best interest of all project team members, and of the project as a whole, to teach all project team members what is expected of them.

There is more than one approach the education and training coordinator can take to train team members. Depending on the level of knowledge needed and the current project design experience of the team as a whole, the coordinator may choose to spend a couple of hours educating the team as a group. The coordinator may also prefer to train team members individually in small, private sessions. The coordinator has the option of obtaining outside training, such as that provided by Novell's design and implementation course, or placing much of the responsibility for learning the design and implementation process onto the shoulders of each individual project team member.

If the first approach is chosen, a short training session of one or two hours can be used to explain systems design briefly (such as the linear method of the system design life cycle) to the project team. From there, the coordinator can explain the NetWare 4 design and implementation process and how it fits into the SDLC. Included in this training session should also be a list of all project team member roles, and a description of what each member is responsible for in relation to the entire team. In addition, a list of documents or types of information each project team member is generally responsible for obtaining, reviewing, analyzing, and sharing with the project team should be included.

If the second approach is chosen, the coordinator is responsible for choosing convenient training times for the project team members, then conducting one-on-one training sessions with them. The information each team member needs is similar to what is provided in the first option, but can be more customized for each member. These individual meetings can include more time in discussing the exact responsibilities of each team member. The primary advantage to this approach is the feedback received by the coordinator, which indicates whether the information is being successfully relayed. This option also enables the team member to ask as many questions as necessary to ensure complete understanding.

The third option can be the most costly of all, both in the cost of the course and in the costs associated with taking the time to attend the course. If this option is chosen, however, all team members will have the opportunity to practice designing and planning for the implementation of a network.

A variation of this third option may also be considered. Instead of sending all team members to the related course taught at a Novell Authorized Education Center (NAEC), the course can be brought to the company. This may reduce some of the cost. In addition, the NAEC may be willing to customize the course so that it uses the company's actual documents rather than those provided for practice in the course itself. Such a customized course may even make it possible for the project team to come away from having taken the course with the first draft of the company's NetWare 4 network design and implementation plans in hand. The project team can then refine those plans and thus be one step closer to implementing the NetWare 4 network, the basic design of which it created in the course.

Note If you are a consultant who is also a Certified Novell Instructor with certification in the NetWare 4.1 Design and Implementation Course, this option is one you can offer to the company when you submit a bid or make a presentation. This option may enable you to obtain consulting jobs for smaller companies that might not otherwise be able to afford your services.

The fourth option may be suitable when team members have some project design or NetWare 4 experience. To implement the fourth option, the education and training coordinator first determines which training aids each project team member needs. Next, the coordinator makes arrangements to obtain those aids and then makes them available to the team members. In addition, the education and training coordinator may also need to work with the testing lab coordinator to provide individual team members with access to a NetWare 4 testing lab so that team members can get some practical, hands-on experience with NetWare 4.

Various training aids are available to the education and training coordinator to help in the process of educating the project team. Several third-party books exist that can be obtained and read by individual project team members. New Riders Publishing has several books that project team members can use to learn about NetWare 4. This book, or portions of it, may also be useful. For example, two of the three appendixes in this book were written specifically to help project team members understand basic networking principals and NDS.

Regardless of which option the education and training coordinator chooses, the project team must have its training needs met. It is the education and training coordinator's responsibility to see to it that the project team receives the training it needs. The project team may not be the education and training coordinator's only responsibility, however. The coordinator may also be responsible for training the personnel who will be administering the network as well as the people who will be using it.

The training coordinator also has several options when deciding how best to educate network administrators and users. The coordinator can develop and teach basic courses, schedule individuals to take courses at NAECs, bring in a CNI to teach in-house NetWare 4 courses, purchase and distribute third-party NetWare books, and so on. The coordinator may also choose to use a combination of approaches.

The needs of the company and its administrators and users, as well as the budget and time constraints, contribute to the approach the coordinator chooses to take. The approach that is most suitable for the company and its personnel is the best approach, but may not always be the one chosen. Ultimately, as long as the education and training needs are met, the best approach is the one that works.

Determining the Approach to Network Design

The first step in network design is choosing the project team and ensuring that all members are aware of the NetWare 4 process and their roles in that process. Next, the relevant information is gathered, analyzed, and shared or discussed among the project team members. Then, project team members are trained as needed. When these three tasks have been accomplished, the project team is ready to determine the approach to be taken when designing the network.

Determining the approach to network design is a process just as the network design and implementation is a process. Its purpose is to establish what the network design process will include and roughly how long it will take to complete the design process. Determining the approach to network design involves three steps:

1. Defining the scope
2. Determining the complexity of the network
3. Defining the schedule for the network's design

A reasonable estimate of the length of time required to design the network is important to company management, including the IS manager. Knowing how long the network design may take is important, because management must budget for the hours and dollars the design process will require.

Defining the Scope

The scope of any project is defined once the length of time and the associated resources are defined. In the NetWare 4 design process, the scope of the design outlines the resources that affect the length of time the design process will take.

Defining the scope of the network design process is important to company management, but it is also important to the project team.

Project team members need to have reasonable expectations related to the design process. Only by determining the scope of the project can the design team have a reasonable understanding of approximately how long the design process will take.

The scope of any project can be affected by any number and type of factors. The scope of designing the NetWare 4 network is primarily affected by the complexity of the network itself.

Determining the Complexity of the Network

To determine the complexity of a network, the project team must first understand what resources are provided by the network. If the network currently exists, the resource lists should provide the necessary information. If the network does not yet exist, the project team first has to make a rough estimate of the resources that should be available on the NetWare 4 network.

There are only a few specific resources that the project team must be concerned with when determining the scope of the project (see fig. 3.5):

- The number of file servers
- The number of company sites or locations
- Whether the company anticipates future growth
- The amount of growth the company expects

Networks with a large number of file servers require more time to design because a greater number of file servers means that all procedures in each phase of the NetWare 4 design process have to be completed. In small networks with a relatively limited number of file servers, some procedures may not have to be executed.

For example, in a small network it may not be necessary to customize partitioning and replication. In many small networks, the default partitioning and replication strategies are likely to be sufficient.

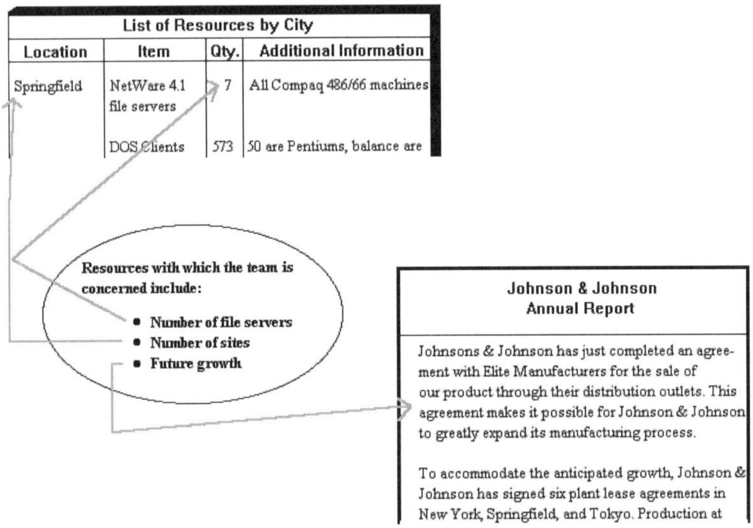

Figure 3.5

Resources associated with defining the project's scope.

The number of sites or locations of offices, retail stores, and so on also affects the time required to complete the network's design. As with small networks, a network with a limited number of sites or locations may not require customization. Accepting the defaults put in place by the NetWare 4 installation program for such things as partitioning, replication, and time synchronization may be a reasonable option for companies that do not have a large number of sites, particularly if those sites are relatively close together, such as you might find in a MAN.

Even networks with a limited number of sites may require a greater amount of design time, however. This is particularly true if the company is anticipating a great deal of growth. During the design of the network, not only must existing company sites and file servers be considered, but so, too, must any future sites and file servers, when they are known.

The time frame in which the growth is expected is also a factor to be considered. If the growth is anticipated to occur in a relatively short period of time, planning must be done now to accommodate the future growth. If the growth is expected to occur more slowly over a greater length of time, less consideration can be given to planning for that growth at this early stage in the design process.

It must not, however, be ignored. Ignoring the potential of future growth now may mean the network will have to be redesigned far earlier than would have otherwise been necessary had the growth been planned for in the early stages of the NetWare 4 design and implementation process.

A more subtle level of complexity, based on a quantity variable, can also be roughly determined. That quantity variable refers primarily to the number of file servers the company has, but may also be applied to the number of sites. For example, a network with only 12 file servers is a relatively simple network. A network with 50 file servers is more complex than the network with only 12 file servers, but the difference may only be slight. A network with 250 file servers starts to become much more complex than one with only 50 servers, however, and a network with 5,000 file servers makes all the other networks seem tiny in comparison.

Is the design of a network with 5,000 file servers more complex and therefore more time-consuming than a network with 250 file servers? The answer is yes, no, and maybe. If the network with 250 servers is spread around the globe, it may be more complex to design than a network with 5,000 file servers located within a relatively small geographic area. If the network with 5,000 file servers is spread around the globe, designing that network will be more complex and time-consuming than designing the network that has only 250 file servers, even though they, too, are spread around the globe.

As you can see, the levels of complexity can vary. Just how complex the network is depends on more than just how many file servers the company has. It also depends on where they are physically located, both on the globe and in relation to each of the company's other file servers. Once the network's complexity is fully defined and understood, however, the project team can then begin determining the schedule for designing the network.

To simplify the process of determining a network's complexity, and thus of determining how long the network's design may take, Novell provides some general recommendations to follow. Those recommendations are based on whether the network is a simple or complex one.

The following are Novell's recommendations for the amount of time required to design a network:

1. If the network has 30 or more file servers, you need time to design configured time sources and set up a test lab, as follows:
   - Simple network, .5 to 1 day
   - Complex network, 2 to 3 days
2. If there are at least 15 file servers on the network that will hold replicas of the NDS database, you need time to design the partitioning and replication strategies, as follows:
   - Simple network, 1 day
   - Complex network, 3 to 4 days
3. If the network has multiple sites and those sites are connected to form a WAN, you need additional time to design the partitioning, replication, and time synchronization strategies, as follows:
   - Simple network, 1 day
   - Complex network, 3 to 4 days
4. If the network will have more than one directory tree, planning for those additional directory trees and the users' access to resources in the other directory trees requires additional design time, as follows:
   - Simple network, .5 day
   - Complex network, 2 days
5. If the company is expecting growth and the network is to be capable of handling that growth, designing the upper layers of the directory tree and providing for the addition of new organizational units and partitions requires additional time, as follows:
   - Simple network, 1 day
   - Complex network, 3 days

To calculate the length of time it will take to design the network, complete the following steps:

1. Assess the level of complexity of the network (simple versus complex).
2. List the factors that affect the network's design, such as the number of network file servers, how many file servers will contain replicas, where the file servers are located, and so on.
3. Add the minimum applicable time estimates for each listed factor.
4. Add the maximum applicable time estimates for each listed factor.

For example, assume the network you are creating a design plan for is a relatively simple one. Assume also that this network contains 500 file servers located within one geographic area, of which only 10 will hold replicas. In addition, assume the company is expecting substantial growth in the next year, but will need only one directory tree. Based on this description of the network, you can estimate that it will take from 1.5 to 4 days to design the network.

Once you work through these steps, you will have a good idea of approximately how long it will take to design the NetWare 4 network. Then, knowing the length of time required to design the network, you can begin preparing a schedule that reasonably reflects the time required for the design process.

Defining the Schedule for the Network's Design

Four primary complexity factors can affect the length of time it will take the project team to design the network. The first three are covered in the last section: the number of file servers and how many of them will have replicas placed on them, the geographic location of the company and its network, and the amount and speed of growth the company anticipates. The fourth factor is whether only a single directory tree or multiple directory trees will be required.

In most cases, Novell recommends that a company's NetWare 4 network be contained within one directory tree. After all, Novell designed NDS around the concept of a single tree to provide several benefits to its users. Most of these benefits are reduced or eliminated when multiple trees are used.

The following are some of the benefits of NDS that a company can reasonably expect to receive when using a single directory tree:

- Centralized network resources
- A modified login process, which requires only a single login allowing authorized access to all available network resources
- A design that is scaleable to accommodate network growth readily
- Centralized file server management
- Automated reconnection to the directory when a connection is lost
- Centralized auditing
- Enhanced security

Designing the network to provide a single directory tree is also necessary if the company chooses to accomplish all the goals associated with designing the directory tree:[4]

- A structure of network resources for ease of access
- A blueprint for the implementation of NetWare 4
- A flexible layout that can be modified to reflect corporate changes
- Secure access to shared resources

There are also reasons why a company may choose to use more than one directory tree. The most common reason for designing and using multiple trees relates to location of network users and the frequency of their access to the network.

Users located in remote sites who do not need to be logged in to the directory to perform most of their daily tasks may be better off using a separate tree. This is especially true if network access would always have to be accomplished across a modem or other relatively slow (256 Kbps) transmission media.

For example, companies with small sales offices who access the directory tree only once a day to pass on daily sales information or receive copies of periodic reports may function more effectively if they have separate directory trees. Their daily work then enables them to log in to their local trees. Relevant information can be passed on to the company on a daily basis, and the only access to the other directory tree will be to log in to pass on or collect information.

Summary

Many factors have to be considered when designing and implementing a NetWare 4 network. Some of those factors include the number of directory trees a company will need, how many file servers the company has, how geographically dispersed the company and its network resources are, and so on.

As this chapter has shown, determining the approach to take in order to design and implement a NetWare 4 network successfully can be a simple or a complex process. Smaller networks enable you to ignore certain design issues such as time synchronization, because acceptable default strategies are provided by NetWare 4 itself. Larger networks, however, often require more design planning, and thus also require more time to implement because the defaults are not sufficient.

This chapter includes the information needed to start the design process—assembling the project team and determining the approach to network design. These two processes are important to ensuring the success of the NetWare 4 design and implementation process, and thus the success of the network as a whole. If the implementation is to be successful, a successful network design must be created before anyone attempts to implement the network. Learning the information and following the guidelines explained in this chapter will get the project design team and the network off to the right start.

Case Study

Alexander, Bachler, and Goldman is a legal defense firm with three offices in Los Angeles. The three offices have four file servers each, used primarily for storing client case information, performing basic word processing tasks, and meeting in-house accounting needs. Until now, all file servers have been running NetWare 2.2. The president of the firm decided to upgrade the company's network to NetWare 4 because it is considering a merger with another law firm.

The other firm already has NetWare 4 installed and has indicated that reductions in nonessential personnel would be required before the merger could be completed. The president of Alexander, Bachler, and Goldman has decided that by upgrading to NetWare 4, two of the current NetWare administrators could be relocated into other positions. The network could then be centrally administered by the remaining administrator.

You have been called to the firm as a consultant and asked to execute the design of the network. The first thing the president wants to know is how long the design process is likely to take. Based on the information the president has just given you about the firm, you tell the president the minimum and maximum lengths of time the network design will take. What minimum and maximum times do you quote the president?

Review Questions

1. If the project team feels that it needs to make an onsite visit to another company that has already completed the process of designing and installing a NetWare 4 network, the responsibility for setting up a visit likely falls to the ___________.

    - A. IS manager role
    - B. server specialist role
    - C. NDS expert role
    - D. testing lab coordinator

2. The responsibility for choosing other team members most often falls to the individual fulfilling the ___________ role.

    - A. IS manager
    - B. server specialist
    - C. NDS expert
    - D. testing lab coordinator

3. The implementation team begins installing the first of the NetWare 4 file servers, only to discover that there is not enough disk space to install NetWare 4. The boss says that heads will roll. Whose head is in eminent danger?

    - A. IS manager
    - B. Server specialist
    - C. NDS expert
    - D. Testing lab coordinator

4. Of the following, which document is used to determine the number of file servers to be upgraded?

    - A. Organization chart
    - B. LAN and WAN topology
    - C. Resource list
    - D. Workflow information
    - E. Company history/background, as follows

5. The NDS expert tells you that, for the team to determine the top layer of the directory tree, the team needs to know what future expansion, growth, or acquisition plans the company has. In which document might you find that information?
   - ○ A. Organization chart
   - ○ B. LAN and WAN topology
   - ○ C. Resource list
   - ○ D. Workflow information
   - ○ E. Company history/background

6. The layout of the existing network is provided by what documents?
   - ○ A. Organization chart
   - ○ B. LAN and WAN topology
   - ○ C. Resource list
   - ○ D. Workflow information
   - ○ E. Company history/background

7. The resource list can provide much of the information needed in order to ___________.
   - ○ A. determine the complexity of the network
   - ○ B. define the scope of the project
   - ○ C. choose project team members
   - ○ D. assess the training needs of network administrators

8. The number of file servers, how many sites or locations the company has, and whether the company anticipates future growth are all resources with which the project team must be primarily concerned when it is trying to ___________.
   - ○ A. determine the complexity of the network
   - ○ B. define the scope of the project

- ○ C. choose project team members
- ○ D. assess the training needs of network administrators

9. If the network for which the scope of the design project is being defined has 61 file servers, for which two procedures must a minimum of one-half day's design time be allotted?
   - ○ A. to design configured time sources
   - ○ B. to design the upper layers of the directory tree
   - ○ C. to set up a test lab
   - ○ D. to plan directory tree mergers

10. Of the following, which is *not* a goal associated with designing the network to function under a single directory tree?
    - ○ A. Ease of access to network resources
    - ○ B. Providing a blueprint for implementation that the company can follow when it is ready to install NetWare 4
    - ○ C. Flexible layout that is easily modified
    - ○ D. Accommodating remote sites using modems when once-a-day access is sufficient

Answers

1. A
2. C
3. B
4. C
5. E
6. B
7. A
8. B
9. A C
10. D

Notes

1. *NetWare 4.1 Design and Implementation Instructor's Guide, Rev. 1.0*. Provo: Novell, Inc., B–1.
2. *Lake Havasu Soccer League, Inc. Constitution By-laws Rules & Regulations, Revised-1993*. Arizona: Lake Havasu Soccer League, Inc., 8.
3. *NetWare 4.1 Design and Implementation Instructor's Guide, Rev. 1.0*. Provo: Novell, Inc., B–15.
4. Hughes, Jeffrey F., and Blair W. Thomas. *QuickPath to NetWare 4.1 Networks*, California: Sybex Inc., 62.

Chapter 4

Chapter Chapter Chapter Chapter Chapter Chapter

Designing and Planning NetWare 4 Local Area Networks

When designing and planning a NetWare 4 LAN, you will find that the process is not much different from the process involved in designing and planning a NetWare 4 MAN. The primary difference is that MANs are more often found in government than in private industry.

For example, a university with multiple campuses in a single geographic area such as a county, may have to implement a MAN rather than a LAN. Network topology becomes more important when designing a MAN than it does when designing a LAN, however. Distances are more limited in a LAN than they are in a WAN but, you can apply the same designing and planning process to both. Thus, although this chapter discusses network design and implementation using a LAN layout, a MAN layout could have been used instead.

When reading and implementing the information contained within this chapter, you should consider whether any differences must be accounted for. If your assignment is the design and implementation of a MAN rather than a LAN, you may need to reference Chapter 6, "Designing and Planning NetWare 4 Wide Area Networks," to ensure that you account for all details. This will be particularly true when planning such things as time synchronization and partitioning and replication strategies, if the defaults that are installed during the NetWare 4 installation process will not be sufficient to accommodate the needs of your WAN.

When you begin the design and implementation process of a NetWare 4 LAN, you need to take into account three issues in particular:

- The process of designing the directory tree
- The approach to take when planning partitions
- The best way to plan and place replicas

This chapter discusses directory tree design in great detail. It includes information on the importance of a correctly designed directory tree and how to approach the design of a directory tree to ensure maximum benefit. It also discusses how to establish and document standards to be applied in the design and implementation of the LAN. In addition, it discusses how to design both the upper and lower layers of the LAN's directory tree so as to take advantage of the benefits associated with a properly designed tree.

The information this chapter provides regarding directory tree design is based on the experience of many companies, as well as the experience of Novell's Consulting Services group. The information related to directory tree design contained within this chapter makes it possible for you to design a LAN or MAN directory tree without having to reinvent the wheel. You can follow the guidelines it provides to design and implement your LAN. If you do, you are likely to end up with a directory tree design that meets the needs of the company for which you are designing the tree, ensures easier access and navigation for network users, and accommodates growth and the easy addition of resources to the network.

This chapter also discusses the design and planning of directory tree partitions and replications. One of the biggest benefits of NetWare 4 is the fault tolerance that its design provides. By properly partitioning the directory tree, and then providing sufficient replicas of each partition placed in strategic locations, the likelihood of a disaster making the entire directory tree inaccessible is practically nonexistent. This benefit, however, does not happen totally by itself.

As you will find when designing NetWare 4 networks, most LANs and MANs can use the default partitioning and replication strategies. The defaults are generally sufficient to ensure fault tolerance. Because this chapter concentrates on designing and planning for LANs, it discusses the default NetWare 4 partitioning and replication strategies. Customization of partitioning and replication is discussed in Chapter 6.

Designing the LAN Directory Tree

Spend whatever time you need to design the directory tree correctly. It is the most important component of your network. A correctly designed directory tree will prevent many problems later on.

One of the most serious problems may not even become evident until the company goes through a growth phase. Company growth may require the addition of one or more Organizational Unit objects at the top of the directory tree, or the merging of one or more trees into a single directory tree. Unless this is planned for ahead of time, adding Organizational Unit objects and merging trees may completely distort the design of your directory tree. Ultimately, a poorly designed tree will make it more difficult for users to navigate the tree, and will not reflect favorably on your network design skills.

Other problems associated with improper tree design may appear at different times. For example, when it comes time to implement network security, you or the individuals implementing security may find the use of Organizational Role objects to be more ineffective than effective in a poorly designed directory tree.

To prevent future problems, which is always less difficult than correcting them after they occur, you should carefully plan the design of the network's directory tree. Careful planning starts with understanding how a correctly designed directory tree structure can benefit the company, the administrators who manage the network, and those users who must access and use the resources it provides.

Besides averting potential problems, there are several benefits associated with designing the tree to meet the company's needs completely. Designing the directory tree right the first time provides some, if not all, of the following benefits:

- Partitioning and replication can be simplified.
- Growth can be readily accommodated.
- Additional network services can easily be added.
- User access can be reduced to the simplest process.
- Navigation of the tree can be more intuitive.

There are several ways in which each of these benefits make it worth the time needed to design the NetWare 4 network's directory tree correctly. You may find it useful to understand just how the design of the NetWare 4 directory tree provides those benefits to the company, its administrators, and its users. This information can prove to be particularly useful if you are asked to justify the time and resources you are spending and requesting for the design and implementation of the NetWare 4 network.

Simplifying Partitioning and Replication

Partitioning the directory tree means dividing the NDS database into a logical organization of containers. These divisions are often referred to as a *subtree* or *branch* of the network.

By partitioning the directory tree, various portions or divisions of the database can be stored on various NetWare 4 file servers (see fig. 4.1). Partitioning the NDS database provides several benefits.

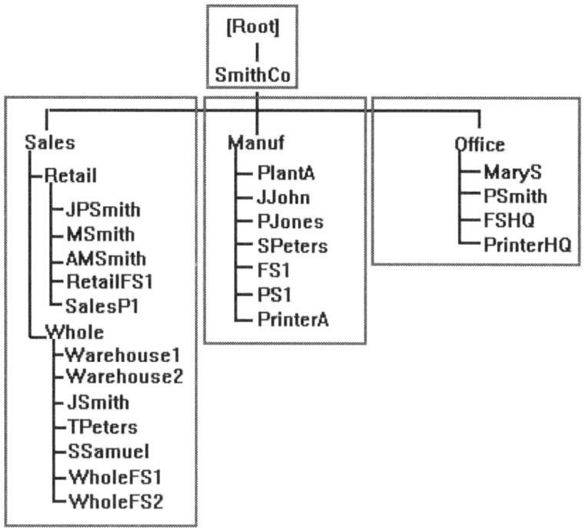

Figure 4.1
Directory tree partitioning.

The first benefit of partitioning the NDS database is that it enables you to divide that database into smaller portions. Smaller portions are easier to spread over different file servers in the network. This benefit is actually a benefit of two parts.

First, by spreading *replicas* (instances of a partition) across the network to different file servers, fault tolerance is provided. If one file server is down, another file server holding a replica of the same portion of the NDS database can be accessed instead.

Second, *writable replicas* (instances of a partition that can be written to) can be placed on the file server closest to the users whose User objects the replica contains. This reduces the time required for a user to log in and be authenticated to the network.

Another benefit of partitioning the network is that it is transparent to network users. Users are not aware that the NDS database is not stored in full on the NetWare 4.1 file server closest to them. This is accomplished because users do not need immediate access to all directory tree partitions. For the most part, and assuming the directory tree design and partitioning has been properly planned and implemented, users generally need access only to the partition of the database that stores the information related to their User object and other objects they regularly use.

Proper directory tree design makes it easier to determine where directory tree partitioning should occur. It also makes it easier to implement those partitions. Proper partitioning makes it easier for users to access the needed resources, and does so transparently to the users. Easy design and implementation of directory partitions is thus a benefit of a properly designed directory tree.

Accommodating Network Growth

Designing the directory tree to accommodate network growth prevents the need for future directory tree redesign. Redesigning a directory tree to accommodate network growth results in a substantial increase in the amount of work required of your network's administrators.

First, network administrators have to make all or part of the network unavailable to users while the redesign and implementation of the redesign is taking place. In addition to being unavailable, network users who otherwise might be able to access the network may not be able to do so until modifications to their workstation's configuration files have been made.

Modifying workstation configuration files on a network of any size can be quite time-consuming. The first problem is determining which network workstations must have modifications made. Next, the changes must be determined, and then the configuration files themselves must be changed.

Another related problem is that users may need to be reeducated. Users who are comfortable with navigating the network and locating resources may have to learn where the resources are now located before they can access them. In addition, users who are comfortable with navigating the network may not even realize that their inability to locate resources is the result of a change, and not the result of some hardware or software problem. Thus, users may waste valuable time trying to determine the source of their inability to access the network resources they used to be able to access.

Easing the Addition of Network Services

A poorly designed network tree may make it difficult to add resources such as Printer or Directory Map objects. Even if adding the objects themselves is not difficult, determining the best location within the directory tree may be a problem. This can be particularly true if the design of the tree makes it necessary to add the same object or additional Alias objects to various containers on the tree.

A good directory tree design considers where users need to have resources placed in order to access those resources easily. Ideally, resources are located closest to those User objects that access them most often. A poor design makes it difficult to ensure that all users have the same access to network resources.

Simplifying User Access

Proper directory tree design also takes into consideration where User objects are located in the tree. As with network resources, User objects should be placed in the container where most of the resources needed by the user are also located. Then, when users log in to the network, they already have easy access to needed resources.

The container holding User objects should also be located within the tree to facilitate the replication of the partition for easy access. Only replicas that permit NetWare to write to them can be used for logging in to the network. If a User object is stored in a partition on a file server containing a read-only replica, NetWare has to search the network for a writable copy of the replica before the user can log in and be *authenticated* (identified to other servers in the tree and verified as to the rights the User object has to use certain resources) on the network.

Making Tree Navigation More Intuitive

When a directory tree has a logical organization to it, users have an easier time understanding that design. Once a user understands the basic tree design, navigating the tree becomes more intuitive. Users can find their way around the network without having to stop and seriously think about it first.

Following the Process for Correctly Designing the Tree

Several steps are involved in the designing of the directory tree. To design the tree correctly requires that you complete these steps, and in a logical order:

- Establishing and documenting naming standards
- Drawing the upper and lower layers of the tree
- Reviewing the directory tree design and revising it to include any other design issues if necessary
- Creating the directory tree structure

After you complete each step, the directory tree design should be sufficient to provide all the benefits associated with a correctly designed directory tree. The tree's design should accommodate future growth for some time, should make it easy for users to access resources, should make network navigation relatively intuitive for users, and should make it easier to add any needed network resources.

Establishing and Documenting Naming Standards

The first step for the project team to take when designing an effective directory tree is that of creating a set of guidelines to be followed when naming objects in the directory tree. The purpose of creating such a document is to ensure that consistency exists throughout the network. Establishing what needs to be done in order to ensure consistency is the responsibility of the project team. As a member of the project team, you are responsible for helping to produce a document that includes guidelines or standards to be followed when naming directory tree objects.

Why Standards Are Necessary

Standards are needed to ensure that all project team members, network administrators, and other individuals responsible for the design, implementation, and management of the NetWare 4 network perform their tasks from the same point of view. Not only does this ensure consistency throughout the network, but it provides other benefits as well.

One benefit is related to the future growth of the network. A network with consistent naming standards is far easier to expand than one where administrators are allowed to implement any standard they feel appropriate. As the network grows, objects must be added. When container objects are added with names that do not meet the set standards, users begin to find network navigation more difficult because it is less intuitive. Standards ease growth and user access.

Some LANs may eventually become part of a larger network, such as a MAN or a WAN. A LAN without naming standards is more difficult to ease into a larger MAN or WAN than one with established naming standards. That does not mean that some of those naming standards may not have to be changed. Having naming standards that have been documented, however, makes it possible to determine which standards can remain, because they already agree with the standards set for the MAN or WAN, and which ones must be changed because they are counterproductive.

You have heard the saying that one person's trash is another person's treasure. This can apply to naming standards as well. It is important that naming standards take as many issues into consideration as possible, to avoid creating a document that seems like a treasure to the project team, but that functions like trash for administrators and users.

Naming Standard Considerations

When preparing to establish naming standards, several issues must be considered. Before reviewing what must be considered or included in a naming standards document, it is important to have a good understanding of the three issues that must be considered, but that may otherwise be neglected:

- Types of network names
- How users navigate the network
- Whether IPX numbering standards should be established

Before creating a naming standards document that specifies object names, you should have an understanding of basic naming standard concepts. Those basic concepts are included here for the benefit of those of you who need additional information or who need a review of network naming concepts.

The following are the naming standards concepts discussed here:

- Common name (CN)
- Context
- Current context
- Distinguished name
- Relative distinguished name

A CN is the name given to a *leaf object,* an object that does not contain any other object. Just as a leaf on a maple tree is found at the end of a branch on a maple tree, a leaf object is found at the end of a branch of the NDS directory tree. As figure 4.2 shows, the common name for the leaf object shown as `.CN=JPSMITH.OU=SALES.O=SmithCo` is `JPSMITH`.

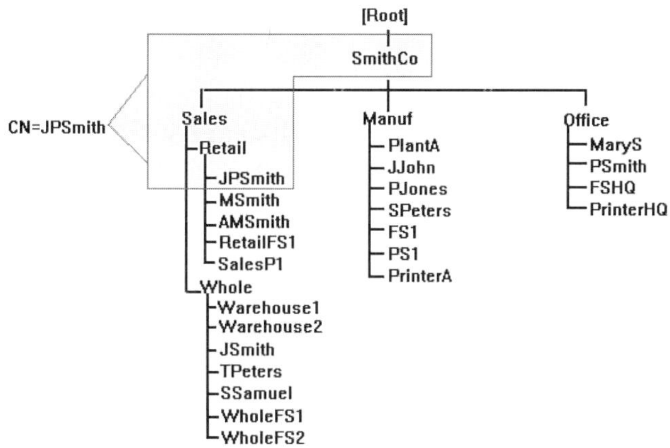

Figure 4.2
Directory tree example to display a common name.

Some of the more common leaf objects are User, Alias, Computer, Directory Map, Group, NetWare Server, Organizational Role, Printer, Print Server, Print Queue, and Volume. Information stored in the NDS database regarding each object is grouped into partitions. Partition information is then copied (replicated) and stored on different NetWare 4 file servers.

It is an object's location within the directory tree that defines its *context*. For example, figure 4.3 shows a portion of a directory tree. This is the context of the SUEM User object:

```
CN=SUEM.OU=USERS.O=BROWN&BROWN
```

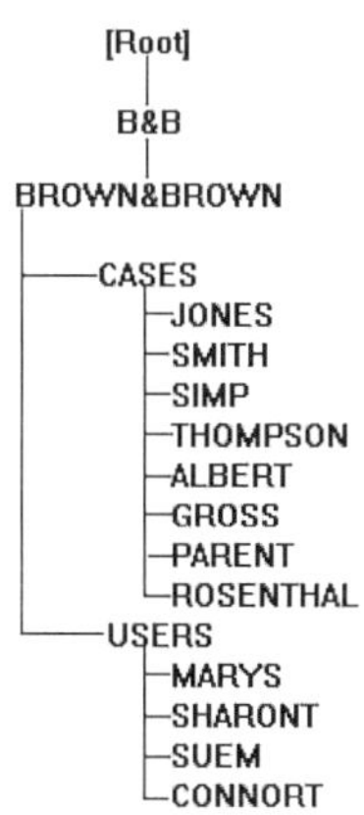

Figure 4.3
Sample section of a directory tree.

The term *current context* refers to the user's current location in the directory tree. Current context is the area in the directory tree to which the user's context is currently set. Current context is similar to the current path or default directory term used in the DOS environment.

Accessing objects in multiple containers is possible and relatively easy if the correct name for that object is used. NetWare needs to know exactly where to look for that object when it cannot be found in the current context. Using the exact name of the object also tells NetWare the object's path. There are two ways in which the exact object name can be provided: *distinguished name* and *relative distinguished name.*

An object's distinguished name is a combination of the object's common name and its context. Distinguished names always begin with a period, commonly referred to as a *leading period*. Objects in a distinguished name are separated with a period.

Distinguished names may be *typeful*, showing the object type followed by the equals sign (=) before the object's actual name, or *typeless*, not using object types or the equals sign. The following two lines show first a typeful distinguished name and then a typeless distinguished name for the same object in the directory tree.

```
.CN=SUEM.OU=USERS.O=BROWN&BROWN

.SUEM.USERS.BROWN&BROWN
```

Every object on the network has a unique distinguished name.

A relative distinguished name lists the path to an object from the user's current context. Relative distinguished names do not use a leading period. Relative distinguished names can, however, use one or more ending periods (also referred to as *trailing periods*) to show the path from the current container to a higher level container in the directory tree, and then back down again to the object. Objects listed in a relative distinguished name are also separated with a period.

Referring again to figure 4.3, the relative distinguished name for user SUEM when another user's current context is set to .0U=CASES.OU=BROWN&BROWN.O=B&B is the following:

CN=SUEM.OU=USERS.OU=BROWN&BROWN.O=B&B

This example of a relative distinguished name uses typeful naming. The same can be accomplished with typeless naming if the object types and equal signs are eliminated. In addition, the trailing period can be used with this relative distinguished name:

SUEM.USERS.

Two trailing periods can be used because both the USERS and CASES containers share the same Organizational Unit above them—BROWN&BROWN. In addition, a second and a third trailing period may be used to indicate the B&B Organizational Unit, and [Root], although it is not necessary in this case.

As a member of the project design team, you must consider how naming standards, as well as the design of the directory tree, affects how users navigate the network in order to access objects in the directory tree. Access can be affected in several ways, the most important of which is often the one based on the geographical distribution of the company and its resources.

For example, users in different geographical locations that perform similar job functions may have to share data. If that is the case, access to that data for users in one geographical area will be different from access to those same resources for a user in another geographical area. In addition, almost all those users are likely to need to access various resources contained within their own *parent containers* (the containers in which their User objects are located). Project team members must consider whether naming standards will accommodate users in different geographic locations. Naming standards should be developed to accommodate a company that has a LAN or a MAN.

Note Mobile or traveling users on the network can also affect how users access network resources, and thus may also affect naming standards. Users who periodically travel between offices or business sites, but who also have a regular office of their own, need dual access to the network. Such users need easy access from their desks, but also need relatively easy access when they are traveling.

If the company utilizes mobile employees, the naming standards document and the network's directory tree design should take this into account. IPX numbering should also be considered.

IPX is the communications protocol used on Novell NetWare networks when data packets are sent across the network to a *node* (termination point on the network cable). IPX ensures that an incoming packet is sent to the correct network node. In order to identify individual file servers and cable segments on the network uniquely, IPX numbers are assigned to each cable segment and file server. Thus, there are two types of IPX network numbers: *internal* and *external*.

Note When designing small networks, which generally means LANs and some MANs, the project team may not have to establish a separate standard for network IPX numbers. The NetWare 4 installation software will assign a random number that can usually be used without creating problems. When networks grow, however, having an established standard for IPX numbers can ease growth. Determining whether to establish IPX numbering standards, therefore, is something the project team must decide when determining other network standards.

An external IPX network number, also sometimes called a *network number* or *network address*, is assigned to each segment of the network's cable. Each external IPX network number must be unique from each other external IPX network number. When multiple *protocols* (conventions or rules used by programs and operating systems to ensure successful communication between points on the network) or *frame types* (packet data formats for a variety of different media such as Ethernet, 802.2, 802.3, token ring, and so on) are used on the same network, each cable segment must have its own external IPX number.

An internal IPX network number uniquely identifies an individual NetWare file server. The internal network number is used to define a logical network through which packets are routed in order to reach their destinations on the physical network to which the NetWare 4 file server is attached.

Both external and internal IPX numbers consist of up to eight hexadecimal digits (the numbers zero through 9 and the letters A through F may be used). Although both external and internal numbers can be randomly assigned, they can also be specified. The external network number is assigned when the IPX protocol is bound to a network board in the file server. The internal network number is assigned when the NetWare 4 file server is installed.

Establishing a standard for external and internal network numbers helps to identify cable segments and file servers when troubleshooting network problems becomes necessary. The drawback is that a successful IPX naming standard requires additional planning initially and careful implementation.

It is the project team's responsibility to decide whether the network will use randomly assigned numbers, or whether an IPX numbering standard will be established. If randomly assigned numbers will be used, the naming standards document should indicate this. If some type of numbering standard will be followed, the naming standard document should specify what comprises that numbering standard.

If the project team decides to require a numbering standard, the naming standard document must include information about, and samples of, how each digit of both types of IPX network numbers is to be assigned.

Figure 4.4 shows a sample portion of a naming standards document, which includes information on a company's standard for IPX internal network numbering.

Figure 4.4
Sample IPX internal network number naming standards document.

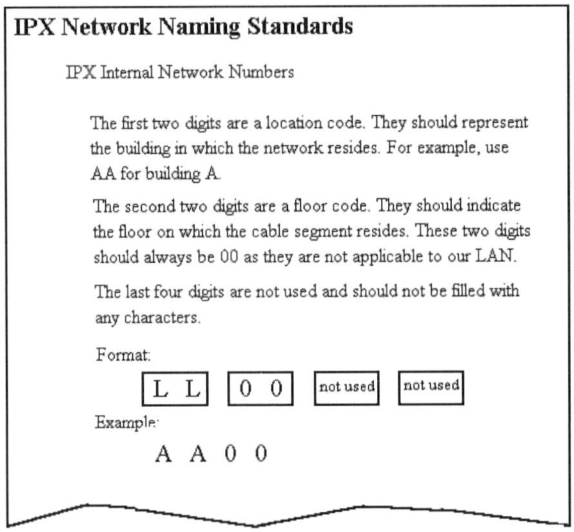

IPX Network Naming Standards

IPX Internal Network Numbers

The first two digits are a location code. They should represent the building in which the network resides. For example, use AA for building A.

The second two digits are a floor code. They should indicate the floor on which the cable segment resides. These two digits should always be 00 as they are not applicable to our LAN.

The last four digits are not used and should not be filled with any characters.

Format:

| L L | 0 0 | not used | not used |

Example:

A A 0 0

Parts of a Naming Standards Document

The naming standards document should include a list of each NDS object that will be assigned a name. Objects included in the naming standards document can be either leaf or container objects. Here are the most common objects included in a naming standards document:

- ◆ Organization
- ◆ Organizational Unit
- ◆ Group
- ◆ Organizational Role
- ◆ Directory Map
- ◆ Profile Login Script
- ◆ File Server

- Volume
- Print Server
- Print Queue
- Printer

For each object type included in the naming standards document, the standard to be followed, any related information, and an example of a correctly named object should be included. Table 4.1 shows how naming standards can be applied to several of the objects commonly included in a naming standards document.

Table 4.1
Example of Naming Standards for Several Common Objects

Object Type	*Standard*	*Example*	*Other Information*
Organization	*CoName_Tree*	B&B_Tree	Use standard abbreviation for the company name, followed by the underscore and the word Tree.
Group	*Workgroup name*	Payroll	Use company workgroup names only.
User	*FLast*	JKing	Use employee's first initial of first name, and last name up to seven characters. If two employees have the same name, use the reverse for the second employee (first name up to seven characters, and first initial of last name for the eighth character). Names are not to exceed eight characters.

continues

Table 4.1, Continued
Example of Naming Standards for Several Common Objects

Object Type	*Standard*	*Example*	*Other Information*
File Server	*LL_NNN*	A1_001	Use two-character abbreviation to specify the building and floor, followed by an underscore and the number assigned to the file server.
Volume	*VOL*	SYS	Use three-character name for each volume. Name should be descriptive; for example, the application volume should be APP, and the User volume should be USR.
Printer	*LL_Type*	A1_HPIII	Use two-character abbreviation to specify the building and floor where the printer is located, followed by an underscore and the type of printer.

In addition to naming standards for these objects, directory tree naming standards should also be included. This is particularly important if your network will initially have more than one directory tree. Most LANs and MANs have only one tree, however, so the name of that tree, along with a brief explanation of why that name was chosen, can be included in the naming standards document.

The naming standards document is very important to the project team and the project as a whole. It helps to focus the project team and gives it a guideline against which it can verify the design of the directory tree. When the project team begins designing the directory tree, a naming standard needs to be in place so that names can be given to the containers included in the tree.

Designing the Top Layer of the LAN Directory Tree

Designing the NetWare directory tree is divided into two parts—designing the top layer of the tree, and designing the lower layers of the tree. Whether the project team is designing the top layer or the lower layers, it needs to give careful consideration to how the tree is designed so that the tree provides the company with maximum benefits and eliminates or reduces potential problems.

As noted in Chapter 3, "Determining the Design and Implementation Approach," there are benefits associated with NetWare 4 and NDS. Several of those benefits also apply to a correctly designed directory tree, which, in turn, makes it possible to accomplish the following:

- Centralize network resources for easier administration and management of network file servers.
- Log in to the entire network with only a single login.
- Readily accommodate network growth without requiring major directory tree design changes.
- Simplify network security.
- Structure network resources for ease of access.
- Provide an effective and functional blueprint for the implementation of NetWare 4.
- Make it easier to modify the directory tree to reflect corporate changes should it become necessary.
- Provide secure access to shared resources.

In order to help companies take full advantage of all these benefits, Novell's NetWare 4 design and implementation process includes guidelines for designing the directory tree. One of those guidelines includes information about what the top layer of the directory tree should include and how it should be designed in order to implement Novell's guidelines successfully.

The Top Layer of the Tree

The directory tree is a hierarchical representation of the objects contained within the NetWare 4 network directory database. As such, the directory tree has different layers. Novell defines two general layers: the top layer and the lower layers.

The directory tree's structure can be created to represent a logical organization of resources or a physical organization of resources. In the smaller local area networks, either approach is generally acceptable, although a physical organization is less likely to be effective. This is true primarily because a LAN is physically located in one area. The logical organization of network resources with the directory tree of a LAN is often more productive.

In a WAN, issues such as the physical structure of the company's WAN, and a reduction of costs associated with network traffic are both reasons to organize the WAN's directory tree structure around the physical resources. Local area networks generally need to be more concerned, however, with other related issues:

- Simplification of partition and replication
- Future changes and needs
- Logical and intuitive organization

In a LAN, the design considerations for partitioning and replicating the tree are minimal. A LAN can generally accept the defaults for partitioning and replication. The network design ends up with a single partition and, by default, three replicas. You may choose to add more replicas, particularly if you have many file servers on the network. As a rule, however, small LANs can work with the defaults.

As a project team member, you do need to consider future company changes and the network's current as well as future needs when designing the upper layers of the directory tree. For example, if you anticipate that the company may someday grow quite large, and thus so will the network, you may decide to design the tree along the guidelines given for designing a WAN, rather than for designing a LAN.

Regardless of whether you consider design issues associated with a WAN or not, you should at least design the directory tree so that its organization is logical and intuitive. When designing the directory tree of a LAN, keep the two primary guidelines discussed in the next section in mind.

Guidelines

There are two guidelines to keep in mind in order to accomplish the task of designing the directory tree so that its organization is logical and intuitive: designing the network in the shape of a pyramid—narrow in the upper layer and wider in the lower layer—and designing the network so that it includes a single organization object.

The more important of the two, for ensuring that the network is easy and intuitive for individuals to use, is the pyramid-like design of the upper layer of the directory tree. This is more important for two reasons. First, partitioning the network is generally easier to do when the directory tree is designed in a pyramid shape. Second, a pyramid-shaped directory tree reduces the number of subordinate reference replicas that must be generated in order to track partitions.

Note

Subordinate reference replicas are replicas that are created automatically by NDS. They are created when a replica of a *child partition* (a partition that is subordinate in the directory tree to another partition) is not stored on the file server containing the child partition's *parent partition*. Subordinate references cannot be created or removed by any network user.

Because NDS has full control over subordinate references, network users cannot specify where subordinate references are placed or how many of them are created. The only way to control subordinate references is by designing the directory tree so it makes best use of subordinate references. To keep the number of subordinate references to a minimum, design the directory tree in a pyramid shape.

Note Directory trees with a single partition do not have child partitions. Without child partitions, no subordinate references are needed, and thus none are created.

Figure 4.5 shows a pyramid-shaped directory tree design. In this figure, only one partition exists; thus, there are no subordinate references.

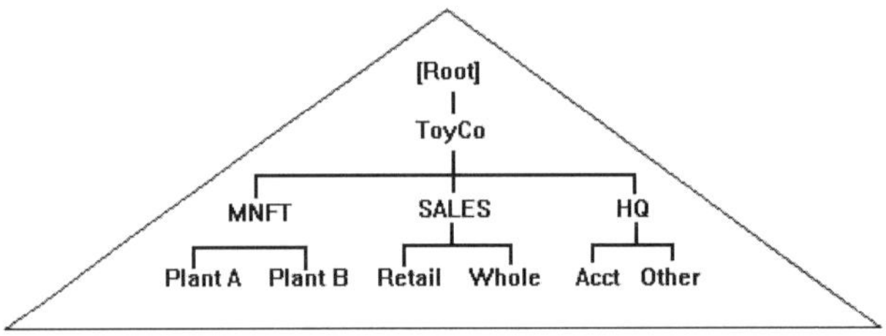

Figure 4.5
Sample pyramid-shaped directory tree.

The second of the two guidelines to help ensure that the network is easy and intuitive for individuals to use is to design the directory tree with only a single Organization object. Using a single Organization object in the directory tree has two advantages, and no real disadvantages.

The first advantage is that it enables you to set rights for the whole company. By giving the rights to the Organization object, all users within the tree will have those rights. For example, you may want to grant the Read file system right to one or more network directories. That right to those directories is then passed on to (inherited by) all network users.

The second advantage is that it makes it easier to merge one tree into another if future growth makes it necessary.

When to Avoid a Pyramid-like Design

There are reasons not to use a pyramid-like design for the directory tree. Some of the reasons apply to wide area networks rather than LANs or MANs. Two reasons, however, can apply to LANs, MANs, and WANs.

First, if the network is located in one geographical area, or high-speed, reliable links are used to connect the network, flattening out the upper layer of the directory tree does not cause problems. Second, if dial-up lines (generally networks connected over longer distances through modems) are used on the network, a drastic increase in network costs would occur if only a single Organization object were used. In this case, multiple Organization units may prove to be less costly.

Note Although not mentioned in this discussion about designing the upper layer of the directory, directory trees always have a single [Root] located at the top of the tree. The Organization object is placed directly below the [Root] object, unless a Country object is used. If a Country object is used, the Organization object is placed below the Country object.

Once the upper layer of the directory tree is designed, the project team can begin designing the lower layers of the tree. The design of the lower layers takes more time than the design of the upper layer, primarily because more issues are involved.

Designing the Lower Layers of the Tree

Unlike designing the upper layers of the tree, design of the lower layers primarily affects the objects at each layer rather than affecting the entire tree structure. This also means that a single general rule can be applied when designing the lower layers of the directory tree. That rule states that you should design the lower layers of the directory tree so that objects with common access needs to other objects are placed in the same container.

Because users with common resource needs are also generally located physically close together in the company, this rule is often easy to follow. It also often results in a directory tree design, which, at the lower levels, resembles the company's organization chart.

If you are not sure whether applying this general rule in the design of your NetWare 4 LAN will be sufficient, there are other considerations you can use as well. Those other considerations can be divided into two categories: current and future.

Current Considerations

Current considerations are those issues that will have an immediate effect on the network's design. Although there may be other current considerations, these are some of the more common ones:

- Whether containers as designed are logical
- Where resources are currently located
- Whether the network will be administered from a central location
- Where partitions will be created
- What types of login scripts will be used
- Whether bindery services will be provided

Logical organization of network containers helps to ensure that user access is relatively easy and as intuitive as possible. Organizing containers around the current location of resources contributes to the logical organization of containers.

How the network will be administered should also be considered when designing the lower layers of the directory tree. There are two possible approaches to directory administration: centralized and distributed.

In the centralized approach, a single department or network administrator takes the responsibility for managing the directory tree for the entire company. To be effective, centralized administration necessitates that the directory tree design have a limited number of lower layers. Fewer layers makes it easier for administrators to navigate the network and view a larger portion of the directory tree at a time.

Centralized administration is easier if all file servers are placed in the same container. This container is referred to as the *server container*. By locating all file servers in one container, it is easier for administrators to track file server activity.

In addition, the use of a file server container is well suited to a LAN or a MAN. With all file servers located in a single container, administration is easier—a big plus for a network with limited administration resources.

Decentralized administration takes the network's manage and monitor functions and spreads them out to administrators in various departments. The decentralized approach may work successfully for larger LANs and MANs, but is more often suited to a WAN. Even large LANs and MANs generally have few people available to handle the daily network administration duties. Decentralized administration requires multiple people to be successful. Small businesses often do not have access to multiple administrators.

Lack of sufficient personnel resources to administer the network from a decentralized location is one drawback of the decentralized approach. A decentralized approach to administration also has a tendency to increase the number of layers at the lower level of the directory tree. More administrators have more control of the network; thus, they often create additional directory tree levels that might not otherwise have been created.

If the network will have more than one partition, the proposed location of the additional partitions may also affect the design of the lower layers of the directory tree. Whenever possible, design partitions so that they contain only the objects and resources the users in the container need. Multiple partitions may also be necessary when such a large number of objects would be in a single container that administration might be unwieldy.

For example, even though a university generally has its own LAN or MAN and is not a part of a WAN, it may have an excessive number of objects. If each student at the university has a corresponding User object in the directory tree, the directory tree could end up with thousands of User objects in a single partition. Because 5,000 objects per partition is the recommended maximum, you may need to create multiple partitions just to break up the number of objects in each partition.

NetWare 4 offers a type of login script not available in previous versions of NetWare—the container login script. Container login scripts can be used to customize a user's environment at the time the user logs in to the network. Because a container login script applies to all users whose User objects are in the container, container login scripts can simultaneously customize the network environment for many different users.

Container login scripts are particularly useful, because in many cases, container login scripts eliminate the need for user login scripts. Managing a single container login script is much easier and less time-consuming than managing multiple user login scripts.

You can use container login scripts for such things as the following:

- Defining drive mappings
- Issuing capture statements
- Calling up menus

- Setting configuration information
- Running executable files
- Displaying messages

If you choose to use container login scripts, the design of the lower layers of the directory tree must take this into consideration. Group users with common resource needs into the same containers so that container login scripts can be used for these users. This approach also means you may need to create additional container objects to accommodate the variety of resource needs through the use of container login scripts.

Bindery services also have an effect on the design of the directory tree. Providing bindery services on the network makes it possible for users to access resources on NetWare 4 file servers when they are currently functioning in a NetWare bindery-based network environment. In addition, bindery services make it possible for applications that are bindery-based rather than NDS-compatible to continue to function in a NetWare 4 network.

To take advantage of bindery services, the directory tree must have bindery context set for each container in which bindery services will be needed. There are some restrictions related to bindery services, the most important of which may be the fact that you cannot have more than 16 bindery contexts set for each NetWare 4 file server.

Note

Versions of NetWare 4 earlier than NetWare 4.1 allowed you to set only a single bindery context per NetWare 4 server. Carefully planning the structure of the lower layers of the directory tree was even more important under that restriction. To work around the limit of one bindery context per file server, designers had to design the network to place all bindery services users into a single container.

With the capability of setting up to 16 bindery contexts per file server, more flexibility in the network's design is provided. That does not excuse the project design team from planning the directory design to consider the needs of bindery-based users. It does, however, make the design process a little less restrictive.

Future Considerations

The most important future consideration associated with designing the lower layers of the directory tree is likely to be the possibility of future growth. If the company is anticipating rapid growth, it may be necessary to approach the design of the lower layers of the directory tree by using an assumption that the company has already expanded. Taking this approach enables the project team to make assumptions and decisions that otherwise might not have been taken into account.

For example, a company anticipating the purchase of another company in a different geographical location may choose to design the lower levels of the tree to accommodate the combining of the two companies. Several questions should be asked and answered if such a major change is anticipated:

- Does the other company already have a network?
- Is the other company's existing network a NetWare 4 network?
- Will the other company's directory tree be merged into the tree presently being planned, or vice versa?
- Will the two directory trees be merged at all, or will they function as separate trees?
- Does the other company have an existing design for the lower levels of its tree that we can duplicate when designing the lower levels of our tree?

Even if the company is not planning on purchasing or being purchased by another company, growth must still be considered. If the company is thinking about expanding its market into the international arena, geography becomes an issue as well. The lower layers of the directory tree may have to be designed to accommodate geographic expansion. Of course, if the company is anticipating geographic expansion when planning the lower layers of the directory tree, it should have also considered geographic expansion when it designed the upper layer of the directory tree.

The best way to determine future changes that may affect the design of the lower layers of the directory tree may be to discuss options or possibilities with company management. Even when management has no plans for acquisition, internationalization, expansion, and so on, things change without notice, and the project team should try at least to consider how changes might affect the design of the directory tree. It is the team's right to choose to assume that few or no changes will occur, but it should at least be aware of changes that are possible and how they may affect the directory tree's design. At least then, if change occurs, the project team can say that it considered the possibility of change and chose, for whatever reason, to design the directory tree as it stands.

Establishing a Partition Approach

Partitions are portions of the NDS directory tree that contain one or more network container objects and the leaf objects contained within those container objects. There are two types of partitions: parent and child.

A child partition is any partition that is subordinate to (immediately below) another partition. A parent partition is any partition immediately above another partition (see fig. 4.6).

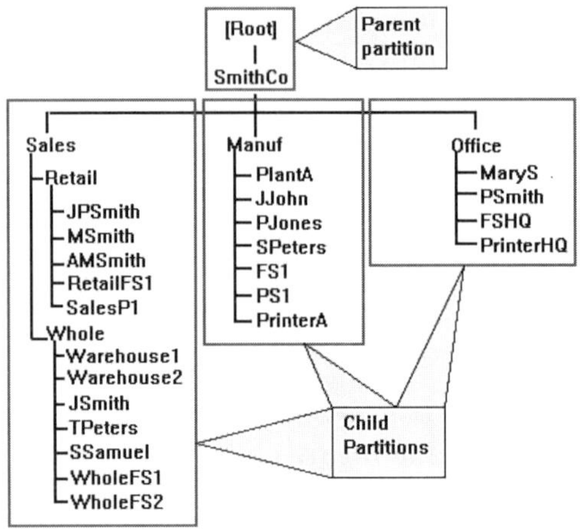

Figure 4.6
NDS directory tree showing parent and child partitions.

Dividing the directory tree into partitions makes it possible to store various replicas on different NetWare 4 file servers throughout the network. Distributing replicas across the network provides fault tolerance and limits network traffic by placing database information close to where it is most needed.

By default, the NetWare 4 installation process creates one partition and places a replica of that partition onto the first three NetWare 4 file servers that are installed in the directory tree. The first NetWare 4 file server to be installed receives the Master replica. The second and third NetWare 4 file servers installed into the directory tree each receive a Read/Write replica of the partition.

In smaller LANs and WANs, generically defined as 15 or fewer file servers with 50 or fewer users, the default partitioning and replication strategy are often sufficient to meet the needs of the network and its users. In larger LANs and WANs, additional partitions and replicas may be required.

It is your responsibility as a member of the project team to help determine whether additional partitions and replicas will be needed. If the team decides that additional partitions and replicas are necessary, the team will also have to determine where the directory tree will be partitioned, how many replicas of each partition should be created, and on which file servers the replicas should be stored. In short, it is your responsibility as a project team member to determine the partition and replication strategy for the network.

Before you can establish a replication strategy, you must first determine how best to partition the network. That decision may mean that you will accept the default of a single network partition. Even in small LANs, however, it is sometimes best to create at least one additional partition to separate the network's [Root] and Organization object from the rest of the network. Doing so protects these two objects from problems associated with other objects on the network, thus substantially reducing the possibility that unrepairable damage to the [Root] object will occur.

Note If the [Root] object, or rather the information contained in the portion of the NDS database where information about [Root] is stored, becomes corrupted beyond repair, it is likely that the entire NDS directory tree will have to be reinstalled. Protecting the directory tree's [Root] is, therefore, a good reason to create a second partition, even in very small local area networks.

There are several guidelines and rules developed by Novell that can be followed to help determine the best partitioning strategy for any given network. Learning, understanding, and following those guidelines and rules helps ensure that the partitioning strategy you develop for the network will be effective and that it will serve the needs of the network for some time to come.

Partitioning Guidelines

There are eight specific guidelines the project team can apply when determining the partitioning strategy for the network:

- Default partitions.
- Do not create partitions across the WAN.

- Consider multiple partitions.
- Eliminate partitions with fewer than 100 objects.
- Plan multiple partitions to keep objects together.
- Group file servers on a single cable segment.
- Design partitions for the upper layer of the tree.
- Avoid increasing administrative overhead.

When the first NetWare 4 file server is installed in the directory tree, a single partition is created. It contains [Root], the Country object (if used), Organization object(s), and any Organizational Units and leaf objects created in the directory tree. This single partition is the default, and may be sufficient for some companies. Assessing whether the default partition is sufficient to meet current and future company needs is the first guideline the project team can use when planning a partitioning strategy for the network.

If you choose to create more than one partition, consider the second guideline—do not create partitions across the WAN. In LANs and MANs, this guideline rarely applies. There may be occasions in small networks, however, when it is necessary to consider the company's physical locations when determining the partitioning strategy for the network. Remember that if the company has offices that are connected to each other over geographic distances, make separate partitions for each office. A single partition should not include more than one geographic region, because the cost of keeping partition replicas updated across the WAN often exceeds the related benefits.

Not spanning the WAN also leads into the third guideline—consider multiple partitions. The directory tree should be partitioned to avoid spanning geographic regions. You should also consider creating additional partitions to help distribute the load associated with storing the NDS database and user access to the database. Distributing the load also helps minimize associated costs and optimize network use.

Each partition on the network should be able to handle 5,000 objects easily—although theoretically, it can handle an unlimited number of objects. More than 5,000 objects, however, becomes unwieldy to manage and may slow network performance or response. You can consider creating additional partitions if your network has more than 5,000 objects. As noted earlier, a university setting with several thousand student User objects is a good example of such a situation.

On the other hand, you do not want to create too many partitions. As the fourth guideline points out, you should eliminate partitions with fewer than 100 objects in them. Partitions this small tend to increase administrative overhead as additional replicas must be managed. In addition, several small partitions increase the time it takes to navigate the directory tree; thus, NDS needs additional time to resolve names when multiple partitions are used. This additional navigation sometimes results in minor increases in network traffic. These issues should be considered and this guideline followed when determining whether and where additional partitions should be created.

Whenever possible, you should also plan multiple partitions to keep objects together. User objects should be located in the same container as the network resources they need to use. Keeping User objects and other network objects in the same partition makes navigation easier for users and name resolution and tree walking easier for NDS.

Grouping file servers on the same cable segment means that, whenever possible, file servers containing replicas of a partition should be kept locally. If all the file servers containing replicas of a partition are connected to the same network cable segment, updating the partition replicas is quicker and more reliable because updates do not have to cross through routers or bridges to reach their destination. The project team should look at a network's topology for such issues as the location of file servers in relation to routers and bridges when determining a partitioning strategy for the network.

When designing partitions, design partitions around the upper layers of the directory tree, flowing down to include lower layers within the partitions. Partition from the top of the tree down, rather than vice versa.

The final guideline—avoid increasing administrative overhead—is rather subjective in nature. There must be some type of tradeoff between designing partitions to meet the network's needs and designing partitions to make administration as simple as possible. Where that tradeoff exists is one of the issues the project team has to deal with when designing the partition strategy. All things being equal, if one partition strategy increases the amount of network administration required, and another approach decreases the amount of network required, choose the approach that limits network administration requirements.

Besides the eight guidelines Novell's Consulting Services group provides for you to use when creating a partitioning strategy, it also has five main rules you need to follow (see fig. 4.7).

Figure 4.7

Guidelines and rules for creating a partitioning strategy.

Partitioning Strategy

Guidelines	Rules
Accept default partitions if appropriate	Partitions hold only NDS information
Do not span the WAN when creating partitions	Each object can be in only one partition
Consider the use of multiple partitions	Each partition is stored on a NetWare 4 file server
Do not create partitions with fewer than 100 objects	Partition boundaries cannot overlap
plan multiple partitions to keep objects together	Each partition must contain a connected subtree
Group file servers on a single cable segment	
Design partitions for the upper layer of the tree	
Avoid increasing administrative overhead if possible	

Rules Associated with Partitioning

The five main rules Novell's Consulting Services specifies regarding the process of designing a network partitioning strategy are as follows:

- Partitions contain only information about the NDS database and no information about the file system. When designing partitions for the directory tree, do not consider the directory structure of a NetWare volume in the design.

- Each NDS object can exist in only one partition. No NDS object can be placed in more than one partition, so partitions cannot cross containers. Just as NDS objects can exist in only one partition, containers can exist in only one container.
- Each partition is stored on a NetWare 4 server. Only NetWare 4 servers can hold partitions. Other versions of NetWare file servers cannot be used to store partitions.
- No partition's boundaries can overlap another partition's boundaries. Objects can be contained within only one partition. Thus, partition boundaries cannot overlap, or objects would be part of more than one partition.
- Each partition must contain a connected subtree. A single container object must have at least one other container or leaf object contained within it before it can be a partition.

When you design partitions, remember that partitions can occur only at containers. You cannot partition leaf objects within a container. In addition, you can only store one replica of a partition on a server. You can have multiple replicas of a partition, but only one replica of each partition can be stored on any given server.

If you design the upper layers of the directory tree to form the shape of a pyramid, the upper layers have only a few containers. The lower layers have more containers and leaf objects. If you create additional partitions, your partitions will also represent a pyramid shape, particularly if you create each partition close to the leaf objects. There are fewer partitions near the upper layers of the directory tree and more partitions at the lower layers. The [Root] object remains as a partition itself.

Planning Replicas and Their Placement

Part of planning partitions is considering where replicas may have to go. Part of planning replica placement is understanding the types of replicas that you can create. The other part of planning replicas and their placement on the network is understanding where to place those replicas in order to facilitate tree walking (accessing specific information in the directory tree, also referred to as the name resolution process).

There are four types of replicas: Master, Read Only, Subordinate Reference, and Read/Write.

The Master replica is the first instance of the partition and is created when the partition is created. The Master replica can be used to log in to the network, add or delete objects, and view directory information. It is stored on the NetWare 4 file server from which the partition itself was created. Only one Master replica can exist on the network for each partition.

The Read Only replica is an exact duplicate of the Master replica. The Read Only replica cannot be used for network login, however, because it cannot be written to. For a user to log in to the network, a writable copy of the partition containing the user's User object must be accessed and written to during the authentication process. Multiple Read Only replicas can be stored on file servers on the network, but only one replica of a partition can be stored on a single file server. Because Read Only replicas cannot be used for network login, it is generally better to use a Read/Write replica rather than a Read Only replica. Read/Write replicas are thus found more often on networks than Read Only replicas.

The Subordinate Reference replica is created by NDS. It cannot be created or changed by any network user. The subordinate reference is also not a duplicate of the Master replica, as are the Read/Write and Read Only replicas. The Subordinate Reference replica is, instead, a pointer. When one of the other three types of replicas (Master, Read/Write, or Read Only) of a child partition is not on the same file server as a replica of that child's parent partition, NDS places a Subordinate Reference replica on the file server holding the parent partition. The Subordinate Reference points to where one of the other three types of replicas for the child partition can be found. The Subordinate Reference does not contain any directory tree database information. Because it is only a pointer, not a copy of the partition, Subordinate Reference replicas cannot be used to log in to the network.

The fourth type of replica, the Read/Write replica, is a writable replica and thus can be used to log in to the network, add or delete objects, and view directory information. Because of its multiple uses and the fact that only one Master replica can exist for each partition on a network, there are several guidelines associated with using Read/Write replicas.

Read/Write Replicas

To ensure fault tolerance on the network, each partition should have a minimum of three replicas placed on different file servers on the network. One replica, the Master, is created by default when the partition is created. Also by default, but only for the first network partition, two Read/Write replicas are created. The first Read/Write replica is placed on the second file server installed in the directory tree. The second Read/Write replica is placed on the third file server installed in the directory tree.

If you create additional partitions above the first partition created by NDS as the default partition, you should also create additional replicas for those partitions. Novell's Consulting Services group recommends that, for fault tolerance, each partition on the network should have a minimum of two replicas in addition to the Master replica.

The project team needs to plan to meet that minimum when it plans its replication strategy. Bearing in mind that only one replica of a partition can exist on a file server, to have three replicas of the first and subsequent partitions requires that the network have a minimum of three file servers in it.

Users should have a writable replica placed on the file server nearest to them to facilitate network login. The guideline that applies here when planning the replication strategy is that the strategy should ensure that replicas are placed on file servers as close to the user as possible.

One other guideline to be remembered when planning replicas is their space requirements. Each replica requires approximately 3 to

5 KB of space on the SYS volume. When planning replica placement, consider the amount of space each file server has on the SYS volume.

Planning Replicas to Facilitate Tree Walking

When planning the replication strategy, you must consider the types of replicas to be used, how many replicas will be used, and on which file servers they will be placed. Project team members must also consider how NDS will perform the name resolution process when planning the network's replication strategy.

The following are issues to consider related to performing the name resolution process:

- Supporting bindery services
- Controlling the number of Subordinate Reference replicas
- Planning and placing replicas to accomplish fault tolerance, easy navigation, and quick access to the network

Of these three issues, supporting bindery context is the most important to users who must log in to and access the NetWare 4 network using bindery services.

Support Bindery Services

NetWare 2 and NetWare 3 users can access resources on a NetWare 4 network if bindery services are installed on the network's NetWare 4 file servers. When bindery services are installed, NDS accepts bindery-based calls made by clients and applications. NDS imitates the flat structure of the NetWare bindery, making it possible for bindery-based applications to make calls to NDS and for bindery-based clients to log in to the NetWare 4 network by using the older NETX shell. By imitating the flat structure of the NetWare bindery, NDS can see bindery objects, users, groups, print queues, print servers, and so on, and respond to requests made from bindery-based applications and clients.

When designing the lower layers of the directory tree, issues related to bindery services need to be considered. The first issue is, of course, whether bindery services will be needed and thus provided for. If all NetWare 2 and NetWare 3 file servers will be upgraded to NetWare 4 within a short period of time (a few days to a few weeks), it may not be necessary to plan for bindery services at all. If, however, the upgrade of all servers to NetWare 4 is expected to take quite some time, plan to include bindery services.

When planning bindery services, remember that where the bindery services feature is enabled (the server's bindery context) is the most important issue. Up to 16 container objects in the NDS tree can have bindery services context set for them. Carefully determine, therefore, which containers need to have bindery services enabled, and plan for it. If necessary, combine objects into fewer containers to accommodate the 16-container limit imposed by bindery services. Carefully determine which applications must be accessed by using bindery services because they have not yet been upgraded to function in the NetWare 4 environment.

Control Subordinate Reference Replicas

As noted previously, a subordinate reference replica is a pointer that ensures that the parent partition and its child partitions have a permanent connection to each other. The subordinate reference is used as a pointer to identify the location of replicas of child partitions when another type of replica for those child partitions is not stored on the same file server as the replica for the parent partition.

Subordinate references are created automatically by NDS. They contain only the *partition root object* (the container object at the top of the partition). The name of the file server is stored in the replica list of the partition.

Proper design of the lower layers of the directory tree helps control the number of subordinate references created by NDS. This is important because too many subordinate reference replicas can increase traffic and—more importantly—provide a single point for network failure, if the majority of the subordinate references end up being stored on a single file server.

As stated, a subordinate reference replica is created when the child partition does not have a replica on the same server as the parent partition. There are three ways to reduce the number of subordinate references. The best way is to reduce the number of file servers holding replicas of the parent partition, beginning with the [Root] partition.

All partitions immediately below the [Root] partition are the [Root] partition's children. If you place a replica of the [Root] partition on three file servers and do not place replicas of each child partition on those same servers, each server has a subordinate reference to each child partition. If you add only a replica of [Root] to a fourth file server, that file server also has a subordinate reference replica of the [Root] partition.

Looking at figure 4.8, you can see that it is possible to place [Root] partition replicas on four file servers. If the Master replica of [Root] is placed on file server AA01 by default, and servers AA02 and AA03 each receive a Read/Write replica of [Root], servers AA02 and AA03 also contain a subordinate reference to the JohnToyCo partition. Adding a fourth replica of [Root] to file server AA04 places a subordinate reference replica on that file server as well. Because three replicas are considered sufficient for fault tolerance, by not placing a fourth replica of the [Root] partition on file server AA04, you control the number of subordinate references on the network.

Another way to reduce the number of subordinate reference replicas on the network is to place replicas of child partitions on the same server as the parent partition. Referring again to figure 4.8, when you create the JohnToyCo partition, the Master replica of the JohnToyCo partition is placed on file server AA01 if that server is used to create the partition.

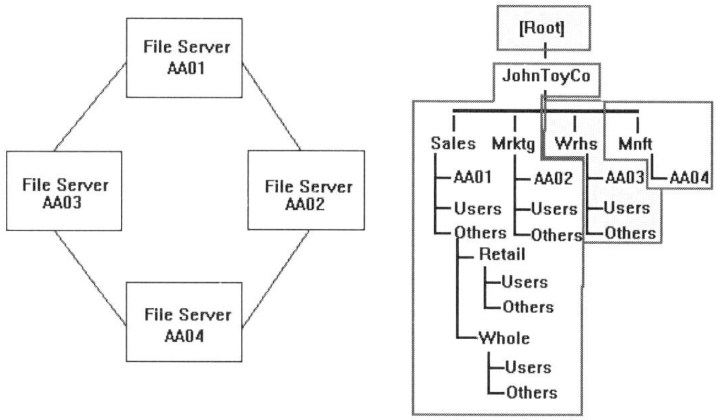

Figure 4.8
Example of a directory tree and network file server layout.

When you create the Wrhs and Mnft partitions, if those partitions are created on file servers AA03 and AA04 respectively, the Master replicas for the Wrhs and Mnft partitions are also on file servers AA03 and AA04, respectively. Because the Wrhs and Mnft partitions are child partitions to JohnToyCo, the AA01 file server contains subordinate references to the Wrhs and Mnft partitions (see fig. 4.9).

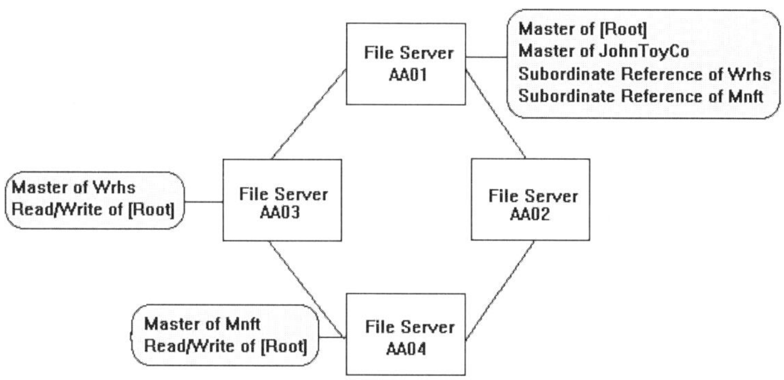

Figure 4.9
Replica placement with subordinate references.

If you want to reduce the number of subordinate reference replicas, there is another approach you can take. This approach is not recommended, because it can actually increase network traffic, but it bears mentioning here.

First, place the Master replicas for the Wrhs and Mnft partitions on file servers AA03 and AA04, respectively. Then, place a Read/Write replica of both the Wrhs and Mnft partitions on file server AA01. When you add the Read/Write replicas to file server AA01, the subordinate references to Wrhs and Mnft on file server AA01 are eliminated. Figure 4.10 shows the final location of partitions for the network displayed in figure 4.9, based upon the completion of this process as described for reducing the number of subordinate reference replicas.

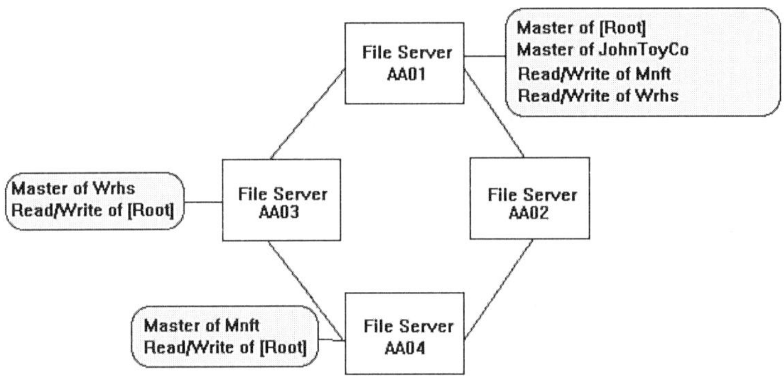

Figure 4.10
Final replica placement.

Plan and Place Replicas

Replicas should be planned and then placed to accomplish fault tolerance, make network navigation easy for users, and provide quick access to the network. To plan and place replicas so as to accomplish these goals, consider the following guidelines:

- Provide a minimum of two Read/Write replicas for each partition. This is in addition to the Master replica created at the time the partition is created.
- Partition the [Root] from the rest of the tree to ensure directory tree integrity and replicate it as recommended in the first guideline.
- If not done at the time each partition was originally created, place replicas of partitions on file servers closest to the users whose User objects and needed resources are contained within the partition.

- Create additional replicas, if necessary, to accommodate bindery services.
- Ensure that the failure of a single file server will not make directory tree access impossible for any or all of the network.

NDS also needs to be able to walk the tree easily when searching for requested resources. Tree walking is generally rather limited in a LAN or MAN, but you may still need to consider this issue when designing the directory tree's lower layers.

Planning Time Synchronization on a LAN

As noted earlier, the purpose of time synchronization is to ensure that all file servers in the directory tree use a coordinated time. NetWare 4 applies a time and date stamp to each network transaction to ensure that transactions are processed in the proper order, which is particularly important to replication, partitioning, and network security.

When planning time synchronization, you should take into account three related aspects:

- Time source
- Time server types
- Time server communication method

In small LANs and MANs, the default time source, time server type, and time server communication method are sufficient. When the LAN or MAN exceeds approximately 30 file servers, or covers multiple sites, advanced time synchronization issues become important. The default time synchronization aspects must be understood and considered when planning time synchronization for a small network.

Time Source

Time synchronization in NetWare 4 keeps NetWare 4 servers synchronized by calculating local time from *Universal Coordinated Time (UTC)*, which is the world time standard coordinated to the zero meridian. To calculate local time, NetWare 4 applies the time zone and daylight savings time settings to the UTC.

To coordinate time across all network servers, at least one NetWare 4 file server must have access to an external time source. An external time source can come from any variety of sources. The file server's hardware clock can be used, as can a radio clock or an atomic clock. You can even use the Internet to obtain an external time source for your network.

Once an external time source is obtained, NetWare calculates the network time. The calculated time is then synchronized across the network. The actual synchronized network time depends on the type of time server.

Time Server Types

There are four time server types. Each falls into one of two categories: time provider or time consumer. A time provider is a server that provides time to any other time provider, time consumer, or workstation requesting time. Three of the four time servers are time providers. A time consumer gets its time from a time provider. Of the four types of time servers, Secondary servers are considered time consumers.

These are the four types of time servers:

- Primary
- Reference
- Single Reference
- Secondary

The Single Reference time server with Secondary time servers are used mostly on small networks. Primary, Reference, and Secondary time servers are generally used on larger WANs.

Primary Time Servers

A Primary time server is a time provider that votes with other time providers to determine network time. During the time synchronization process, the Primary time server polls other time servers to see to what time they are set; then the time providers vote on an average network time. Next, the Primary time server adjusts its internal clock to correct its time. It only corrects its time up to 50 percent of the discrepancy, however.

The next and each subsequent time a polling of time servers occurs, the Primary time server votes with other time servers on a network time, then adjusts its internal clock accordingly, but again only up to 50 percent of the discrepancy. After multiple polling and synchronization processes, the Primary time server eventually displays the same time on its internal clock as that recorded on the internal clocks of other time providers. Once the Primary time server is in exact synchronization with at least one other time provider, the Primary time server indicates its synchronization by raising its time synchronization flag. The Primary time server is then synchronized.

Reference Time Servers

A Reference time server votes with other time servers to establish a common network time. Whereas each Primary time server carries a voting weight of one, the Reference time server has a weight of 16. By giving the Reference time server greater weight in the voting, other time servers eventually converge to that of the Reference server, because the Reference server never adjusts its internal clock.

Because a Reference time server eventually dictates network time, you should use only one Reference server on your LAN or MAN. All other time servers eventually synchronize to the Reference server. This also means that, although you can use the Reference time server's internal clock, you should use an external time source. That external time source should be the most reliable time source available to your network.

Single Reference Time Servers

A Single Reference time server is a sole time provider. All other network time servers are installed as Secondary time servers by default after the first file server is installed (see fig. 4.11). The first file server installed into the NetWare 4 network is installed as a Single Reference time server, also by default.

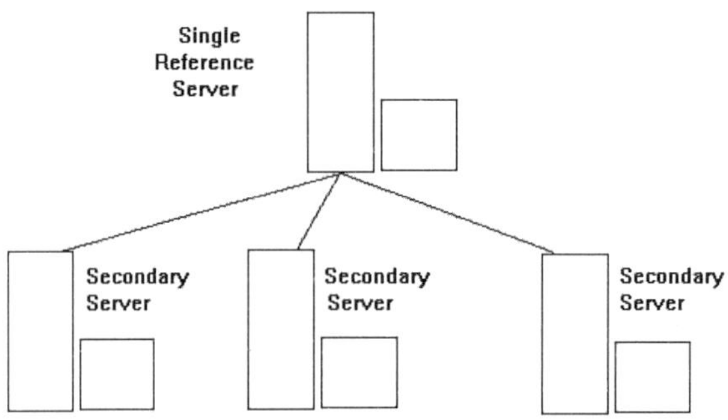

Figure 4.11
Default time synchronization strategy.

The Single Reference time server is synchronized the moment that installation is complete, because it does not have to synchronize with any other time server. It does not poll other time servers to determine network time. It raises its synchronization flag without ever communicating with other time servers.

Although the Reference time server functions as a dictator, the Single Reference time server is less like a dictator and more like a beloved monarch. All other time servers, as well as workstations, seek out the Single Reference time server for their time. With Reference time servers, polling, voting, and dictating time are needed to synchronize time providers across the network. This is not the case for Single Reference time servers. Because Single Reference time servers do not need to obtain time from any other time source to become synchronized, only Secondary time servers can function on the same network or within the same time provider group as Single Reference time servers.

Secondary Time Servers

A Secondary time server is a time server that always adjusts its time to a time provider. It is known as a time consumer. A Secondary time server can adjust its time to the time ultimately specified (dictated) by a Reference server to that which is provided through the voting process (Primary time server), or to the time specified by a beloved monarch (Single Reference time server). The Secondary time server's goal is to remain synchronized to the providing time server.

The majority of time servers on the network are time consumers, or Secondary time servers. It is the responsibility of the Secondary time servers to request time from a time provider, then synchronize themselves to the time made available to them by the time provider. Their time adjustment, therefore, is 100 percent, unlike the 50 percent adjustment that Primary time servers make. Secondary servers also provide time to workstations on the network.

When determining the best time synchronization approach to use for your network, consider using the default of one Single Reference time server and multiple Secondary time servers. Then, consider which communication method is best suited to your network.

Time Server Communication Methods

Time servers must communicate with each other either to provide or to consume time. There are two communication methods used for time synchronization:

- Service Advertising Protocol (SAP) method
- Custom configuration method

The SAP method is the default method. It is the easiest to work with because it does not require any special configuration or manipulation in order to function effectively. To use the SAP method also does not require the use of a TIMESYNC.CFG file, although you can issue some related SET TIMESYNC commands at the file server console to perform some configuration. The custom configuration method requires the use of a configuration file called TIMESYNC.CFG.

In the SAP method of time server communication, Primary, Reference, and Single Reference servers use SAP to announce their presence on the network. Time consumers accept the SAP announcements, but do not use SAP to communicate with time providers on the network.

The custom configuration method uses a list of time providers to determine which time servers should communicate with which other time servers. Using the custom configuration method allows absolute control over network time server communication. The actual use of the utility associated with time configuration (SERVMAN) is relatively simple and easy.

The biggest problem with using custom configuration is that no time server communication occurs if the time server included on another time server's list cannot be located. Mistakes in the time server configuration list can also affect time synchronization, as can the use of a time server that is providing an incorrect time as the time provider. In this situation, time synchronization on the network may be seriously and negatively impacted.

When determining the best time synchronization strategy for your LAN or MAN, if possible, accept the default of one Single Reference server, with all other file servers being Secondary servers. If your network has more than 30 file servers, or is geographically dispersed, you can customize time synchronization through the use of time provider groups (discussed in detail in Chapter 6).

Developing the Accessibility Plan

When developing the NetWare 4 network accessibility plan, you need to review users' needs, as well as to consider the needs of applications and other resources on the network. For example, you need to consider whether some of your network users need to access the network while they are at home or traveling. You also need to consider whether all the application programs used on the network are capable of functioning in a NetWare 4 environment. If they are not, you need to consider how you are going to make those applications available to users on the network. You also need to consider what basic guidelines or standards for accessibility you and the project team will establish and follow.

Basic guidelines or standards for accessibility may include information about the use of common login scripts and what they may contain, and also may include a list of settings to be included in each workstation's NET.CFG file. Other basic guidelines may include the following:

- A design strategy for dealing with traveling or mobile users
- An approach or strategy for designing the network to accommodate bindery services
- A strategy for ensuring network security, including information on different levels of network administrators and the rights that should be assigned to them

There are several issues that must be considered when creating a NetWare 4 network accessibility plan. You deal with many of these issues merely in the course of designing the network, but there are also some specific issues that must be considered related to creating the accessibility plan itself.

Creating an Accessibility Plan

Issues to consider when creating a NetWare 4 network accessibility plan for a small LAN or a MAN should include at least the following:

- Workstation types
- NetWare operating system versions on the network
- Resources requiring bindery-based access
- Applications used on the network
- Hardware resources
- Network administration

Not all NetWare 4 network workstations are IBM-compatible Personal Computers with an Intel 80486 or higher microprocessor, 8 MB of RAM, and a 120 MB hard disk. Some network workstations are 80386 machines, Macintosh, or maybe even UNIX workstations. Each and every piece of network hardware has to be considered when developing an accessibility plan for the network.

The resource list that the project team obtained early in the design and implementation process should provide you with a pretty good idea of what hardware currently exists on the network. From that list you should be able to determine at least which hardware can be used on the NetWare 4 network and which has to be eliminated or replaced.

Other accessibility issues should be considered as well, particularly issues related to how specific objects and their properties should be handled.

Accessibility Guidelines for Particular Objects or Properties

There are several accessibility issues to consider:

- Group object standards may include information about the model to be followed when naming Group objects.

- Profile object standards may specify when a Profile login script should be used, and what should generally be included in a Profile login script. The Profile object can also be used to specify the purpose for or reason behind the use of a specific Profile login script.
- Organizational Role standards may specify how the Organizational Role object will be used, how a user is to qualify for inclusion in an Organizational Role, what various levels of Organizational Role objects can exist, and what their security access should include.
- Directory Map objects point or refer to a specific directory on a network volume. Directory Map objects do not let users view the directory itself, but do allow them to run an executable file stored in the directory structure to which the Directory Map object points. Directory Map object standards should indicate to what types of directories the Directory Map object can point, such as applications, NetWare utilities, and so on.
- An Inherited Rights Filters (IRF) exists for every object in the NetWare directory tree. An IRF also exists for every directory and file in each NetWare volume's directory structure. When the IRF should be used, when it should not be used, and how administrators will prevent others from accidentally or deliberately cutting off sections of the NDS directory tree from other administrators should be included in the IRF standards. In addition, if some sections of the tree should be cut off from anyone other than those specifically chosen to have access to it, how to accomplish that should also be included in a discussion of the IRF standards.
- User Login Scripts standards specify whether User login scripts should be used, as well as when and how they should be used. The kinds of information or types of commands that can be included, or that must not be included, in User login scripts should also be specified in the related standards.
- Alias objects are leaf objects that point to the original location of an object in the directory tree. Aliases are used to make it

easier for users to access objects in containers other than their parent containers. For example, an Alias object can be created in one container to point to a Printer object in another container. That way, users in both containers can have easy access to the Printer object. When Alias objects will be used, the types of leaf objects they can point to, and similar issues should be discussed when specifying standards for Alias objects.

- Security-related issues should also be specified in the network standards document, including information such as the levels of container administrators that are to be created on the network, which rights should be assigned to the Organization object to enable those rights to flow to all users in the network, and other security-related issues.

There are several issues that should be discussed in a network standards document. Naming standards for objects and IPX network number standards are only two of those issues. Other issues that, if applicable, the project team should include in the company's standards document for a company with a LAN or MAN, include the following:

- Network structure overview
- Installation standards and procedures
- Object naming and property values
- Print services naming conventions
- Security configurations
- Time synchronization standards
- Partitioning and replication standards

These general categories of information need to have details related to them specified in the company standards document.

For example, you should include information in the company standards document about the assignment of standard object names and their associated property values, if this has not been covered in detail in a separate naming standards document. The information about assigning object names should discuss details about different objects, such as User objects. You should also include information about how a user's login name is to be defined, how the user's last name will be entered (uppercase only, lowercase only, upper- and lowercase), whether user's phone numbers will be separated by dashes, and so on.

Special object naming may be specified separately within the company standards document, as in the case of printing services objects. If the project team prefers, however, all objects may have their specifications included under a single heading in the company's standards document. The best approach to choose is the one that best meets the company's needs.

Overview of the Network's Structure

Some space within the company's standards document should be devoted to providing an overview of the network's structure. Information about the structure might include any of a variety of information, as applicable, but should include at least a diagram of the network cabling system, including the location of each file server on the network (see fig. 4.12).

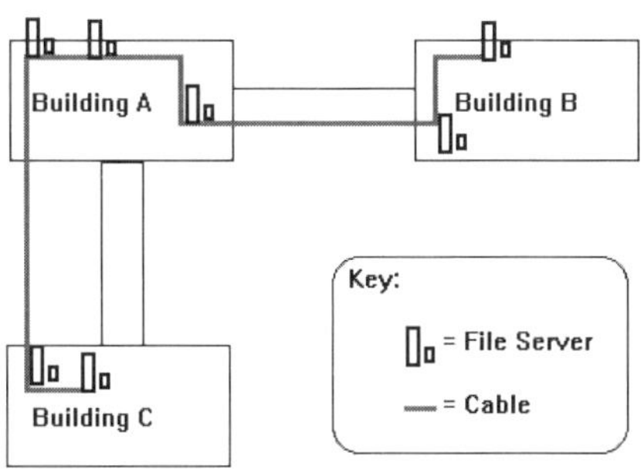

Figure 4.12
Sample network diagram.

Some of the information that may eventually be included in this portion of the company's standards document includes a description of the network as a whole. In some ways, the information that may be included in the overview of the network's structure may be discussed in the naming standards document, but applies more to the network as a whole. This provides the project team with some place to locate information about the design of the network that can be referenced later on as needed.

There is one thing in particular that should be noted about the overview of the network's structure portion of the company's standards document. This portion of the document may have to be completed either as the project team proceeds with the network's design or after the design (and possibly the implementation) of the network has been completed. Some of this information simply cannot be provided until other phases of the NetWare 4 network design and implementation process have been completed.

The following is other information relevant to the network's structure that you could include as part of the overview of the network's structure portion of the company's standards document:

- A brief description of the reasoning behind the design of the network
- A copy of the directory tree as designed, with updates that reflect the final design if modifications are eventually required
- Information about the protocols and frame types used on the network
- Explanations of why portions of the network were not upgraded to NetWare 4 during the implementation process, if this is the case
- Any other information that seems relevant and that may be of value to individuals who will be implementing the design of the network

Some of the information that you may choose to include in the overview is general network documentation. It may be included in other company documents as well or provided only as part of the company's standards document.

How do you know what should be included in the company's standards document? As with other aspects of the network's design, the project team should always seek to meet the company's needs. Choose what to include in the company's standards document based on the needs of those individuals who will be implementing the network, as well as those who will be managing and monitoring the network. The overview of the network's structure portion of the company's standards document will then be sufficient.

Installation Standards and Procedures

Some guidelines for installing NetWare 4 file servers into the directory tree may be useful in the company's standards document, and might include such items of information as the following:

- Who is responsible for installing NetWare 4 file servers
- Whether any formal protocol must be followed before, during, or after installation of a file server
- Whether the file server's IPX address is to be registered, and if so, how to register it
- Whether naming standards apply to file servers, and if so, how file servers whose names do not meet those standards will be treated
- How partitioning and replication is to be handled for newly installed file servers, and who is responsible for dealing with this issue

Installation standards may also include other types of information. For example, if the Admin User object that is created at the time of the new file server's installation will have restricted rights, this information may be included. Even information such as the maximum number of replicas to be stored on a file server can be included in this portion of the company's standards document. Any information related to file server installation that the project team determines to be appropriate may be included in the company's standards document.

Assignment of Standard Object Names and Property Values

The assignment of standard object names and property values section of the company's standards document is likely to be the longest of all the sections, and may, in some companies, actually be a separate naming standards document. If it is not, it will be included in the company's standards document as a section of that document. It contains information related to each object on the network, with the possible exception of objects related to print services. Print services object standards may be covered in a separate portion of the company's standards document.

In addition, this section of the company's standards document includes information about some of the properties of various objects. For example, the User object has many properties that lend themselves to standards. The login name is probably the most likely to require a naming standard. Information such as what should be used to make the login name (first initial followed by first seven characters of the last name, or something similar) may be specified.

Objects that are likely to be included in this section along with descriptions of and information about those objects include the following:

- User
- Group
- Organizational Role
- Profile
- Directory Map

Standards provided regarding User objects generally reflect the properties of User objects. For example, the Department property may be specified as mandatory, optional, or required. Then, a description of the type of information that should be included in the Department property may also be included. Finally, an example of the property may be included where an example is applicable.

Some of the other User object properties that may be included in the standards for User objects are shown in table 4.2. Also shown in this table is information about whether these properties are mandatory, optional, or required in order to create a User object successfully. In addition, a description and an example of the property may also be included.

Table 4.2
User Object Properties Standards

Property	*Mandatory*	*Description*	*Example*
Last name	X	User's surname	`Smith`
Full name	X	First name, middle initial, last name	`John L. Smith`
Title	X	Official position title	`Clerk Typist I`
Telephone	X	User's extension	`x5217`
E-mail address		User's electronic mail address	`JSmith@BB.COM`
Network address		IPX node address of user's workstation	`AA110123`
Postal Address	X	User's mail stop	`A-123`

As previously noted, Group object standards may include information about the model to be followed when naming Group objects. For example, the first four characters of the Group object may be used to specify the function or primary job responsibility associated with the group, followed by three characters that represent the department in which these users work.

The following is an example of a Group Object for a group of users functioning as graphic designers in the documentation department:

```
DSGNDOC
```

Organizational Role standards may specify such things as when the Organizational Role object will be used. For example, a statement similar to the following may be included:

> Use the Organizational Role object whenever administrative rights must be granted to more than one network user. In addition, whenever a role is filled frequently by multiple people, the Organizational Role object can also be used.

Guidelines for naming Organizational Role objects may also be included in the naming standards document. For example, a specific name may be required when using the Organizational Role object to grant administrative rights, such as ADMINOR.

The Profile object provides a login script that can be used by groups or users who have the same login script requirements. Standards for using the Profile object may include such things as guidelines for naming Profile objects or information about commands that are not to be used in Profile login scripts.

The Directory Map object is an NDS leaf object that points to a specific directory on a NetWare volume. The company's standards document may specify how Directory Map objects are to be named.

For example, you may write the company's standards document to indicate that all Directory Map objects be given the full name of the directory containing the application to which it points. If you make this part of the naming standard, the Directory Map object pointing to the directory containing the WordPerfect 6 executable file requires a name of WordPerfect6.

Print Services Naming Conventions

In smaller local area networks, the Quick Setup option in the PCONSOLE utility may be used to establish basic printing services. If the Quick Setup option of PCONSOLE is to be used, the company's standards document can indicate that.

In addition, if there will be too many print services objects with the same common name from installing print services using the

Quick Setup option, other standards may also be included. For example, information specifying that print services objects be renamed from the default after installation may also be included.

The guidelines to follow when renaming print services objects may include information such as: how many characters each object's name must include, which characters should be used to indicate differences between types of printing services objects (print queues, print servers, or printers), and other related items.

Security Default Configurations

Companies with small LANs or MANs usually also have a small number of network administrators. Defining security configurations for network administrators when there are only a few of them becomes relatively simple.

When the first NetWare 4 file server is installed and the NetWare directory tree created, a single network administrator exits (Admin User object) by default. If only one person will be administering the network, the default of the single Admin User object is sufficient.

When more than one network administrator exists or is needed, the network's management can be easily divided using the Organizational Role object. The Organizational Role object can be given any appropriate name when it is created, but a name such as `Container Admin` makes it easy to understand the function of that Organizational Role object quickly.

Note

As the network and thus the need for additional administrators grows, multiple Organizational Role objects can be created throughout the tree. More information about creating additional Organizational Role objects and assigning various levels of administration responsibility to those objects is provided in Chapter 6.

If you choose to use Organizational Role objects to assist in the administration of the directory tree, that decision needs to be documented in the naming standards document. In addition, the project team may also choose to specify where in the directory tree the Organizational Role object is to be placed and how many users should be assigned to an Organizational Role object.

Another item of information regarding the Organizational Role object you may choose to include in the company's standards document is a list of containers to which the Organizational Role object should be made a trustee. In addition, you may also include the rights that are to be granted to the Organizational Role object for those containers.

Because LANs and MANs are generally relatively small networks, some consideration should be given to the procedure for handling administrators who are on a leave of absence. Questions such as whether another user should be temporarily assigned to the Organizational Role object, and, if so, what criteria should be used for choosing a temporary replacement may be answered in the company's standards document.

Security associated with network users should also be discussed in this section of the company's standards document. In LANs and MANs, the user account security defaults may be sufficient. If that is the case, placing a statement in the company's standards document that indicates that the security defaults are to be accepted at the time of User object creation is sufficient. It is better to be a little more thorough than that in your documentation, however. Including a list of the security defaults in the company's standards document leaves no room for error.

If a change to the defaults is needed, those changes can be included in the company's standards document as well. Here are some changes you may want to make in even small networks:

- Limit Concurrent Connections: Yes
- Maximum Number of Connections: 2
- Require Password: Yes
- Minimum Password Length: 6

- Detect Intruder: Yes
- Lock Account After Detection: Yes

There are other changes you may choose to make as well. These are generally sufficient for smaller LANs and MANs. Additional changes, which most often apply to larger WANs, are discussed in Chapter 6.

Default Time Synchronization Standards

Novell's NetWare 4 network time synchronization strategy ensures that all file servers in the directory tree are using the same time (adjusted for varying time zones and daylight savings time). Time synchronization enables NetWare to time stamp and date stamp each network transaction. Doing so helps ensure that each transaction is processed in the same order in which it was conducted.

Note Time stamping becomes particularly important when replication and partitioning is involved, because transactions such as these can have a profound effect on the network's functionality.

When NetWare 4 and the directory tree are installed, default time synchronization standards are implemented. During installation, the installer is prompted to provide the type of time server the file server is to provide. The default time source is Single Reference, but the installer can choose from Single Reference, Primary, Reference, or Secondary time server options.

If the file server being installed is the first NetWare 4 file server, it should be designated as a Single Reference server. This is the default, so you simply need to accept the default to install the server as a Single Reference time server. All other NetWare 4 file servers should be designated as Secondary time servers when they are later installed. This approach to time synchronization is sufficient for LANS, and generally for MANs as well.

Using the default time synchronization strategy of one Single Reference time server used with multiple Secondary time servers is the most appropriate choice when the following are true:

- The company has fewer than 30 file servers.
- All file servers are in one location.

If your LAN or MAN has more than 30 file servers, a different approach to time synchronization may be appropriate. Chapter 6 explains the approach to take for WANs. This approach may also be suitable when you have a larger LAN (more than 30 file servers).

Note If you use a Single Reference time server, do not use Primary or Reference time servers on the LAN. Primary time servers should be used on larger networks, such as WANs.

In addition to accepting the default for time servers, the method of communication must also be chosen. There are two options: SAP and Custom.

SAP communication is the default, and should be the method most often chosen for a LAN or MAN. SAP communication is simple and provides its own configuration. By default, the network's Single Reference server will use SAP to advertise itself to all Secondary servers on the network.

If the defaults of Single Reference server with Secondary servers and SAP communication are chosen, note that increased network traffic may occur. SAP communication for time synchronization causes additional SAP traffic on the network. In a LAN or MAN with only a few SAP devices, the traffic will not be a problem, however. The real problem comes when the time on the Single Reference server is not correct. An error in time on the provider server (the Single Reference server) propagates itself to other time servers on the network and may disrupt time synchronization.

Whether the default time synchronization standards are accepted or the project team chooses to customize time synchronization, the chosen standard needs to be explained in the company's standards document. In addition, the location of each time server should be noted so that those implementing the network know which servers should be set as time providers and which ones should be time receivers.

How the project team decides to present this information is up to the project team. One way of providing the information, which is relatively easy, starts with a map of the network. Each NetWare 4 file server is identified on the map. Then, the type of time server each server is to become is also noted. Figure 4.13 shows a sample of this approach.

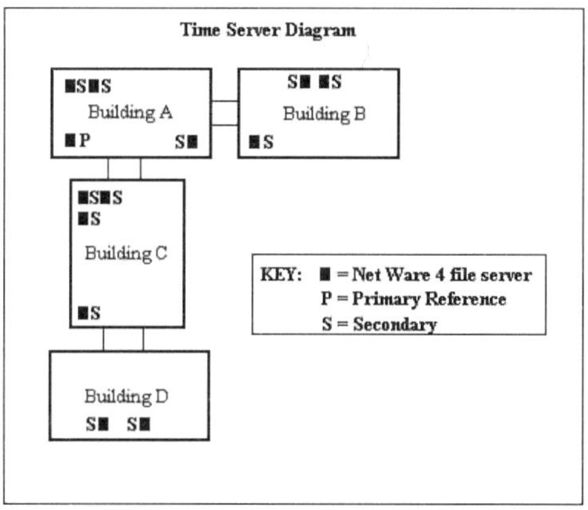

Figure 4.13

Sample network map displaying time server approach.

Default Partition and Replication Standards

NetWare 4 automatically creates one partition when the first file server is installed and the directory tree created. All file servers are then placed into that one partition. For small networks, a single partition is generally sufficient. The default single partition can be used and no additional partitioning will be needed until the network grows sufficiently to require additional partitions.

If the network has more than 15 file servers, however, or spans geographic locations, as a WAN does, more than one partition may be required. In that case, information on how many partitions and what containers they should include has to be discussed in the company's standards document.

By default, the first three file servers installed into the directory tree receive a copy—a replica—of the NDS database for the default partition. The first file server receives the first replica, the Master replica. The next two file servers installed into the directory tree each receive a Read/Write replica.

The default of one partition and three replicas is designed to provide minimum fault tolerance for a small network. When changes are made to the NDS database, those changes are sent to all the related replicas. NDS automatically performs this updating, so no manual effort on the part of the network administrator is required.

When a network begins to outgrow its LAN status, or when it begins to have more than 15 file servers, it may be time to consider splitting the directory tree into two or more partitions. It will also be necessary to consider adding more replicas to network file servers. Administrators may also want to add replicas to additional network file servers for another reason.

In order for a user to log in to the network, the network must be able to access a writable copy (the Master or a Read/Write replica) of the portion of the NDS database containing information about the User's object. When a LAN is spread out among different buildings or even just among different floors in the same building, it may be more expedient to place writable replicas on at least one of the file servers closest to a given group of users. This prevents NetWare from having to search very far to find a usable replica with which to log in users and authenticate them to the network.

As you can see, there are a variety of issues to be considered when creating a company's standards document. Some of the information that goes into the company's standards document may not even be fully accurate until the implementation of the NetWare 4 network is almost complete. The important issue, however, is that a standards document is created and that it include naming standards and other standards that can be followed when designing and implementing the NetWare 4 network.

Much of the information contained within the company's standards document will be useful to the project team from the very beginning.

Summary

Designing and planning a NetWare 4 local area network or a regional area network is phase two of the NetWare 4 design and implementation process. In phase two, as well as in the process of designing and planning a NetWare 4 LAN or MAN, you and the project team must accomplish four major NetWare 4 design and implementation procedures. Each of those four procedures is covered in this chapter, specifically from the point of LAN and MAN networks:

- Designing the directory tree
- Creating a partition and replication strategy
- Planning a time synchronization strategy
- Developing an accessibility plan

During the discussion of each of these four procedures, many suggestions, guidelines, rules, and requirements are put forth. Their purpose is to help you better understand these four procedures associated with the NetWare 4 design and implementation process and to learn to apply them in the successful design of a NetWare 4 LAN or MAN.

The balance of the summary of this chapter is presented in the form of a checklist. The purpose of this approach to summarizing this chapter is first to help you review and remember those procedures and their associated suggestions, guidelines, rules, and requirements. It also is provided in this format to give you a quick checklist of things to do and remember when you begin designing NetWare 4 LANs and MANs.

This chapter gives you the basic information you need to understand why the efficient and effective design of NetWare 4 LANs and MANs is so important. In addition, this chapter provides the information you need to know how to design the right LAN or MAN so that it fills the needs of the company for which it is designed. Finally, after reading this chapter, you should know what you can do to help ensure the project's success, whether you have full or partial responsibility for designing and implementing a small local area network or a larger regional area network.

When you are designing NetWare 4 LANs and MANs, you can use this checklist to help you remember all or at least most of the little details, consider the important issues, and design a network the company considers successful:

- ☐ Design the NetWare 4 LAN or MAN directory tree
    - ☐ Ensure fault tolerance by distributing replicas
    - ☐ Use writable replicas to simplify network access
    - ☐ Provide an Organization object for future growth
    - ☐ Place resources for easy user access
    - ☐ Group user resources in a container with User object
    - ☐ Organize objects for intuitive access
    - ☐ Establish and document naming standards
        - ☐ Consider typeless versus typeful naming
        - ☐ Consider how users navigate the network
        - ☐ Determine whether IPX numbering standards will be used
        - ☐ Develop and provide example and additional information for each naming standard
    - ☐ Design upper layers of directory tree
    - ☐ Provide logical resource organization or geographical approach
    - ☐ Ensure that partitioning and replication will be relatively simple

- ☐ Consider future changes and needs
- ☐ Determine whether organization is intuitive
- ☐ Design to form a pyramid shape
  - ☐ Unless network is located in one geographic area
  - ☐ Unless dial-up lines are used on the network
- ☐ Include a single Organization object

☐ Design lower layers of the directory tree

- ☐ Ensure that objects with common access needs are placed in the same container
- ☐ Develop lower layers to resemble the company's organization chart
- ☐ Consider current, related issues
  - ☐ Logical container design
  - ☐ Current location of physical resources
  - ☐ Central versus distributed network administration
  - ☐ Planned location of partitions
  - ☐ Types of login scripts to be used
  - ☐ Needs of bindery-based users and resources
- ☐ Consider future issues
  - ☐ Existing networks
  - ☐ Possible directory tree mergers

☐ Create a partition strategy

- ☐ Consider whether default is sufficient
- ☐ Eliminate partitions that will cross the WAN
- ☐ Determine whether multiple partitions are necessary to accomplish the following
  - ☐ Keep objects to 5,000 or fewer per partition
  - ☐ Keep related objects together

- ☐ Group file servers on a single cable segment
- ☐ Design partitions from the upper layer down
- ☐ Avoid increasing administrative overhead
- ☐ Follow rules for creating partition strategy
    - ☐ Partitions contain NDS information only
    - ☐ Each object can exist in only one partition
    - ☐ Partitions can be stored only on NetWare 4 file servers
    - ☐ Partition boundaries cannot overlap
    - ☐ Each partition must contain a connected subtree

☐ Create a replication strategy

- ☐ Consider the four types of replicas—Master, Read/Write, Read Only, and Subordinate Reference
- ☐ Ensure fault tolerance by providing a minimum of three replicas for each partition
- ☐ Place writable replicas on file servers closest to users to facilitate login
- ☐ Allow 3 to 5 KB of space on the SYS volume for each replica
- ☐ Consider NDS's need to walk the tree
- ☐ Support bindery services
- ☐ Control the propagation of Subordinate References
- ☐ Partition the [Root] separately to protect it
- ☐ Ensure that failure of a single file server will not make the network inaccessible

☐ Plan a time synchronization strategy

- ☐ Consider the default time synchronization strategy
- ☐ Consider the default SAP communication method

- ☐ Plan to use `SET TIMESYNC` commands as needed
- ☐ Customize time synchronization using TIMESYNC.CFG if necessary

☐ Develop an accessibility plan

- ☐ Review user's needs as well as the needs of applications and other network resources
- ☐ Establish basic accessibility guidelines to follow:
  - ☐ A design strategy for mobile users
  - ☐ Guidelines for accommodating bindery services
  - ☐ Guidelines that will ensure network security

☐ Consider other issues, including the following:

- ☐ Workstation types
- ☐ NetWare OS versions and other network OSs
- ☐ Bindery services requirements
- ☐ Application needs
- ☐ Hardware resources
- ☐ Network administration

☐ Consider the use of various network objects, but in particular consider objects such as the following:

- ☐ Alias
- ☐ Group
- ☐ Organizational Role
- ☐ Directory Map
- ☐ Inherited Rights Filter
- ☐ User Login Scripts

☐ Consider security-related issues

- Consider other issues that the project team included in the network's standards document, which should include the following:
  - Network's structure
  - Installation standards and procedures
  - Object naming and property value
  - Print services naming conventions
  - Security configurations
  - Time synchronization strategy
  - Partitioning and replication standards

Use this checklist to help you complete the case study in this chapter. Then you will be ready to use this checklist to design and implement local and municipal area networks in real life.

Case Study

You have been drafted by the mayor of Apple Town (a personal, long-time friend of yours) to design a NetWare 4 network for Apple Town. The mayor has no money in this year's budget to pay for a consultant, but he has told you that if you can help him prepare the documents he will need to sell the city council on funding a NetWare 4 network, he will make sure you get a fair chance at bidding for the job once the council approves the network. Considering the following information, design the upper and lower layers of the directory tree for Apple Town. This information, along with other relevant information the mayor has gathered, will be included in a special presentation the mayor is preparing for the city council.

Apple Town is a small, nonincorporated community with three public offices located in two buildings next to each other at the town's center. The two buildings contain the city's volunteer fire department, public library, and town office. You have been hired by the town mayor to connect the four computers in two of these three offices—the library and town office—with the intent of eventually adding the volunteer fire department.

The town office houses the mayor, one assistant, and two city workers (maintenance technicians level I) who handle all city maintenance. The public library has one paid librarian and three volunteer library aids. The fire department has a fire chief and five firemen, all volunteer. See figure 4.14 for the town's organization chart.

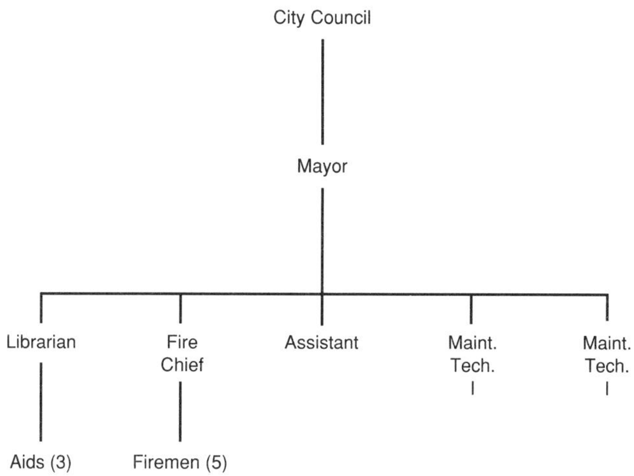

Figure 4.14
Organization chart for Apple Town.

Two of the four computers are located in the town office. The mayor uses one of the computers and the assistant uses the other. The mayor's computer contains a personal scheduling application and a word processing package. The assistant's computer has only a word processing package. The maintenance personnel have been asking for software to help them track the city's maintenance.

The library is currently using a manual card system, but has just received two new Compaq 486DX/66 machines with special library software—a library checkout and inventory tracking system. No one at the library has yet learned how to operate the computers.

The Mayor is planning on adding two computers at the library, two computers at the town office, and one computer at the fire department. The equipment request has been included in next year's budget, but has not yet been approved by the city council.

Review Questions

1. If a network grows substantially in the first year after it is implemented, but no significant problems occur as a result of this growth, it indicates that ___________.

   ○ A. the directory tree was well designed

   ○ B. default partitioning was sufficient

   ○ C. enough Read/Write replicas were created

   ○ D. the consultant was not paid enough money

2. What is the proper order of the following steps associated with the directory tree design phase:

   ◆ Create directory tree structure.

   ◆ Draw upper and lower layers.

   ◆ Review and revise directory tree design.

   ◆ Establish and document naming standards.

   ○ A. 1234

   ○ B. 3241

   ○ C. 2134

   ○ D. 4231

3. Naming standards can be affected by ___________.

   ○ A. profile login scripts

   ○ B. internal IPX numbers

- ○ C. mobile users
- ○ D. object types

4. *Three* reasons to consider organizing a LAN's directory structure around physical resources are ____________.

- ○ A. to simplify partition and replication
- ○ B. to shape the tree like an inverted pyramid
- ○ C. to plan future changes and needs
- ○ D. to organize the tree to be logical and intuitive

5. You do not have to shape the directory tree like a pyramid if (choose *two*) ____________.

- ○ A. the network is all in one geographic location
- ○ B. you want to set some rights for the whole company
- ○ C. the top should have only a single Organization object
- ○ D. the network uses high-speed reliable links

6. You may need to have multiple partitions in a small LAN if ____________.

- ○ A. container login scripts will not be needed
- ○ B. the administrator does not want to use a file server container
- ○ C. administration will be centralized
- ○ D. there are over 5,000 objects on the network

7. Which *three* should be considered when planning time synchronization?

- ○ A. time source
- ○ B. time server types
- ○ C. time server communication method
- ○ D. time replicas

8. The default time synchronization includes which *two* time server types?
   - A. Primary
   - B. Reference
   - C. Secondary
   - D. Single Reference

9. The time server type that is a sole time provider is ___________.
   - A. Primary
   - B. Reference
   - C. Secondary
   - D. Single Reference

10. More than one partition may be required if ___________.
   - A. the network has more than 15 file servers
   - B. the network has fewer than 5,000 objects
   - C. the first three file servers installed already hold a replica of the first partition
   - D. the LAN spans more than one floor in a building

Answers

1. A
2. D
3. C
4. B
5. A D
6. D
7. A B C
8. C D
9. D
10. A

Chapter 5

Chapter Chapter Chapter Chapter Chapter Chapter

Implementing the NetWare 4 Local Area Network Plan

Implementing the network plan that you and the project team developed is the next phase of the NetWare 4 design and implementation process. As you learned from Chapter 2, "Understanding the NetWare 4 Network Design and Implementation Process," there are three primary procedures associated with the implementation phase of the NetWare 4 design and implementation process:

- Develop a migration strategy
- Create an implementation schedule
- Implement NetWare 4

The main purpose of the implementation phase, and thus the main goal to be accomplished during this phase, is to make the process of setting up, upgrading, or migrating an existing network, or installing a new NetWare 4 network, proceed as smoothly as possible.

If the migration strategy is carefully planned, and a reasonable implementation schedule developed, those assigned to implement the network should be able to implement the network design successfully with few, if any, problems. To help you prepare for and complete the implementation of a NetWare 4 network, this chapter discusses the three basic procedures associated with the implementation phase of the NetWare 4 design and implementation process—developing a migration strategy, creating an implementation schedule, and implementing NetWare 4.

Developing the Migration Strategy

When developing your strategy for migrating an existing network, you must consider a variety of issues related to the existing network, if one exists. If no network yet exists, you must still consider almost all, if not all, of these same issues. The main difference is that if the network does not already exist, you may also have to determine what hardware and software will have to be purchased to create the network.

Before you can develop the migration strategy, there are several issues that you need to consider. For example, you need to determine what network operating systems exist and which ones will be migrated.

Migration Considerations

During the NetWare 4 implementation phase, you need to consider whether existing NetWare 2 and NetWare 3 file servers will be migrated to NetWare 4. In addition, if non-NetWare file servers exist on the network, you also need to decide whether those file servers will be migrated or replaced. If new file servers are added, you must also consider where those file servers will be installed and how soon.

Which file servers will be migrated, which file servers will be replaced, and when those file servers will be migrated or replaced are not the only considerations, however. You must also consider whether bindery services will be provided, and if so, where. In addition, you must consider whether all types of workstations (DOS, Windows, Macintosh, UNIX, and so on) will be used in the NetWare 4 network, and you must plan accordingly.

You must consider which applications are NetWare 4 compatible, and which are not. Then you must decide whether those applications that are not compatible will continue to require network support. If the answer is yes, bindery services have to be provided for those applications and considered when planning the implementation.

Once those types of decisions have been made or at least considered, you are ready to develop the migration strategy. With the migration strategy developed, you can then create an implementation schedule. Then, with the implementation schedule in place, you can begin implementing the NetWare 4 network as designed.

In order to plan the network's migration properly, the project team should collect and review several items of information. Just as the migration process itself can be divided into three categories, so too can the related information. Those categories are the following:

- File server information
- Workstation information
- Application information

In addition to issues that should be considered when planning the migration strategy, the types of information to be reviewed and considered for each of these three categories are listed and discussed in the following sections of this chapter.

Migrating Applications

If you are designing and implementing a network that currently exists but must be upgraded to NetWare 4, many of the existing network applications may already be NetWare-aware, (capable of running on a NetWare network). They probably function sufficiently in a NetWare 2 or NetWare 3 network, but still may not be compatible with NetWare 4, because NetWare 4 is substantially different from earlier versions of NetWare. The major difference is, of course, NetWare 4's use of the NDS database, instead of the flat bindery used by earlier versions of NetWare.

To accommodate the applications that can function in the bindery environment but that have not yet been upgraded to function in NetWare 4's hierarchical NDS database environment, NetWare 4 provides bindery services. Bindery services make it possible for users and applications that are not NetWare 4-aware to make calls to NetWare 4 file servers. With bindery services set, the operating system treats certain objects that existed in a NetWare 3 bindery, but that are now in a NetWare 4 container, as if they were still bindery objects. The following are the bindery objects for which NetWare 4 provides bindery services:

- User
- Group
- Print Queue
- Print Server

By setting bindery services, applications that are not NetWare 4-aware but were NetWare 3-aware can access print queues and print servers as they did before. In addition, users, groups, and bindery-based applications can access NetWare 4 servers as if they were bindery-based servers.

Planning for and implementing bindery services makes it possible for the company to continue to receive the benefit of using existing applications. Eventually, applications will have to be upgraded to NetWare 4 compatibility, but until then, companies do not have to put out additional funds for application upgrades.

Bindery-based applications function as if they are running on a NetWare 3 file server, even though they are actually running on a NetWare 4 file server.

As a member of the project team, you must decide which network containers will have a bindery context set for them. Those users in containers with bindery context set are then able to access the NetWare 3-aware applications.

Note In NetWare 4.1, you can set bindery context up to 16 containers. Earlier versions of NetWare 4 enabled bindery context to be set only on a single container.

The strategy you develop for migrating applications is only part of developing the network's entire migration strategy. Which applications can and should be migrated and which applications can and should be eliminated, replaced, or updated must be considered when you and the project team establish the migration strategy. Therefore, when planning the network's migration strategy, remember to consider and plan for what must be done with, to, or for existing network applications. Determine also in what time frame the changes, upgrades, replacements, and so on are to be performed.

To help make all the decisions related to the network's application migration strategy, gather information that will be useful. Information that you and the project team should gather and consider when determining the migration of applications should include at least the following:

- Which existing applications are already compatible with NetWare 4 and thus will not have to be upgraded or migrated?
- Which applications are not compatible with NetWare 4 but must continue to be accessible once the network is upgraded and thus will require bindery services?

- Which users need to access those applications that are not NetWare 4-aware?
- Which existing menus are used to call applications that are not NetWare 4-aware and thus will have to be modified to access those applications?
- What context will be used for locating applications requiring bindery services, and where will the bindery services context be set?

Once you establish the approach to take for migrating network applications, you can continue with determining the strategy to follow or the approach to take for migrating workstations.

Migrating Workstations

Upgrading network workstations to a NetWare 4 environment also needs to be considered when developing the network's migration strategy. For DOS and Windows workstations, the migration process is likely to include upgrading from the NetWare shell (NETX) to the NetWare DOS Requester.

Before deciding what should be included in the workstation migration process, there are several items of information the project team may find useful to collect and review. Questions may include the following:

- What operating systems and their version numbers are currently being used on workstations?
- What client networking software is currently being used on workstations, and what is its version number?

To obtain answers to these questions, you can review existing network documents. If a resource list exists, you can find the answers to many questions on this list (see fig. 5.1).

Resource List

Location	Server/Client Type	Hardware	Applications
Bldg.A	NetWare 3 file servers (5)	80386 (2) 12MB (3) 16MB RAM	WordPerfect 5.2 Accounting Payroll
Bldg.B	NetWare 3 file servers (2)	80386 12 MB	Accounting Database
	Workstations (11)	(3) 80286 (8) 80386	
	Printer	HPIII (3)	

Figure 5.1

Sample resource list.

For example, the total number and types of workstations should be included on the resource list. Information such as what versions of operating system the workstations are running is also generally found in the resource list.

There are other questions you will need answered that are not as likely to be found on the resource list. For these questions, you may have to conduct a survey of network users:

- Are workstation configuration files currently set up for network access, and if so, which ones will have to be modified to accommodate NetWare 4?
- Will any network management tools be used for workstation management?
- Will Large Internet Packet (LIP) or packet burst be set for use at workstations?
- Are any applications currently being stored on individual workstations, and if so, which applications?
- Are any applications on workstations to be used in the NetWare 4 environment, and if so, are they compatible with NetWare 4?
- Which protocols are currently being used by network workstations?

- Do any of the workstations already have a NetWare 4-compatible version of the NetWare DOS Requester?
- Who is currently responsible for handling workstation-related problems, and is workstation support sufficient?
- Will additional workstation support be needed during the transition to NetWare 4?
- Will workstations be backed up by using SMS-compliant backup software?
- Will information sent between NetWare 4 file servers and workstations require encryption?

One other issue with which you and the project team may have to deal is the level of users' networking experience. In addition to preparing workstations for network access, you may also have to train users to access and use the network. If planning for training is to be included in the migration strategy, you and the project team must be aware of how extensive that training may have to be.

To obtain answers to these and other types of questions and thus accomplish the development of a migration strategy, the project team can begin completing several tasks. The first task is assessing existing network clients. In this case, both workstations and users have to be assessed.

Assessing Network Clients

The project team needs to assess which operating systems are being used on network workstations (DOS, Windows, and so on), what versions of those operating systems are being used, the current status of workstation configuration files, and the user's level of networking expertise.

The first issue is to determine which operating systems are currently being used on workstations. This is an important issue because not all versions of workstation operating systems are compatible with NetWare 4.

For example, some LANs have workstations running both Microsoft (MS) DOS 5 and MS-DOS 6. Because both are compatible with NetWare 4, there will not be any problems. If some of the workstations are running versions of MS-DOS that are earlier than version 3.1, however, it might be necessary to upgrade the operating system on those workstations to prevent conflicts. You and the project team need to assess whether this is the case so that you can plan for this in the migration strategy.

Workstation configuration files, such as AUTOEXEC.BAT, CONFIG.SYS, NET.CFG, and STARTNET.BAT, should be checked. The first thing to check for is whether all these files exist. If no STARTNET.BAT file exists, it is likely that the workstation is running the older NetWare shell (NETX) instead of the NetWare DOS Requester. Even if the STARTNET.BAT file does exist, it needs to be checked to determine whether it contains the required information, as do the other configuration files.

For example, the STARTNET.BAT file should load the network communication files if the AUTOEXEC.BAT file is not being used to load them. It should load the most current NetWare 4-compatible versions of the following:

- LSL.COM
- The network board driver (such as NE2000.COM)
- IPXODI.COM
- VLM.EXE

You also need to determine how much experience users have with networks and networking. Most companies will find their users have varying levels of experience. If the company has some users who are very experienced, these users may be recruited to help with the workstation migration. If the company's users are all inexperienced, additional workstation help personnel may be required during the migration.

Determining Typical Workstation Configurations

Once workstation and user assessment is complete, determining the configuration of VLMs as well as the NET.CFG file is the first of the next steps. Next, workstation migration options need to be tested and evaluated and the best method chosen.

When you determine the configuration of VLMs and the NET.CFG file, the decision should be made based on the network's needs. Although not all VLMs may be necessary, it is generally easier to load all VLMs. Installing all VLMs is the default, and is less likely to cause problems on your LAN.

The NET.CFG has some minimum requirements. Those minimum requirements are also met by default when the NetWare DOS Requester is installed. The NetWare DOS Requester creates a NET.CFG file if one does not exist. If one does exist, the DOS and Windows Client installation program will modify it if you choose to have it modified, or you can do it manually later.

Workstation migration can be handled in several different ways. The following are migration method options from which to choose:

- Accessing the network from each workstation and running the DOS and Windows Client Installation INSTALL program (discussed in detail in the Implementing NetWare 4 section later in this chapter)
- Running a special batch file created specifically to upgrade each workstation, from either the workstation or from the file server (by using the system login script)
- Running WSUPDATE or WSUPGRD (also discussed in detail in the Implementing NetWare 4 section later in this chapter)

It is possible to test each migration method, but it may be more reasonable and is definitely less time-consuming to choose one or two options that hold the most promise for migrating workstations and test those options only.

After testing the most likely upgrade options, review and evaluate the results. Seek to determine which of the options is the quickest and most accurate. Unless some unforeseen circumstance makes the quickest and most accurate method unacceptable, choose that method for migrating workstations.

Sharing Client Software with Administrators

Once you choose the most appropriate method for migrating workstations, you must then share the migration strategy with those who are likely to be responsible for implementing it. In LANs and MANs, that will probably be one or more network administrators.

Sharing the chosen method for migrating workstations includes training the administrators to perform the migration process. It also includes training them to troubleshoot and deal with potential problems. Most of the problem resolution training you can provide will be the result of the implementation tests the project team ran. Unfortunately, if the implementation tests went smoothly, you may have little problem resolution data to use.

You have another option, however. You can establish a training lab, then train the administrators on migrating typical workstation configurations. The training lab itself will provide administrators not only with experience in migrating the workstations, but with experience in troubleshooting migration-related problems.

If the migration method you choose is to run the INSTALL program, part of training the network administrators includes preparing a sample INSTALL.CFG file. You may also have to prepare different INSTALL.CFG files if your network clients do not all have the same physical configuration.

Another way of training administrators is to assign them the responsibility for upgrading their own workstations. Then they will become familiar with client architecture, the client installation process, and how to use the chosen migration method.

Creating User Training

As with other aspects of designing and implementing a NetWare 4 network, there is a process that can be applied to creating user training. That process is shown in figure 5.2.

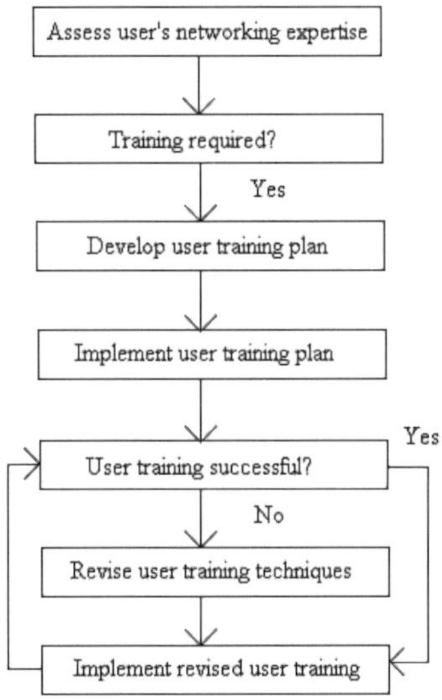

Figure 5.2
User training process.

Administrators are not the only ones who will need training. Users may need training as well. Part of your assessing existing network clients is assessing the level of users' networking expertise. That assessment should lead you to determine what the user's network training needs are. From there, a plan for creating user training should be developed.

When developing user training, do not think only in terms of conducting formal training classes, although this may be a viable option. Consider alternatives as well. For example, simple e-mail messages can be composed and distributed to users to provide training on some aspects of the network. You may choose to use e-mail to explain the new lines contained within their workstation's configuration files.

Other options for user training may include the use of written documents, both formal and informal. In addition, quick reference materials such as cards or foldouts can be used. It may even be an option to conduct no formal or informal training at all, but merely to let users learn about NetWare 4 networking on their own.

Once a training approach is chosen, it should be tested. Typical network users should be chosen for the test. The type of test you conduct depends on the type of training method you choose. For example, if you choose to distribute an e-mail message, you let the test users know ahead of time that you are sending them a message, the purpose of which is to test the effectiveness of the message, not the intelligence of the user. You might include a list of questions at the end of the e-mail message for the user to answer and return to you. This helps you know whether the training by the use of this particular e-mail message was effective or needs to be revised.

After testing the training approach on typical users, revise it, if necessary, to make it as effective as possible. Then test it again. Once its effectiveness is determined, implement the training for all affected network users.

Upgrading Clients

The last task to be completed in the development of a client migration strategy is to begin upgrading clients. Document all problems you encounter as you go along. Document also what it took to repair or get around the problem successfully. With this information in hand, you can then migrate all network clients when the time comes.

When developing the migration strategy for network clients, remember that the greater the number of workstations to be upgraded, the more time will be required for migrating. You can reduce the time required to upgrade the network's clients by assigning multiple people to assist with the upgrade. If only a few people are available to conduct the upgrade, however, your migration plan has to take that into consideration. It may even mean that you have to train additional people—network administrators and users—to perform the workstation migration.

Keep in mind that if you conduct training sessions for users, you can include having those users migrate their own workstations, solving all problems that occur. You then can have those users help other users migrate their workstations. If following this approach makes it possible for you to cut the required upgrade time sufficiently, you can include this approach as the best one to follow in your workstation migration strategy.

There are a variety of ways to accomplish the workstation migration. Choosing the best approach is the project team's—and thus your—responsibility. The best approach has to be determined based on available resources, network needs, and time available. Choose what seems to be the best approach for your network, then plan the migration of workstations accordingly.

Migrating File Servers

Both file servers running non-NetWare operating systems and file servers running versions of the NetWare operating system that are earlier than NetWare 4.1 may have to be upgraded. Upgrading file servers helps ensure their successful migration into the NetWare 4.1 network.

As a member of the project team, it is your responsibility to help determine how network file servers will be migrated. In order to accomplish the migration of network file servers successfully, there is a series of tasks that must be performed. After completing these tasks, you will have successfully planned, tested, scheduled, and prepared for migrating your network file servers.

The following are tasks that must be performed in order to prepare for a successful migration of the network file servers:

- Review current file server configurations.
- Establish a testing lab.
- Discuss downtime and migration with management.
- Choose the file server migration method.

- Obtain NetWare 4.1 software and licenses.
- Schedule and perform pilot migrations.
- Train users in the pilot department.
- Schedule migration for the balance of the network.

As with most tasks, there are various steps or methods of accomplishing them. In addition, there is information you need to know about each task that will help you perform those tasks successfully.

Reviewing Current File Server Configurations

Before you determine the best approach to migrating file servers, there is some relevant information you may need to find out. As with migrating workstations, some of that information will be available on the network resource list. Other items of information may require additional research. However you approach the process of gathering, reviewing, and analyzing relevant information, you should gather appropriate information to answer some, if not all, of the following questions. Doing so will help you develop the best file server migration strategy for your network.

Some of the most common questions you should be able to answer before developing and implementing a file server migration strategy may include the following:

- What other versions of the NetWare operating system are currently being used on the network?
- Will other versions of NetWare still have to be supported for a period of time?
- Will bindery services to support users and applications be required?
- What file servers will need to have bindery services provided?
- What hardware is currently being used for NetWare file servers?

- Will additional hardware be purchased for NetWare 4 file servers, and if so, what will be purchased?
- Do all the existing file servers have hardware that is compatible with NetWare 4 and thus that can be upgraded to NetWare 4?
- Are other non-NetWare network operating systems currently in use on the existing network?
- Will file servers running non-NetWare operating systems also be migrated to NetWare 4?
- Which network administrators will require NetWare 4 training, and how will that training be accomplished?
- Should any hardware and software testing be done?
- Will a testing lab be available?

Even if all this information is not available, you need the minimum following information, by department:

- Names of existing file servers
- Current type and version of operating system running on each file server
- Disk storage capacity (size of hard disk, such as 1,000 MB)
- Amount of file server RAM (such as 12 MB)
- Microprocessor (such as Intel 80486)

You also need to know whether any of these file servers will be replaced with upgraded equipment, whether that equipment has been ordered or has arrived, and if on order, when it will arrive.

After gathering the answers to these and other relevant questions, you should be able to continue with the process of determining the best strategy for migrating the network's file servers. The next step to take in that process is establishing a testing lab.

Establishing a Testing Lab

A testing lab may be as small as one NetWare file server or as large as one or more file servers of each type found on your network. The testing lab may be located in any convenient location in your company. Although the environment of the testing lab should emulate the actual environment of the company, it should not be part of the actual company network to prevent your testing from interfering with daily network activity.

The purpose of the testing lab is threefold. The first purpose is to let you check out the migration options you are considering using to migrate the network. That means you will need a minimum of one of each type of file server to be migrated. Those test file servers should be configured to reflect the most typical network configuration.

For example, if you are running NetWare 3 and IBM LAN servers on your network, you should have a minimum of one of each of these types of file servers set up in your testing lab. They should be configured to match the typical configuration used on the real network.

The second purpose of establishing a testing lab is to evaluate the migration process. You want to determine which method yields the best results as far as speed and accuracy are concerned. You may determine you have to trade a little speed to get greater accuracy, or vice versa. You will not know what your options are, however, unless you test the migration methods you are considering using.

The third purpose of establishing a testing lab is to train administrators to perform the migrations. If you are trying to decide which migration option is best for each file server, you should set up enough of each type of file server to test the migration. If equipment is limited, you may have to use the same hardware each time, installing the typical current network operating system, then migrating it, recording the results, and starting the process again with a different operating system. Network administrators can be trained to do this. Then, when the final option is chosen, each network administrator can receive additional training in the lab on the migration method chosen. Network administrators will thus get to see and understand why the chosen method was selected and have more than one experience with migrating file servers using that approach.

The approach you choose will depend on how much time, equipment, and personnel you have available for the testing lab. Regardless of the limitations placed on you by these resources, you should test migration before you determine which approach to take. Testing migration options in a nonproduction lab before trying it out on the live network will save you time and headaches later when the real network migration process begins.

Discussing Downtime and Migration with Management

After you test the migration methods, you are then ready to discuss with management the approach you believe will be best for migrating network servers. The purpose of this discussion is primarily to determine when management believes network downtime will be most acceptable (because downtime for migrating the file servers will be required) and which file servers are to be migrated. If necessary, the data contained on a file server to be migrated can first be transferred to another file server so that it is still available while the file server is being migrated. That data can be transferred back once the migration is complete.

Choosing a File Server Migration Method

Several upgrade methods are available for migrating both NetWare and non-NetWare operating systems. You and the project team are responsible for choosing the option that best suits the network's needs. The option (or options) you choose will depend on the type and version of the network operating system you must migrate. Four specific options for migrating network operating systems are available (see fig. 5.3):

- *Across-the-wire.* Use this option to upgrade Banyan Vines, IBM PC LAN (PCLP) v1.3 Extended Services, IBM LAN Server v1.0 to v1.3, Microsoft LAN Manager v2.0, and NetWare versions 2.1x, 2.2, 3.1x, and 4.0x to NetWare 4.1.
- *Same-server.* Use this option to upgrade Banyan Vines, IBM PC LAN (PCLP) v1.3 Extended Services, IBM LAN Server v1.0 to v1.3, Microsoft LAN Manager v2.0, and NetWare versions 2.1x, 2.2, 3.1x, and 4.0x to NetWare 4.1.
- *In-place upgrade.* Use this option to upgrade NetWare 2.1x and NetWare 2.2 file servers to NetWare 4.1.
- *NetWare 4.1 Installation.* Use the Upgrade menu option of the NetWare 4.1 Installation program to upgrade NetWare 3.1x and 4.0x to NetWare 4.1.

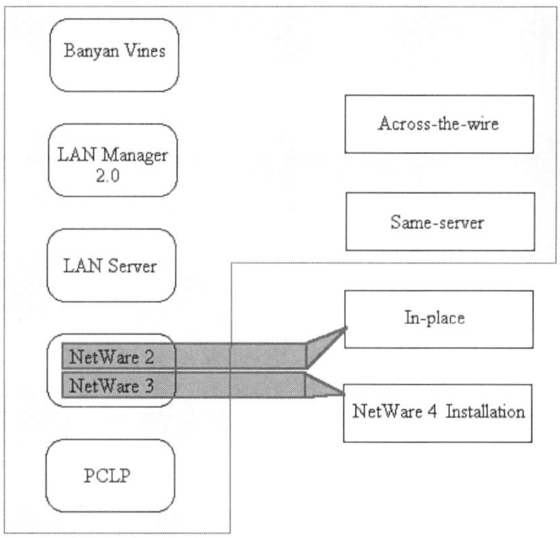

Figure 5.3
File server migration options.

As you can see, more than one option is available for upgrading network file servers, regardless of the type and version of operating system they are currently running. Of the four available options, using the across-the-wire method to another server is the safest one because it is actually performed on a different server. It keeps the contents of the original server intact until you have the opportunity to verify that the upgrade was successful. This option may not be readily available in smaller LANs, however, if hardware is limited. If that is the case, the across-the-wire to the same-server method can be used.

The same-server method uses only one file server and one workstation. Even though it is not as secure an option as the across-the-wire method, it is a viable option for a small network with limited equipment.

The in-place upgrade is the least safe method because the only way you can restore the old file server is by using backup media. If you choose to use this method, the file server must already have an existing DOS partition; you cannot create one during the in-place upgrade.

The NetWare 4 installation migration option may be a good choice for smaller networks as well. It enables you to install NetWare 4 on existing compatible hardware with another NetWare operating system already installed. The NetWare 4 Simple Installation option is also available for existing compatible hardware.

Obtaining NetWare 4.1 Software and Licenses

It is generally not the responsibility of project team members to order the NetWare 4.1 software and licenses. Many times the ordering responsibility falls to the accounting department or other similar department. The project team is responsible for knowing what needs to be ordered, when it must arrive, and who should be asked to place the order.

The project team may also be responsible for following up to ensure that the software arrives on time and that it is as ordered. It is important that you and the project team ensure that you order what is needed and have it available to you well before you attempt to begin testing file server migrations.

Scheduling and Performing Pilot Migrations

Part of the process of scheduling your NetWare 4 network is determining how to implement the migration to the NetWare 4 network. Like all the other tasks, there are items of information that must be reviewed, issues that must be considered, and procedures that must be followed.

Scheduling the migration of file servers for the balance of the network requires that you and the project team complete the following general tasks:

- If needed, schedule extra personnel to help administrator and users migrate network file servers.
- Clean up binderies.
- Back up all file servers and test the backup media to ensure that it is a usable backup.
- Migrate the first file server in the pilot department.
- Log any problems and their solutions.
- Revise the migration procedure as needed.

In small LANs and MANs, scheduling extra personnel may not be possible because they may not be available. You can consider hiring from outside the company on a temporary basis, or you can plan the implementation to be performed with the available personnel.

Cleaning up NetWare binderies should be done before file servers are migrated, to make the migration go as smoothly as possible and the end result as error-free as possible. A cleaned-up NetWare bindery should contain the following:

- Only names that conform to the naming standards established by the project team.

- No duplicate user, group, print queue, print server, or other names on a single server, or on multiple servers across the network. Duplicate names for the same object type are merged into one container during migration. Duplicate names for different object types will have only the first occurrence of the object migrated to the NDS database. Subsequent occurrences will not be migrated.
- Only current user and other objects with the access rights they are intended to have, and no other.

Novell provides two utilities to help you clean up the NetWare bindery. The first utility is called SECURITY.EXE. It provides information about NetWare 3 binderies to help you find and correct potential security problems. This utility is included with NetWare 3. The second utility is called DUPBIND. It can be used to display duplicate names in the NetWare bindery. This utility does not ship with NetWare, but it is available on NetWire through CompuServe.

All data and software on the file server, including the NetWare operating system and related programs, should be backed up to another medium before migrating the file server. In addition, the backup should be tested for validity by restoring it. If the restore is successful, the next step can be performed on that file server.

Migrate the first file server in the pilot department, using the chosen migration method. Keep a log of any problems encountered and how you solved those problems during the migration. After the first file server is successfully migrated and running, you can migrate the remaining file servers. You can choose to migrate the file servers one at a time, or you can have multiple people migrate several servers at the same time. Note, however, that if you choose to migrate multiple file servers simultaneously, you may find that it takes longer to synchronize the NDS database than it would if you migrate servers one at a time.

If necessary, revise the migration procedures as you go about migrating file servers. You may find that one approach to file server migration works best for NetWare 3 file servers, and another approach or a slight modification to the first approach works better for migrating NetWare 2 file servers.

The ultimate goal of migrating the pilot department is to work out all the problems you may encounter when performing the migrations and then find the best way to migrate servers. This information can be used to the company's advantage when migrating the remainder of the company network to NetWare 4.

Training Users in Pilot Departments

As with the client migration strategies, users require some training on the new network. The training may be limited to an explanation of NetWare 4 and how it differs from NetWare 3, at least from the user's perspective. The training may be more extensive, including in-house training sessions with hands on experience in a lab or any variety of training alternatives. Training alternatives such as those discussed for client migration strategies may also prove effective for training users in the file server migration process.

The training alternatives discussed in client migration strategy include the following:

- The composition and distribution of simple e-mail messages to users to provide training on some aspects of the new NetWare 4 network
- Written documents, both formal and informal, that explain information that the user may need to know about the NetWare 4 network
- Quick reference materials, such as cards or foldouts, that users can keep at hand to find information related to the NetWare 4 network when problems or questions arise
- No formal or informal training at all, although encouragement for users to learn about NetWare 4 networking on their own

If the last option—letting users figure it out on their own—is chosen as the preferred method of training users, the users should at least be told where they can find the information they need. Instructions for accessing the online help information should be provided to the users. If necessary, their workstations can be set up for them to enable quick access to Dynatext.

Additional information in paper form (the third-party books provided by companies such as NRP, for example) can be made available to users. The project team may choose to provide a list of NetWare 4 networking books that users can reference, such as the following from New Riders Publishing: *Migrating to NetWare 4.1* and *Inside NetWare 4.1, Second Editon.*

Most of these publications can be found at local bookstores. If you cannot find one that you need, contact NRP at the following address or telephone number: 201 West 103rd Street, Indianapolis, IN 46290, 800-653-6156.

Scheduling Migration for the Balance of the Network

Scheduling the migration for the balance of the network uses the same process you use to schedule migration for the pilot department, which includes the following steps:

- Scheduling extra personnel to help administrators and users migrate network file servers
- Cleaning up the NetWare binderies to eliminate duplicates, old and unused user and other types of objects, and to ensure that user security was complete and appropriate
- Backing up all file servers and testing the backup media to ensure it is a usable backup
- Migrating file servers
- Logging any problems and their solutions
- Revising the migration procedure as needed

The last three steps are, of course, part of the implementation phase of the NetWare 4 design and implementation process. The migration itself is the most important aspect of the implementation phase and is discussed in detail in the last section of this chapter, Implementing NetWare 4.

Once you gather and analyze all related file server information, you then set up a lab and test migration configurations. Once you determine which migration methods are appropriate for your network, you verify with management which departments will be affected and how much downtime is acceptable. From that point, you select the best migration method, obtain the NetWare 4.1 software and licenses, then schedule and perform the pilot migrations. Once pilot migrations have proven themselves effective and helped you work out any unforeseen problems associated with migration, you train the users in the pilot department. The final step then is to create an implementation schedule for migrating the rest of the network.

Creating an Implementation Schedule

Many tasks lead to the procedure of creating a schedule for implementing the NetWare 4 network. The tasks you have to complete depend on the size of your network, its geographical location, the types and versions of workstation and file server operating systems on the existing network, and a variety of other issues. There are also many tasks that you must do in order to complete the seventh procedure associated with designing and implementing a NetWare 4 network—creating an implementation schedule.

To create and implement a schedule that will be successful for your network, these are the procedures you have to perform:

- Identifying all the tasks that must be completed in order to create an implementation schedule and successfully implement the NetWare 4 network
- Creating a schedule to ensure the successful implementation of the network design
- Coordinating the schedule with schedules for other groups that are also responsible for network migration, and then revising the original schedule if needed
- Conducting a pilot test to pinpoint and solve any potential implementation problems
- Proceeding with the implementation as scheduled

Identifying which tasks need to be performed in order to implement the network plan is often the most difficult part of the implementation process. The list of tasks to be completed may vary somewhat from one company to another. This is due at least in part to several issues, the first of which are the individual needs of each company. Although the needs of one company may be similar to the needs of another company, several issues affect those needs.

The most likely factor to determine what tasks a company will have to complete is the size of the company. For example, a company with only 1 department, 7 file servers, and 15 employees is not likely to have the resources (equipment or personnel) to set up a migration testing lab. The approach that a company of this size may have to take is to transfer all relevant data from a single file server to another file server on the network, then use an in-place upgrade to upgrade the first file server. The testing may have to be done on a production file server, rather than in a testing lab.

On the other hand, a larger LAN with 50 file servers, 200 employees, and 4 departments may have the resources needed to set up a testing lab. It may choose, however, to hire out migration testing in order to save time and keep its available resources centered on production work.

It is the project team's—and thus your—responsibility to determine which tasks must be completed in order to implement the NetWare 4 network. After identifying these tasks, they must be placed in the order in which they must be completed if the implementation is to be successful. With the identified tasks in their appropriate order, the schedule for completing those tasks can then be determined.

Identifying Tasks

As noted earlier, the most difficult part of creating an implementation schedule may well be the process of identifying all the tasks that must be completed in order to implement your NetWare 4 network successfully. To help you identify tasks that may be required to implement NetWare 4 in your network environment, this section of this chapter contains a detailed list of tasks that may be required.

As far as possible, those tasks are listed in the logical order in which they may have to be completed. Because each network is different, however, there may be other tasks you need to include in your list, and some you need to eliminate. In addition, you may need to modify the order of these tasks to accommodate differences or glitches that are specific to your network's implementation. Consider the following list of tasks to be a guideline from which you can create your own list:

- Assess workstation and file server upgrade requirements.
- Select the team to conduct the network migration.
- Begin training the migration team.
- Place purchase orders for any additional workstation software that may be needed.

- Place purchase orders for any hardware needed to upgrade existing workstations.
- Place purchase orders for the NetWare 4.1 software.
- Place purchase orders for any hardware needed to install new file servers.
- Decide what workstation configuration files need to be created or modified, what those files should contain, and whether workstations will be upgraded to the NetWare 4 default Ethernet frame type of 802.2.
- Set up a testing lab.
- Test applications and workstation communication software configurations against NetWare 4.1.
- Complete training for the migration team.
- Upgrade workstations for the pilot implementation area of the company's network.
- Train users in the pilot area on using the new workstation software and accessing the migrated network.
- Determine which applications must be upgraded.
- Place purchase orders to upgrade applications that are not NetWare 4-compatible.
- Begin training network administrators, starting with upgrade and installation procedures if administrators will be helping with the migration process.
- Install the first network file server and set up the NDS directory tree as designed, including creating container objects as designed.
- Install network communication software on workstations in pilot implementation areas, modifying workstation configuration files as needed.
- Upgrade the hardware on network file servers and workstations that were identified as needing upgrades and for which additional hardware was ordered and received.

- Perform a backup of each pilot area's network file servers in its present state.
- Review the bindery on existing NetWare 2 and 3 file servers to eliminate objects no longer being used, and to check for and then correct object names that do not conform to naming standards developed by the project team.
- Run DUPBIND, or manually review the binderies on NetWare file servers that will be migrated during the pilot implementation, to find and eliminate duplicate objects such as users and print queues.
- Run SECURITY.EXE on NetWare file servers being migrated during the pilot implementation to detect any existing potential security violations, and then clean up any security violations detected.
- Run BINDFIX to find and correct any potential problems with bindery files on NetWare servers being migrated during the pilot implementation.
- Perform another backup of existing NetWare network file server operating systems and other program files for those file servers being migrated during the pilot implementation.
- Clean up the file system on those NetWare 2 and NetWare 3 file servers being migrated during the pilot implementation.
- Complete a separate backup of the file system directories and data files stored on those NetWare file servers that will be migrated during the pilot implementation.
- Migrate existing file servers in the pilot implementation area to NetWare 4.1 and log the results.
- Install any new NetWare 4.1 file servers in the pilot implementation area and log the results.
- Review the logs for the workstation and file server pilot implementation.
- Modify the installation and migration approach as needed to correct or prevent problems noted in the pilot migration logs.

- Upgrade workstations for the balance of the company's network.
- Train the company's remaining network users.
- Perform a backup of the company's remaining network file servers in their present states.
- Review the binderies on the balance of the existing NetWare 2 and 3 file servers to eliminate objects no longer being used, and to check for and then correct object names that do not conform to naming standards developed by the project team.
- Run DUPBIND, or manually review the binderies of the remainder of the company's existing NetWare file servers, to find and eliminate duplicate objects such as users and print queues.
- Run SECURITY.EXE on the balance of the company's NetWare file servers to view existing potential security violations, then clean up any security violations detected.
- Run BINDFIX to find and correct any potential problems with the binderies on the remainder of the company's network file servers.
- Perform another backup of the existing network file server operating system files and other program files for the rest of the company's network.
- Clean up the file system on existing NetWare 2 and NetWare 3 file servers for the remaining file servers on the company's network.
- Complete a separate backup of the file system directories and data files stored on existing NetWare file servers for the remainder of the company.
- Upgrade remaining file servers in the company, following a workgroup, geographic location, or other method that is most appropriate for the company.

- Upgrade any applications that were ordered and received as the result of migrating the network to NetWare 4.
- Determine, then document, how new user training and the addition of network workstations, file servers, and applications will be handled in the future.
- Review the complete workstation and file server migration process once network migration is complete, noting what went right and what went wrong, as well as what may be improved and how it might be improved the next time a network migration is done.
- Correct any problems or idiosyncrasies and train any untrained users or administrators that still exist.
- Celebrate the successful implementation of the NetWare 4 network.

Once the list of tasks to be completed has been determined, you can now create a schedule to show when those tasks will be completed, and by whom.

If you have not already done so, arrange the tasks to be performed in an approximate order of priority. Some tasks will also have to be performed in parallel with other tasks, although a straight task list does not easily represent that fact. Once you start adding start dates and time to complete estimates, overlapping tasks will become more obvious.

Assess the approximate length of time it will take to complete each task. Next, create a timeline or schedule for completing those tasks. Then, assign individuals to be responsible for completing each of those tasks. Finally, document the migration schedule and share that schedule with everyone who will be involved in, is responsible for, or has a need or right to know about the scheduled implementation of the NetWare 4 network.

Conducting a Pilot Test

For smaller LANs and MANs, the pilot test may be performed on a single NetWare file server. Taking one file server out of production to conduct the pilot test may be the only option. If the company has a larger network, however, the pilot test may proceed the same way it would for a wide area network, involving an entire department or at least a single workgroup.

The purpose of the pilot test is similar to that of the testing lab—to test existing applications against NetWare 4. In the pilot test, the testing is performed on a production server, which may have to be isolated from the remainder of the network, particularly if no testing lab was available to test NetWare 4 and bindery services before installing NetWare 4 on a production file server. Conducting a pilot test is an important step in establishing compatibility with both NetWare 4.1 and bindery services in order to make the migration go as smoothly as possible.

Once you implement the first NetWare 4 file server in your production network, you can accept that as sufficient and implement the remainder of the network if you choose. You may prefer, however, to continue the pilot test by implementing one or more additional file servers before proceeding with the complete network implementation.

There are other benefits to be gained and issues to be resolved during the pilot test, including the following:

- Completion of the final tests on production servers before performing the entire network migration
- Resolution of file server migration and compatibility issues prior to involving the entire network and its administrators and users
- Refinement of the procedure for helping and supporting network administrators and users
- Revision of client installation and migration to accommodate unforeseen problems or idiosyncrasies

- Additional experience for the migration team, network administrators, and possibly for network users, depending on their level of involvement

Which file servers you choose for pilot testing may be dictated by the network itself. For example, if your network has only three file servers, your choice is substantially limited. If you have the opportunity to make a choice, try to choose the file server that your most experienced network administrators or migration team members regularly use. You will encounter few user types of problems, which can be a blessing when pilot testing your first one or two file servers.

Coordinating the Schedule with Others

Coordinating the implementation schedule may range from simple to arduous. Most of the time, the smaller the network, the fewer the number of people who have to be involved in the migration. This usually means there will also be fewer scheduling conflicts. It may also mean, however, that there are fewer experienced people to help with the scheduling and implementation. This may mean that some of the issues that should have been dealt with early in the process may not become evident until it is much too late to accommodate them, or to accommodate them to the full satisfaction of all those involved in the migration process.

The best way to head off this kind of situation is to involve everyone who may be affected by the network in the implementation process reasonably early. If possible, at least a representative handful of people should be included in discussions regarding the migration of the network. This helps ensure that at least the majority of issues are raised, even if all issues cannot be accommodated.

Part of coordinating the implementation schedule with others is to ensure that those others are invited to project team meetings. The invitation to these individuals should be extended as soon as the project team has an idea of what will be involved in the migration process. This may mean people should be included in the actual scheduling of the implementation tasks, which should begin as soon as those tasks are identified.

Others who may be affected by the implementation but who are not already part of the project team or the implementation team can be asked to observe the lab testing and pilot implementation. Doing so helps those individuals get a feel for what their areas or departments can expect to see happen when implementation begins in earnest for them. Knowing what to expect also makes it possible for these people to contribute to the scheduling activity from a reasonable knowledge base, instead of having to depend on their own "guesstimates."

Once those who may be affected by the implementation are brought into the process, the implementation scheduling process can begin.

Completing the Implementation Schedule

The entire implementation scheduling process requires that you and the project team do the following:

- Establish a list of tasks that must be completed in order to implement the NetWare 4 network successfully.
- Determine the order in which each task must be performed.
- Calculate the approximate length of time each task will require.
- Establish dates by which each task must be completed.
- Assign the responsibility for the completion of each task to the appropriate individual.
- Create an implementation schedule that is realistic to follow.
- Coordinate the implementation schedule with others who may be affected by or need to participate in the upgrade or installation of the NetWare 4 network.
- Proceed with the implementation of the NetWare 4 network.

After the implementation schedule is created and coordinated, responsibility for each task is assigned, the pilot test has been successfully conducted, and the schedule coordinated with others, the only remaining issue is that of implementing the NetWare 4 network design, following the schedule as outlined—or at least as closely as possible. The project team then has only two remaining tasks:

- Review and document the successes and failures of the network implementation and complete any final tasks that are needed.
- Celebrate the successful design and implementation of the NetWare 4 network.

In this case, the best part of implementing the NetWare 4 network—celebrating the success—comes last, with one possible exception. The best part may actually be the success of the network itself, and how well it performs the tasks for which it was designed and implemented. Of course, for that to occur, the network must be implemented.

Implementing NetWare 4

The process of implementing the NetWare 4 network is more than just upgrading a few workstations and file servers, although that certainly is an important part. Implementing the NetWare 4 network requires that a variety of tasks be completed:

- Creating the NDS directory structure
- Installing and migrating NetWare 4 file servers
- Upgrading workstations

There is more than one way to perform these tasks. For example, you can use either the Simple Installation option or the Custom Installation option of the NetWare 4 INSTALL program to install new NetWare 4 servers. You also can use various migration techniques, such as the across-the-wire method discussed previously, to migrate existing NetWare file servers to NetWare 4.

To help ensure that the methods you choose for creating the NDS directory structure, installing and migrating NetWare 4 file servers, and upgrading workstations are relatively easy to follow, those methods that are most appropriate to a LAN or MAN implementation are discussed in this section. Each method is explained in detail so that you can follow the process yourself, or use the following pages to guide others to perform the related tasks.

The methods discussed are: the process to follow for creating the NDS directory structure, how to use the NetWare Simple Installation option to install NetWare 4, how to upgrade NetWare 3 Servers to NetWare 4 by using the in-place upgrade method, and how to upgrade DOS and Windows workstations to access the NetWare 4 network.

Creating the NDS Directory Structure

Creating the NDS directory structure requires that, at a minimum, you create container objects, partition the directory tree, and provide fault tolerance by replicating partitions in strategic locations across the network. Much of this work may be performed by network administrators, but if you and the project team are responsible for the initial implementation of the NetWare 4 network, some or all of these tasks may become your responsibility. This section explains the process required in order to create NDS container objects, partition the directory tree, and create replicas of partitions. With these three tasks accomplished, others can then continue the implementation of the directory tree by adding additional objects, such as users and printers, and expanding the lower layers of the directory tree as needed.

Creating NDS Container Objects

There are three types of NDS objects you have to create in order to implement the directory tree as designed. The first is the [Root] object. As you know, only one [Root] object may exist per NDS directory tree, and that [Root] object is created when the first

NetWare 4 file server is installed. Whoever is responsible for installing the first NetWare 4 file server is the individual who installs the [Root] of the tree.

The two other types of NDS objects you have to create are called container and leaf objects. There are three types of container objects. Those three types are Country, Organization (O), and Organizational Unit (OU). Unless the project team decides to use a Country object in the design of the directory tree, which is not generally recommended, you do not have to worry about the Country object. Most of the time, you have to create Organization and Organizational Unit objects.

There are 17 leaf objects, most of which are commonly created and managed by network administrators, and thus they may or may not have to be created by those responsible for the initial implementation of the NDS directory tree. There are two leaf objects, however, that you may choose to create as part of the initial implementation of the NDS directory tree. By creating these two leaf objects, you then make it possible for other individuals to continue the implementation of the NDS directory tree as designed. Those two objects are the User object, and the Organizational Role object.

You can use either the DOS-based NETADMIN utility, or the Microsoft (MS) Windows-based NetWare Administrator utility to create NDS objects. Only the second option, the NetWare Administrator utility, is discussed here. Creating Organization and Organizational Unit objects is discussed first, followed by instructions for creating User and Organizational Role objects.

To create NDS Organization and Organizational Unit objects using the NetWare Administrator utility, you must first log in to the network as a user with the appropriate rights to create NDS objects. Initially, only the ADMIN user exists and thus is the only user with rights to create NDS objects.

Once you have logged in to the network, run MS Windows. Next, choose the NetWare Administrator icon to start the NetWare Administrator utility. Then, complete the following steps:

1. Open the Browser window (choose Browser from the Tools pull-down menu).
2. With [Root] highlighted, or other container into which the new container is to be placed highlighted, choose Create from the Object pull-down menu.
3. Select (highlight) Organization in the New Object list (see fig. 5.4), and choose OK.

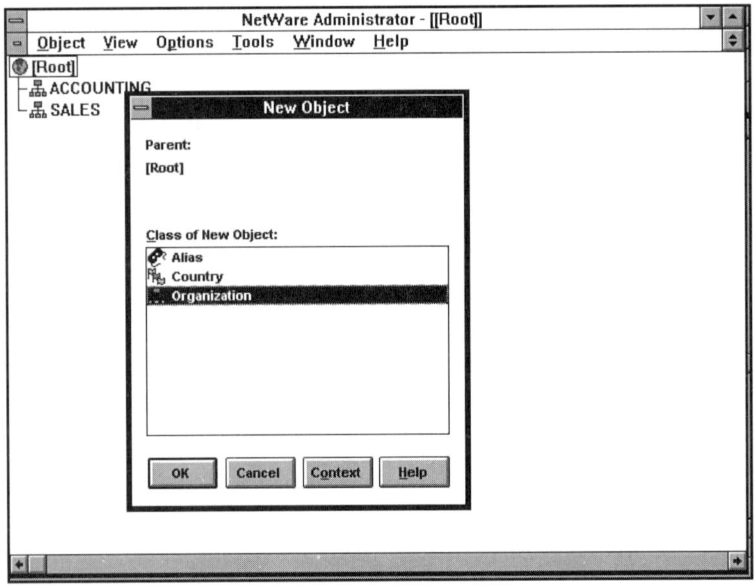

Figure 5.4
New Object list with Organization object selected.

4. When the Create Organization dialog box opens, type a name for the Organization object, place an x in the Define Additional Properties box (click on the box), then choose OK (see fig. 5.5).
5. When the Identification page opens for this Organization object, fill in any needed information (see fig. 5.6).

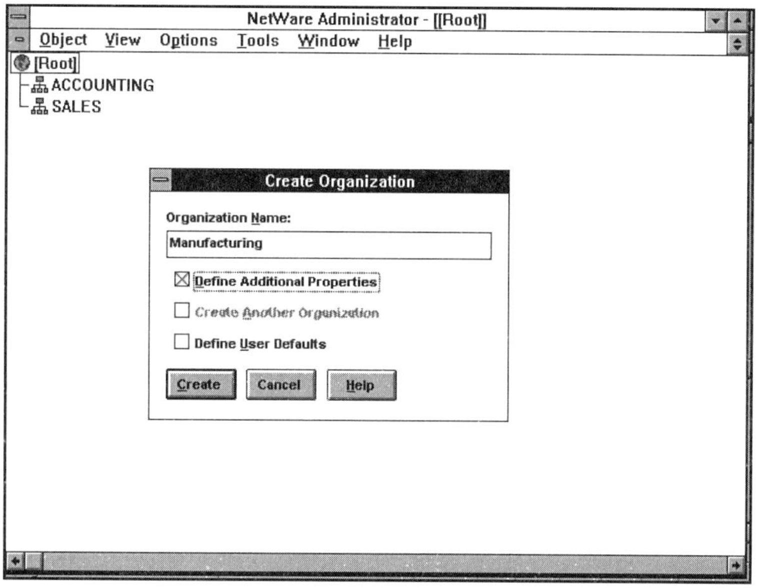

Figure 5.5

Create Organization dialog box.

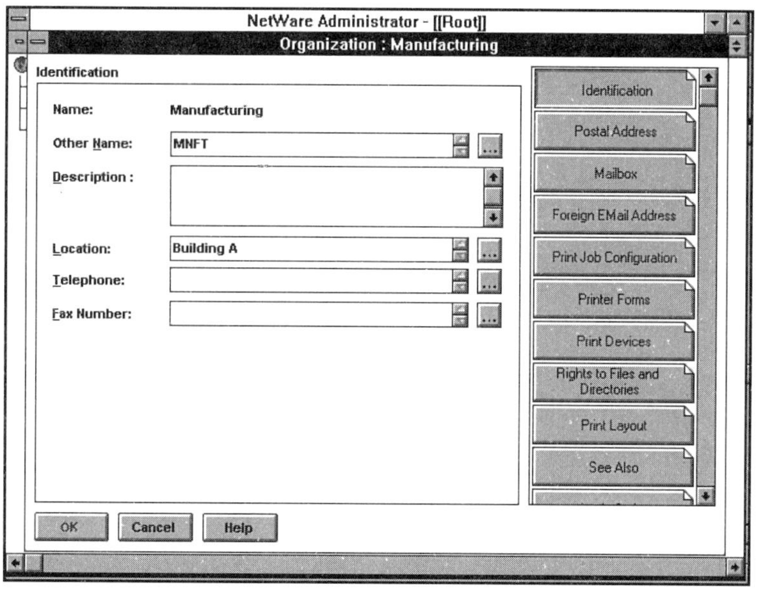

Figure 5.6

Manufacturing Organization object identification page.

6. Continue with the object's creation by choosing any of the associated pages and filling in the needed information. (Choose from the row of page buttons down the right side of the window. For example, choose the Postal Address or Mailbox page to record a mailing address for deliveries and an electronic address for e-mail.)
7. When all needed information for all pages has been filled in, choose OK to create the object.

You create Organizational Unit objects the same way you create Organization objects. The types of information you provide vary somewhat. Instead of choosing Organization from the New Object list, you choose Organizational Unit.

Creating NDS User Objects

You create User and Organizational role objects the same way you create Organization objects. Again, the types of information you provide vary somewhat, and you choose User or Organizational Role from the New Object list instead of choosing Organization; otherwise, the process remains the same.

Remember that when creating any NDS objects, the important thing is to highlight the container where the object is to exist before you choose Create from the Object pull-down menu. If you do not have [Root] or a Country object highlighted before attempting to create an Organization object, you cannot create it. If you do not have an Organization object highlighted before attempting to create an Organizational Unit object, you also cannot create it. Finally, if you do not have an Organization or Organizational Unit highlighted before attempting to create a leaf object, you cannot create it.

When you create a User object, you must provide a Login Name and Last Name at the minimum. You also can mark the Use User Template, Define Additional Properties, and Create Home Directory boxes so that you can provide additional information regarding the user, including the location in the directory tree where a home directory should be created for this user. If you created a template for User objects, you can specify that the template be used to create this user.

With a template, you can define such things as Login Restrictions, Group Memberships, and other items you want to have associated with each new User object.

Partitioning the Directory Tree

In small LANs and MANs, the default partitioning strategy of a single network partition is often sufficient to meet a company's needs. When one partition is not enough and additional partitions have been defined, those partitions are created by using the MS Windows NetWare Administrator utility or the DOS-based version of the partition manager called PARTMGR.

Because small LANs generally do not need additional partitions, the process for partitioning a tree is not described in this chapter, but is described in Chapter 7, "Implementing the NetWare 4 Wide Area Network Plan," because WANs more commonly have several network partitions.

Replicating Partitions

As is true with partitioning LANs and MANs, the default of one Master and two Read/Write copies of the sole partition as the replication strategy for a LAN or MAN is also likely to be sufficient. The process of replicating partitions by using the NetWare Administrator utility, therefore, is also discussed in Chapter 7, because it more readily applies to WANs than to LANs or MANs.

Installing and Migrating NetWare 4 File Servers

In a wide area network, you may find it necessary to perform custom installations and to exercise full control over the migration of file servers. In a LAN or MAN, installing and migrating file servers should be as simple as the network design will allow. The best approach to take when installing new NetWare 4 file servers into a LAN or MAN is likely to mean that you run the NetWare 4 INSTALL program and choose the Simple Installation of NetWare 4.1 option provided with the NetWare 4 operating system.

Before installing NetWare 4.1, you must first create a small DOS partition (a bootable DOS partition) and a large NetWare partition (a secondary DOS partition) on the computer's hard disk using the DOS FDISK command. (If necessary, refer to your DOS manual for information on how to create partitions.)

The installation process then begins by inserting the NetWare 4.1 CD-ROM into the CD-ROM drive on the computer that is to become the NetWare 4 file server. Next, change to the drive containing the NetWare 4.1 installation CD-ROM disk and complete the following steps:

1. Type INSTALL, and press Enter.
2. Choose NetWare Server Installation from the menu (see fig. 5.7).
3. Choose NetWare 4.1 from the NetWare Installation Utility menu.
4. Choose Simple Installation of NetWare 4.1.
5. Type a name to be used for the NetWare 4.1 file server, then press Enter.
6. When the Copy server boot files to DOS partition screen opens, modify the Source path or Destination path as needed.
7. After the NetWare server files are copied to the DOS partition and the NetWare Server Installation 4.1 NetWare Loadable Module screen opens, choose the server disk driver from the list of known drivers.
8. When prompted to Verify/Enter the driver parameters to be sure that they match the hardware in this computer, verify or change the related parameters as needed.

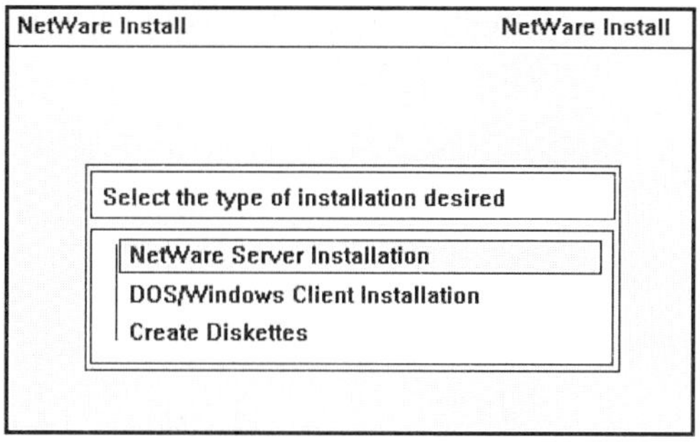

Figure 5.7
First of the NetWare 4.1 Installation screens.

9. After all disk drivers are installed, choose No when prompted to install additional disk drivers.
10. When prompted to Verify/Enter the driver parameters to be sure that they match the hardware in this computer, verify or change the related parameters if any parameters need to be changed. Then, choose Save parameters and continue.
11. Choose Yes when prompted with `Do you want to select an additional network driver?`, if there are other drivers to be installed. Otherwise, choose No.
12. When prompted to change drivers or continue, choose Continue installation from the Driver Actions menu.
13. Wait while the installation software performs a variety of tasks, including checking for conflicts, then read the Warning message that appears and continue the installation process by choosing Continue accessing the CD-ROM via DOS.
14. Ignore the warning that some disk partitions already exist, because you created those deliberately with FDISK so that both a DOS and non-DOS (NetWare) partition would be available. Instead, simply press Enter to continue with the installation.
15. When prompted to `Delete existing non-bootable disk partitions?`, choose Yes.
16. When prompted to specify the path from which license files will be installed (drive A is the default, press F3 to specify a

different location), insert the licensing disk into drive A, then press Enter to continue.

17. When prompted to Install NetWare Directory Services (NDS), choose Yes, this is the first NetWare 4 server to install the first NetWare 4.1 file server, or choose No, connect to existing NetWare 4 networks, if this is the second or subsequent file server being installed into this directory tree.
18. When prompted, choose a time zone from the list of time zones.
19. When prompted for an Organization Name, type in the name you have chosen to represent your organization and press Enter.
20. Type the ADMIN user's password, and press Enter.
21. When prompted, retype the password and press Enter again.
22. When the NetWare Directory Services and other related NetWare 4 files have been copied to their assigned location, read the For your information window that opens, then press Enter to continue.
23. When the balance of the files are copied, choose Continue Installation from the Other Installation Actions menu.
24. Press Enter to exit to the system console screen.

Once you finish this process, you have completed the installation of a NetWare 4.1 file server. The process can be repeated to install as many new NetWare 4.1 file servers into the directory tree as are available. If the network already exists and it has NetWare 3 file servers that will be upgraded to NetWare 4, follow the steps in the next section to perform an in-place upgrade on each of these file servers.

Upgrading NetWare 3 Servers to NetWare 4 Using the In-Place Upgrade

Using the in-place upgrade makes it possible for you to migrate your NetWare 3 file servers to NetWare 4 file servers. This migration process takes the existing NetWare 3 bindery information and merges it into the NetWare 4 NDS database. Therefore, it is important that you clean up the bindery files on your NetWare 3 file servers before you perform the in-place upgrade. In addition, back up your file server to prevent an unforeseen problem from irreplaceably wiping out your file server files. Be sure also to back up all data on the file server in a separate backup. That data can then be restored to the NetWare 4 server after the in-place migration has been completed.

To run the in-place migration, after performing all of the premigration tasks just discussed, complete the following steps:

1. Place the NetWare 4.1 CD-ROM in the CD-ROM drive.
2. Change to the drive where the MIGRATE.EXE file is located, type `MIGRATE`, and press Enter.
3. When the Select the type of migration menu appears, choose the Same-Server migration option.
4. Choose NetWare 3x from the Select the source LAN type menu.
5. Choose NetWare 4.*x* from the Select the destination LAN type menu.
6. Complete the Migration Utility Configuration form (see fig. 5.8).
7. Choose Exit (return to DOS).

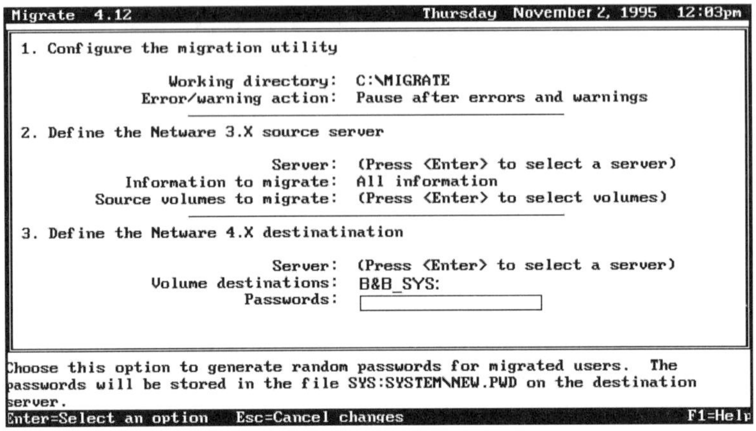
Migrate 4.12 Thursday November 2, 1995 12:03pm

1. Configure the migration utility

Working directory: C:\MIGRATE
Error/warning action: Pause after errors and warnings

2. Define the Netware 3.X source server

Server: (Press <Enter> to select a server)
Information to migrate: All information
Source volumes to migrate: (Press <Enter> to select volumes)

3. Define the Netware 4.X destinatination

Server: (Press <Enter> to select a server)
Volume destinations: B&B_SYS:
Passwords:

Choose this option to generate random passwords for migrated users. The passwords will be stored in the file SYS:SYSTEM\NEW.PWD on the destination server.
Enter=Select an option Esc=Cancel changes F1=Help

Figure 5.8
Migration utility configuration form.

Upgrading Workstations

Workstations on the NetWare 4 network need to run the Requester. For DOS and Windows workstations, that means the NetWare 4-compatible version of the NetWare DOS Requester needs to be installed on each workstation. The NetWare DOS Requester may be installed across the network, or from disk.

To install the NetWare DOS Requester across the network, log in to the network, map a drive to SYS:PUBLIC on the NetWare 4 file server, set that network drive as the default drive, then change to the CLIENT\DOSWIN subdirectory.

To install the NetWare DOS Requester from disk, create the appropriate disks from the NetWare 4.1 INSTALL program. Next, insert the NetWare Client for DOS and MS Windows Disk 1 (WSDOS_1) disk into the drive, swapping out disks WSDOS_1 through WSDOS_5 when prompted.

To complete the installation, whether performed across the network or from disk, execute the following steps:

1. Type INSTALL, then press Enter.
2. When the NetWare Client Install screen opens (see fig. 5.9), choose step 1 and either press Enter to accept the default of C:\NWCLIENT for the destination directory and move the highlight to the next line, or type in a new directory, then press Enter.

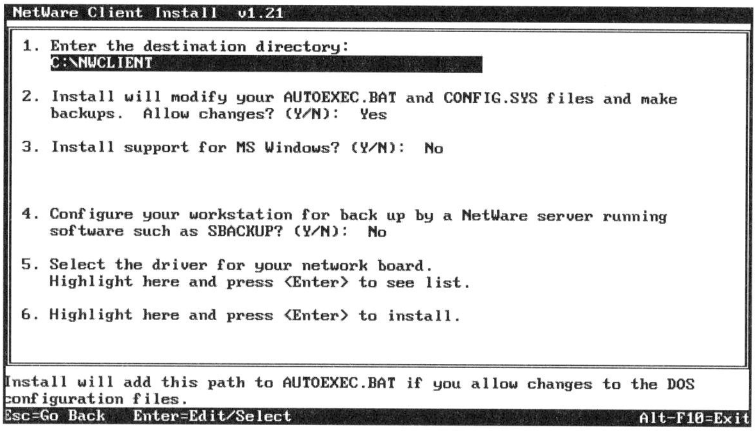

Figure 5.9

NetWare Client Install v1.21 screen.

3. Select step 2. Press Enter to choose Yes, thus allowing the installation program to make changes to the AUTOEXEC.BAT and CONFIG.SYS files. If you want to modify those files manually, choose No. The existing files will not be changed. New files are created in their place with a .NEW extension (AUTOEXEC.NEW and CONFIG.NEW).

   If you prefer to make the changes to the workstation configuration files manually, the following changes must be made:

   - AUTOEXEC.BAT. Add the `C:\NWCLIENT\STARTNET.BAT` line at the end of this file to load the NetWare DOS Requester and related files.
   - CONFIG.SYS. Add the `LASTDRIVE=Z` command.
   - NET.CFG. Add the LAN driver information under the `Link Driver driver_name` heading. Include the `PREFERRED TREE=` or `PREFERRED SERVER=` and `FIRST NETWORK DRIVE=` statements under the `NetWare DOS Requester` heading. If you want the workstation to be backed up by a NetWare server, include the TSA-related information associated with this process.
   - STARTNET.BAT. Include commands to load the files required for network connection from the AUTOEXEC.BAT file. The files to be loaded should include LSL.COM, the LAN driver (such as NE2000), IPXODI.COM, and the NetWare DOS Requester (VLM.EXE).

4. Select step 3. If the workstation has Windows running on it, type `Y` to change the default of No to Yes. The Windows files will be installed on this workstation.

   When you choose Yes, the default directory of C:\WINDOWS is placed on the `Enter MS Windows directory:` field, and another field (`Highlight here and Press <Enter> to customize.`) is made available. You can choose that field and modify the directory to that directory that contains this workstation's MS Windows files.

5. Accept the country codes default of No. Change this default to Yes at the `Do you plan to use more country codes than the one currently running on your machine? (Y/N):` prompt, if needed.

6. If you want this workstation to be able to access a shared directory, set the `For network administrators only: Do you want to set the shared MS Windows path? (Y/N):` field to Yes, and provide the path for this directory.

   When you have finished modifying the Customize Support for MS Windows screen, press F10 to save your changes.

7. Set the `Configure your workstation for back up by a NetWare server running software such as SBACKUP? (Y/N):` field to Yes if you want to be able to back up the hard disk(s) on this workstation by using the file server's backup software. Otherwise, leave the default set to No.

8. Select step 5. Press Enter. Enter the network board configuration information or accept the information provided. Press Enter to continue.

9. Select the `Highlight here and press <Enter> to install` field, and press Enter to start the file copy and configuration process.

10. When The Install Utility is finished screen is displayed, the installation is complete. Press Enter to exit to DOS, or press Ctrl+Alt+Del to reboot the workstation and load the configuration files.

Using *WSUPDATE* and *WSUPGRD*

You can also use the WSUPGRD and WSUPDATE utilities to simplify the process of updating the same files on multiple workstations. Use WSUPGRD to update the IPX LAN driver if the current LAN driver is not ODI compliant. WSUPDATE is run from the network.

Type the following:

```
WSUPGRD [path] [/options]
```

at the command line and press Enter. Replace `[path]` with the path pointing to the complete driver name, and replace `[/option]` with any of the following available options as needed:

- `/C` exits the utility with an error code of level `1` instead of `0` when the upgrade does not complete successfully.
- `/E0`, `/E1`, or `/E2` specifies whether no changes should be made to the AUTOEXEC.BAT file (`E0`), or the IPX driver command in the AUTOEXEC.BAT file should be replaced with the commands to load the ODI driver (`E1`), or the IPX driver command in the AUTOEXEC.BAT file should be removed and a call added to the NWSTART file that is then created and will be called to load the ODI drivers (`E2`).
- `/I` places the hardware ID in the master configuration table for the ODI driver.
- `/N` saves the old copy of the IPX driver.
- `/S` prevents the NET.CFG file from being generated with the information contained in the original IPX driver's configuration table.

Note You can also place this command into a login script so that it runs automatically when users log in to the network.

Type the following:

```
WSUPDATE [network_path] [drive.|volume:] [client_path\filename]
[/options]
```

at the command line and press Enter. Replace [network_path] with the location of the new file. Replace [drive.¦volume:] with the mapped drive letter pointing to the old file, or use the /ALL option instead. Replace [client_path\filename] with the name of the old file being replaced by the new file. Replace [/option] with any of the following options:

- /ALL to search all mapped drives
- /C to copy the new file over the old without a backup
- /E to erase the existing file
- /F=[path\file] to have the command ignore other options
- /LOCAL to search the workstation's drives
- /L=[path\file] to specify the location and name of the log file
- /P to have the user proceed with or abort the update when there are no files to update
- /O to update all files
- /R to rename the old version of the file with an .OLD extension
- /S to search for copies of the file to be updated
- /? to view online help information about this utility

As with the WSUPGRD command, you can also place the WSUPDATE command into a login script to have it run automatically when users log in to the network.

Summary

Once you and the project team have developed the network's design, the next phase of the project requires that you implement the NetWare 4 network. The main goal to be accomplished during this phase is to make the process of setting up, upgrading or migrating an existing network, or installing a new NetWare 4 network proceed as smoothly as possible. To accomplish this goal, the project team must successfully complete three procedures: develop a migration strategy, create an implementation schedule, and implement NetWare 4, which are explained in detail in this chapter.

After having read and understood the information contained within this chapter, you should be ready to implement a fully designed NetWare 4 local area network as well as a municipal area network in one or more companies. The balance of the summary of this chapter is, therefore, presented in the form of a checklist to help you review and remember the procedures associated with implementing a NetWare 4 network.

If you combine this checklist with the one found in the Summary in Chapter 4, "Designing and Planning NetWare 4 Local Area Networks," you should find it easier to remember most of the details of designing and implementing NetWare 4 LANs and MANs.

- ☐ Develop a migration strategy
    - ☐ Review migration-related information
    - ☐ Assess application needs
        - ☐ Will bindery services be required?
        - ☐ Will any applications have to be upgraded?
        - ☐ Are applications called from existing menus?
        - ☐ Which users access applications requiring bindery services?
- ☐ Assess network clients/workstations
    - ☐ Note which operating systems are being used
    - ☐ Decide whether workstation configuration files need to be modified
    - ☐ See whether any workstations currently run NETX

    - ☐ Determine whether the workstations load the latest version of VLMs
    - ☐ Check to see whether LIP is being used
    - ☐ Consider the use of network management tools
    - ☐ List protocols being used
    - ☐ Decide whether workstations will be backed up
- ☐ Consider approach to upgrading workstations
    - ☐ Find out who currently provides workstation support
    - ☐ Determine typical workstation configurations
    - ☐ Share client software with administrators
    - ☐ Create user training
    - ☐ Begin upgrading workstations
- ☐ Assess network file servers
    - ☐ Review current file server configurations
        - ☐ Note which operating systems are being used
        - ☐ Log names of current file servers
        - ☐ Determine whether sufficient disk storage and RAM exist
        - ☐ Determine whether the microprocessor meets minimum requirements for NetWare 4
    - ☐ Determine which file servers will be upgraded
    - ☐ Decide which file servers must be replaced
- ☐ Begin migrating file servers
    - ☐ Establish a testing lab
        - ☐ Set up testing lab for typical network configuration
        - ☐ Test migration methods to determine which will be suitable
        - ☐ Train administrators to perform migrations

- ☐ Discuss potential downtime with management
- ☐ Choose the most appropriate migration method
- ☐ Obtain NetWare 4.1 software and licenses
- ☐ Schedule and perform pilot migrations
  - ☐ Obtain additional personnel to assist with the migration, if needed
  - ☐ Clean up NetWare binderies
    - ☐ Ensure that names conform to naming standards
    - ☐ Eliminate duplicate object names (DUPBIND.EXE)
    - ☐ Remove unused objects
    - ☐ Ensure that all objects have appropriate rights (SECURITY.EXE)
  - ☐ Back up file servers
  - ☐ Test backup media to ensure usability
  - ☐ Migrate the first file server
  - ☐ Log all problems and the chosen solution
  - ☐ Revise the migration procedure as needed
  - ☐ Train users in the pilot department
- ☐ Choose training method (e-mail, written documents, quick reference materials, hands-on, or self-study using third-party books)
- ☐ Implement training method
- ☐ Review success of training method
- ☐ Revise training method if needed, then review again

- ☐ Schedule migration for balance of the network
  - ☐ Obtain additional personnel to assist with the migration, if needed
  - ☐ Clean up NetWare binderies
    - ☐ Ensure that names conform to naming standards
    - ☐ Eliminate duplicate object names (DUPBIND.EXE)
    - ☐ Remove unused objects
    - ☐ Ensure that all objects have appropriate rights (SECURITY.EXE)
    - ☐ Back up file servers
    - ☐ Test backup media to ensure usability
    - ☐ Migrate the first file server
    - ☐ Log all problems and the chosen solution
    - ☐ Revise the migration procedure as needed
- ☐ Create an implementation schedule
  - ☐ Identify implementation tasks
    - ☐ Assess workstation, application, and file server migration requirements
    - ☐ Assemble and train migration team
    - ☐ Order needed hardware and software, including NetWare 4 and licenses
    - ☐ Upgrade workstations in the pilot test area, including their configuration files
    - ☐ Establish a testing lab and test applications, workstation communication software and migration methods, and log results only
    - ☐ Prepare file servers in the pilot test area for migration
    - ☐ Migrate file servers in the pilot test area and log results

- ☐ Train users, support personnel, and administrators in the pilot test area
- ☐ Upgrade workstations in the remainder of the company, including their configuration files
- ☐ Prepare file servers in the rest of the company for migration
- ☐ Migrate file servers in the remainder of the company, logging problems and corrections as they occur
- ☐ Train the company's remaining users, support personnel, and administrators
- ☐ Document the results of the migration and procedures for dealing with any issues that develop as a result of the migration

- ☐ Schedule each task
  - ☐ Assess approximate length of time required to complete each task (assume 15 minutes minimum per workstation and one to 10 hours per file server, depending on how much bindery and file system cleanup is required)
  - ☐ Create a timeline or schedule of tasks
  - ☐ Assign responsibility for each task
  - ☐ Document the schedule
- ☐ Coordinate the schedule with others

- ☐ Implement NetWare 4
  - ☐ Create the NDS directory structure
    - ☐ Create NDS Container objects
    - ☐ Create NDS User and other objects (optional, because it may be performed by network administrators once the implementation is complete)
    - ☐ Partition the directory tree (if needed)
    - ☐ Replicate partitions (if needed)

- ☐ Install and migrate to NetWare 4 file servers
    - ☐ Create hard disk partitions if needed (FDISK)
    - ☐ Install NetWare 4 on new file servers (generally by using the Simple Installation option for LANs and MANs)
    - ☐ Migrate NetWare and non-NetWare file servers using across-the-wire, same-server, in-place upgrade, or NetWare 4.1 INSTALL's upgrade menu option
- ☐ Upgrade workstations
    - ☐ Run NetWare Client Installation, WSUPDATE, or WSUPGRD software
    - ☐ Modify workstation configuration files manually if you choose not to let the NetWare Client Installation software modify them
        - ☐ STARNET.BAT to load communication files
        - ☐ AUTOEXEC.BAT to call STARTNET.BAT
        - ☐ NET.CFG to include LAN driver information, `PREFERRED TREE` or `PREFERRED SERVER` statement, `NAME CONTEXT` statement, and `FIRST NETWORK DRIVE` statement
        - ☐ CONFIG.SYS to include `LASTDRIVE=Z`
- ☐ Ensure that users are sufficiently trained

Case Study

Southtown Health Center is a nonprofit organization with one clinic in a small rural community. They provide free-to-low-cost medical care. They draw from all surrounding communities. Patients have come to the clinic from as far away as 129 miles. Southtown Health Center believes it may soon have to open a second clinic, although funds have not yet been made available.

Southtown's Chief Executive Officer, Ms. Alberta Smiles, has hired you to help her volunteer staff determine the steps that will be necessary to implement a NetWare 4 local area network for Southtown. Ms. Smiles has provided you with the following information about Southtown:

> 2 Compaq Presario 486 PCs, which are to become file servers
>
> 7 IBM-compatible 386 PCs to be used as workstations, one of which already holds a custom medical program. The medical program was written three years earlier when Southtown was considering the installation of a NetWare 3 network. The medical program was written to be used in the NetWare bindery environment. Its author is a volunteer nurse who says she can upgrade the software to be NetWare 4-compatible, but that it will take her about one year to upgrade the software.
>
> Southtown has already paid to have network boards and Ethernet cabling installed. They also have already purchased NetWare 4 and a network version of WordPerfect 6.1.

Given this information, write a list of tasks that are likely to have to be performed by Southtown's volunteer staff before NetWare 4.1 will be up and running.

Review Questions

1. Which of the following is *not* an object type that requires bindery services?

   ○ A. User

   ○ B. Group

   ○ C. Print Server

   ○ D. Alias

2. In NetWare 4.1, you can set bindery context on only ____________ container(s).
   - A. 1
   - B. 6
   - C. 12
   - D. 16
3. The last task to be completed in the development of a client migration strategy is ____________.
   - A. to begin migrating clients
   - B. to set a timeline for migrating clients
   - C. to determine which clients should be migrated first
   - D. to determine into which container each client should be placed
4. When preparing for a successful migration of the network file servers, you should discuss downtime and migration with management before you ____________.
   - A. establish a testing lab
   - B. review current file server configurations
   - C. choose the file server migration method
   - D. upgrade any network clients
5. To upgrade a NetWare 2.1*x* file server without the aid of any other file servers or workstations, use the ____________ method.
   - A. across-the-wire
   - B. same-server
   - C. in-place
   - D. upgrade menu

6. The factor most likely to influence which tasks a project team will have to complete when migrating its network is ___________.

   - A. the size of the company
   - B. how many team members will help with the migration
   - C. the design of the directory tree
   - D. the physical distance between network file servers

7. To check for more than one User object with the same name on an existing NetWare 3 file server, run the ___________ utility.

   - A. SECURITY
   - B. DUPBIND
   - C. BINDFIX
   - D. UPGRADE

8. Which of the following is *not* a task associated with completing the implementation scheduling process?

   - A. establishing a list of tasks to be completed
   - B. assigning completion dates to tasks
   - C. training network users
   - D. calculating the length of time each task requires

9. Establishing a second partition when only a single network partition will not be sufficient is part of which NetWare 4 implementation tasks?

   - A. creating the NDS directory structure
   - B. installing NetWare 4 file servers
   - C. migrating non-NetWare file servers
   - D. upgrading workstations

10. When installing the NetWare DOS Requester, if you do not allow the program to modify configuration files, which command do you have to add manually to the workstation's CONFIG.SYS file?
    - ○ A. `PREFERRED SERVER=`
    - ○ B. `FIRST NETWORK DRIVE=`
    - ○ C. `NAME CONTEXT=`
    - ○ D. `LASTDRIVE=`

Answers

1. D
2. D
3. A
4. C
5. B
6. A
7. B
8. C
9. A
10. D

Chapter 6

Chapter Chapter Chapter Chapter Chapter Chapter

Designing and Planning NetWare 4 Wide Area Networks

NetWare 4 WANs generally encompass a large geographic area. A WAN may span one or more continents or simply include only one country or multiple states. Although some smaller companies have WANs, many WANs are also found in larger companies, such as those included on the Fortune 500 list.

Regardless of the size of the WAN, the process developed by Novell's Consulting Services group for designing and planning a WAN is almost the same as that of designing and planning a LAN or a MAN. There are some other factors associated with designing a WAN, however, that are not applicable to designing a LAN or a MAN. This chapter discusses the similarities and differences of those factors between LAN or MAN design and planning and WAN design and planning. No step in the process should be left out, unless it is not applicable, when designing and planning a WAN.

If you are primarily designing and planning WANs, you need the information in this chapter, as well as in Chapter 7, "Implementing the NetWare 4 Wide Area Network Plan," more than you will need the LAN and MAN information. On the other hand, if you are primarily designing LANs and MANs, you may need to become very familiar with Chapter 4, "Designing and Planning NetWare 4 Local Area Networks," and Chapter 5, "Implementing the NetWare 4 Local Area Network Plan." If you are studying to take the CNE examination for the NetWare 4.1 Design and Implementation course, having the needed information presented as it relates to LANs and MANs, and then again as it relates to WANs, should help you get a better grasp of the overall material and be better prepared for the examination.

As noted, designing and implementing a NetWare 4 WAN is very similar to designing and implementing a NetWare 4 LAN or MAN. The process designed by Novell's Consulting Services group is also the same. That also means that each of the phases and associated procedures are the same.

As with designing and implementing a LAN, the design and implementation process of a NetWare 4 WAN requires that you take into account three related issues. Those three issues are the main topics of this chapter:

- Designing the WAN directory tree
- Planning partitions
- Planning and placing replicas

This chapter discusses directory tree design, including information on designing a WAN directory tree for maximum benefit, and explains the process of establishing and documenting naming and network standards as part of the process of designing and implementing WANs. This chapter then discusses how to design the directory tree, including both the upper and lower layers, to ensure that the company receives the advantages associated with a properly designed tree and avoids the problems associated with a poorly designed directory tree.

As with designing and planning LANs and MANs, the WAN's directory tree design is based on experience. Many different companies helped Novell's Consulting Services group to assess and then determine the best approach to take when designing and planning NetWare 4 wide area networks. That combined information and experience is thus shared by Novell with NetWare 4 designers, consultants, and other interested parties—and is presented here—to help ensure that NetWare 4 networks meet the needs of the companies that install it.

Properly planned and implemented NetWare 4 directory trees help ensure network fault tolerance, thus substantially reducing the likelihood that a major disaster or sabotage could render the entire directory tree inaccessible.

Although NetWare 4 software makes it possible for you to ensure a fault-tolerant network, you must do the up-front and continuous work to ensure that NetWare 4 performs at its best. You need to understand how to modify the default partitioning and replication strategies to accommodate a wide area network. Unlike designing and planning a LAN or MAN, using NetWare 4's default partitioning and replication strategies to create a WAN will not be sufficient to ensure fault tolerance. This chapter, therefore, concentrates on designing and planning for WANs and the steps you must take above and beyond the defaults installed by NetWare 4, beginning with the design of the directory tree for a NetWare 4 wide area network.

Designing the WAN Directory Tree

If careful design of a NetWare 4 directory tree is important to developing a LAN or MAN, it is even more important when developing a WAN. A poorly designed directory tree can result in branches of the WAN being impractical, if not unusable. A poorly designed directory tree may

- Not be able to provide complete fault tolerance
- End up restricting rather than simplifying network access

- Make it difficult if not almost impossible to administer and maintain network security correctly
- Eventually result in a network that is too costly to maintain

Although these problems may not be immediately evident, they will become so as the WAN is implemented and when it begins to grow. It is important, therefore, to understand the benefits and factors associated with the correct design of a NetWare 4 WAN directory tree, and to apply the skill and knowledge needed to develop an effective directory tree.

Benefits of a Correctly Designed Tree

Preventing potential problems from becoming problems is a benefit of a correctly designed directory tree. It is not the only benefit, however. There are other benefits associated with designing the WAN directory tree right the first time:

- Partitioning and replication strategies that are easy to implement and relatively simple to maintain
- Network growth that is easily accommodated
- Network services that are readily maintained and easily added to the network
- User access that is reduced to the simplest of processes
- Directory tree navigation that is relatively intuitive for network users and administrators

If you want to design the most effective NetWare 4 directory tree for your WAN, you may find it helpful first to understand how proper directory tree design can benefit the network.

Simplifying Partitioning and Replication

When you partition the directory tree, you are creating logical divisions within the NDS database, which contains all information about the network itself, excluding the directory and file structure contained within each NetWare 4 file server. When you partition the directory tree, you are dividing the NDS database into several smaller sections. If you then make copies (replicas) of those partitions, and store the replicas on different NetWare 4 file servers, you are ensuring fault tolerance. Because the entire database is not stored on one single NetWare file server, and copies of each portion of the NDS database exist on multiple file servers, there is no single point of failure on the network.

Partitioning the NDS database and then replicating those different partitions provides several benefits:

- Easier handling of the database because it has been divided into smaller sections (multiple network administrators can be used instead of a single network administrator)
- Fault tolerance (no section of the directory tree can be completely lost due to the failure of a single NetWare 4 file server)
- Reduced login and authentication time (writeable replicas placed on the file server closest to the users whose User objects are contained within that partition reduces the time it takes for NetWare to find User object information and thus the length of time it takes to log users into the network and get them authenticated)
- Easier access to the network for network users (users are not aware that the NDS database is distributed, nor does it matter to them because most users do not need immediate access to all directory tree partitions)

Accommodating Network Growth

Redesigning a directory tree to accommodate network growth not only results in a substantial increase in the amount of work required of your network's administrators, but may also interfere substantially with the ability of network users to do their jobs. Part of the network will be unavailable to users while the redesign and implementation is taking place. In addition, workstation configuration files may have to be modified before users can access the network at all. If the WAN is substantially large, modifying workstation configuration files can be a very time-consuming task. It may not be possible to automate the process because it will be necessary first to determine which network workstations must have their configuration files modified. Once the workstations are identified, the changes must be determined. Finally, the configuration files themselves must be modified, which may require manual intervention.

Network menus may also require modification. If users currently access applications through menus using Directory Map objects, those menus may have to be changed if network design changes move Directory Map or User objects from one container to another. It may be as simple as changing the Directory Map object's pointer, but even simple changes take some time and may also necessitate that users be reeducated.

Easing the Addition of Network Services

A poorly designed network tree can make it difficult to add resources. Printer or Directory Map objects may have to be created where none existed before. If the possibility of adding such objects at a later time is not considered, adding them later may make the directory tree more difficult to administer.

This could be particularly true if a large number of objects has to be added to a given container. Although NetWare 4 theoretically can handle an unlimited number of objects in a container, placing more than 5,000 objects in a single container may make it quite difficult to administer the container. In addition, network replication can be very time-consuming if the container has many simultaneous object additions or changes made to it.

Even though the process of adding an object to a container is not a difficult one, choosing the best location within the directory tree for that object may be a problem. This can be particularly true if the design of the tree makes it necessary to add the same object or additional Alias objects to various containers on the tree.

Simplifying User Access

A successful directory tree design also considers where users need to have resources placed for easy access, ideally located closest to those User objects that will access them. To accomplish this, directory trees should be designed so that the User object and the various network resources are placed in the same container in the tree. If this design approach is taken, users will have easy access to needed resources as soon as they log in to the network.

Because users must have available to them, at login time, a writable replica of the container where their User object is located, the directory tree design should take into account what type of replica will be used, and where it will be placed on the network. Unless a writable replica is on the file server the user's workstation will first access upon login, NetWare has to search the network for a writable copy of the replica before the user can log in and be authenticated (identified to other servers in the tree and verified as to the rights the User object has to use certain resources) on the network.

Making Tree Navigation More Intuitive

When a directory tree has a logical organization to it, users have an easier time understanding that design. With that understanding comes easier network navigation. If users need to find their way around the network tree when their current context is not sufficient, they will be able to spend less time trying to figure out how to find and then access the resources they need, and more time working.

Process for Correctly Designing the Tree

When preparing to design the directory tree, following the Novell Consulting Services recommended steps to tree design helps ensure that the directory tree is designed to meet the network's needs. Here are the steps associated with correctly designing a NetWare 4 directory tree:

- Establishing and documenting naming standards
- Drawing the upper and lower layers of the tree
- Reviewing and revising the tree design
- Creating the directory tree structure

Completing the proper process associated with designing the NetWare 4 WAN directory tree helps to ensure that future growth and access to network resources for users will be as simple as possible and that network navigation will be relatively intuitive for users.

Establishing and Documenting Naming Standards

As with designing and planning the NetWare 4 LAN or MAN, the first step you must take in order to design an effective NetWare 4 WAN directory tree successfully is to create a set of guidelines to be followed when naming objects. These guidelines will then be followed by the project team, as well as by any network administrators responsible for maintaining the network once it is implemented.

The naming standards document ensures consistency throughout the network and throughout the project team. Establishing naming standards helps to coordinate all project team members, network administrators, and other individuals responsible for the design, implementation, and management of the NetWare 4 network. A coordinated team working from the same set of standards makes it possible for all members of the team to perform their tasks from the same point of view.

Besides naming standards, there are other issues with which you must be concerned when designing and planning a NetWare 4 WAN:

- Naming standards concepts
- Network navigation
- IPX numbering standards

These issues are only briefly reviewed here because they are discussed in detail in Chapter 4, "Designing and Planning NetWare 4 Local Area Networks," followed by information about what naming standards documents should include. Please refer to Chapter 4 if you need more detailed information.

The following are naming standards concepts with which you need to be familiar and which are reviewed here:

- Common name
- Context
- Current context
- Distinguished name
- Relative distinguished name

A common name (CN) is the name given to a leaf object such as a User, Alias, Computer, Directory Map, Group, NetWare Server, Organizational Role, Printer, Print Server, Print Queue, or Volume object. For example, the common name for a User leaf object of a person whose real name is Sue Martin may be shown as SUEM.

The context of an object is its location within the directory tree. For example, here is the context for the SUEM User object with the directory tree shown in figure 6.1:

```
CN=SUEM.OU=USERS.O=BROWN&BROWN
```

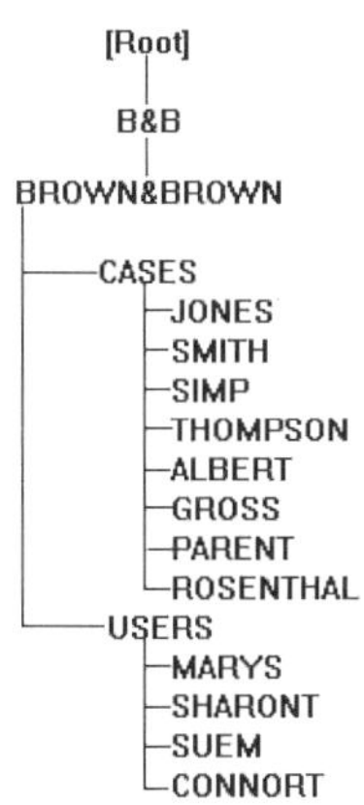

Figure 6.1

Sample section of a directory tree.

Current context is the location in the directory tree to which the user's context is currently set, similar to the current path or default directory term used in the DOS environment.

An object's distinguished name is a combination of the object's common name and its context. Distinguished names always begin with a period, commonly referred to as a leading period. Objects in a distinguished name are separated with a period. Distinguished names may be typeful, showing the object type followed by the equal sign (=) before the object's actual name, or typeless, not using object types or the equal sign. For example, a typeful distinguished name may appear as follows:

```
.CN=SUEM.OU=USERS.O=BROWN&BROWN
```

A typeless distinguished name may appear as follows:

```
.SUEM.USERS.BROWN&BROWN
```

A relative distinguished name is a name that lists the path to an object from the user's current context. Relative distinguished names do not use a leading period, but can use one or more ending periods (trailing periods) to show the path from the current container to a higher-level container in the directory tree, and then back down again to the object. Objects listed in a relative distinguished name are also separated with a period.

Referring again to figure 6.1, the following is the typeful relative distinguished name for user SUEM when another user's current context is set to .0U=CASES.OU=BROWN&BROWN.O=B&B:

```
CN=SUEM.OU=USERS.OU=BROWN&BROWN.O=B&B
```

Network navigation is the second issue that needs to be discussed when designing and planning a NetWare 4 WAN. The ways in which users navigate the network to access objects in the directory tree affect the naming standards you set, as well as the design you establish for the directory tree. The geographical distribution of the company and its resources affect network access, and thus affect tree design. Designing the upper layers of the tree to resemble the physical organization of the tree is often the easiest way to accommodate a user's need to navigate the network. The geographical distribution of the company is particularly important in wide area network design. When users in different geographical locations perform similar job functions and share data, access to that data for users in one area is different from access to those same resources for a user in another area, but the tree must be designed to accommodate both. You and the project team must consider, therefore, how to develop naming standards to accommodate users in different geographic locations.

Mobile or traveling users on the network may also affect how users access network resources, and thus may also affect naming standards. For example, if the company has multiple users who periodically travel between offices or business sites, they are likely to need easy access to the network from multiple locations. Not only do these users need to access the network from their own desks, but they must also be able to access the network from any location when they are traveling. If the company for whom you are designing the network, and thus creating a naming standards document, utilizes mobile employees, the naming standards document and the directory tree design must be developed to accommodate mobile users.

The use of IPX numbering standards should also be considered when designing and implementing a WAN. Recall that IPX is the communications protocol used on Novell NetWare networks when data packets are sent across the network to a node (termination point on the network cable). It is IPX's responsibility to ensure that each incoming packet is sent to the correct network node. Each network file server and segment of the network cable must have unique IPX numbers assigned to them.

There are two types of IPX network numbers: external and internal. An external IPX network number, also sometimes called a network number or network address, is assigned to each segment of the network's cable. If multiple *protocols* (conventions or rules used by programs and operating systems to ensure successful communication between points on the network) or *frame types* (packet data formats for a variety of different media such as Ethernet, 802.2, 802.3, token ring, and so on) are used on the same network, each cable segment is given its own external IPX number.

An internal IPX network number uniquely identifies an individual NetWare file server. The internal network number is used to define a logical network through which packets are routed in order to reach their destination on the physical network to which the NetWare 4 file server is attached.

Both external and internal IPX numbers consist of up to eight hexadecimal digits (the numbers zero through 9 and the letters A through F may be used), which can be either specified or randomly assigned during installation of NetWare 4.

It is the project team's responsibility to decide whether the network will use randomly assigned numbers or whether an IPX numbering standard will be established. If randomly assigned numbers are to be used, the naming standards document should indicate this. If some type of numbering standard is to be followed, the naming standard document should specify how that naming standard is to be implemented.

It is also important to identify the contents of a naming standards document so that you and the project team understand what should be included. The naming standards document should include a list of each NDS object that will be assigned a name, regardless of whether those objects are leaf or container objects. In addition, the standard associated with each object and any related information should also be included. Many naming standards documents also show an example of a correctly named object for each object type specified in the naming standards document.

Note

Table 4.1 in Chapter 4 shows how naming standards can be applied to several of the objects commonly included in a naming standards document.

Use the naming standards document to help focus the project team and guide it in the design and planning of the NetWare 4 network. Because a major part of designing the directory tree includes assigning names to container objects, guidelines for assigning names must exist before the directory tree design begins. Once naming standards are in place, you can begin the design of the top layer of the directory tree.

Designing the Upper and Lower Layers of the Tree

The NetWare directory tree has both top and bottom layers, because it is hierarchical in nature. When designing the WAN directory tree, therefore, it is easiest to design the tree one layer at a time, starting at the top. Both layers of the directory tree must be carefully designed to make it possible to do the following:

- Centralize network resources.
- Take advantage of the single login feature of NetWare 4.
- Accommodate network growth without major redesign of the directory tree.
- Simplify the design and implementation of network security.
- Ease access to network resources.
- Provide a successful blueprint for implementation.
- Simplify directory tree modification when changes within the company itself make directory tree changes necessary.
- Provide secure access to shared resources.

To ensure the successful implementation of a NetWare 4 WAN, guidelines for designing the directory tree are available. Guidelines include information about what the top and lower layers of the directory tree should include, as well as how they should be designed in order to implement NetWare 4 successfully in a wide area network. Give careful consideration to the design of the top layer of the tree before designing the lower layers.

There are issues with which you must be concerned when designing the top layer of the directory tree. In a wide area network, the top layer of the directory tree should be designed to reflect the physical layout (topology) of the company itself. You organize the WAN's directory tree structure around the physical resources for the following reasons:

- To reflect the physical structure of the company's WAN
- To restrict expenses associated with network traffic across geographically dispersed communication links
- To accommodate the dynamic nature of NetWare Directory Services

For the most part, designing the WAN directory tree around the company's geographic topology will result in a pyramid-shaped directory tree (see fig. 6.2).

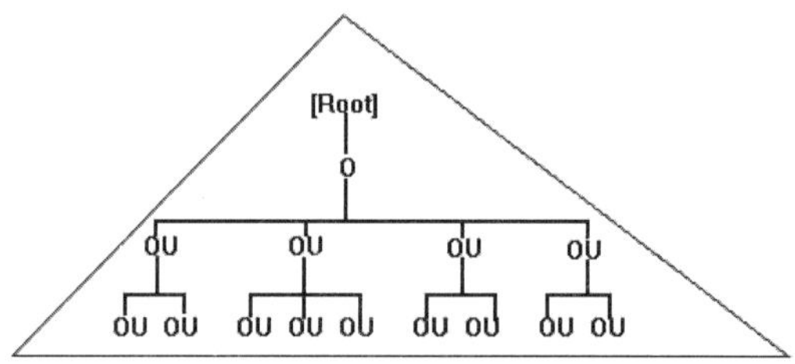

Figure 6.2
Pyramid-like structure of a WAN directory tree.

The [Root] object is at the top of the tree. Below the [Root] object, you should place either a Country object or an Organization (O) object. Most often, the Country object is omitted and a single Organization object, named for the company itself, is placed below [Root].

Note

There are two advantages to using a single Organization object in the directory tree, but no real disadvantages. First, having only one Organization object enables you to set rights for the whole company simply by assigning those rights to the sole Organization object. Second, having a single Organization object makes it easier to merge one tree into another if the present network design requires the temporary use of multiple trees, or future growth and expansion makes necessary the merging of trees.

Below the Organization object there generally are several Organizational Unit (OU) objects. Most often in a WAN, the OU objects are used to represent geographical regions within which the company does business.

For example, if a company called BigTech has offices, warehouses, manufacturing sites, and so on in two areas of the world, the Western hemisphere and the Middle East, you should design the top layer of the directory tree to reflect that same logical organization of the company's physical resources. To accomplish this, you create two OU containers, one for the West and one for the Mideast, directly below the Organization container located at the top of the tree (see fig. 6.3). Each of those Organizational Units then represents one of the two regions of the world where the company does business.

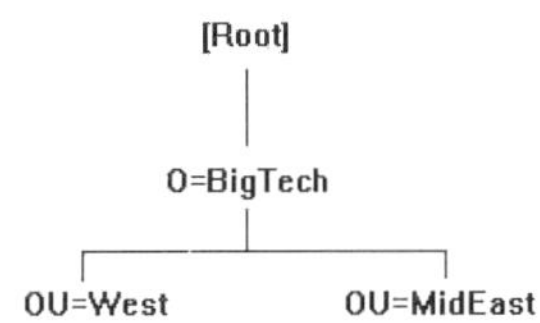

Figure 6.3
Example of the top layer of BigTech's directory tree.

Note

Designing the top layer of the directory tree to represent a pyramid shape helps prevent potential problems with partitioning. It also helps reduce the number of subordinate reference replicas that are generated automatically by NDS for each child partition when a file server contains a replica of a parent partition, but not of the parent's child partitions.

If you prefer, you can design the top layer of the directory tree to provide multiple Organization objects. There is no NetWare 4 requirement that only one Organization object be used. There are some good reasons not to create the directory tree so that it is narrow at the top layer and wider in the lower layers:

- *The company has two or more distinct business units that function more like separate companies than as part of the one company.* This typically describes the larger corporation, which may function as much as a holding company as it does a working company. Companies with this type of structure may have business and management philosophies that are in conflict. Trying to force a directory tree with a single Organization object onto a company of this nature may doom the entire network migration process to failure.

  All companies are different, as are their needs. It is best to consider whether these separate business units share resources (other than e-mail) and the same WAN or LAN infrastructure before deciding whether to create one or multiple Organization objects. If too many incompatibilities exist, or almost no resources are shared, there is no real reason to create a single Organization object for this company. Multiple Organization objects would be appropriate.

- *The entire network is located in one geographical area, and no future expansion is expected or planned.* In this case, a container to specify location is not needed. Instead, the directory tree may be designed by corporate function rather than by location.

- *The network uses high-speed, reliable links for connection.* The fast, reliable links generally enable the network to function more like a LAN than a WAN. If this is the case, a location-based design is less important. Because users tend to share network resources within their own locations, however, you may still want to use a location-based directory tree design or a combination approach—organization and corporate function.

- *Dial-up lines (generally using modems) are used on the network.* If the network utilizes dial-up lines and those geographic areas of the network are included in the same directory tree, a drastic increase in network costs would occur if only a single

Organization object were used. In this case, multiple Organization units may prove to be less costly because NDS database updates will not have to be done across slower communication links. If the remote locations require constant access to the directory tree, rather than once a day or periodic access, you may have to consider including them in the directory tree. If only occasional access is needed, you can consider providing a separate directory tree for each remote location. NetWare 4 would be installed in these sites, so each location could still access the primary directory tree on the same schedule as before, but with reduced costs.

Whether you use a single or multiple Organization objects, you must then decide how to design the next level of the top layer of the directory tree. There are three approaches to designing the second level of the top layer of the directory tree, the Organizational Unit objects:

- Physical approach
- Functional approach
- Combination approach

Each approach has benefits and drawbacks associated with it. The approach you choose should depend on what best meets the needs of the company for whom you are designing the directory tree.

If you choose to use the physical approach to designing the Organizational Unit level of the top layer of the directory tree, you create an Organizational Unit object for each of the company's physical locations. For example, a company called Partners, Incorporated, with offices in Germany, Mexico, and the United States could have an Organizational Unit for each of those locations. These would be considered regional locations or regional units (see fig. 6.4).

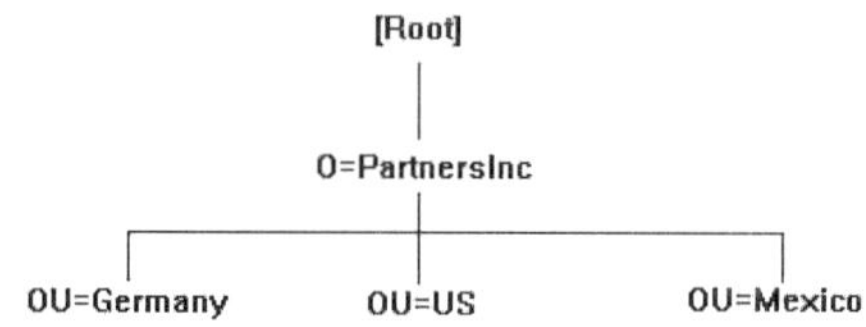

Figure 6.4
Physical directory tree organization by region.

Below these regional units, the directory tree would contain Organization units by more localized areas such as city (see fig. 6.5). This designs the directory tree so that, as much as possible, it matches the physical design of the company itself.

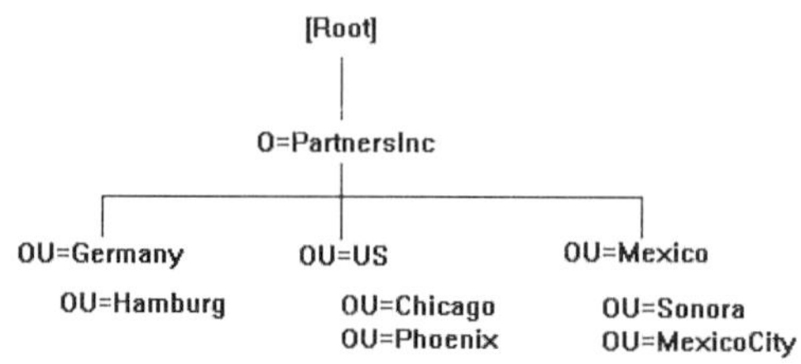

Figure 6.5
Physical directory tree organization with city containers.

To design the directory tree so that it matches the company's organization, you need to see what the company's organization looks like. You should review different company documents, but primarily the company's organization chart.

Although you may consider including different offices or buildings for Organizational Unit objects in the tree, this is generally not a practical approach to take. The biggest problem with using buildings is that they are not very descriptive of a company's location. In addition, they may not be very stable, because companies often change locations or add buildings as the company expands.

If the physical approach to organizing the directory tree does not appear to be practical for a company, you can use the functional approach instead. This approach may use departments rather than locations as Organizational Units (see fig. 6.6).

The functional approach to directory tree design is best used when the company has no WAN links, or when it has only a single NetWare 4 file server. In other words, this approach is more appropriate for a LAN than for a WAN.

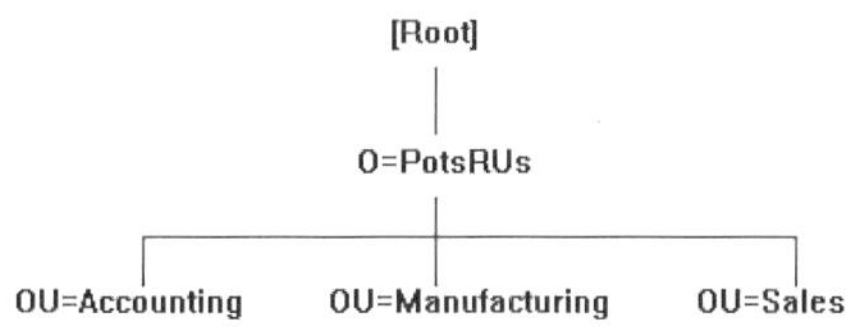

Figure 6.6
Functional directory tree organization.

You may occasionally find that a combination of the physical and functional approaches to designing a wide area network directory tree is the best approach to take. A combination approach can be particularly effective when a company has all its general business offices in a single location, with other aspects of the business more geographically dispersed.

For example, a generic company that raises specialty edible plants called EdiGrows, Inc., could have its headquarters in Tucson, Arizona, with sales offices throughout the major U.S. cities. In this case, the top layer of the directory tree may be organized to be mostly regional, but by division at the headquarters office (see fig. 6.7).

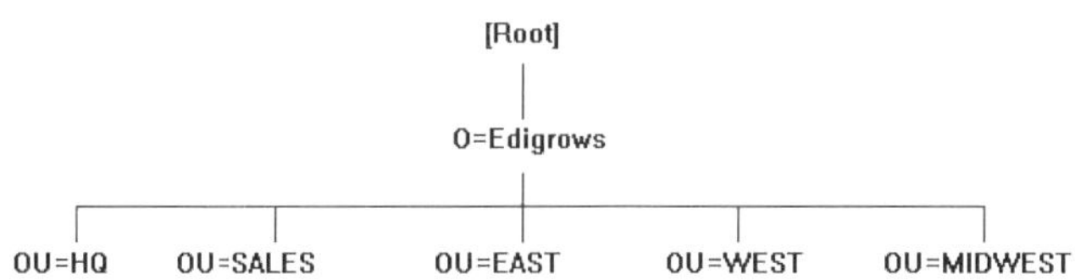

Figure 6.7
Combination directory tree organization.

A combination approach is less commonly used in WANs. This approach is probably more useful in smaller regional networks such as MANs, where some geographic and functional distribution is more suitable.

When designing the top layers of the directory tree structure for a company with a wide area network, the location approach is the most commonly used and generally the most effective approach to take. It is the approach Novell recommends most.

As a general rule, Novell recommends that you design the top layer of the WAN directory tree with the following in mind:

- The [Root] object is always at the top of the tree, and only one [Root] object exists on a tree.

- Do not use Country objects unless there is a valid reason for using them, because they add little to the design of the tree, but do add an additional tree layer.
- WAN directory trees must have a unique name of the physical network. This name is the name you assign to the Organization unit, located directly below the [Root] object if no Country object is used.
- The Organization object name should represent the company's name.
- Place the first layer of Organizational Unit objects below the Organization object, and assign those objects names that reflect a regional location, such as a country.
- Place the second layer of Organizational Unit objects below the first layer of Organizational Unit objects and assign those objects names that reflect a more limited location, such as a city.
- Verify that the directory tree design resembles the shape of a pyramid, except when the company has two or more distinct business units that function like separate companies. The directory tree also may not resemble a pyramid when the entire network is located in one geographical area and no future expansion is expected or planned, or when the network uses high-speed, reliable links for connection. In addition, if parts of the network use dial-up lines (generally requiring modems) to connect distant offices, a pyramid shape may not be appropriate.

As you design the top layer of the WAN directory tree, consider any planned future changes, anticipated growth, acquisitions, and so on. Then, design the tree along the guidelines given for designing a WAN. Once the upper layer of the directory tree is designed, you and the project team can begin the design of the lower layers of the tree. As long as you design the directory tree following Novell's recommendations, its organization will be reasonably logical and intuitive.

A logical and intuitive pyramid-like design is important for two reasons. First, partitioning the network is generally easier to do when the directory tree is designed in a pyramid shape. Second, a pyramid-shaped directory tree reduces the number of subordinate reference replicas that must be generated in order to track partitions.

Designing the Lower Layers of the Directory Tree

Unlike designing the upper layers of the tree, the design of the lower layers can have a substantial effect on all the objects within the tree, because the lower layers of the tree encompass all other objects on the network. To ensure that the effect is positive, design the lower layers of the directory tree so that users with common access needs to various objects are placed in the same container. Users with common resource needs are also generally located physically close together in the company. It is, therefore, often easier to design the lower layers of the directory tree to follow the company's organization chart.

Using the company's organization chart makes it easier to group objects together within network containers. It also makes it easier to group objects for common access. Designing the upper layer of the WAN directory tree to resemble the geographical distribution of the company is Novell's recommended method. Designing the lower layers of the WAN directory tree to follow the company's organization chart is also Novell's recommendation. Once you have designed the upper and lower layers of the directory tree to follow these recommendations, you are then ready to review and, if needed, revise the tree design.

Reviewing and Revising the Tree Design

As stated, the first draft of the upper layer of the WAN directory tree should follow the geographic distribution of the company. For example, the first layer of Organizational Units could be divided into regions when the company covers multiple countries.

The lower layers of the WAN directory tree should follow the company's organization chart. For example, Organizational Units could reflect departments or divisions within the company. Put together, the initial draft of the directory tree design will likely include four or five layers, starting at [Root] and ending at company departments or divisions.

The tree design should not include containers for individuals. Corporate vice presidents, for example, should not be the key to directory tree organization. The Organizational Unit should reflect the division, or department, not the vice president in charge of that division (see fig. 6.8).

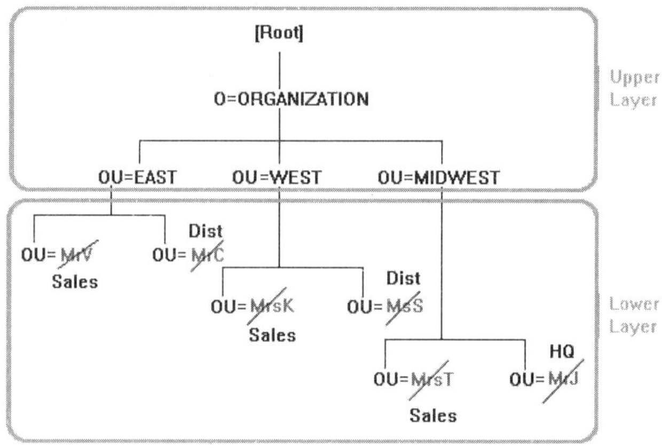

Figure 6.8
The right and wrong ways to name containers.

After ensuring that the upper layer and first couple of levels of the lower layer of the directory tree's design reflect the company's topology and corporate organization, the next step is to apply any special design considerations that may be applicable. To do that, you need to review the tree design, then review special considerations. Special considerations include the following, and should be applied to the design of the directory tree when they are applicable:

- *Whether containers as designed are logical, based on where resources are currently located.* Containers designed to follow a logical organization help ensure that user access is relatively easy and intuitive. To ensure that containers are logically organized, consider the current physical location of network resources.

For example, assume that a company's accounts payable personnel are all located in one office area and that their printers and NetWare 4 file servers are also located in the same physical area. It is therefore logical to organize a portion of the directory tree to include a container for the accounts payable group, and then to place all the accounts payable group User, Printer, and File Server objects into that container.

- *Whether the network will be administered from a central location or spread out among network administrators located in various geographical areas.* The use of centralized versus decentralized administration affects the lower layers of the directory tree design as well. If administration will be centralized, the directory tree design should have a limited number of lower layers. The fewer the layers, the easier it will be for administrators to navigate the network and even just to view a larger portion of the directory tree at a time.

  Centralized administration is easier to handle if all file servers are placed in the same container, referred to as the server container. By locating all file servers in one container, network administrators find it easier to track file server activity. The use of a file server container, however, is better suited to a LAN or a MAN than it is to a WAN, because WANs generally have substantially more file servers to be administered.

  Decentralized administration spreads the network's manage and monitor functions out to administrators in various departments. This approach is particularly effective for WANs, because larger companies have not only a greater number of objects to administer, but they also have a greater number of people who can help administer the network. The decentralized approach to administration also often results in an increase in the number of layers at the lower level of the directory tree. Each network administrator has the right to create additional directory tree levels as needed, thus more directory tree levels are likely to be created when decentralized administration is used.

- *Whether multiple partitions will be created.* WANs require the use of multiple partitions. How many partitions and where they are located can affect the design of the lower layers of the directory tree. Whenever possible, design the lower layers of the directory tree so that partitions have containers for shared objects and resources, and so that partitioning will be easy.

  The number of objects within a partition will also affect how many partitions are necessary. When an excessive number of objects (5,000 or more) is in a single partition, it is easier to administer than if it is broken up into two or more partitions.

- *Whether and what types of login scripts will be used.* The container login script is a NetWare 4 login script that enables you to customize the environment for all users within that container. The customization occurs at the time each user logs in to the network. Because a container login script applies to all users whose User object is in the container, container login scripts can be used to customize the network environment for many different users.

  The use of container login scripts almost eliminates the need for user login scripts. Because managing a single container login script is much easier and less time-consuming than managing multiple user login scripts, you should design the lower layers of the directory tree to take advantage of container rather than user login scripts, whenever possible.

  As with user login scripts, you can use container login scripts to accomplish a variety of tasks. For example, use container login scripts to define drive mappings, issue capture statements, call menus, set configuration information, start executable files, and display messages.

  To use container login scripts successfully, group users with common resource needs into the same containers. If necessary, create additional container objects to accommodate the variety of resource needs through the use of container login scripts.

- *Whether bindery services will be provided.* Adding bindery services to the network makes it possible for users in a bindery-based (NetWare 2 or NetWare 3) environment to access resources on NetWare 4 file servers. Bindery services also accommodates the requirements of bindery-based applications that are not NDS-compatible to continue to function in a NetWare 4 network.

  To take advantage of bindery services, the directory tree must have bindery context set for each container in which bindery services will be needed. When designing the lower layers of the directory tree, consider whether bindery services will be needed, and for which containers bindery services will be activated (a maximum of 16 containers per NetWare 4.1 file server).

- *The possibility of future growth.* If you know the company is expecting to experience rapid growth, you should design the lower layers of the directory tree with that information in mind. Consider whether additional containers will be needed, where they are likely to go, whether another partition or two will be required, how many file servers will be added, how many other objects will be added, and so on.

  Even if the company presently has no major plans for growth, growth must still be considered when designing the lower layers of the directory tree. They may have to be designed to accommodate the possibility of geographic or resource expansion.

  The best way to determine future changes that may affect the design of the lower layers of the directory tree may be to discuss options or possibilities with company management. Even when management has no plans for acquisition, internationalization, expansion, and so on, things change without notice, and the project team should try to at least consider how changes might affect the design of the directory tree.

Start tree design with the upper layer and design it so that it resembles the company's regional distribution. Next, design the tree's lower layers to reflect the company's organization chart.

Then, review the entire directory tree design and revise if needed to accommodate the type of administration the network will receive. Review the design and revise as needed to accommodate partitioning, the location of physical devices on the network, login script usage, and bindery services.

Once you take all these factors into consideration, the final task in the design process is that of creating the directory tree's structure.

Creating the Directory Tree Structure

To create the NDS directory tree structure, you can install or migrate the first NetWare 4 file server, then create the container objects you designed for the upper and lower layers of the directory tree. If you do not yet want to migrate or install a NetWare 4 production file server, you can create the directory tree structure on a file server in the lab. When you are ready to begin migrating the network, you can place the lab file server into production. The directory tree structure will then already be in place when you begin installing and migrating NetWare 4 file servers.

If you prefer not to create the directory tree using a lab server or a production server, there is another option. You can use an automated NDS modeling and migration program. Novell and a company called Preferred Systems worked together to codevelop an NDS modeling and migration product called DS Standard. You can use DS Standard (available from Novell) to create the WAN directory tree structure.

You can use DS Standard to create the objects needed to establish the WAN directory tree structure and also to capture existing bindery-based file servers and automate the analysis and migration of their flat database files into the NDS database.

If you choose to use DS Standard, you can do so without interfering with normal network production activities, because it uses a back-end database that will not interfere with the network database on your existing production network. Once you run DS

Standard and create the WAN directory tree structure, you can move the DS Standard database into the live NetWare 4 network environment.

Although DS Standard does not support every NetWare 4.1 object property, it is still sufficiently functional. You can use it as a tool to create the basic directory tree structure. You will have to purchase DS Standard separately, however, because it does not ship with NetWare 4.

DS Standard is relatively easy to use. A brief description of how to use it is included here to help you determine whether you might want to take a look at it. Providing basic information here lets you get a glimpse of DS Standard, without all the associated marketing hype.

DS Standard is relatively easy to install and use. It is an MS Windows-based program, so it is installed by choosing the Run option from the MS Windows Program Manager File pull-down menu. To install DS Standard, run the SETUP.EXE file, contained in the DSSTD directory on the DS Standard CD-ROM.

To create the WAN directory tree by using DS Standard, you first connect to the network. You must have the NetWare DOS Requester loaded on the workstation. Next, you use the Discover process to collect information from the binderies on existing NetWare 3 file servers, as well as from the NDS database on existing NetWare 4 file servers. DS Standard then uses this information to create the mockup of the directory tree. This entire process is a passive one because it makes no changes to the production environment. It only models the existing production environment to create the DS Standard version of the NDS directory tree.

To start DS Standard once it is installed, choose the DS Standard icon from the DS Standard group. Once the DS Standard window opens, choose New View from the File pull-down menu. Next, fill in the Enter New View Information window and choose OK (see fig. 6.9).

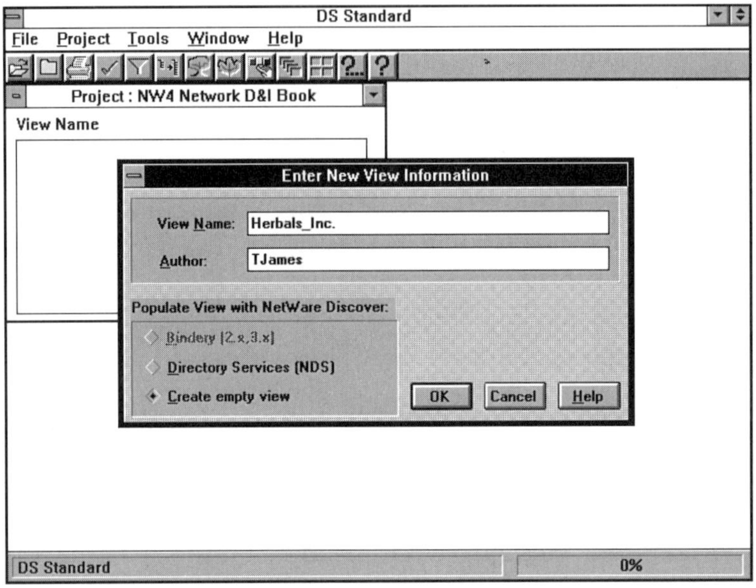

Figure 6.9
DS Standard's Enter New View Information dialog box.

When filling in the Enter New View Information window, give the directory tree design you will be creating a View Name, then fill in the Author Name field. Next, choose from the darkened button options. If you are currently logged into a NetWare network that is bindery-based, you can choose to read the bindery to help create the directory tree structure. If you are logged in to a bindery-based network, the Bindery [2x,3x] button will be darkened. If you are logged into an existing NetWare 4 network, the Directory Services [NDS] button will be darkened. If you prefer to create a view manually, without taking information from the existing network, mark only the Create Empty View button, which will also be darkened, indicating that it is an available option.

Once you choose OK to create the view, the process that occurs depends on the buttons that you marked. For example, if you marked the Directory Services [NDS] button, the discovery process occurs, and the [Root] object of the tree is placed into the view. If you then choose the Expand Tree button from the NDS Discover window, the full NDS tree is displayed (see fig. 6.10).

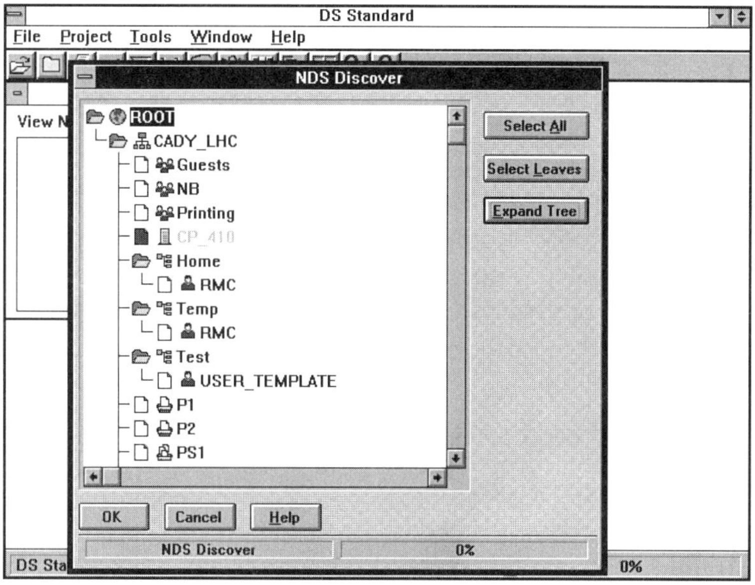

Figure 6.10

NDS Discover window.

You can then save the resulting view, modify it as needed, or exit DS Standard (choose Cancel) to close the view without saving it.

Using DS Standard helps you create the directory tree structure without affecting your existing network. This can be a particularly useful tool for those of you who are consultants, resellers, and so on, and those who are responsible for creating NetWare 4 networks for multiple companies.

Besides creating the directory tree, you may be called upon to create and implement partitions, as well as to establish and place the replicas. Running DS Standard will not do this for you. You must either implement the partitioning and replication strategy yourself or turn that part of network design and implementation over to the network administrators who will be responsible for the network. Either way, before the partitions can be created and replicated, you and the project team must determine the partitioning and replication strategy that best suits your network.

Establishing a Partition Approach

Partitions are portions of the NDS directory tree that contain one or more network container objects and the leaf objects contained within those container and various leaf objects. There are two types of partitions: parent and child. A child partition is any partition that is subordinate to (immediately below) another partition. A parent partition is any partition immediately above another partition.

To partition the directory tree, you divide it into sections. Replicas (copies of partitions or instances of the NDS tree) of each partition can then be stored on different NetWare 4 file servers throughout the network. Distributing replicas across the network provides fault tolerance and limits network traffic by placing database information close to where it is most needed.

By default, the NetWare 4 installation process creates one partition and places first the Master replica, and then two Read/Write replicas onto the first three NetWare 4 file servers installed into the directory tree. This default partitioning and replication strategy is usually sufficient for small networks, but it is not sufficient for WANs. You must, therefore, consider where partitions will be placed and how many partitions are to be used. In other words, you and the project team are responsible for determining the approach you will take to establish partitions on the directory tree.

To protect the [Root] from irreparable damage, it may be best to begin by separating [Root] into its own partition. The [Root] partition may also include the Country object, if used, and the company Organization object.

When deciding the best approach to take to partition the network, there are several other guidelines and rules to follow. The most important of these rules is simply stated as *Do not span the WAN.* This means that a single network partition should include only one geographic region.

There are eight guidelines you should follow when establishing a partitioning approach for your wide area network. Following these guidelines helps to ensure that the partitioning approach continues to serve the needs of the network for some time to come.

Guidelines for Partitioning the WAN Directory Tree

The following are eight guidelines that Novell recommends for determining the best partitioning strategy for a wide area network:

- Use default partitions where appropriate.
- Do not create partitions across the WAN.
- Consider using multiple partitions if needed.
- Eliminate partitions with fewer than 100 objects.
- Plan multiple partitions to keep objects together.
- Group file servers on a single cable segment.
- Design partitions for the upper layer of the tree.
- Avoid increasing administrative overhead.

As explained in Chapter 4, when the first NetWare 4 file server is installed into the directory tree, a single partition is created. It contains the [Root] object, the Country object (if used), Organization object(s), and any Organizational Units and leaf objects created in the directory tree. The use of a single partition is the default, but it is insufficient for wide area networks. You and the project team must, therefore, determine how best to modify the default partitioning approach to accommodate a WAN.

Most likely, you will need to create multiple partitions in order to accommodate the size of most WANs. You probably need to create multiple partitions for the directory tree if you can answer no to any one or more of the following questions:

- Is the entire network physically situated in a single geographic location?
- Does the network have 15 or fewer file servers that will hold replicas?
- Does the network contain fewer than 5,000 objects per partition?

Adding partitions to the network is necessary to accommodate a geographically dispersed network, which is just what a wide area network generally is. You should also add partitions if there are more than 15 network file servers being used to store partition replicas or more than 5,000 objects in the default partition.

As part of the partitioning approach, you should also be able to determine when you may have designed too many partitions. Having too many partitions on the network has costs associated with it. The more partitions you add, the greater the network administration. Each additional partition requires that three replicas exist for it if the network is to be considered sufficiently fault tolerant. Each replica, including associated subordinate references, has to be managed by NDS. The more partitions on the network, the more replicas. The more replicas on the network, the more NDS administration required to manage those replicas.

The more partitions the network has, the more partitions NDS must navigate in order to locate the resource for which it is searching. This fact slows the process of locating resources and causes NDS to take longer to resolve names when multiple partitions exist.

In some instances, the additional management overhead and tree navigation result in increased network traffic. Much of the time, users will not notice the increased network traffic, but network administrators may.

The ultimate goal is to design the partition approach so that it makes the network more efficient. You merely need to balance the overhead associated with an increased number of partitions against the benefits.

The second guideline—do not create partitions across the WAN—is particularly important when determining the partitioning strategy for the network. When applying this principle, remember that if the company has offices that are connected to each other over geographic distances, make separate partitions for each office. A single partition should not include more than one geographic region, because the cost of keeping partition replicas updated across the WAN often exceeds the related benefits.

Create additional partitions to help distribute the workload associated with storing the NDS database and user access to that database. Creating additional partitions to distribute NDS' workload also helps to minimize associated costs and optimize network use.

When choosing to create additional partitions, you should also consider the following information:

- Each partition on the network should be able to handle 5,000 objects easily—although theoretically, it can handle an unlimited number of objects. More than 5,000 objects, however, becomes unwieldy to manage and may slow network performance or response.
- Do not create or eliminate partitions with fewer than 100 objects. Partitions of this size tend to increase administrative overhead, increase the time it takes to navigate the directory tree, and sometimes increase network traffic.
- Plan multiple partitions to keep objects together. User objects should be located in the same container as the network resources they need to use to make navigation easier for users and name resolution and tree walking easier for NDS.
- If possible, group file servers on the same cable segment so that replicas of a partition will be kept locally. Keeping the file servers containing replicas of a partition on the same network cable segment means that replica updates will be quicker and more reliable because routers and bridges will not have to be crossed when updating occurs.

- When possible, design partitions around the upper layers of the directory tree, flowing down to include lower layers within the partitions. Partitioning from the top of the tree down, rather than vice versa, helps maintain the integrity of tree design, and makes the process of creating partitions much easier. It also helps prevent you from creating too many partitions, or from creating partitions where they may not really be needed.

To avoid increasing administrative overhead, consider what trade-offs can be utilized between designing partitions to meet the network's needs and designing partitions to make administration as simple as possible. What trade-offs may exist and how they can best be used is one of the issues that you and the project team must work on in order to design the most effective partition strategy for your network.

Rules Associated with Partitioning

When creating a partitioning strategy, there are five main rules that you must follow, in addition to the eight guidelines previously discussed:

- Partitions will contain only information about the NDS database. No information about the file system is stored in the NDS database, even though you can see the file system by using the NetWare Administrator utility. When designing partitions for the directory tree, therefore, do not consider the directory structure of a NetWare volume in the design.
- Each NDS object, including container objects, can exist in only one partition. No NDS object can be placed in more than one partition; thus partitions cannot cross containers.
- Replicas of NDS partitions are stored on NetWare 4 file servers. Only NetWare 4 servers can hold NDS partitions. Other versions of NetWare file servers cannot be used to store partitions.

- No partition's boundaries can overlap another partition's boundaries. Objects can be contained within only one partition. Thus, partition boundaries cannot overlap, or objects would be part of more than one partition.
- Each partition must contain a connected subtree. A single container object must have at least one other container or leaf object contained within it before it can be a partition.

When designing partitions, also remember that partitions can be created only at the container level. You cannot create partitions at a leaf object. In addition, also remember that, although you can store multiple replicas on a single file server, you can only store one replica of any single partition on a server.

By designing the upper layers of the directory tree to form the shape of a pyramid, there will be only a few containers in the upper layers. There will be fewer partitions near the upper layers of the directory tree and more partitions at the lower layers. The lower layers will thus contain the majority of the container and leaf objects. Because of the pyramid shape of the tree, your partitions will also follow a pyramid shape, particularly if you create each partition close to the leaf objects.

If you choose, you can also let the [Root] object remain as a partition itself. This helps ensure that transactions and problems on the network cannot corrupt the directory tree's [Root] partition. A [Root] partition that is corrupted beyond repair, or for which no usable replica is available, requires that the entire directory tree structure be recreated in order to once again have a usable NDS directory tree.

Planning Replicas and Their Placement

Part of planning partitions is considering where replicas will be placed. Part of planning replica placement is understanding the types of replicas that you can create. The other part of planning replicas and their placement on the network is understanding where to place those replicas in order to facilitate tree walking (accessing specific information in the directory tree, also referred to as the name resolution process).

Because Chapter 4 discussed replica types in detail, only a quick review of replica types is provided here. From that review, you can then begin to plan replicas for your network.

There are four types of replicas: Master, Read Only, Subordinate Reference, and Read/Write.

The Master replica is the first instance of the partition. It is created when the partition is created and can be used by NDS to log a user in to the network. It is stored on the NetWare 4 file server from which the partition itself was created. Only one Master replica can exist on the network for each partition.

The Read Only replica is an exact duplicate of the Master replica, but it cannot be used for network login because it cannot be written to, a prerequisite for NDS' login of a network user.

The Subordinate Reference replica is created by NDS and cannot be created or changed by any network user. The subordinate reference does not contain object information. Instead, the Subordinate Reference replica is a pointer, indicating where one of the other three types of replicas (Master, Read/Write, or Read Only) of a child partition can be found, when one of the other types of replicas does not exist on the same file server as a replica of that child's parent partition.

The Read/Write replica is an exact duplicate of the Master replica, and because it is a writable replica, it can be used by NDS to log a user in to the network. As with the Master replica, the Read/Write replica can also be used to add or delete objects and view NDS directory information.

Only one Master replica for a partition can exist on the network. Multiple Read/Write replicas for a partition can exist on the network, although only one copy of any type of replica for a single partition can exist on a single file server.

Because of their flexibility, Read/Write replicas are found more often on the network than any of the other types of replicas. The Read/Write replica, therefore, is the type of replica most often created and placed by network administrators. That also makes it the replica that requires the most placement planning.

You must consider where Read/Write replicas will be placed when determining the network's replica strategy. To determine successfully how many Read/Write replicas should be used and where they should be placed, there are several issues to consider:

- Develop the partition strategy to ensure fault tolerance. Plan for a minimum of three replicas per partition. Those three replicas must be placed on three different file servers on the network. The Master replica is created by default when the partition is created, so the project team has to determine where to place a minimum of two Read/Write replicas.

Note By default also, but only for the first network partition, two Read/Write replicas are created. The first Read/Write replica is placed on the second file server installed in the directory tree. The second Read/Write replica is placed on the third file server installed in the directory tree. Thus, you will have to plan additional replicas only for additional partitions, or to place writable replicas on file servers close to users to expedite the login process.

- If you create more partitions than those created by NDS by default, create additional replicas for those partitions.
- Develop the partitioning strategy to consider the NDS restriction that only one replica of a partition can exist on a file server.
- Place a writable replica on file servers closest to users to facilitate network login.

One other guideline to remember when planning replicas is their space requirements. Each object contained within a replica requires approximately 3 to 5 KB of space on the SYS volume. When planning replica placement, consider the amount of space each file server currently has available on the SYS volume.

When planning the replication strategy, you must consider the types of replicas to be used, how many will be used, and on which file servers they will be placed. In addition, other items of import must be considered. Consider how the replication can be designed and implemented to facilitate tree walking, support bindery services, and control Subordinate References.

Facilitating Tree Walking

The simplest way to facilitate tree walking when developing the replication strategy is to place writable replicas of the partition containing the User object and other resource objects the user needs to access on a file server closest to the user's physical location. If a copy of the replica is located close to the user, NDS does not have to look very far to find the information it needs to log users in and authenticate them to the network.

In addition, you should originally design network partitions to keep related objects together within partitions. For example, users who need access to a specific printer and application program should have the related printing services objects in the same container as their User objects. They should also have at least a Directory Map object pointing to the location of the application contained within the same container as the User object.

Support Bindery Services

NetWare 2 and NetWare 3 users can access resources on a NetWare 4 network if bindery services are installed on the network's NetWare 4 file servers. When bindery services are installed, NDS accepts bindery-based calls made by clients and applications. NDS imitates the flat structure of the NetWare bindery making it possible for bindery-based applications to make calls to NDS, and for bindery-based clients to log in to the NetWare 4 network using the older NETX shell. By imitating the flat structure of the NetWare bindery, NDS can see bindery objects, users, groups, print queues, print servers, and so on, and respond to requests made from bindery-based applications and clients.

When developing the network's replica strategy, consider where bindery services need to exist on the network in order to provide the support that users and applications will need.

When planning bindery services, also remember that the most important issue is where the bindery services feature is enabled (the server's bindery context). Up to 16 container objects in the NDS tree can have bindery services context set for them. Carefully determine, therefore, which containers need to have bindery services enabled—and plan for it.

Control Subordinate References

As noted previously, a subordinate reference replica is a pointer that ensures that the parent partition and its child partitions have a permanent connection to each other. The subordinate reference is used as a pointer to identify the location of replicas of child partitions when another type of replica for those child partitions is not stored on the same file server as the replica for the parent partition.

Subordinate references are created automatically by NDS. They contain only the *partition root object* (the container object at the top of the partition). The name of the file server is stored in the replica list of the partition.

To prevent too many subordinate reference replicas from being created by NDS and thus increasing network traffic, try to design the replication strategy so that there will not be a large number of child partitions without replicas other than the Subordinate Reference replica on the same file server. Where possible, condense the file servers that hold replicas. Use only a few reliable file servers to hold replicas.

There are other ways to reduce the number of subordinate references; the best way is to reduce the number of file servers holding replicas of the parent partition, beginning with the [Root] partition. Group storage of replicas onto a few file servers whenever possible. This approach must be considered against the need for writable replicas located on file servers close to users. If possible, accomplish both goals when you design the replica strategy.

Another way to reduce the number of subordinate reference replicas on the network is to place Read/Write or Read Only replicas of child partitions on the same server as the parent partition. Be careful, however, not to create too many of these replicas. Because Subordinate Reference replicas are only pointers, only changes in the location of the other types of replicas generally require that the Subordinate Replica be updated. Changes such as expanding or decreasing the border of a partition can require updates of other types of replicas.

Remember that replicas should be planned and then placed to accomplish fault tolerance, make network navigation easy for users, and provide quick access to the network. When planning replicas and where they should be placed, you can accomplish these goals if you attempt to design and implement a replica strategy that considers the following guidelines:

- Provide a minimum of two Read/Write replicas for each partition. This is in addition to the Master replica created at the time the partition is created.
- Partition the [Root] from the rest of the tree to ensure directory tree integrity, and replicate it as recommended in the first guideline.
- If not done at the time each partition was originally created, place replicas of partitions on file servers closest to the users whose User objects and needed resources are contained within the partition.
- Create additional replicas if necessary to accommodate bindery services.
- Ensure that the failure of a single file server will not make directory tree access impossible for any or all of the network.

Once the replica strategy is created, you can then move to the next procedure in the Design phase of the NetWare 4 network design and implementation process—planning time synchronization.

Planning Time Synchronization on a WAN

As noted earlier, the purpose of time synchronization is to ensure that all file servers in the directory tree use a coordinated time. NetWare 4 applies a time and date stamp to each network transaction. This is then used to ensure that each transaction is processed in the proper order. Time synchronization is particularly important when it comes to NDS directory replication and partitioning.

When planning time synchronization for a WAN, you need to consider three related items:

- Time source
- Time server types
- Time server communication method

These three items were discussed in some detail in Chapter 4. There is one additional issue to explore here, however—the time provider group.

Unlike a LAN or MAN, which generally finds the default of one Single Reference time server and multiple Secondary time servers to be acceptable, WANs generally do not. On a WAN, if you used the default approach, time synchronization would occur across the WAN for many networks. Not only would this be a costly approach to time synchronization, it would also cause increased network traffic. For a WAN implementation, the best time synchronization approach is generally to use a time provider group.

A *time provider group* consists of a combination of Reference, Primary, and Secondary time servers (see fig. 6.11). Single Reference time servers are never included in a time provider group because they are sole time providers (dictators).

Figure 6.11
Sample time provider group.

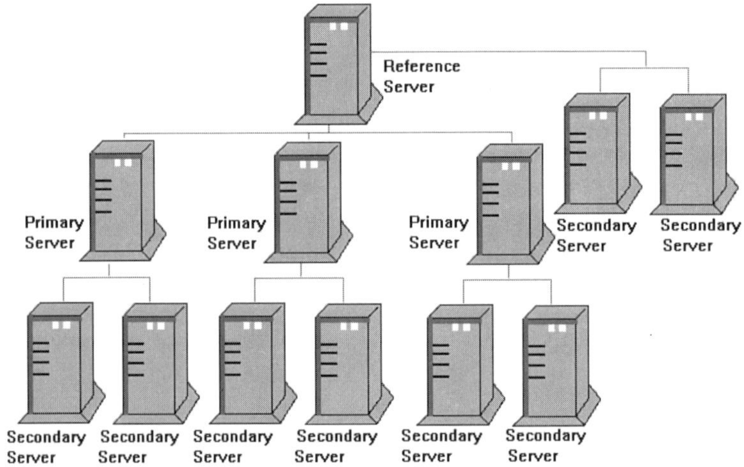

In a time provider group, Primary and Secondary servers can synchronize time with Reference servers. Secondary servers can also synchronize time with Primary servers. The Reference server provides time to which all other time servers (as well as client workstations) can synchronize.

The Reference server is synchronized to an external time source. The Reference server acts as the central point by which to set network time. Primary servers synchronizing with a Reference server will eventually have their time set based on the time established by the Reference server, because Reference servers do not adjust their internal clocks, but Primary servers do.

In many WANs, a single Reference server is used to synchronize time for the entire network. When WANs are substantially geographically dispersed, it may be better to use more than one Reference server, thus creating more than one time provider group. If you decide to use multiple time provider groups, ensure synchronized network time by using the same external source from which the Reference servers obtain their time.

Remember when designing the time synchronization approach that Primary and Reference time servers must be able to contact each other for time polling and voting. Thus, Primary and Reference servers must be connected with a permanent connection. In other words, it is impractical to attempt to connect Primary and Reference servers across a dial-up line.

When designing a time synchronization strategy for the WAN, remember that Secondary time servers do not participate in polling and voting. They do need to contact a Primary or Reference server, however, in order to synchronize time. Keeping Secondary time servers in relatively close proximity to Primary or Reference servers should also be considered when designing the network's time synchronization strategy.

Time Server Communication Methods

In addition to the types of time server and time provider groups you will use on the network, you must also consider communication issues when determining the network's time synchronization strategy. Time servers must communicate with each other in order to either provide or consume time. There are two communication methods used for time synchronization:

- Service Advertising Protocol (SAP) method
- Custom configuration method

The SAP method is the default method. It is the easiest to work with because it does not require any special configuration or manipulation in order to function effectively. The SAP method also does not require the use of a TIMESYNC.CFG file, although you can issue some related `SET TIMESYNC` commands at the file server console to perform some configuration. The custom configuration method requires the use of a configuration file called TIMESYNC.CFG.

In the SAP method of time server communication, Primary, Reference, and Single Reference servers use SAP to announce their presence on the network. Time consumers accept the SAP announcements, but do not use SAP to communicate with time providers on the network.

The custom configuration method uses a list of time providers to determine which time servers should communicate with which other time servers. Using the custom configuration method enables absolute control over network time server communication, which is the main reason the custom configuration method is generally used when creating the time configuration strategy for WANs.

The greatest drawback associated with custom configuration is that no time server communication will occur if the time server included on another time server's list cannot be located. Mistakes in the time server configuration list can, therefore, substantially affect time synchronization. If a time server exists on the network and is providing an incorrect time, time synchronization on the network may be seriously and negatively impacted.

When determining the best time synchronization strategy for your WAN, consider using the time provider groups as mentioned previously, which also generally require that you use custom TIMESYNC.CFG files.

Use TIMESYNC.CFG files and thus custom configuration when your WAN has more than 30 file servers or is geographically dispersed. To customize time configuration successfully by using the TIMESYNC.CFG file, place the following two types of SET parameters into the TIMESYNC.CFG file:

- Parameters that control how time synchronization functions
- Parameters that determine how time synchronization is handled

Note Time synchronization parameters can also be placed in the AUTOEXEC.NCF file, but not in the STARTUP.NCF file, because the TIMESYNC.CFG file is read after the STARTUP.NCF file.

Most of the time servers on the network use the same TIMESYNC.CFG file. The one difference is likely to be in the `SET TIMESYNC` *`time_source`* parameter where the *`time_source`* (name of the file server that is to be contacted in order to obtain time for synchronization) specifies the exact file server being used to provide time to this file server.

`SET` commands to be used in the configuration file on a WAN are likely to be the following:

- `SET TIMESYNC Service Advertising = OFF`
- `SET TIMESYNC Configure Sources = ON`
- `SET TIMESYNC` *`time_source`*
- `SET TIMESYNC Add Time Source`
- `SET Default Time Server Type`

Setting service advertising to `OFF` prevents the use of SAP for time synchronization. This parameter affects only time providers, however, and does not affect time consumers (Secondary time servers).

Setting configure sources to `ON` causes time servers to ignore SAP information. They listen instead only to those time providers that are included in their configuration list.

The `SET TIMESYNC` *`time_source`* parameter specifies which file server this file server is to use to obtain the time for synchronization. The `SET TIMESYNC Add Time Source` also causes the file server to select a time source from its configuration file before listening to any SAPs that may be sent across the network.

The `SET DEFAULT Time Server Type` can be used to override the Secondary default time server type on a file server.

When planning time synchronization on a NetWare 4 wide area network, keep the following in mind:

- Use Reference, Primary, and Secondary time servers on a WAN to prevent crossing the WAN to synchronize network time.

- Because Single Reference server is a time dictator, it cannot share time with other providers. Do not, therefore, use a Single Reference server on a WAN. The loss of the Single Reference server means time synchronization will be temporarily lost.
- Use a reliable time keeper for the Reference time server, and as far as possible, place it in a central location on the network.
- When the WAN has multiple sites, use multiple Reference servers that are all synchronized to the same precise external clock to ensure accurate synchronization. Using multiple Reference servers will prevent time synchronization traffic from having to cross a WAN link.
- When using multiple Reference servers, use a configured list of servers between sites to ensure that Reference servers communicate with Primary and Secondary servers only, and not with other Reference servers.
- Include a second Primary time server after listing the Reference server in the configuration file of each Reference server. If the Primary server loses its connection to the Reference server, the Primary server can contact another Primary server to continue the time synchronization process.
- Do not include more than seven Primary servers in a time provider group. Instead, create multiple time provider groups.

Most of the time providers on the network will be Secondary time servers. Secondary time servers can use either SAP for communication or a configured list. Enabling Secondary servers to use SAP for communication reduces the time synchronization maintenance network administrators may be required to perform, but does not provide absolute network control. As long as Primary and Reference servers are using configured lists for time synchronization, there should be no problem with using SAP communication for Secondary servers on a WAN.

Developing the Accessibility Plan

When developing the NetWare 4 network accessibility plan, first review users' needs and the needs of applications and other resources on the network. Consider whether all the application programs used on the network are capable of functioning in a NetWare 4 environment. If they are not, consider how you will make those applications available to users on the network.

You also need to consider what basic guidelines or standards for accessibility you and the project team will establish and follow. Once you determine the basic guidelines or standards for accessibility, document those guidelines in a company standards document. Be sure to include all guidelines or standards that may be applicable.

The document that specifies basic guidelines or standards for accessibility may include any or all of the following:

- If, how, and where login scripts will be used
- What settings will be placed in each workstation's NET.CFG file
- How accessibility will be provided for traveling or mobile users
- How the network will be designed to accommodate bindery services
- How network security will be provided

There also are several issues that must be considered when creating an accessibility plan, which often include the following:

- Workstation types
- NetWare operating system versions on the network
- Resources requiring bindery-based access

- Applications used on the network
- Hardware resources
- Network administration

In addition, guidelines for particular objects or properties may also have to be considered. The following are objects that may require special attention when developing accessibility guidelines:

- Group object standards may include information about the model to be followed when naming Group objects.
- Profile object standards may specify when a Profile login script should be used, and what should generally be included in a Profile login script.
- Organizational Role standards may specify when and how an Organizational Role object will be used, and how a user is to qualify for inclusion in an Organizational Role.
- Directory Map objects are used to point or refer to a specific directory on a network volume, and thus what they will be used for should be specified.
- An Inherited Rights Filters (IRF) exists for every object in the NetWare directory tree. Thus, the following should be included in the IRF standards: when the IRF should be used, when it should not be used, and how administrators will prevent others from accidentally or deliberately cutting off sections of the NDS directory tree from other administrators.
- User login scripts standards specify whether User login scripts should be used, when and how they should be used, and the kinds of information or types of commands that can be included or that must not be included.
- Alias objects are leaf objects that point to the original location of an object in the directory tree. When Alias objects will be used, the types of leaf objects they can point to, and similar issues should be discussed when specifying standards for Alias objects.

- Security-related issues should also be specified, including information such as the levels of container administrators that are to be created on the network, which rights should be assigned at the Organization object to enable those rights to flow to all users in the network, and other security-related issues.

As previously noted, part of developing the accessibility plan includes documenting all the decisions the project team has made regarding the network and how it is to be accessed. The following are most, if not all, of the decisions that should have information included about them in the standards document:

- Network structure overview
- Installation standards and procedures
- Object naming and property values
- Print services naming conventions
- Security configurations
- Time synchronization standards
- Partitioning and replication standards

The contents of each of these general categories of information are basically the same for WANs as they are for LANs and MANs, with a couple of exceptions. Chapter 4 discussed these general categories of information in detail; please refer to that chapter for details. The following discussion expands on that information specifically to relate to WANs.

Additional information associated with creating guidelines for accessibility for WANs falls into the following four categories:

- The network's structure
- Customized print services
- Customized security configurations
- The mobile network user

The next sections discuss each of these four accessibility issues based on how they affect or relate to a wide area network.

Overview of the WAN's Structure

By its nature, the network's structure determines at least some of the system requirements. For example, minimum hardware requirements for file servers must be met in order to load NetWare 4 onto a network file server. The fact that the network will be structured to run NetWare 4 thus sets minimum hardware equipment requirements.

The system's structure requirements can be divided into several categories. The most common categories of requirements that may need to be defined for a wide area network are the following:

- General network
- Network management
- Application
- Printing
- Information access
- Resource access
- Standards

General network requirements may address such issues as whether NetWare 4.1 will be required throughout the WAN, or whether NetWare 3 file servers can remain part of the network. Issues such as whether support for the MS Windows environment and applications designed to run in MS Windows will be provided may also be discussed as part of general network requirements.

Network management requirements may specify such things as whether management agents will be loaded on NetWare servers, and if so, which utility will be used. These requirements may also specify which network management alarms may be set and where alarms will be sent (management console, pagers, and so on).

Network infrastructure requirements may indicate the media to be used for production servers and network routers. They may also specify which routing protocol to use for each network protocol. For example, NLSP may be specified for IPX.

Application requirements may be used to specify the basis for or purpose of applications. For example, application requirements may specify that all or only some applications will be made readily available to network users. Which applications must be integrated into the network, or what applications other applications must be compatible with, may also be specified when application requirements are defined.

Printing requirements are likely to specify issues such as the use of point and click captures as a requirement. Other printing requirements may include the capability of dragging and dropping files onto printer objects as a method of sending a print request.

Information access requirements may specify how help information is to be provided to network users, such as through the use of online documentation. Other requirements may include information about Fax services, e-mail, and remote connectivity.

Resource access requirements may specify such things as what naming standards document is to be used when implementing e-mail. This requirements document may also specify such things as when and how the scheduling of resources should be handled.

Standards requirements may define requirements for hardware standards, file server uptime, and the use and reuse of equipment. This section may even define how standards requirements will be determined or modified, such as through a committee or by dictate.

Customized Print Services

In the NetWare 4 network, printing can be customized for users and applications that rely either on DOS or MS Windows. In NetWare 4 wide area networks, the default installation of print services is insufficient. Print services must be customized.

The first step in customizing print services for a WAN is to create the necessary NDS objects—Printer, Print Server, and Print Queue—being careful to locate them in the needed containers. Once print services objects are created, various NetWare utilities can be used to customize printing.

Printer control is provided to DOS applications using various NetWare utilities, the more common of which are the following:

- PRINTDEF is used to create custom definitions for network printers and forms.
- PRINTCON is used to establish print job configuration files, which then can be used by the CAPTURE, NPRINT, and PCONSOLE utilities to run custom print jobs (see fig. 6.12).
- CAPTURE is used to customize the network users' printing environments and accomplish a variety of printing-related tasks.
- NPRINTER is used to connect printers to workstations, which can then be accessed by other network users.
- NETUSER is used to add, modify, or delete print jobs.

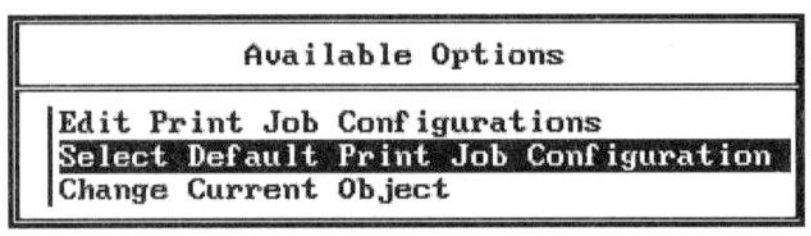

Figure 6.12
PRINTCON Available Options menu.

An MS Windows-based print services utility, called the NetWare Administrator, is also available to customize the network printing environment. By using this utility, you can create and administer printing services in the NetWare 4 environment, as well as accomplish all the following tasks:

- Create, control, monitor, and manage print queues
- Create, control, monitor, and manage print servers
- Delete, change, monitor, and reorder print jobs
- Assign print queue objects to printers and printer objects to print servers

In addition to the NetWare Administrator utility, you can also use MS Windows 3.1 to customize printing for each application requiring print support. If correctly set up and print customization information is not available elsewhere (such as in memory), MS Windows checks for print settings established in the WIN.INI file and uses those. If unavailable, MS Windows then uses the defaults in its own setup to complete a print request. To take full advantage of MS Windows printing, you may need to set up printing using the Printers dialog box in the MS Windows control panel (see fig. 6.13).

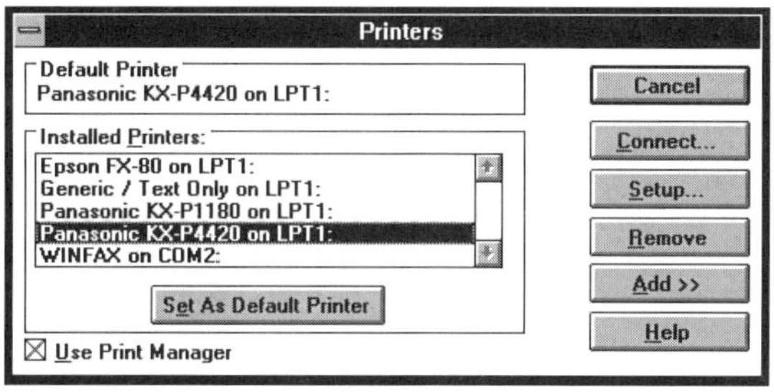

Figure 6.13
MS Windows Printers setup and configuration windows.

Regardless of the utilities that eventually will be used to customize printing in the NetWare 4 environment, customizing printing services is necessary in a NetWare 4 network. What, where, and how printing services customization will be done must therefore be considered and planned for when developing the network's accessibility plan.

Customized Security Configurations

Wide area networks generally require the use of multiple Organizational Role objects created throughout the tree to make it possible to utilize decentralized administration. Using Organizational Role objects makes it possible to assign various levels of administration responsibility to different containers on the network.

When needed, an Organizational Role object should be created for each network container. That object can then be given container administrative rights to the container in which it resides. The rights given to the Organizational Role object are then automatically granted to any user who is made an occupant of that role.

Varying levels of rights can be given to an Organizational Role object to control how much or how little administrative control the occupants of that role will have over the container. Each level can be referred to by a level number such as 0, 1, 2, and so on, or by a title. Title examples might include Admin (at the least restrictive level of 0), or Container Admin (which can be set to the most restrictive level of 5, or which can be set to a less restrictive level).

The least restrictive Admin level would be given full object and file system rights, beginning at the [Root] of the NDS tree. This Organizational Role object would have complete and total control over the NDS directory tree, including all objects contained within the tree and the directory and file system structure located on every volume on every file server in this tree. This Organizational Role object should thus be placed in a hidden directory tree location, preferably where no user except those with proper security access could ever see.

The least restrictive Admin level of the Organizational Role object should have only network-wide or enterprise-wide administrators assigned as occupants of that role. This Organizational Role object should never be occupied by any network administrator who does not have the complete confidence and support of the company's leading executive (chief executive officer, corporate president, and so on).

The most restrictive Organizational Role object should be reserved for occupants who require access to only a single container on or area or portion of the NetWare directory tree. The Container Admin assigned to this role may be given minimal rights to NDS objects within the specified container, being allowed to, for example, assign members to groups and modify login scripts. In addition, the user assigned to this role may or may not be given any rights to the file system.

Other examples of uses for Container Admins occupying special Organizational Role objects include help desk personnel, workstation specialists, application specialists, and printer specialists. Each of these network users may have some associated administrative responsibility. Defining what the Organization Role can and cannot do within the container to which it is assigned provides great flexibility when it comes to network security.

Accommodating the Mobile User

There are two types of mobile users on the NetWare 4 network: the remote user and the true mobile user. The remote user is a network user who accesses the network from a remote location by using a dial-in method such as a modem. Remote users, although dialing in from the outside, always access their *home containers* (the containers in which their User objects and needed resources are located).

The true mobile user may access the network either by using a dial-in method or directly from a workstation connected to the network. The main difference is that the true mobile user will be accessing whatever container can be accessed in order to locate needed resources. That container often is not the mobile user's home container.

Because the remote user has little impact on the network or its design, little consideration needs to be given to remote users when dealing with network design issues. The true mobile user, however, may have a substantial impact on the network and thus must be considered when dealing with network issues.

The true mobile user may be someone such as an account executive who is traveling to different company accounts. While on the road, the account executive may have a laptop for use from a hotel room. The account executive may also have a local workstation setup for use while on location.

Administering the network to accommodate mobile users can be accomplished in one of three ways:

- To train users to understand NDS, user login, and naming context, and to require them to set the correct context on whatever computer they use to log in to the network when they are traveling
- To set up login scripts that rely on a site location variable in the computer's CONFIG.SYS file to designate a home site name that makes it possible for users to log in from any location and still have the correct drive mappings established for them
- To create an Alias object below the Organization object for each mobile user on the network, and then have that Alias object point to the container within the directory tree where the traveling user's User object exists

Training mobile users may be a viable option in a WAN, but is not as reliable or permanent a method as are either of the other two. Employees come and go. Designing the company's mobile user strategy based on training individual users may mean that training mobile users is an ongoing process, depending on the length of time typical users who fill the mobile user spot stay with the company.

If you create a login script that mobile users can take advantage of, a single login script might suffice for all mobile users. Administering a single login script is simpler than continually training mobile users. It is an approach worth taking when the WAN has a large number of mobile users.

Creating an Alias object for each mobile user on the network and using those Alias objects to point to the mobile user's home directory may be effective. The problem is that its use is limited. Once the network begins to exceed 20 mobile users, creating and maintaining an Alias object for each mobile user can become very restrictive, time-consuming, and impractical.

Implementation strategies for mobile users on the network are shown in table 6.1.

Table 6.1
Mobile User Guidelines

Access Method	*Strategy*	*Associated Guidelines/Notes*
Laptop used for logging in anywhere	NET.CFG file	Set `Name Context=` parameter in the NET.CFG file on the laptop.
	Login script	Place the following lines into a container or Profile login script for a mobile user: `IF "%NETWORK_ADDRESS"="address" THEN; MAP INS S1:=server\SYS:PUBLIC; MAP G:=server\SYS:home_directory\ %LOGIN_NAME; END` *Note:* Use this when an IPX standard is used. Repeat these lines for each network address.
Alternative method for logging in from anywhere, using a laptop	AUTOEXEC.BAT	Place `SET NW_SITE=site`
	User login script on laptop	IF <NW_SITE>=="site" THEN BEGIN MAP ROOT M:=S4:= server\SYS:dir_path\app_file MAP ROOT W:=S16:= server\SYS:dir_path\app_file END EXIT *Note:* Use this alternative when the file system structure is the same throughout the network, replacing server with a file server name, SYS:dir_path with the volume and directory name where the

continues

Table 6.1, Continued
Mobile User Guidelines

Access Method	*Strategy*	*Associated Guidelines/Notes*
		application program is located, and app_file with the name of the executable program that runs the application. Repeat these lines for each application program to be run.
Logging in from anywhere, using local PC	CONFIG.SYS	Place `SET NW_SITE=`*`site`*

	Container or Profile login script	`IF <NW_SITE>=="`*`site`*`" THEN BEGIN`
		`MAP ROOT M:=S4:=`
		`server\SYS:dir_path\app_file`
		`MAP ROOT W:=S16:=`
		`server\SYS:dir_path\app_file`
		`END`
		`EXIT`
		Note: Very similar to previous method, but set the location variable in the CONFIG.SYS file instead of the AUTOEXEC.BAT file.

User Alias Object	Limited number of users	Place Alias objects for each mobile user under the Organization object, when 20 or fewer mobile users exist.
	Users splitting time between offices	Place Alias object in container where needed resources are located for containers that are not the mobile user's home container.

To accommodate mobile users on the network, also consider the location of partition replicas when planning for mobile user network access. When possible and reasonable, place a Read/Write replica of the container where the mobile user's User object exists on a file server close to where that user will be accessing the network when traveling. Bear in mind that if the replica is placed in a remote location, network traffic associated with database synchronization will increase.

When planning for mobile users, also consider the mobile user who has a dockable notebook or laptop computer. Because dockable workstations often function as regular workstations when the laptop computer is docked, and some manufacturers provide commands to determine whether the laptop is docked, special commands may need to be placed in the STARTNET.BAT file on the dockable computer. The relevant lines are placed after the command that loads the LSL.COM file, and they replace the standard command used to load the network board. These are the commands that may have to be placed in the STARTNET.BAT file on a dockable computer:

```
IF %DOCKED%==YES driver_name

IF %DOCKED%==NO NRN

IF %DOCKED%==NO DIALCON
```

Note In the first line, replace `driver_name` with the executable file that loads the network board driver for this computer. For example, if the network board installed in this computer is the NE2000 board, replace `driver_name` with `NE2000`.

Regardless of the approach you choose, you must establish a method for handling remote users. If your network has both types of traveling users—remote and mobile—you may want to specify how network access should be provided for each user.

Summary

The process of designing and planning a NetWare 4 wide area network is the second phase in the NetWare 4 design and implementation process. During this phase, you and the project team must accomplish the following four major NetWare 4 design and implementation procedures if the NetWare 4 network is to be beneficial to the company for which it was installed:

- Designing the WAN directory tree
- Establishing a partition and replication approach
- Planning a time synchronization strategy
- Developing an accessibility plan

There are a variety of procedures associated with this phase of the NetWare 4 design and implementation process. It is important to the network's success, however, that each procedure is given careful attention and that you and the project team learn how to follow the procedures associated with the NetWare 4 WAN design and implementation process.

To help you complete the design phase of the NetWare 4 design and implementation process successfully for every company with which you work, this chapter provides the details you need to know. Now that you have read and learned the material contained within this chapter, you should feel more confident about designing a NetWare 4 wide area network. To help ensure that you are as successful in the design and implementation of a NetWare 4 network as possible, this chapter summary provides a checklist to guide you when you design a NetWare 4 wide area network. This approach will help you review and remember the procedures, suggestions, guidelines, rules, and requirements associated with designing a NetWare 4 wide area network.

After having read this chapter, you should understand why the efficient and effective design of NetWare 4 WANs is important, and what you can do to help yourself and others be successful at designing the right WAN for each company. Use the following checklist to guide you.

- Design and plan the NetWare 4 WAN
  - Ensure fault tolerance by partitioning and distributing replicas
  - Provide for network growth through
    - The use of an Organization object at the top of the directory tree
    - Modifications in menus to ensure continued access to applications
    - The addition of Directory Map objects where appropriate
  - Simplify the addition of network services, such as applications and printers
  - Simplify network access for users by placing writable (Master or Read/Write) replicas containing User objects on file servers closest to the user
  - Organize objects for intuitive access
- Establish and document naming standards
  - Consider naming standard concepts that may affect design, such as the use of typeless versus typeful names, context, current context, common names, and distinguished versus relative distinguished names
  - Consider how users navigate the network as well as design issues that may affect it, such as the geographic distribution of the company and its resources and network access by traveling users
  - Determine whether IPX numbering standards will be used, or if randomly assigned IPX numbers are acceptable, for both of the following:
    - Internal IPX numbers
    - External IPX numbers

- ☐ Determine what will be placed into a naming standards document, then provide guidelines for each item and, where applicable, examples and additional information for each naming standard guideline

☐ Design upper layers of the directory tree to do the following:

- ☐ Follow a regional/geographical approach that reflects the network's topology and that will help reduce expenses associated with network traffic and accommodate the dynamic nature of NDS
- ☐ Make partitioning and replication as simple as possible while still providing sufficient fault tolerance
- ☐ Accommodate network growth and the potential for future changes and needs
- ☐ Be intuitive to use
- ☐ Provide secure access to shared resources
- ☐ Form a pyramid shape unless the following are true:
  - ☐ Network is located within one geographic area
  - ☐ Dial-up lines are used on the network
- ☐ Include a single Organization object instead of multiple Organization objects when the following does not apply:
  - ☐ The company has two or more distinct business units that function more like separate companies than as part of a single company
  - ☐ The entire network is located in one geographical area and no future expansion is planned or expected
  - ☐ The network uses high-speed, reliable links for all its network connections
  - ☐ The network includes dial-up lines, and those geographic areas using dial-up lines will be included in the directory tree

- Reflect one of the following three possible approaches when creating Organizational Unit (OU) objects below the Organization object:
  - Physical, which requires that an OU be created for each of the company's physical locations
  - Functional, which places OUs below the Organization object that reflect the operations or workgroups within a company that does not have WAN links
  - Combination, which uses a variety of OUs, some that may reflect the company's physical location and some that may reflect the company's operations or workgroups
- Follow Novell's recommended design guidelines:
  - The [Root] object is always at the top of the tree, and only one [Root] object exists on a tree
  - Do not use Country objects unless there is a valid reason for using them, because they add little to the design of the tree but do add an additional tree layer
  - WAN directory trees must have a unique name on the physical network. This name is the name you assign to the Organization unit located directly below the [Root] object if no Country object is used
  - The Organization object name should represent the company's name
  - Place the first layer of Organizational Unit objects below the Organization object and assign those objects names that reflect a regional location, such as a country
  - Place the second layer of Organizational Unit objects below the first layer of Organizational Unit objects and assign those objects names that reflect a more limited location, such as a city
  - Verify that the directory tree design resembles the shape of a pyramid, except as noted

- ☐ Design the lower layers of directory tree
  - ☐ Ensure that objects with common access needs are placed in the same container
  - ☐ Resemble the company's organization chart
  - ☐ Consider current and related issues, including the following:
    - ☐ Logical container design
    - ☐ Current location of physical resources
    - ☐ Central versus distributed network administration
    - ☐ Planned location of partitions
    - ☐ Types of login scripts to be used
    - ☐ Needs of bindery-based users and resources
- ☐ Consider future issues
  - ☐ The possibility of combining existing networks
  - ☐ The possibility of directory tree mergers
- ☐ Review and revise the directory tree design if the following are true:
  - ☐ It does not follow a geographic distribution at the upper layers and the company organization chart at the lower layers, but geographic and company organization would be most suitable
  - ☐ Changes are necessary to accomplish the following:
    - ☐ Ensure a logical design based on where current resources are located
    - ☐ Accommodate decentralized versus centralized administration
    - ☐ Ensure that a sufficient number of properly located partitions can be created

    - Accommodate the use of login scripts
    - Provide bindery services where needed
    - Enable future growth and expansion of the network
- Create the directory tree structure by using a lab server, a production server, or software, such as DS Standard, that enables you to model and migrate the existing network without interfering with the network's current operations
- Establish a partitioning approach
  - Consider whether default is sufficient
  - Eliminate partitions that will cross the WAN
  - Determine whether multiple partitions are necessary in order to accomplish the following:
    - Keep objects to 5,000 or fewer per partition
    - Keep related objects together
    - Eliminate partitions with fewer than 100 objects
  - Group file servers on a single cable segment
  - Design partitions from the upper layer down to the lower layers
  - Avoid increasing administrative overhead when no substantial benefits will result from that increase
- Follow rules for creating partition strategy
  - Partitions contain NDS information only
  - Each object can exist in only one partition
  - Partitions can be stored only on NetWare 4 file servers
  - Partition boundaries cannot overlap
  - Each partition must contain a connected subtree
- Create a replica strategy

- ☐ Consider the four types of replicas—Master, Read/Write, Read Only, and Subordinate Reference
- ☐ Ensure fault tolerance by providing a minimum of three replicas for each partition
- ☐ Place writable replicas on file servers closest to users to facilitate login
- ☐ Allow 3 to 5 KB of space on the SYS volume for each object contained within each replica
- ☐ Consider NDS's need to walk the tree
- ☐ Support bindery services
- ☐ Control the propagation of Subordinate References
- ☐ Partition the [Root] separately to protect it
- ☐ Ensure that failure of a single file server will not make the network inaccessible

☐ Plan a time synchronization strategy

- ☐ Consider the default time synchronization strategy
- ☐ Consider the use of a custom communication configuration method instead of the default SAP communication method
- ☐ Customize time synchronization by using TIMESYNC.CFG files as needed, including parameters that do the following:
  - ☐ Control how time synchronization functions
  - ☐ Determine how time synchronization is handled
  - ☐ `SET TIMESYNC Service Advertising = OFF`
  - ☐ `SET TIMESYNC Configure Sources = ON`
  - ☐ `SET TIMESYNC` *`time_source`*
  - ☐ `SET TIMESYNC Add Time Source`
  - ☐ `SET Default Time Server Type`

- Ensure that the following issues are kept in mind when planning time synchronization for a WAN:
  - Reference, Primary, and Secondary time servers should be used to prevent crossing the WAN when synchronizing network time
  - Single Reference servers should not be used on a WAN because they dictate rather than negotiate time, and the loss of the Single Reference server means time synchronization will also be lost
  - Use a reliable time keeper for the Reference time server, placed in a central location
- Use multiple Reference servers, all synchronized to the same precise external clock, to ensure accurate synchronization and to prevent time synchronization traffic from having to cross a WAN link
- When using multiple Reference servers, use a configured list of servers between sites to ensure that Reference servers communicate with Primary and Secondary servers only, and not with other Reference servers
- Include a second Primary time server after listing the Reference server in the configuration file of each Reference server to ensure that the Primary server can connect to another Primary server if the Primary server loses its connection to the Reference server
- Use multiple time provider groups if more than seven Primary servers in a single time provider group would otherwise be necessary

- Develop an accessibility plan
  - Review users' needs as well as the needs of applications and other network resources
  - Establish and document basic accessibility guidelines to be followed

- ☐ If, how, and where login scripts will be used
- ☐ Settings to be used in workstation configuration files
- ☐ Approaches to follow so that mobile users can be accommodated
- ☐ How and where bindery services will be accommodated
- ☐ Ways to customize security configurations

☐ Consider other related issues, such as workstation types, NetWare OS versions, bindery-services requirements, and so on

☐ Consider the use of various network objects, but in particular, consider objects such as Aliases, Directory Map, Groups, Inherited Rights Filter, login scripts, and Organizational Role

☐ Consider security-related issues, including in particular, the use of multiple Organizational Role objects created throughout the tree

☐ Consider how mobile users will be accommodated when the following are true:

- ☐ A laptop is used for logging in to the network from any location
- ☐ A local PC is used by traveling users when they are away from home and at other company offices
- ☐ Fewer than 20 mobile users exist on the network and Alias objects can be used to accommodate them
- ☐ A dockable laptop is used by mobile users

☐ Consider other issues that the project team included in the network's standards document, which should include the network's structure, installation standards and procedures, object naming and property value, print services naming conventions, security configurations, time synchronization strategy, and partitioning and replication standards

Case Study

The BJB company has 1,500 network users, a corporate office in Michigan, one sales office in Mexico, one in Canada, and one in the United States, and a manufacturing plant in Mexico. All offices and the manufacturing plant are connected through high-speed WAN links.

The directory tree consists of a single BJB Organization followed by an Organizational Unit for the Canada sales office. It also has a United States OU object and a Mexico OU object below the BJB Organization object. Below the Mexico OU object, two additional OU objects exist: one for the manufacturing plant (MNFT), and one for the sales office (SALES). Below the United States OU, two additional OUs exist: one for the sales office (SALES), and the other for the corporate office in Michigan (HQ).

There are four sales managers whose home office is in the Michigan office. These sales managers each have their own laptops, which they take with them on regular visits to the sales offices in the United States, Mexico, and Canada. These sales managers also make regular visits to suppliers throughout the United States and Mexico, as well as on-site visits to customers to ensure customer satisfaction.

As a consultant to the BJB company, you have been hired to develop a strategy for the network's enterprise administrator to implement, which will accommodate the four traveling sales managers. You must prepare a one-page overview of what the network's enterprise administrator must do in order to simplify access to the network by the traveling sales managers.

Review Questions

1. Which of the following is not associated with the process for correctly designing the directory tree?
   - A. establishing and documenting naming standards
   - B. organizing the upper layer of the directory tree around the company's geographical distribution
   - C. creating User objects
   - D. creating the directory tree design
2. The *two* advantages associated with using a single Organization object at the top of the directory tree are ___________.
   - A. rights can be set at the Organization object to affect all network users
   - B. it is the best way to design the network if you want to partition off the directory tree [Root]
   - C. merging directory trees is easier
   - D. it makes it possible to use a Country object
3. The ___________ directory tree organization approach is best used when the company has no WAN links or when only a single NetWare 4 file server exists on the network.
   - A. physical
   - B. functional
   - C. regional
   - D. combination
4. When designing the lower layers of a WAN, the most common approach is to ___________.
   - A. include an OU for each country in which the company does business
   - B. employ only three layers

- ○ C. design these layers in an inverted pyramid
- ○ D. follow the company's organization chart

5. When planning WAN partitions, ___________.

- ○ A. design them to reflect the upper layer of the tree
- ○ B. always use default partitioning
- ○ C. limit partitions to no more than 100 objects
- ○ D. regardless of the size of the WAN, group all file servers on the same cable segment

6. Which *three* of the following are rules associated with partitioning a NetWare 4 wide area network?

- ○ A. Directory information is stored in NDS.
- ○ B. Replicas can be stored only on NetWare 4 file servers.
- ○ C. Partition boundaries cannot overlap.
- ○ D. Each partition must contain at least one connected subtree.

7. The time server type *not* generally used on a WAN is the

- ○ A. Primary
- ○ B. Reference
- ○ C. Single Reference
- ○ D. Secondary

8. A collection of file servers used to provide time synchronization on a WAN is referred to as ___________.

- ○ A. a time provider group
- ○ B. a time synchronization group
- ○ C. a time reference group
- ○ D. a time server group

9. Which of the following is *not* generally included in an accessibility plan?
   - ○ A. settings that should be placed into workstation NET.CFG files
   - ○ B. the method for providing network security
   - ○ C. which login script types will be used
   - ○ D. a list of User objects to assume the Organizational Role

10. Which of the following is not a recommended option for dealing with mobile users?
    - ○ A. Train users to understand NDS, including context and how to navigate the network.
    - ○ B. Set up login scripts, which rely on a site location variable.
    - ○ C. Create Alias objects for mobile users to access.
    - ○ D. Set up a special container for remote users who access only their own home container.

Answers

1. C
2. A C
3. B
4. D
5. A
6. B C D
7. C
8. A
9. D
10. D

Chapter 7

Implementing the NetWare 4 Wide Area Network Plan

The NetWare 4.1 process associated with implementing the NetWare 4 WAN is identical to that of implementing the NetWare 4 LAN. Some of the procedures and steps that must be performed for a WAN implementation, however, are different from those followed in order to implement a LAN. In addition, there are some other differences.

For example, when implementing a WAN, some NetWare 4.1 file server installations may require the use of the Custom Install option rather than the Basic Installation option. In addition, wide area networks also often have non-NetWare file servers that will be upgraded to NetWare 4.1. WANs also frequently have a greater variety of workstation types, many of which include Macintosh or OS/2 workstations.

All of these differences, as well as the similarities, must be considered when implementing the NetWare 4 wide area network. This chapter discusses the process associated with implementing a NetWare 4.1 wide area network. Where appropriate, it revisits issues discussed in Chapter 5, "Implementing the NetWare 4 Local Area Network Plan," which relate to WANs as well as to LANs and MANs.

This chapter discusses the implementation phase of the Novell NetWare 4.1 Design and Implementation process, especially phase 6, Developing a Migration Strategy, and phase 7, Creating an Implementation Schedule of the NetWare 4 Design and Implementation process. In addition, and unlike the Novell NetWare 4.1 Design and Implementation course, this chapter also discusses the eighth phase, Implementing NetWare 4.

After reading this chapter, you will understand the procedures and steps associated with developing a migration strategy for a wide area network, creating an implementation schedule for a wide area network, and implementing NetWare 4 on a wide area network.

Developing the Migration Strategy

The first step required in order to develop a successful migration strategy for a NetWare 4 wide area network is to understand the process associated with it. Novell's Consulting Services group has defined three required procedures and one conditional one associated with developing a migration strategy:

- Creating a migration strategy for workstations
- Creating a migration strategy for file servers
- Creating a migration strategy for applications
- Setting up a testing lab

With a carefully planned migration strategy and implementation schedule in hand, those assigned to implement the network should be able to do so with few problems. The first step, therefore, is to create migration strategies for the three network resources that must be migrated—workstations, file servers, and applications.

Part of creating a migration strategy for these resources is verifying that the resources can be successfully migrated to NetWare 4. This is where a testing lab can be quite useful. As part of the migration process then, you should set up and utilize a testing lab. As the migration strategy is developed, the testing lab will help you verify that the strategy will be successful in the migration of the actual network.

Creating a Migration Strategy for Workstations

Developing a migration strategy for network workstations involves four major steps:

- Assessing existing network clients
- Determining typical workstation configurations
- Sharing new client software with administrators
- Creating the appropriate level of user training

To accomplish the first step—assessing existing network clients—you must determine what clients currently exist on the network. A list of existing network workstations is generally part of the network resources document and should have been made available to the project team early in the design and implementation process. Once this document is in hand, you must review it to obtain answers to a variety of related questions.

The following are questions related to existing network workstations that you need to answer in order to develop a successful workstation migration strategy:

- The total number of workstations on the network
- The types of workstations on the network
- The different types of operating systems that the workstations are currently running
- The version of each type of operating system currently used on workstations
- The client networking software (the older NetWare shell, an earlier version of the DOS Requester, and so on) currently used on workstations
- The version number or level of client network software currently used on each network workstation

There are other questions you need to ask and have answered in order to develop a strategy for migrating network clients. These questions are not as likely to be found on the resource list. User surveys, access of workstations using management software, and other approaches may have to be used to answer these questions. The following are some of the questions for which you may have to seek alternative methods of answering:

- Whether existing workstation configuration files are currently set up for network access
- Of the existing workstation configuration files that accommodate network access, which ones have to be modified to accommodate NetWare 4
- Whether network management tools are currently used
- What network management tools are currently used
- If network management tools are currently used, whether they will be used on the migrated network and whether they are NetWare 4-compatible
- Whether Large Internet Packet (LIP) or packet burst will be set for use at workstations
- Whether any applications are currently being stored on individual workstations, and if so, which applications

- Whether any applications on workstations are also to be used in the NetWare 4 environment and, if so, whether they are compatible with NetWare 4
- Which protocols are currently being used by network workstations
- Who is currently responsible for handling workstation-related problems and whether current workstation support will be sufficient when migration begins
- Whether workstations will be backed up by using SMS-compliant backup software
- Whether information sent between NetWare 4 file servers and workstations will require encryption

In addition to being able to answer these questions, you also need to know the current level of networking experience for each of the network's users. You may find that it will be necessary to train users to access and use the network. Part of developing a migration strategy for workstations may, therefore, include developing a related strategy for training network users. The company is not likely to be as successful at implementing the training strategy as it could be if you do not determine the user's level of networking knowledge before determining how to train network users. If planning for training is to be included in the migration strategy, therefore, you and the project team must be aware of how extensive that training may have to be.

To obtain answers to these and other types of questions and thus accomplish the development of a migration strategy, the project team must begin by assessing existing network clients, including workstations and users.

Assessing Network Clients

The first step in assessing network clients is to determine which operating systems are currently used on network workstations. Operating systems used may include MS DOS, Windows, Macintosh, and so on. Besides knowing what operating systems are being used, you must also know what versions of those operating systems are being used, because multiple versions of the same operating system are frequently found on workstations within wide area networks.

You must also assess the current status of workstation configuration files and determine whether they are compatible with NetWare 4. Most often, workstation configuration files will have to be modified. The minimum modification will include this command added to the NET.CFG file on the user's workstation to set the user's network name context:

```
Name Context = "user_context"
```

For example, if user TROSE's User object is in container SALES under the REGION1 container for BIG_SHOES, the name context statement would appear as the following:

```
Name Context = "OU=SALES.OU=REGION1.O=BIG_SHOES
```

Assessing existing clients means that other workstation configuration files, such as AUTOEXEC.BAT, CONFIG.SYS, and STARTNET.BAT, may need to be checked as well. You should check the workstations to determine whether these files exist at all, then proceed accordingly. Determining the existence and content of these files will answer questions for you, such as whether the workstation is currently using the NetWare shell or a version of the NetWare DOS Requester.

Note

If no STARTNET.BAT file exists, it is likely that the workstation is running the older NetWare shell (NETX.COM) rather than the NetWare DOS Requester. Even if the STARTNET.BAT file does exist, it needs to be checked to determine whether it contains the required information, as do the other configuration files.

For example, the STARTNET.BAT file should load the network communication files if the AUTOEXEC.BAT file is not being used to load them. It should load the most current NetWare 4-compatible versions of the following:

- LSL.COM
- The network board driver (such as NE2000.COM)
- IPXODI.COM
- VLM.EXE

In addition to assessing the workstation based on the presence of configuration files and their content, you also need to determine how much experience users have with networks and networking. Most companies will find their users have varying levels—from very inexperienced to experienced. The greater the number of inexperienced users, the greater the likelihood that additional personnel will be needed to assist in the migration of network workstations.

After assessing network workstations, the configuration files they use, and the level of networking experience of the users who work from those workstations, you need to determine whether a typical workstation configuration exists.

Determining Typical Workstation Configurations

Determining whether a typical workstation configuration exists will help you decide the best approach to take to update workstations. The approach you use for updating one workstation may not be the same one you use for updating another workstation, unless the configuration of the two workstations is the same.

For example, you may have some workstations that already use the NetWare DOS Requester for network access and some that still use the NetWare shell. You may choose not to update those that use the NetWare shell immediately, but rather to update those using the NetWare DOS Requester to the latest version of the Requester.

The NET.CFG file has some minimum requirements, which are met by default when the NetWare DOS Requester is installed. The NetWare DOS Requester creates a NET.CFG file if one does not exist. If one does exist, the DOS and Windows Client installation program will modify it if you choose to have it modified, or you can do it manually later.

Assessing the current typical workstation configuration helps you decide the best way to configure the VLMs to load, what should be included in the NET.CFG and other workstation files, and how much work may be required to update current network workstations. Knowing the typical workstation configurations also helps when determining how each network workstation should be migrated.

There are several ways in which network workstations can be migrated. Before the project team can decide on the best method, you need to ensure that you and the team understand the different options from which you can choose. Depending on the current status and configuration of your network's workstations, network workstation migration options may include the following:

- Running the DOS and Windows Client Installation INSTALL program at each workstation
- Running a special batch file from the file server's system login script, created specifically to upgrade workstations when users log in to the network
- Running the same special batch file for upgrading workstations, but running it at each workstation rather than from the file server's system login script
- Running the WSUPDATE or WSUPGRD programs

Choosing one or more of these upgrade options is part of developing the migration strategy. On large or varied networks, more than one migration method may be suitable. To determine which migration methods are most suitable, the project team may choose to test each migration method.

After testing those workstation migration methods that seem most suitable for your network, review and evaluate the results of those tests. Evaluating those tests should help you determine which of the migration options is the quickest and most suitable for your network. The migration methods you deem to be most suitable should then be specified as the methods to use when migrating network workstations.

The project team is responsible for the phases of the NetWare 4 design and implementation process that proceed through, but do not include, the implementation phase. Thus, project team members may not be responsible for conducting the actual network migration. Because project team members are generally chosen from company personnel, however, many of the project team members may also share in the responsibility of performing the actual migration. Whether this is the case or not, network administrators often perform the migration. Therefore, the decisions, and thus the software needed for migrating network clients, must be shared with the network's administrators.

Sharing Client Software with Administrators

Sharing the chosen method for migrating workstations includes training network administrators to perform the migration process. It also includes training them to troubleshoot and deal with potential problems. Most of the problem resolution training you can provide will be the result of the implementation tests the project team ran. Fortunately—or unfortunately, if the implementation tests went smoothly—you may have little problem resolution data to use.

You can, however, establish a lab from which you can train the administrators and any other involved personnel on the process chosen for migrating typical workstation configurations. A training lab provides administrators with experience in migrating the workstations and troubleshooting migration-related problems. It may also help find migration-related problems that did not occur during the testing of migration options.

The training you implement in the training lab will be determined, at least in part, by the migration method you choose. For example, if you choose to run the DOS and Window Client

Installation software, part of training the network administrators will include preparing a sample INSTALL.CFG file. You may also have to prepare different INSTALL.CFG files if your network clients do not all have the same physical configuration.

If not all administrators can train and prepare for workstation migration in the training lab, you can follow another approach by letting administrators be responsible for upgrading their own workstations. By upgrading their own workstations, they become familiar with client architecture, the client installation process, and how to use this workstation migration method.

Creating User Training

In addition to training network administrators to migrate workstations, users must be trained to use their workstations once they have been migrated. If the migration is as successful as planned, and part of the planning process included making network access reasonably transparent, not much user training will be necessary. If users want or need to know about the effect the workstation migration has on their access to the network, training will be needed.

As with other aspects of designing and implementing a NetWare 4 network, there is a process that can be applied to creating user training. This process includes several steps:

- Assess user's network expertise.
- Decide whether training will be required.
- Determine for what topics training should be conducted.
- Develop a training plan and associated materials.
- Conduct the first training session.
- Evaluate the results of the first training session.
- Revise the training techniques and associated materials if needed.
- Conduct another training session.

- Reevaluate the results of the training session and revise if needed.
- Continue conducting training sessions until all users have been trained.

When determining what user training should be conducted, you have a variety of options. Of course, you can conduct formal training sessions. They can be very costly on a large network, however, as well as very time-consuming. Therefore, formal training sessions may not be justified.

In addition, the amount of training each user needs should be relatively limited, assuming that the training is conducted only to explain the changes associated with accessing the network. If the training also includes details about NetWare 4, some formal training may be required. You do not have to think only in terms of conducting formal training classes, however, when determining what training should be provided to network users.

Training alternatives are available and should be considered. The following are some additional training options:

- E-mail
- Memos and other formal or informal written documents
- Quick reference materials
- Self-study materials
- Online documentation

If your company has an existing electronic mail software package and most network users are familiar with its use, you can use e-mail as a user training method. You merely need to compose and distribute e-mail messages to users that provide them with training on those aspects of the network on which training is needed. For example, you can use e-mail to explain the new lines contained within their workstations' configuration files, to show them how to log in using the `/b` option if they are still accessing the network from a workstation running the old NetWare shell, or even merely to tell them where to obtain more information on these and other network-related topics.

Other options for user training may include the use of written documents, both formal and informal. Formal documents may include such things as training manuals prepared either by company personnel or by an outside firm, worksheets, or NetWare 4 documentation. Informal documents may include a bulleted list of related information, a memo explaining one or more issues related to workstations or NetWare 4, or any other type of written documentation not prepared as part of a formal company process.

Quick reference materials may also be used for training and may include such things as review cards, foldouts, or bullet lists of information. In addition, quick reference materials can include posters, small handbooks, and so on. If the material contains limited or abbreviated information, it can generally be considered as quick reference material.

Self-study materials may be used as well. Most self-study materials are third-party books, such as this one, that discuss the information the reader needs to know. Users may also choose to read one or more of Novell's documentation manuals, such as the *NetWare Client for DOS and Windows User Guide.*

In addition to or instead of self-study materials, users may access Novell's online documentation to learn what they need to know about the network. Novell's online documentation set includes an electronic copy of each book in the complete NetWare 4.1 documentation set (see fig. 7.1). It also includes a search feature that enables a user to search a single book or the entire collection of books to find information about a specific topic.

Once a training approach is chosen, it should be tested to determine whether it is suitable and sufficient. To test the chosen training approach, select one or more typical network users, and conduct a test of the training materials with these users. The type of test you conduct depends, of course, on the type of training method you choose.

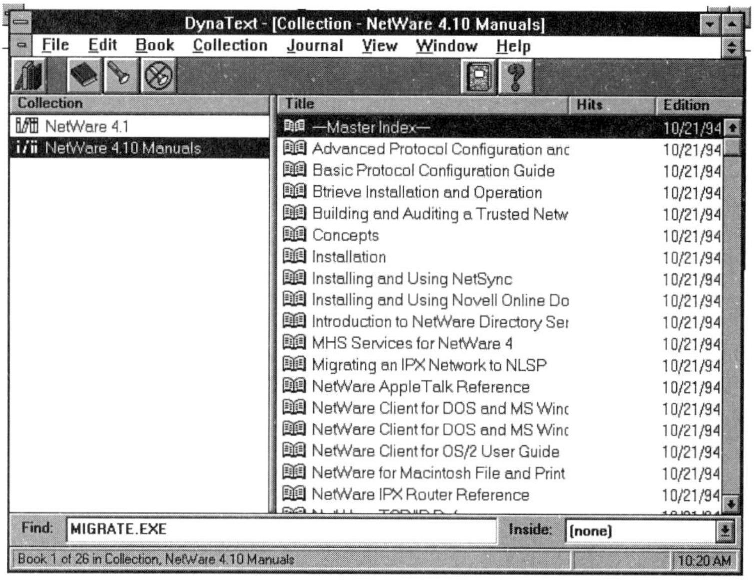

Figure 7.1
Novell's online documentation set.

For example, if you choose to distribute an e-mail message, you let the test users know ahead of time that you are sending them a message, the purpose of which is to test the effectiveness of the message, not the intelligence of the user. You might include a list of questions at the end of the e-mail message for the user to answer and return to you. This helps you know whether the training by the use of this particular e-mail message was effective or needs to be revised.

If you want to conduct a more formal test, you may consider preparing a list of questions for the user to answer, or problems for the user to solve. With the list of questions or problems in hand, provide a sample group of typical users with the appropriate documentation. Next, ask each user to attempt to find an answer to each question or solution for each problem on the list. Observe users as they attempt to answer each question or find a solution for each problem. Document the process users go through during this test, then revise the process to correct any problems the users may have encountered.

After testing the training approach on typical users, revise it, if necessary, to make it as effective as possible. Then, also if necessary, test it again. Once its effectiveness is determined, implement the training for all affected network users.

Once the level of user knowledge related to workstation network access is sufficient, you can begin migrating workstations. Even though the network itself has not yet been upgraded to NetWare 4, you can begin migrating workstations if you choose. The NetWare 4-compatible version of the NetWare DOS Requester can be used in the bindery environment. If you choose, you can upgrade workstations early and begin training users. This gives users a little time to get used to accessing the network by using the NetWare DOS Requester before the network is migrated.

Creating a Migration Strategy for File Servers

Developing a migration strategy for network file servers begins with obtaining answers to various questions such as the following:

- What versions of NetWare currently exist on the network?
- Are other network operating systems currently being used?
- Will all network file servers be migrated to NetWare 4?
- Is hardware currently available for setting up a testing lab?
- How will a testing lab be configured so that testing can be conducted?
- Will data have to be migrated in addition to the network operating system?
- Is there a database on the network that can be used to import objects into NDS?

During the NetWare 4 implementation phase, you need to consider all these questions and more. Issues such as whether existing NetWare 2 and NetWare 3 file servers will be migrated to NetWare 4, eliminated altogether, or left with the current network operating system running on them need to be decided. In addition, if non-NetWare file servers exist on the network, you need to know what network operating system types and versions are running so you can decide whether those file servers will be migrated or replaced. If new file servers are going to be added, you must also consider where those file servers will be installed and when.

Which file servers will be migrated, which file servers will be replaced, and when those file servers will be migrated or replaced are not the only considerations, however. You must also consider whether bindery services will be provided, and if so, where. In addition, you must consider whether all types of workstations (DOS, Windows, Macintosh, UNIX, and so on) will be used in the NetWare 4 network and plan accordingly.

File servers running non-NetWare operating systems and file servers running versions of NetWare earlier than NetWare 4.1 may have to be upgraded. Upgrading file servers helps ensure their successful migration into the NetWare 4.1 network.

As a member of the project team, it is your responsibility to help determine how network file servers will be migrated. In order to execute the migration of network file servers successfully, there is a series of tasks that must be performed. After completing these tasks you will have successfully planned, tested, scheduled, and prepared for migrating your network file servers.

The following are tasks that must be performed in order to prepare for a successful migration of the network file servers:

- Review current file server configurations.
- Establish a testing lab.
- Discuss downtime and migration with management.
- Choose the file server migration method.
- Obtain NetWare 4.1 software and licenses.
- Schedule and perform pilot migrations.

- Train users in the pilot department.
- Schedule migration for the balance of the network.

As you can see, the tasks to be performed are the same for WANs as they are for LANs and MANs. The amount of work increases substantially when you are dealing with WANs, however. For example, in a wide area network there are many more file servers, thus more configurations to review, more licenses to purchase, and a larger number of workstations and file servers to migrate.

All these tasks require a variety of steps in order to accomplish them. The first associated step is that of collecting and reviewing relevant information. That information is available to you in a variety of forms and documents.

For example, the resource list will tell you what file server configurations currently exist on the network. This book as well as the Novell documentation set provides you with the information you need regarding which migration options are available and which ones can be used to migrate different network operating systems successfully. It is your responsibility to review this information and then begin the process of developing a migration strategy.

Reviewing Current File Server Configurations

As you review relevant information, your goal is to determine the best approach to take to migrate existing and new network file servers to NetWare 4. Some of the information you need will be available on the network resource list. Other documents may also have to be gathered, reviewed, and then analyzed for relevant information. In working toward the goal of planning a successful network migration to NetWare 4, the information you gather and review should provide you with answers to most of the following common questions:

- What other versions of the NetWare operating system are currently being used on the network?
- Will other versions of NetWare still have to be supported for a period of time?

- Will bindery services be required?
- What file servers will need to have bindery services provided, and where will bindery services context have to be set?
- What hardware is currently being used for NetWare file servers, and is it sufficient for upgrading to NetWare 4?
- If existing hardware is not sufficient, what additional hardware will have to be purchased?
- Are there other network operating systems currently in use on the existing network?
- Will file servers running other network operating systems be migrated to NetWare 4 or eliminated?
- Which network administrators will require NetWare 4 training, and how will that training be accomplished?
- What configuration should be set up in the testing lab to accommodate hardware and software testing?
- Will a testing lab be available, and how will it be configured to be representative of the current network topology?
- What are the names of each of the existing file servers?
- What type and version of network operating system is currently running on each file server?
- What is the disk storage capacity of existing file servers?
- How much file server RAM is currently available on each file server, and will additional RAM be needed to accommodate the minimum requirements for NetWare 4?
- What microprocessor exists on each of the network file servers?
- Will any of these file servers be replaced with upgraded equipment?
- Has any of that equipment already been ordered or received, and if not yet received, when it will arrive?

After gathering the answers to these and other relevant questions, you should be able to continue the process of determining the best strategy for migrating the network's file servers, the next step of which involves testing.

Establishing a Testing Lab

When you have the answers you need to the questions you have asked, you should have a pretty good idea of what your existing network file server structure looks like. You should know whether or not the existing file servers meet NetWare 4's minimum hardware configurations and whether new file server equipment will be available. Now it is time to establish a testing lab.

The purpose of the testing lab is to let you set up hardware that resembles a scaled-down version of your existing network so that you can test typical configurations. The lab should have representative examples of hardware and software from your current environment.

For example, if the majority of file servers on the network use IBM-compatible 80386 computers, your testing lab should contain mostly IBM-compatible 80386 computers. If MS DOS 6 is the most common DOS being used on the network, the workstations and file servers you set up in the lab should also be running MS DOS 6. If the current network operating system running on the majority of your network file servers is NetWare 3, file servers in the lab should also be running NetWare 3.

The testing lab should be set up to enable you to test the most common or typical configuration. You may also choose to set up the testing lab to include some of the less-common configurations.

For example, assume your wide area network has 350 file servers, 15 of which are currently running NetWare 2 and the balance of which are running NetWare 3. You obviously want to set up the majority of the file servers in the testing lab with NetWare 3. You probably should also consider, however, setting up one or two lab file servers to run NetWare 2 so that you can test the migration of your NetWare 2 file servers as well.

Once the testing lab is set up, you begin testing the different migration options available to you. The purpose is to determine which migration option is the quickest and most accurate, based on your network's current configuration.

The testing lab can serve another function in addition to helping you determine a migration strategy. The testing lab can also be used to educate network administrators and other individuals who will be participating in the migration process.

By the time you have determined which migration option is most suitable for your network, you may also have determined one other issue. You may now have a good idea of just how long it will take to migrate the network's file servers to NetWare 4. This is information you are likely to need when you complete the next migration task.

Discussing Downtime and Migration with Management

After you test the migration methods, you are then ready to discuss with management the approach you believe will be best for migrating network servers. You also will be able to give management a rough estimate of how long it will take to migrate the network's file servers, based on the results you noted when migrating lab servers.

Informing management of rough estimates is not the real purpose of this meeting, however. The true purpose of this discussion with management is to find out at what time management believes network downtime will be most acceptable. In order to migrate network file servers, each file server has to be removed from production.

Before each file server's network operating system is migrated, it may be necessary to migrate the data originally contained on each file server as well. If separate migration of network data will be needed, accommodations for this must be made even before the file server's network operating system is migrated. One successful approach to migrating network data is to copy it to another file server; then once the network file server is migrated, the data can be transferred back to the migrated file server. The migrated file server can then be returned to its original production status.

In order to perform each of these tasks, you need to know when the file server can be removed from production and cause the least amount of interference. The best way to determine when down-time would be the least problematic is to meet with management and ask.

You should also find out from management which file servers are to be upgraded. It may be that some of the existing file servers are not to be migrated, but are to be replaced or combined with other file servers. If this is the case, you need to know it. Decisions such as this are often left up to management, although the project team is likely to have some influence on these types of decisions.

Choosing the File Server Migration Method

Several upgrade methods are available for migrating both NetWare and non-NetWare file servers (see fig. 7.2). You and the project team are responsible for choosing the option that best suits the network's needs. The option (or options) you choose will depend on the type and version of the network operating system you must migrate. It also will depend on the results of the lab testing you conducted.

Recall that there are four options for migrating network operating systems:

- Across-the-wire
- Same-server
- In-place upgrade
- NetWare 4.1 Installation

The across-the-wire and same-server migration methods can be used to upgrade any of the following network operating systems:

- Banyan Vines
- IBM PC LAN (PCLP) v1.3 Extended Services

- IBM LAN Server, version 1.0 through version 1.3
- Microsoft's LAN Manager version 2.0
- NetWare versions 2.1*x* and 2.2
- NetWare version 3.1*x*
- NetWare version 4.0*x*

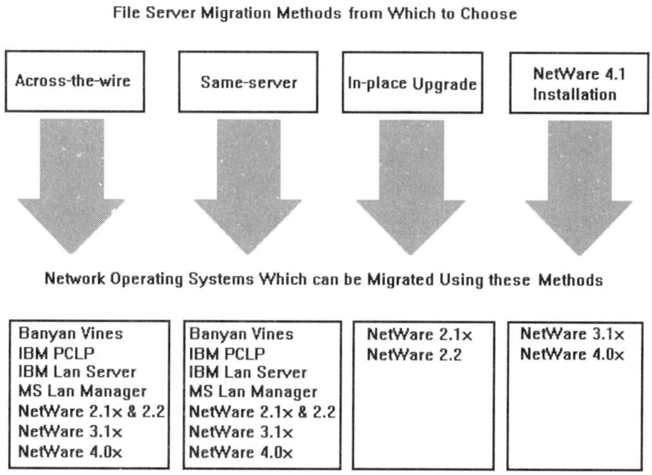

Figure 7.2
File server migration methods.

The primary difference between the across-the-wire and same-server migration methods is the end result. During the across-the-wire migration, information is transferred across the network to another file server. The across-the-wire method is considered to be the safest upgrade method because it is actually performed on a different server, keeping the contents of the original server intact until you have had the opportunity to verify that the upgrade was successful.

The same-server method uses only one file server and one workstation, because the existing file server network operating system is upgraded on the existing file server. Even though this is not as secure an option as the across-the-wire method, it is a viable option particularly on some of the smaller sections of the wide area network where equipment availability is more limited.

The in-place upgrade is used to upgrade NetWare 2.1*x* and NetWare 2.2 file servers to NetWare 4.1. Of the four migration options, the in-place upgrade is the least safe method. If something goes wrong during the migration process when the in-place upgrade is being used, the only way you can restore the old file server software is through the use of backup media. It is important, therefore, that you conduct and verify the usability of a complete backup of any file server to be upgraded by using the in-place upgrade method.

If you choose the in-place upgrade method, ensure that the file server already has an existing DOS partition. Unlike the fourth migration option—the NetWare 4 installation migration option—you cannot create a DOS partition during the in-place upgrade. Thus, if a DOS partition does not already exist on a file server to be upgraded by using the in-place upgrade method, create one. First, back up the file server, then run `FDISK` and partition the hard drive. Then you may begin the in-place upgrade.

The NetWare 4 installation migration option is used to upgrade existing NetWare 3.1*x* or NetWare 4.0*x* file servers to NetWare 4.1. The NetWare 4 installation migration option enables you to install NetWare 4 on existing compatible hardware, even when another NetWare operating system is already installed. The NetWare 4 Simple Installation menu option is also available, as is the Custom Installation menu option.

These four migration options, or a selection from these four, should be tested on the appropriate file servers in the testing lab. Before you can test them, however, you need to know which options are available. With the results of migrating network file servers from lab testing in hand, you can then choose the most appropriate migration options for migrating your network.

Obtaining NetWare 4.1 Software and Licenses

Whether migrating a LAN, MAN, or WAN, it is generally not the responsibility of project team members to order the NetWare 4.1 software and licenses, although it may be. Regardless of who does the actual ordering, however, it is the project team's responsibility to determine what needs to be ordered, when it must arrive, and who should be given the responsibility for ensuring that the order is placed and received.

Although it may be assigned to a non-project team member, it is generally someone on the project team who is responsible for following up to ensure that the software arrives on time and that it is what was ordered. It is important, therefore, that you and the project team ensure that you order what is needed and have it available to you well before you attempt to begin testing file server migrations.

Scheduling and Performing Pilot Migrations

Even before the NetWare 4.1 installation and licensing software arrives, you can begin planning migration of file servers within the pilot department. Of course, to plan migration of the pilot department's file servers, you must first choose which department is to become the pilot department.

The pilot department does not have to be a complete network department. The size of the WAN, the structure of the company, the number of individuals available to conduct the pilot migration, and any number of other issues will help determine what portion of the company will function as the pilot department.

Many large companies have IS departments, which often have a key role in the migration of the network to NetWare 4. Under these circumstances, the IS department itself may be used as the pilot department. There are other factors as well that may help to determine whether the IS department becomes the pilot department.

For example, the IS department must have or be able to obtain hardware for file servers and workstations that meets the minimum requirements for NetWare 4. In addition, IS department personnel must be trained to implement NetWare 4 in their departments if they are going to be responsible for implementing NetWare 4 throughout the network.

Often, another reason for choosing the IS department for the pilot implementation is the level of technical knowledge department personnel already have. Almost all the IS department's technical staff will have some experience with troubleshooting and solving equipment and software problems. That capability makes them a logical choice for piloting the NetWare 4 implementation.

If the company does not have an IS department, or the IS department does not seem to be the best choice for pilot implementation, another choice will have to be made. Here are some factors to consider when choosing a department, workgroup, or section of the company as the pilot department:

- Sufficient quantity of hardware that meets the minimum NetWare 4 migration and installation requirements
- Area of the network that can be relatively isolated from the rest of the network during pilot implementation
- Employees who have a positive attitude toward the implementation of NetWare 4
- Enough employees to assist in the implementation and troubleshoot and solve problems as they arise

The department, workgroup, or section of the company chosen as the pilot department should also be representative of the typical workstation and file server configuration found throughout the company. In addition, it should be physically located within a reasonable distance of the project team and those who will be responsible for conducting the pilot implementation. The department where the pilot implementation occurs should not be left to deal with migration issues itself. All involved personnel should be actively participating in the pilot migration.

Finding problems, documenting those problems, finding ways to solve problems, and documenting the solutions are all part of the pilot implementation. It takes many people working together to conduct a successful pilot implementation, and without it, there will be no successful network migration.

Training Users in the Pilot Department

It is not just those responsible for implementing the pilot department's migration who must understand the migration process. The pilot department's network users must also understand the migration process and the impact it has on their daily work. A plan for training users in the pilot department must be created and implemented. The implementation plan is part of the pilot migration, and it should be carried out as such.

Just as the pilot department should not be left to conduct the pilot migration on its own, the pilot department's users should not be left on their own to learn about the migration and how it affects them. Instead, the pilot department's users should be trained.

The project team may choose to look upon this training issue as just another problem to deal with. It is instead truly an opportunity. In a wide area network, there are generally hundreds or even thousands of users who will have to be given some type of training. That training may consist of nothing more than a couple of e-mail messages. On the other hand, it may require that each network user be given a copy of a third-party book, such as NRP's *CNE 4 Short Course,* along with instructions as to special sections to read and study. Training may consist of anything between or beyond these options. The project team needs to decide how the users will be trained and then plan accordingly.

Training the pilot department is an opportunity, because it lets the project team test the training method and materials it has chosen. This opportunity gives the project team a chance to determine whether the chosen training method will be successful. If the chosen training method is not successful, it is better to know it after having trained a handful or two of people than after having trained thousands. Training users in the pilot department is, therefore, an important part of conducting a pilot implementation.

The other important part of conducting a pilot implementation is, of course, the success of the implementation itself. After the pilot department has been successfully migrated to NetWare 4, the NetWare 4 network design begins to receive its first true test. If the file server and workstation migration is successful, users in the pilot department should be able to access all necessary network resources and have a general knowledge of how to use the fully migrated network once it is available.

Scheduling Migration for the Balance of the Network

After the pilot department has been successfully migrated, the project team can begin scheduling the migration of the remainder of the network. Scheduling the migration requires that the project team determine whether different departments or areas of the company's network will be migrated before other departments or areas or whether the entire network will be simultaneously migrated. There are merits to both approaches. There are also drawbacks.

Migrating the network one department or area at a time allows a little extra time for finding and working out any problems associated with migrating the network. On the other hand, this approach may also cause the migration of the network to drag out substantially longer than the company considers reasonable.

Migrating one department or area at a time gives you greater control over the migration process. If only a few individuals are given the responsibility for migrating the entire company, those few will become quite expert at migration. On the other hand, the company will be wholly dependent upon these individuals for the success of the migration.

Having to train a limited number of people to perform the migrations can provide a cost savings. It is initially less expensive to send 5 people out for special training than it would be to send 50, but costs may add up elsewhere when this approach is used.

For example, with only a handful of people performing the migration, these people have to travel extensively in order to migrate the entire network. Travel expenses can be quite costly, thus increasing the overall cost to the company.

As you can see, there are tradeoffs regardless of the choice. One option that works on WANs that are particularly large is to provide a team of individuals to implement each geographic region. Those teams, or at least a representative from each team, can be brought to the headquarters office, or sent to special training, to learn what needs to be done to migrate the portion of the network for which they are responsible. These individuals then return to their own region, and in return, educate those individuals who will help them migrate the network. Travel costs are contained, training costs are contained, but sufficient training occurs to accomplish the task.

Another benefit to this approach is that it enables the network to be simultaneously migrated. At least, the migration can be done on each area of the network in a time span close enough that the migration is almost simultaneous, or so that it does not drag on for weeks or even months.

Once the project team determines how the implementation is to take place and who will be handling it, it can schedule the migration of the file servers for the remainder of the network.

Creating a Migration Strategy for Applications

Of course, workstations and file servers are not the only items for which a migration strategy must be developed. The project team must also create a migration strategy for existing network applications.

Before the project team can create a migration strategy for existing network applications, it must know what applications exist on the network. The project team must then determine which of the existing network applications are NetWare 4-compatible, and which are not. Then finally, the project team must decide whether applications that are not compatible with NetWare 4 will be upgraded at all, when they will be upgraded, and whether they will require continued network support until the upgrade can occur.

If those applications that are not NetWare 4-compatible will continue to be used on the network for a period of time, you must plan for and take steps to ensure that those applications can still be used on the migrated NetWare 4 network. This means that you have to plan where and how you will provide continuing support for these applications when developing a migration strategy for the network. It also means that you must use the testing lab to verify that these applications will function on the network, with bindery services in place on the network.

As you learned in Chapter 5, NetWare 4 provides bindery services to provide continuing support for applications that can function only in the bindery environment. Bindery services makes it possible for users and applications that are not NetWare 4-aware to make calls to NetWare 4 file servers. With bindery services set, the operating system treats certain objects that existed in a NetWare 3 bindery, but which are now in a NetWare 4 container, as if they were still bindery objects.

By setting bindery services, applications that are not NetWare 4-aware but that were NetWare 3-aware can access print queues and print servers as they did before. In addition, users whose workstations cannot be immediately upgraded to the newer VLM client can access NetWare 4 services as if they were accessing bindery-based services.

Properly planning for and implementing bindery services ensures that the company and its employees continue to receive the benefit of using existing applications.

Note

Bindery services are, however, provided in NetWare 4 only as an interim measure. Novell has indicated that bindery-based applications and other network resources will eventually have to be upgraded to NetWare 4. The interim use of bindery services ensures that companies will not have to put out additional funds for application upgrades immediately.

If you activate bindery services on your NetWare 4 network, bindery-based applications will function as if they were running on a NetWare 3 file server, even though they are actually running on a NetWare 4 file server. Setting bindery services on the migrated network also makes it possible for users to continue to use bindery-based applications on the NetWare 4 network.

For bindery-based applications to perform as though they are still being run on a NetWare 3 file server, you must set a bindery context. Setting a bindery context makes NetWare 4 aware of where bindery-based users (any network user who accesses the network from a workstation using the NetWare Shell instead of the NetWare Requester) are located on the network.

As a member of the project team, you must decide which network containers will have a bindery context set for them. In NetWare 4.1, you can set bindery-context up to 16 containers. Earlier versions of NetWare 4, however, allowed bindery context to be set on only one container.

There are three methods that you may use to set bindery context on a NetWare 4 file server. Following the first method, you issue a SET command at the file server console one time for each container on which bindery services is to be set. To use the SET command at the file server console, you type the following line, replacing *context* with the context of the container for which bindery services is to be activated:

```
SET BINDERY CONTEXT=context
```

Then press Enter. For example, if the CHICAGO OU, and LA OU objects under the US OU object for the BILLCO company are to have bindery services set, you type the following two lines at the file server console, pressing Enter after each line:

```
SET BINDERY CONTEXT=OU.CHICAGO.OU=US.O=BILLCO
SET BINDERY CONTEXT=OU=LA.OU=US.O=BILLCO
```

Following the second method, you place the same SET commands into the file server's STARTUP.NCF file, using an editor from the DOS prompt. Each time the file server is booted, these SET commands are executed and bindery services are set for each of the specified containers. If you choose to use this second method, you have to reload the NetWare operating system for the changes you placed into the STARTUP.NCF file to be activated.

Following the third method, you run the INSTALL utility while the NetWare 4 file server is running. To use INSTALL, you run it (type `LOAD INSTALL` at the file server prompt and press Enter) then choose the NCF Files Option from the Installation Options menu (see fig. 7.3). You can then edit the STARTUP.NCF file and save your modifications to this file when you exit INSTALL.

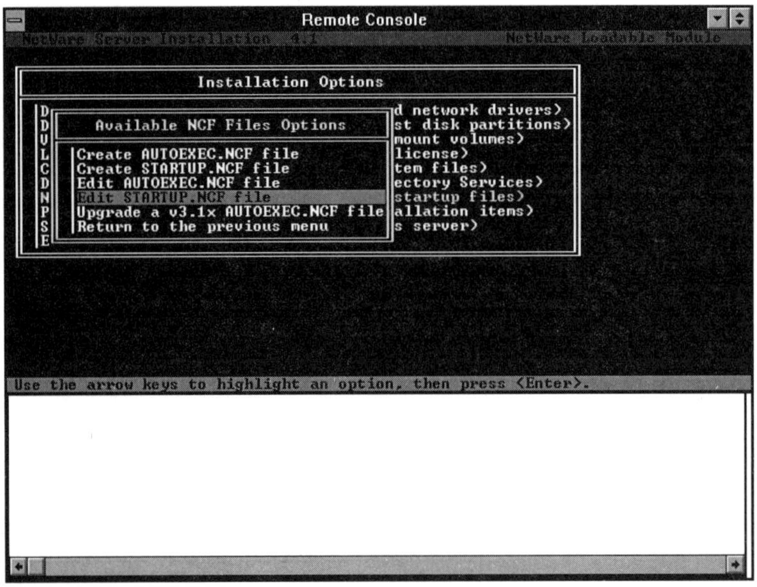

Figure 7.3
INSTALL's Available NCF Files Options menu.

Once bindery context is set, users who log in to the network by using NETX.COM instead of VLM.EXE, and whose User object is located in a container with the bindery context set, are able to access the NetWare 3-aware applications.

Note When a NetWare bindery-based user logs in to the NetWare 4 network, that user must modify the login process slightly. The user must add the `/b` option to the login statement, which tells NetWare that this user is logging in to the network as a bindery-based instead of NDS-based user.

For example, a user named `JKING` used to log in to the NetWare 3 bindery-based network by typing `LOGIN JKING` and pressing Enter. That same user must type `LOGIN JKING/b` and press Enter to log in to the NetWare 4 network.

Setting bindery context is only part of the process associated with developing the strategy for migrating applications. Before you determine where to set bindery context, you need to know whether you even need to set it. In addition, you need to determine which applications can and should be migrated and which applications can and should be eliminated, replaced, or updated. When planning the network's migration strategy, therefore, remember to consider and plan for what must be done with, to, or for existing network applications—and within what time frame.

To help make all the decisions related to the network's application migration strategy, gather information that will be useful in helping you make those decisions. Whether you are planning a LAN, MAN, or WAN, the information that you and the project team should gather and consider when determining the migration of applications is still the same, and it should include at least the following questions:

- Which applications currently exist on the network?
- Which of the existing applications are compatible with NetWare 4 and thus will not have to be upgraded or migrated?
- Which applications are not compatible with NetWare 4, but must continue to be accessible once the network is upgraded and thus will require bindery services?

- Which users need to access bindery-based applications?
- Which existing menus that call bindery-based applications will have to be modified to access those applications?
- What changes might have to be made to existing menus to accommodate their use on the migrated network?
- What context will be used for locating applications requiring bindery services?

Once you establish the approach to take for migrating network applications, you have finished establishing the approach to take for migrating the majority of network resources. It will now be your responsibility to determine where and how a testing lab will be set up, what it will include, who will be responsible for running it, and so on.

Setting Up a Testing Lab

As discussed previously in this chapter, the primary purpose of setting up a testing lab is to let you check out the migration options you are considering using to migrate the network. The testing lab you set up may be as small as one NetWare file server or large enough to include one or more file servers of each type found on your network.

The testing lab may be located in any convenient location within your company. Although the environment of the testing lab should emulate the actual environment of the company, it should not be part of the actual company network. Keeping it separate ensures that your testing will not interfere with daily network activity. It also allows those who are running migration tests to make as many mistakes as needed, without fear of causing permanent problems on the network.

The testing lab has two purposes other than testing various migration options. The second purpose is to evaluate the migration process you have chosen. You want to determine which method yields the best results as far as speed and accuracy are concerned.

You may determine that you have to trade a little speed to get greater accuracy, or vice versa. You will not know what your options are, however, unless you test the migration methods you are considering using.

The third purpose of establishing a testing lab is to train administrators to perform the migrations. If you are trying to decide which migration option is best for each file server, you should set up enough of each type of file server to test the migration. If equipment is limited, you may have to use the same hardware each time, installing the typical current network operating system, then migrating it, recording the results, and starting the process over again with a different operating system. Network administrators can be trained to do this. Then, when the final option is chosen, each network administrator can receive additional training in the lab on the migration method chosen. Network administrators will thus get to see and understand why the chosen method was selected and have more than one experience with migrating file servers by using that approach.

The approach you choose will depend on how much time, equipment, and personnel you have available for the testing lab. Regardless of the limitations placed on you by these resources, you should test migration before you determine which approach to take. Testing migration options in a nonproduction lab before trying it out on the live network will save you time and headaches later when the real network migration process begins.

Creating an Implementation Schedule

Sooner or later the project team has to determine exactly what the migration of the network will involve and how long each process will take. It is at this point that the project team must create the implementation schedule.

Many tasks lead to the process of creating a schedule for implementing the NetWare 4 network. Which tasks are completed depend on the size of your network, its geographical location, the types and versions of workstation and file server operating systems on the existing network, and a variety of other issues. There are also many tasks that you must do in order to complete the seventh procedure associated with designing and implementing a NetWare 4 network—creating an implementation schedule.

To create and implement an implementation schedule that will be successful for your network, you have to execute the following procedures:

- Identify all the tasks that must be completed in order to create an implementation schedule and successfully implement the NetWare 4 network.
- Estimate approximately how long each identified task will require to complete.
- Create a schedule to ensure the successful implementation of the network design.
- Coordinate the schedule with schedules for other groups who are also responsible for network migration.
- Revise the original schedule, if needed.
- Conduct a pilot test to pinpoint and solve any potential implementation problems.
- Proceed with the implementation as scheduled.

Identifying which tasks need to be performed in order to implement the network plan is often the most difficult part of the implementation process. This is particularly true because the task to be completed may vary somewhat from company to company. Although the network design and implementation requirements of one company may be similar to those of another company, there are several issues that cause variations in needs.

The size of the company is often the biggest factor affecting the needs of each individual company. For example, a small company with a limited number of departments, file servers, and employees is less likely to have the all the equipment and personnel resources they need in order to set up a full migration testing lab. The smaller company may, therefore, have to test migration on production file servers. The process is likely to include transferring all relevant data from one production file server to another, then running an in-place upgrade to upgrade the first file server, and copying the data back on to the now-migrated production file server. This procedure may end up being the only migration testing the company can do, before migration of the remainder of the production file servers becomes necessary.

It is the project team's—and thus your—responsibility to execute the following:

- Identify which tasks must be completed in order to implement the NetWare 4 network successfully.
- Arrange the tasks to be completed in the order in which they must be done.
- Determine approximately how long each task will take.
- Identify any tasks that rely on other tasks for their successful completion.
- Schedule start and finish dates for each task identified on the list.

Identifying Tasks

The most difficult part of creating an implementation schedule may well be the process of identifying all the tasks that must be completed in order to implement your NetWare 4 network successfully. The next most difficult task is estimating how long each task will take to complete.

Factors that affect the first difficulty include such things as the size of the company's network (LAN, MAN, or WAN); which of the existing file servers, workstations, and applications will be migrated; and the amount of experience and knowledge the project team has with systems design, project planning, and other functions similar to that of planning a NetWare 4 network's implementation.

The primary factor that may affect the second difficulty—identifying the order in which the tasks must be completed—is the knowledge level of project team members. Project team members who have studied or experienced the process of migrating a NetWare 4 network will have a basic understanding of which steps must be finished before the next steps can begin. In some cases, however, tasks can be performed simultaneously. These can be the most difficult tasks to schedule because the pattern of events may be less obvious.

The implementation phase of the NetWare 4 design and implementation process is basically the same regardless of whether you are implementing a LAN, a MAN, or a WAN. Only the size of the project differs significantly. Consequently, the list of tasks that may be required in order to implement a wide area network within your company is basically the same.

This section of the chapter is designed to help you identify tasks that may be required to implement NetWare 4 in your network environment. Whenever possible, each task included in this list is arranged in the logical order in which it may need to be completed. Because each network is different, however, there may be other tasks you need to include in your list or some you need to eliminate. In addition, you may need to modify the order of these tasks to accommodate anything that is specific to your network's implementation.

When planning to implement your own NetWare 4 network, use the following list as a guide. When appropriate, modify the list to create a list that fully meets the needs of your company.

The following are tasks that may be included on the implementation schedule for implementing a NetWare 4 wide area network:

- Assess workstation and file server upgrade requirements.
- Select the team to conduct the network migration.

- Begin training the migration team.
- Place purchase orders for any additional workstation software that may be needed.
- Place purchase orders for any hardware needed to upgrade existing workstations.
- Place purchase orders for the NetWare 4.1 software.
- Place purchase orders for any hardware needed to install new file servers.
- Decide what workstation configuration files need to be created or modified, what those files should contain, and whether workstations will be upgraded to the NetWare 4 default Ethernet frame type of 802.2.
- Set up a testing lab.
- Test applications and workstation communication software configurations against NetWare 4.1.
- Complete training for the migration team.
- Upgrade workstations for the pilot implementation area of the company's network.
- Train users in the pilot area on using the new workstation software and accessing the migrated network.
- Determine which applications must be upgraded.
- Place purchase orders to upgrade applications that are not NetWare 4-compatible.
- Begin training network administrators, starting with upgrade and installation procedures if administrators will be helping with the migration process.
- Install the first network file server and set up the NDS directory tree as designed, including creating container objects as designed.
- Install network communication software on workstations in the pilot implementation area, modifying workstation configuration files as needed.

- Upgrade the hardware on network file servers and workstations that were identified as needing upgrades and for which additional hardware was ordered and received.
- Perform a backup of each pilot area's network file servers in its present state.
- Review the bindery on existing NetWare 2 and 3 file servers to eliminate objects no longer being used and to check for and then correct object names that do not conform to naming standards developed by the project team.
- Run DUPBIND, or manually review the bindery on NetWare file servers that will be migrated during the pilot implementation, to find and eliminate duplicate objects, such as users and print queues.
- Run SECURITY.EXE on NetWare file servers being migrated during the pilot implementation to detect any existing potential security violations and then clean up any security violations detected.
- Run BINDFIX to find and correct any potential problems with bindery files on NetWare servers being migrated during the pilot implementation.
- Perform another backup of existing NetWare network file server operating systems and other program files for those file servers being migrated during the pilot implementation.
- Clean up the file system on those NetWare 2 and NetWare 3 file servers being migrated during the pilot implementation.
- Complete a separate backup of the file system directories and data files stored on those NetWare file servers that will be migrated during the pilot implementation.
- Migrate existing file servers in the pilot implementation area to NetWare 4.1 and log results.
- Install any new NetWare 4.1 file servers in the pilot implementation area and log results.

- Review the logs for the workstation and file server pilot implementation.
- Modify the installation and migration approach as needed to correct or prevent problems noted in the pilot migration logs.
- Upgrade workstations for the balance of the company's network.
- Train the company's remaining network users.
- Perform a backup of the company's remaining network file servers in their present states.
- Review the bindery on the balance of the existing NetWare 2 and 3 file servers to eliminate objects no longer being used and to check for and then correct object names that do not conform to naming standards developed by the project team.
- Run DUPBIND, or manually review the binderies of the remainder of the company's existing NetWare file servers, to find and eliminate duplicate objects, such as users and print queues.
- Run SECURITY.EXE on the balance of the company's NetWare file servers to view existing potential security violations, then clean up any security violations detected.
- Run BINDFIX to find and correct any potential problems with the binderies on the remainder of the company's network file servers.
- Perform another backup of the existing network file server operating system files and other program files for the rest of the company's network.
- Clean up the file system on existing NetWare 2 and NetWare 3 file servers for the remaining file servers on the company's network.
- Complete a separate backup of the file system directories and data files stored on existing NetWare file servers for the remainder of the company.

- Upgrade remaining file servers in the company, following a workgroup, geographic location, or other method that is most appropriate for the company.
- Upgrade any applications that were ordered and received as the result of migrating the network to NetWare 4.
- Determine, then document, how new user training and the addition of network workstations, file servers, and applications will be handled in the future.
- Review the complete workstation and file server migration process once network migration is complete, noting what went right and what went wrong, as well as what may be improved and how it might be improved the next time a network migration is done.
- Correct any problems or idiosyncrasies and train any untrained users or administrators that still exist.
- Celebrate the successful implementation of the NetWare 4 network.

Once the list of tasks to be completed has been determined, you can create a schedule to show when those tasks will be completed, and by whom.

If you have not already done so, arrange the tasks in the approximate order in which they must be performed. Some tasks will also have to be performed in parallel with other tasks, although a straight task list does not easily represent that fact. Once you start adding start dates and time-to-complete estimates, overlapping tasks will become more obvious.

Assess the approximate length of time it will take to complete each task. Next, create a timeline or schedule for completing those tasks. Then, assign individuals to be responsible for completing each task. Finally, document the migration schedule and share that schedule with everyone who will be involved in, is responsible for, or has a need or right to know about the scheduled implementation of the NetWare 4 network.

To summarize, once you identify those tasks relevant to the migration of your network to NetWare 4, you must do the following:

- Arrange the tasks in the order in which they must be done.
- Determine approximately how long each task will take.
- Identify tasks that are dependent upon the completion of other tasks.
- Schedule start and finish dates for each task.

After you follow these steps to develop an implementation schedule for your network, you must then coordinate that schedule with any other department, workgroup, or area of the company with responsibility for part of the network migration.

Coordinating the Schedule with Others

Coordinating the implementation schedule may range from simple to arduous. Most of the time, the smaller the network, the fewer the number of people who have to be involved in the migration—thus, the fewer the number of scheduling conflicts. It may also mean, however, that there are fewer experienced people to help with the scheduling and implementation, thus some issues that should have been dealt with earlier in the process may not become evident until it is much too late to correct or accommodate them to everyone's satisfaction.

The best way to prevent this kind of problem from occurring is to involve everyone who may be affected by the network in the implementation process as early as is reasonably possible. If possible, include a representative from each affected group in the meetings that discuss the implementation. This helps ensure that at least the majority of issues are raised, even if all issues cannot be accommodated, and company departments can't complain that they were not included in the process.

If having all concerned parties attend the implementation meetings is not feasible, consider having one or more of them participate in the lab testing and pilot implementation. Doing so helps those individuals get a feel for what their areas or departments can expect to see happen when implementation begins in earnest for them.

Completing the Implementation Schedule

The entire implementation scheduling process requires that you and the project team do the following:

- Establish a list of tasks that must be completed in order to implement the NetWare 4 network successfully.
- Determine the order in which each task must be performed.
- Calculate the approximate length of time each task will require.
- Establish dates by which each task must be completed.
- Assign the responsibility for the completion of each task to the appropriate individual.
- Create an implementation schedule that is realistic to follow.
- Coordinate the implementation schedule with others who may be affected by or need to participate in the upgrade or installation of the NetWare 4 network.
- Proceed with the implementation of the NetWare 4 network.

After the implementation schedule is created and coordinated, responsibility for each task is assigned, the pilot test has been successfully conducted, and the schedule coordinated with others, the only remaining issue is that of implementing the NetWare 4 network design. Implementation should follow the schedule as outlined, as closely as possible. Then, during the implementation, the project team needs to review and document the successes and failures of the network implementation and complete any final tasks that may be required.

Implementing NetWare 4

Implementing the NetWare 4 migration strategy requires that you follow as closely as possible the migration strategy you developed and the implementation plan you devised. This means that each aspect of the network for which you developed a plan and scheduled implementation must be completed.

Implementing NetWare 4 means that you must execute the following:

- Upgrade network connection software on each network workstation.
- Migrate each network file server to NetWare 4.
- Install new NetWare 4 file servers where needed.
- Accommodate network applications.

Implementing NetWare 4 then requires that you implement the strategies you developed for migrating each network resource.

Upgrading Connection Software on Network Workstations

The last task to be completed in the development of a client migration strategy is to begin upgrading clients. Document all problems you encounter as you go along, including what it took to repair or get around the problem successfully. With this information in hand, you can then successfully migrate all network clients.

When developing the migration strategy for network clients, remember that the greater the number of workstations to be upgraded, the more time for migrating is required. You can reduce the time required to upgrade the network's clients by assigning multiple people to assist with the upgrade. If only a few people are available to conduct the upgrade, however, your migration plan will have to take that into consideration. It may even mean that you have to train additional people—network administrators and users—to perform the workstation migration.

Keep in mind that if you conduct training sessions for users, part of the sessions can include having those users migrate their own workstations, solving all problems that occur. You can then have those users help other users migrate their workstations. If following this approach makes it possible for you to cut the required upgrade time sufficiently, you can include this approach as the best one to follow in your workstation migration strategy.

There are a variety of ways to accomplish the workstation migration. Choosing the best approach is the project team's—and thus your—responsibility. The best approach has to be determined based on available resources, network needs, and time available. Choose what seems to be the best approach for your network; then plan the migration of workstations accordingly.

Workstations on the NetWare 4 network need to run the Requester. For DOS and Windows workstations, that means that the NetWare 4-compatible version of the NetWare DOS Requester needs to be installed on each workstation. The NetWare DOS Requester may be installed across the network or from disk.

To install the NetWare DOS Requester across the network, log in to the network, map a drive to SYS:PUBLIC on the NetWare 4 file server, set that network drive as the default drive, then change to the CLIENT\DOSWIN subdirectory.

To install the NetWare DOS Requester from disk, create the appropriate disks from the NetWare 4.1 INSTALL program. Next, insert the NetWare Client for DOS and MS Windows Disk 1 (WSDOS_1) disk into the drive, swapping out disks WSDOS_1 through WSDOS_5 when prompted.

To complete the installation, whether performed across the network or from disk, follow these steps:

1. Type `INSTALL`, then press Enter.
2. When the NetWare Client Install screen opens (see fig. 7.4), choose step 1 and either press Enter to accept the default of

C:\NWCLIENT for the destination directory and move the highlight to the next line, or type in a new directory, then press Enter.

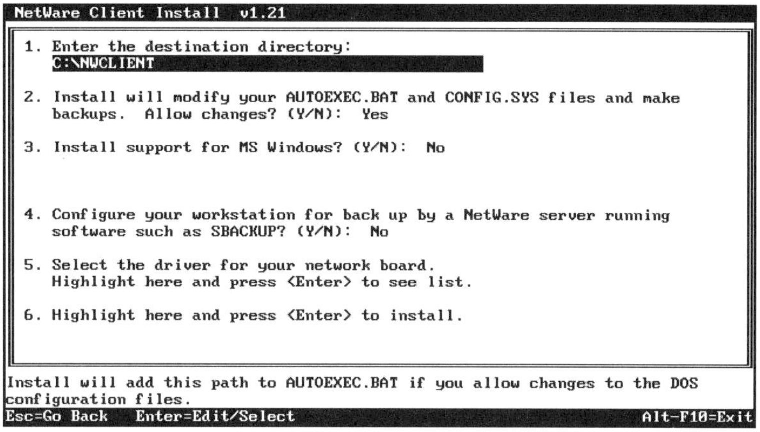

Figure 7.4
NetWare Client Install v1.21 screen.

3. Select step 2. Press Enter to choose Yes, thus enabling the installation program to make changes to the AUTOEXEC.BAT and CONFIG.SYS files. If you want to modify those files manually, choose No. The existing files will not be changed. New files are created in their place with a .NEW extension (AUTOEXEC.NEW and CONFIG.NEW).

   If you prefer to make the changes to the workstation configuration files manually, the following changes must be made:

   - AUTOEXEC.BAT. Add the `C:\NWCLIENT\STARTNET.BAT` line at the end of this file to load the NetWare DOS Requester and related files.
   - CONFIG.SYS. Add the `LASTDRIVE=Z` command.
   - NET.CFG. Add the LAN driver information under the Link Driver driver_name heading. Include the PREFERRED TREE= or PREFERRED SERVER= and FIRST NETWORK DRIVE= statements under the NetWare DOS Requester heading. If you want the workstation to be backed up by a NetWare server, include the TSA-related information associated with this process.

- STARTNET.BAT. Include commands to load the files required for network connection from the AUTOEXEC.BAT file. The files to be loaded should include LSL.COM, the LAN driver (such as NE2000), IPXODI.COM, and the NetWare DOS Requester (VLM.EXE).

4. Select step 3. If the workstation has Windows running on it, type `Y` to change the default of No to Yes. The Windows files will be installed on this workstation.

   When you choose Yes, the default directory of C:\WINDOWS is placed on the `Enter MS Windows directory:` field, and another field (`Highlight here and Press <Enter> to customize.`) is made available. You can choose that field and modify the directory to that directory that contains this workstation's MS Windows files.

5. Accept the country codes default of No. Change this default to Yes at the `Do you plan to use more country codes than the one currently running on your machine? (Y/N):` prompt if needed.

6. If you want this workstation to be able to access a shared directory, answer the `For network administrators only: Do you want to set the shared MS Windows path? (Y/N):` prompt with Yes and provide the path for this directory.

   When you finish modifying the Customize Support for MS Windows screen, press F10 to save your changes.

7. Answer the `Configure your workstation for back up by a NetWare server running software such as SBACKUP? (Y/N):` prompt with Yes if you want to be able to back up the hard disk(s) on this workstation by using the file server's backup software. Otherwise, leave the default set to No.

8. Select step 5. Press Enter. Enter the network board configuration information or accept the information provided. Press Enter to continue.

9. Select the `Highlight here and press <Enter> to install` field, and press Enter to start the file copy and configuration process.
10. When The Install Utility is finished screen is displayed, the installation is complete. Press Enter to exit to DOS, or press Ctrl+Alt+Del to reboot the workstation and load the configuration files.

You can also use the WSUPGRD and WSUPDATE utilities to simplify the process of updating the same files on multiple workstations. Use WSUPGRD to update the IPX LAN driver if the current LAN driver is not ODI-compliant. WSUPDATE is run from the network.

Type the following:

```
WSUPGRD [path] [/options]
```

at the command line and press Enter. Replace `[path]` with the path pointing to the complete driver name, and replace `[/option]` with any of the following available options as needed:

- `/C` exits the utility with an error code of level `1` instead of `0` when the upgrade does not complete successfully.
- `/E0`, `/E1`, or `/E2` specify, respectively, whether no changes should be made to the AUTOEXEC.BAT file, the IPX driver command in the AUTOEXEC.BAT file should be replaced with the commands to load the ODI driver, or the IPX driver command in the AUTOEXEC.BAT file should be removed and a call added to the NWSTART file, which is then created and will be called to load the ODI drivers.
- `/I` places the hardware ID in the master configuration table for the ODI driver.
- `/N` saves the old copy of the IPX driver.
- `/S` prevents the NET.CFG file from being generated with the information contained in the original IPX driver's configuration table.

Note You can also place this command into a login script so that it runs automatically when users log in to the network.

Type the following:

```
WSUPDATE [network_path] [drive.¦volume:] [client_path\filename]
[/options]
```

at the command line and press Enter. Replace `[network_path]` with the location of the new file. Replace `[drive.¦volume:]` with the mapped drive letter pointing to the old file or use the `/ALL` option instead. Replace `[client_path\filename]` with the name of the old file being replaced by the new file. Replace `[/option]` with any of the following options:

- `/ALL` to search all mapped drives
- `/C` to copy the new file over the old without a backup
- `/E` to erase the existing file
- `/F=[path\file]` to have the command ignore other options
- `/LOCAL` to search the workstation's drives
- `/L=[path\file]` to specify the location and name of the log file
- `/P` to have the user proceed with or abort the update when there are no files to update
- `/O` to update all files
- `/R` to rename the old version of the file with an .OLD extension
- `/S` to search for copies of the file to be updated
- `/?` to view online help information about this utility

Note As with the `WSUPGRD` command, you can also place this command into a login script to have it run automatically when users log in to the network.

Migrating Network File Servers to NetWare 4

You can use either the in-place upgrade or the across-the-wire upgrade to migrate file servers to NetWare 4. Using the in-place upgrade makes it possible for you to migrate your NetWare 3 file servers to NetWare 4 file servers. This migration process merges the existing NetWare 3 bindery information into the NetWare 4 NDS database. Therefore, it is important that you clean up the bindery files on your NetWare 3 file servers before you execute the in-place upgrade. In addition, back up your file server to prevent an unforeseen problem from irreplaceably wiping out your file server files, and be sure to back up all data on the file server in a separate backup. That data can then be restored to the NetWare 4 server after the in-place migration has been completed.

To run the in-place migration, after executing all the premigration tasks just discussed, complete the following steps:

1. Place the NetWare 4.1 CD-ROM in the CD-ROM drive.
2. Change to the drive where the MIGRATE.EXE file is located, type `MIGRATE`, and press Enter.
3. When the Select the type of migration menu appears, choose the Same-Server migration option.
4. Choose NetWare 3.x from the Select the source LAN type menu.
5. Choose NetWare 4.x from the Select the destination LAN type menu.
6. Complete the Migration Utility Configuration form (see fig. 7.5).
7. Choose Exit (return to DOS).

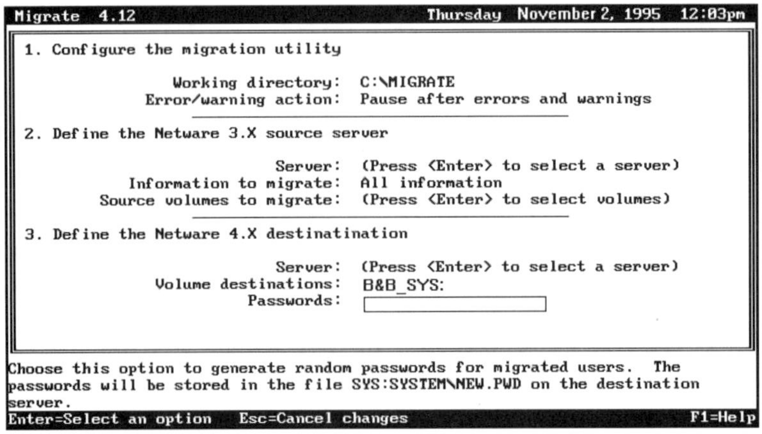

Figure 7.5

Migration utility configuration form.

You can run the across-the-wire upgrade to migrate bindery information and data from a NetWare 3 file server (source) to a NetWare 4 file server (destination). This process uses the MIGRATE.EXE utility included with NetWare 4, which enables you to choose which information in the NetWare 3 bindery and which data files will be upgraded. The process results in the creation of a customized NetWare 4 server.

The process itself involves the following steps:

1. The bindery information to be migrated is transferred to a working directory on the workstation.
2. The transferred bindery information is converted into a format that the NetWare 4 NDS database can understand.
3. The converted information is transferred to the NetWare 4 server by using bindery services, an emulation of the flat bindery structure found in pre-NetWare 4 file servers.
4. The transferred objects are placed into the NDS database and become part of the NDS tree.

Note

Any NetWare 3 user names that are the same as user names in the NetWare 4 NDS database are merged. In addition, NetWare 3 system files, including the system login script, are not migrated, although user login scripts are migrated. You can also use Novell's UIMPORT utility to convert the NetWare 3-based login scripts to NetWare 4.

Data files with the same name on both the NetWare 4 and NetWare 3 file servers are not copied to the NetWare 4 destination server, and the fact that they were not copied is noted in the migration report.

If a directory on the destination server has the same name as a directory on the source server, all files within the directory on the source server are merged into the same-name directory on the destination server. To prevent files from being merged, you must rename one or the other of the directories before migrating the file server.

Because user names are also merged when the migration is performed, eliminate duplicate names before running the migration. If you do not eliminate duplicate names ahead of time, invalid user account information may be transferred to the NetWare 4 server if the users are not actually the same.

To execute an across-the-wire migration, complete the following steps:

1. Have all users log out of the network.
2. Perform any or all of the following tasks to clean up the NetWare 3 file server's bindery and file system:
   - Delete any files you do not want to migrate.
   - Delete any files with a .VAP extension, because they are not NetWare 4-compatible.

- Rename files or directories that do not follow the DOS naming standard.
- Reduce the number of levels on the source server's directory structure so that no more than 25 levels exist.
- Run BINDFIX to clean up the NetWare 3 bindery.
- Delete the following files from the SYS:SYSTEM directory, if they exist:
    - LARCHIVE.EXE
    - LRESTORE.EXE
    - MACBACK.EXE
    - NARCHIVE.EXE
    - NRESTORE.EXE

3. Log in to the NetWare 4 server using bindery emulation (/B).
4. Change the drive to the directory where the MIGRATE.EXE file is located, then type MIGRATE and press Enter.
5. Choose Across-The-Wire migration from the Select the type of migration menu (see fig. 7.6).

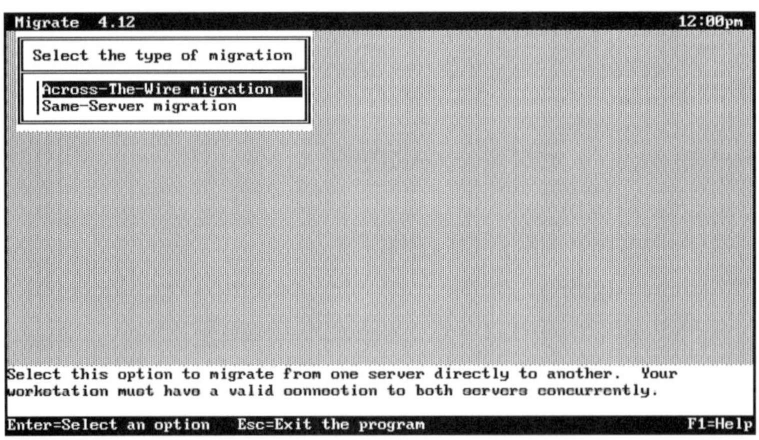

Figure 7.6
Select the type of migration menu.

6. Choose NetWare 3.x from the Select the source LAN type menu.
7. Choose NetWare 4.x from the Select the destination LAN type menu.
8. Fill in any needed information on the Migration Utility Configuration form, then press F10 (see fig. 7.7).

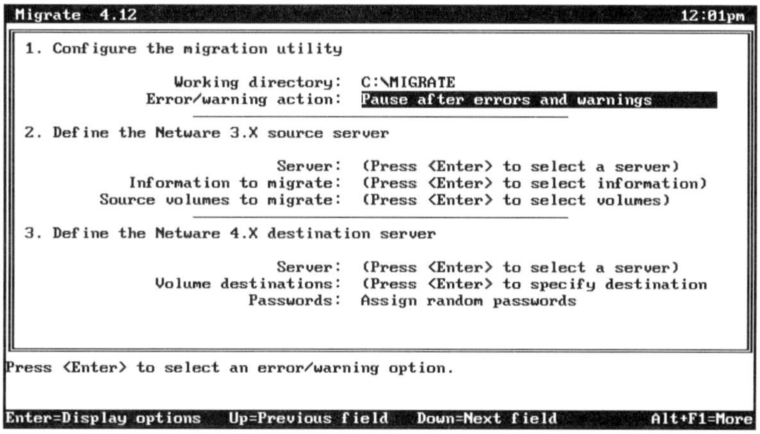

Figure 7.7
Migration utility configuration menu.

9. From the Select a Migration Action menu, choose Start the Migration.
10. When the migration is complete, choose View Migration Reports from the Select a Migration Action menu, then choose Exit to DOS to exit from this program.

Running MIGRATE does not migrate the NetWare 3 printing services to NetWare 4. If you also need to migrate printing services, run the MIGPRINT utility by typing the following:

```
MIGPRINT /s=source /d=destination /VOL=Q_volume /O=file
```

and pressing Enter. Replace `source` with the name of the source server, `destination` with the name of the NetWare 4 destination server, `Q_volume` with the name of the print queue volume if not using SYS:, and `file` with the name of a file to migrate to if you do not want to use the default file.

To complete the process, follow the instructions provided on the MIGPRINT screen, then exit MIGPRINT and perform any necessary cleanup.

Installing New NetWare 4 File Servers Where Needed

You have two options to choose from when installing NetWare 4 file servers by using the NetWare 4 Installation software. You can use the Simple Installation option or the Custom Installation option. In a wide area network, you may find it necessary to run the Custom Installation option, which is described in this section.

If you prefer or can use the Simple Installation option instead, do so by running the NetWare 4 INSTALL program and choosing the Simple Installation of NetWare 4.1 option provided with the NetWare 4 operating system. Chapter 5 explains how to install NetWare 4 using that option.

To begin installing NetWare 4.1 by using the Custom Installation option, place the NetWare 4.1 CD-ROM into the CD-ROM drive on the computer that is to become the NetWare 4 file server. Next, change to the drive containing the NetWare 4.1 installation CD-ROM disk and complete the following steps:

1. Type INSTALL and press Enter.
2. Choose NetWare Server Installation from the Select the type of installation desired menu.
3. Choose NetWare 4.1 from the NetWare Installation Utility screen.
4. Choose Custom Installation of NetWare 4.1 from the next NetWare Installation Utility screen that opens.
5. When prompted, type in the name to be assigned to this file server and press Enter. Ensure that the name complies with the naming standards established by the project team.

6. When the randomly generated internal IPX number is displayed, type in a hexadecimal number that follows the naming standards established by the project team, then press Enter.
7. When prompted, press Enter to begin copying the server boot files.
8. Once the server boot files are copied, accept the defaults for Country Code, Code Page, and Keyboard Mapping by pressing Enter.
9. When prompted, choose DOS filename format (recommended).
10. Choose No when prompted with `Do you want to specify any special startup set commands?` (see fig. 7.8).

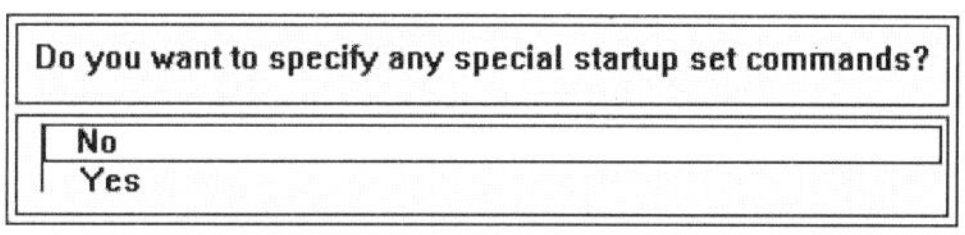

Figure 7.8
Specify set commands screen.

11. Choose either Yes or No when prompted with `Add commands to AUTOEXEC.BAT to load SERVER.EXE?`.
12. When prompted with `Choose the Server Drivers - Disk Drivers`, choose the appropriate server disk driver from the list of known drivers.
13. Choose Save parameters and continue when prompted by the Driver driver_name Parameter Actions menu.
14. Answer No when prompted with `Do You Want to load an Additional Disk Driver?`, unless this file server has more than one type of hard disk installed.
15. When `Choose the Server Drivers - Network Drivers` is displayed, choose the LAN driver for this computer.
16. When prompted, modify the parameters to represent the settings on this computer's network board, then press F10 to save the parameter settings and choose Save parameters and continue.

17. Choose No when prompted with `Do You Want to load an Additional LAN Driver?`.
18. Choose Continue Installation.
19. Accept the default number for binding the protocol to the network board for each protocol you are using, or modify it as needed.
20. Choose Continue accessing the CD-ROM via DOS after the warning message regarding access to the CD-ROM drive is displayed.
21. When prompted to `Create NetWare disk partition`, choose Automatically, which opens the `Choose the Server Drivers - Disk Drivers` prompt. If you prefer, you can choose Manually, then set the partition size, hot fix, and mirroring configurations yourself.
22. Choose Continue with Installation from the Disk Partition Options menu (see fig. 7.9).

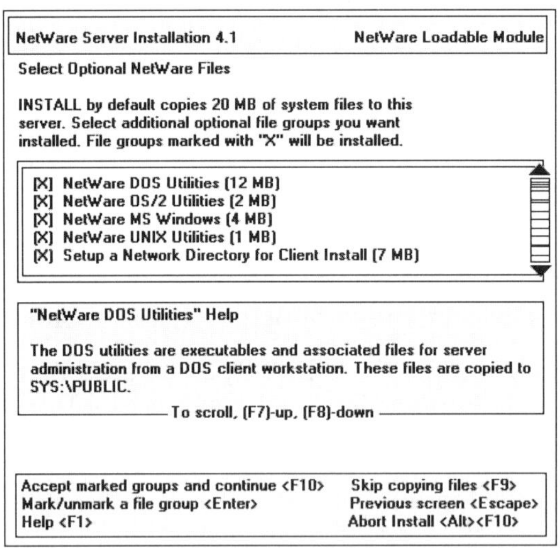

Figure 7.9
Disk partition options.

23. Make changes to NetWare volumes as needed, then press F10 to continue.
24. Press Enter to start the installation of the NetWare files.
25. When the Select Optional NetWare Files window opens, unmark the boxes associated with those groups of files that you do not want to have installed.
26. When prompted with `Install NetWare Directory Services (NDS)`, choose one of the following options:

    ```
    Yes, this is the first NetWare 4 server

    No, connect to existing NetWare 4 networks
    ```

    If this is the first server being installed in this NetWare 4 directory tree, choose the Yes option and continue. If it is not the first NetWare 4 file server installed in this directory tree, choose the No option.
27. Choose a time zone from the list of time zones.
28. Type in an Organization name, following the standards established by the project team, and press Enter. The screen displays the following message:

    ```
    The organization name:
    - Is typically your company name but may also be a
         division or department name.
    - Uniquely identifies your NetWare 4 network (tree).
    - Should not be lengthy (abbreviate if necessary).
    - Cannot contain spaces.
    ```
29. Type in the administrator's password at the `Admin Password:` prompt and press Enter.
30. Retype the password when prompted and press Enter.
31. Press Enter to continue. Then, when all files are copied and the Other Installation Options screen opens, choose any one of four Other Installation Items/Products if needed; otherwise, choose Continue Installation from the Other Installation Actions menu.

The following are Other Installation Items/Products options:

- Create a Registration Diskette
- Upgrade 3.1x Print Services
- Create DOS/MS Windows/OS2 Client Installation Diskettes
- Create NetWare UPGRADE/MIGRATE Diskettes
- Install Online Documentation and Viewers
- Create NetWare BOOTDISK Diskettes
- Install NetWare for Macintosh

You complete the installation once you choose to Continue Installation. You can then press Enter to exit the installation program and return to the system console screen. Repeat this process to install each new NetWare 4.1 file server into the directory tree by using the Custom Installation option.

Upgrading Applications

Completing the migration process includes upgrading any network applications that are not compatible with NetWare 4. Immediately upgrading applications may not be possible, however, because not all software developers may have upgraded their applications. If this is the case, you have two choices.

First, you can leave the existing applications in place and ensure that bindery services are provided on the network for the benefit of these applications and users. You can then upgrade these applications when an upgraded version becomes available. This option is satisfactory for a period of time, but as more users become comfortable with using NetWare 4, they will want the applications upgraded. Novell also has indicated that bindery services is only an interim solution to applications that are not compatible with NetWare 4.

The second choice is to replace existing applications that are not compatible with NetWare 4, and for which there are currently no upgrades, with other applications that are compatible. This involves removing the other applications, converting database or other data files to the new applications, installing the new applications, and training users to use them. This approach may be both too labor- and cost-prohibitive. It is an alternative, however.

Regardless of what you do about migrating applications, you must consider what can be done and make a choice. Then you include the migration of applications in your migration strategy.

Summary

When implementing the NetWare 4.1 WAN, the process followed as defined by Novell's Consulting Services group is the same as that for implementing the NetWare 4 LAN, although some of the procedures and steps may vary. To implement the NetWare 4 WAN, you must develop a migration strategy, create an implementation schedule, and implement NetWare 4.

With designing, planning, and implementing NetWare 4 LANs and MANs, as well as with designing and planning NetWare 4 WANs, a checklist can be quite useful when you begin implementing a NetWare 4 WAN. This summary, therefore, provides you with a checklist to follow as you implement various NetWare 4 wide area networks. If you combine this checklist with the one found in the Summary section of Chapter 6, "Designing and Planning NetWare 4 Wide Area Networks," you should find it easier to remember most of the details of designing and implementing a NetWare 4 WAN.

- ☐ Develop the migration strategy
  - ☐ Create a migration strategy for workstations
  - ☐ Assess existing network clients to determine the following:
    - ☐ The total number of workstations on the network
    - ☐ The types of workstations on the network
    - ☐ The types and versions of operating systems on each workstation
    - ☐ The current type and version of network communication software running on each workstation (NetWare Shell versus the Requester)
    - ☐ Whether existing workstation configuration files are set up for network access
    - ☐ Whether network management tools are being used, the type being used, and whether they will be compatible with NetWare 4
    - ☐ Whether LIP will be set for workstations
    - ☐ Whether packet burst will be set for workstations
    - ☐ Whether any applications currently exist on workstations that will be used in the NetWare 4 environment
    - ☐ Which protocols are currently used by workstations
    - ☐ Who currently handles workstation support, and whether current support will be sufficient when migration begins
    - ☐ Whether workstations will be backed up by SMS-compliant backup software
    - ☐ Whether information transferred between file servers and workstations will have to be encrypted
    - ☐ Current level of each user's networking experience

- ☐ Determine typical workstation configuration
- ☐ Check existing hardware to identify the following:
    - ☐ The microprocessor (80386, 80486, and so on)
    - ☐ The amount of RAM
    - ☐ The amount of hard disk space
    - ☐ Current protocol
- ☐ Check existing software files, including the following:
    - ☐ NET.CFG
    - ☐ AUTOEXEC.BAT
    - ☐ CONFIG.SYS
    - ☐ STARTNET.BAT
- ☐ Identify and become familiar with options for migrating workstations, including the following:
    - ☐ DOS and Windows Client Installation
    - ☐ Batch file in system login script
    - ☐ Batch file run at workstations
    - ☐ WSUPDATE
    - ☐ WSUPGRD
- ☐ Test most logical options
- ☐ Review and evaluate results of testing
- ☐ Choose best method(s)
- ☐ Share client software with network administrators
    - ☐ Allow administrators to work in a testing lab
    - ☐ Have administrators migrate their own workstations

- ☐ Create user training
    - ☐ Assess user's expertise
    - ☐ Determine whether training will be required
    - ☐ Determine what topics should be included in training
    - ☐ Develop a training plan, choosing from various training options, including the following:
        - ☐ E-mail
        - ☐ Formal and informal written documents
        - ☐ Quick reference materials
        - ☐ Self-study materials
        - ☐ Online documentation
        - ☐ Formal training sessions, in-house or at an outside training facility
    - ☐ Conduct the first training session
    - ☐ Evaluate the results of the first training session
    - ☐ Revise training techniques and associated training if needed, conduct another training session, evaluate, and repeat the process until the training program and materials are sufficiently successful

☐ Create a migration strategy for file servers

- ☐ Gather and review relevant information to answer basic questions, including the following:
    - ☐ What versions of NetWare and other operating systems are currently used on the network?
    - ☐ Will all file servers be migrated to NetWare 4?
    - ☐ Is hardware currently available for establishing a testing lab?
    - ☐ How will the testing lab be configured to best represent the existing network?

    - ☐ Will network data on file servers have to be migrated separately from and in addition to the network file server operating systems?
    - ☐ Is a database of user information available from which to create part of the NDS database by using the UIMPORT utility?
- ☐ Establish a testing lab to accomplish the following:
    - ☐ Help determine the most appropriate file server migration strategy
    - ☐ Train administrators and other personnel who will be responsible for migrating file servers on the migration option(s) chosen
- ☐ Discuss downtime and migration with management
- ☐ Choose the most appropriate file server migration method(s) from the following options:
    - ☐ Across-the-wire
    - ☐ Same-server
    - ☐ In-place upgrade
    - ☐ NetWare 4.1 installation
- ☐ Obtain NetWare 4.1 software and licenses
    - ☐ Schedule and perform pilot migration
    - ☐ Choose the pilot department by using the following issues to guide your choice:
        - ☐ Whether sufficient hardware exists in the pilot department to run the migration
        - ☐ Whether the area on the network can be somewhat isolated to keep from disturbing the remainder of the network
        - ☐ Whether employees in the pilot department have a positive attitude and are open to being the pilot test users

- Whether enough employees exist in this department to assist with troubleshooting and problem resolution during the pilot test
- Train users in the pilot department
- Schedule migration for the balance of the network, choosing from the following:
  - Migrating a single area of the company at a time until all areas have been migrated
  - Simultaneously migrating the entire company by using a large number of personnel to perform the migration

- Create a migration strategy for applications
  - Gather relevant information, such as the following:
    - A list of applications on the existing network
    - A list of which existing applications are NetWare 4-compatible and which are not
    - A list of which users must continue to function as bindery-based users for a period of time
    - A list of which existing menus call bindery-based applications and thus will have to be modified
    - In what context bindery-based users exist
  - Decide the approach to take to migrate applications, choosing from the following:
    - Immediately upgrade or replace all applications that are not NetWare 4-compatible
    - Provide bindery services for applications and users that must continue to function as if they were still on a bindery-based network

- Set up a testing lab to do the following:
  - Verify that applications will run with NetWare 4
  - Evaluate the chosen migration process
  - Train administrators to migrate applications
- Create an implementation schedule
  - Identify all tasks that must be completed
  - Organize tasks in the most logical order
  - Estimate approximate length of time each task will require
  - Prepare a preliminary implementation schedule, assigning planned start and complete dates to each task and who will be responsible for completing each task
  - Review the preliminary implementation schedule with all affected departments
  - Revise the implementation schedule, if needed, and obtain final approval from all affected departments
- Implement NetWare 4
  - Upgrade each network workstation to the latest connection software by running the following:
  - The DOS and Windows Network Client installation software
    - WSUPGRD
    - WSUPDATE
  - Migrate each file server to NetWare 4 and install new NetWare 4 file servers as needed by using the following:
    - NetWare 4 Simple Installation
    - NetWare 4 Custom Installation
    - MIGRATE.EXE

- Accommodate network applications, whether bindery-based or NetWare 4-compatible
- Accommodate network users who must temporarily continue to function as though they were part of a bindery-based network

Case Study

The Xtra Company is in the business of providing classroom training on three common application programs: WordPerfect, Dbase, and Lotus 1-2-3. The Xtra Company currently runs NetWare 3.12 on two file servers in the Sales department and NetWare 3.11 on all its other file servers. Xtra is planning on migrating all 47 file servers to a NetWare 4 network.

The project team has determined that there are four typical file server configurations on the existing network, all of which exist within three departments: Training, Sales, and Business.

The Training department has the majority of file servers, a total of 31. All file servers except one within the training department contain 80386 microprocessors, with 12 MB of RAM and 80 MB hard disks. The one different file server has an 80486 microprocessor, with 16 MB of RAM and a 200 MB hard disk.

The Sales department has 11 file servers, 9 of which have 80386 microprocessors with 12 MB of RAM and 120 MB hard disks. The other two file servers have 80486 microprocessors with 16 MB of RAM and 200 MB hard disks. These two file servers are the ones that are running NetWare 3.12.

The Business department has only five file servers, all of which have 80386 microprocessors, with 16 MB of RAM and 200 MB hard disks. The Business department will be used for the pilot implementation because it contains the fewest number of file servers, with the largest amount of RAM and disk storage space. Sales will be migrated second, and Training will be migrated last.

According to the naming standards document developed by the project team, all file servers will be renamed to include the first four letters of the department in which the file server is located, followed by a three-digit number assigned randomly to each file server. The three-digit number will be used by the company to track inventory and has no purpose other than to identify the hardware associated with each file server. Thus, the number portion of the file server's name will be assigned starting at 001 for the first file server installed, followed by 002 for the second, and so on until all file servers are named with a department abbreviation and sequential number.

Given the above information, Xtra's owner has asked you to provide her with a full file server migration configuration. The file server migration configuration document was started by another consultant who took ill and was forced to withdraw from the project. Because the cost of migrating the network is a big expense for Xtra this year, the owner has asked you to pick up where the previous consultant left off and complete the file server migration document, rather than making any changes or starting over. To accomplish this task, you must fill in the missing information on the following file server migration summary document. Each file server being migrated is listed in the order in which it is to be migrated.

Xtra Company File Server Migration Summary

Department	*Server Name*	*OS*	*Configuration*
Business	BUSI_001	3.11	80386, 16 MB RAM, 200 MB HD
	BUSI_002	3.11	80386, __ MB RAM, 200 MB HD
	________	3.11	80386, 16 MB RAM, 200 MB HD
	BUSI_004	3.11	80386, 16 MB RAM, ___ MB HD
	BUSI_005	____	80386, 16 MB RAM, 200 MB HD
Sales	________	3.12	80486, 16 MB RAM, 200 MB HD
	BUSI_006	3.12	80486, __ MB RAM, 200 MB HD

continues

Xtra Company File Server Migration Summary

Department	Server Name	OS	Configuration
	BUSI_007	3.11	80386, 11 MB RAM, 120 MB HD
	BUSI_008	3.11	80386, 11 MB RAM, 120 MB HD
	BUSI_009	3.11	80386, 11 MB RAM, 120 MB HD
	BUSI_010	3.11	80386, 11 MB RAM, 120 MB HD
	________	3.11	80386, 11 MB RAM, 120 MB HD
	BUSI_012	3.11	80386, 11 MB RAM, 120 MB HD
	BUSI_013	3.11	80386, 11 MB RAM, 120 MB HD
	BUSI_0__	3.11	80386, 11 MB RAM, 120 MB HD
_________	BUSI_014	____	80386, 12 MB RAM, 80 MB HD
	BUSI_015	3.11	80386, 12 MB RAM, 80 MB HD
	________	____	____________________________
	________	____	____________________________
	BUSI_016	3.11	_____, 16 MB RAM, 200 MB HD
	________	____	____________________________
	________	____	____________________________
	________	____	____________________________
	________	____	____________________________
	________	____	____________________________
	________	____	____________________________
	________	____	____________________________
	________	____	____________________________
	________	____	____________________________
	________	____	____________________________
	________	____	____________________________

__________	_____	________________________________
__________	_____	________________________________
__________	_____	________________________________
__________	_____	________________________________
__________	_____	________________________________
__________	_____	________________________________
__________	_____	________________________________
__________	_____	________________________________
__________	_____	________________________________
__________	_____	________________________________
__________	_____	________________________________
__________	_____	________________________________
__________	_____	________________________________
__________	_____	________________________________
__________	_____	________________________________

Review Questions

1. Developing a list of file servers and the type and version of network operating system running on those file servers, is part of the ____________ task.

   ○ A. assess current server configurations

   ○ B. set up a testing lab

   ○ C. schedule and perform pilot implementation

   ○ D. choose the best migration method for each server

2. If you are beginning the training of administrators to perform file server migration, you are in the process of ____________ for file server migration.

- A. assessing current server configurations
- B. setting up a testing lab
- C. scheduling and performing pilot implementation
- D. choosing the best migration method for each server

3. The safest of the file server migrations is the ____________ method.

- A. across-the-wire
- B. same-server
- C. in-place
- D. NetWare 4.1 Install

4. To migrate a NetWare 4.0*x* file server, you must use the ____________ migration method.

- A. across-the-wire
- B. same-server
- C. in-place
- D. NetWare 4.1 Install

5. Which of the following is *not* a consideration when developing a migration strategy for network workstations?

- A. whether network management tools will be used on the network
- B. whether workstation backups will be performed using SMS-compliant backup software
- C. whether LIP or packet burst will be used
- D. whether binderies will need to be cleaned up

6. If no STARTNET.BAT file exists, it is likely that the workstation is ____________.

- A. not going to be migrated
- B. already upgraded to function in a NetWare 4 environment

- ○ C. running the older NetWare Shell
- ○ D. using a NetWare 3.12 version of the NetWare DOS Requester

7. Of the following, which *three* statements are true regarding setting bindery services on the migrated network?
   - ○ A. Bindery services make it possible for users to continue to use bindery-based applications on the NetWare 4 network.
   - ○ B. If bindery services are to be used, you must set the bindery context for all containers, or for no containers.
   - ○ C. Setting a bindery context makes it possible for bindery-based applications to perform as though they are still being run on a NetWare 3 file server.
   - ○ D. Setting a bindery context makes NetWare 4 aware of where bindery-based users are located on the network

8. Running the across-the-wire upgrade to migrate bindery information and data from a NetWare 3 file server to a NetWare 4 file server uses the ____________ utility.
   - ○ A. UPGRADE.EXE
   - ○ B. MIGRATE.EXE
   - ○ C. WSUPGRDE.EXE
   - ○ D. WSUPDTE.EXE

9. Which *two* functions can a testing lab serve?
   - ○ A. testing migration options
   - ○ B. verifying hardware configuration
   - ○ C. educating users
   - ○ D. training network administrators

10. Which of the following are factors to consider when choosing a department, workgroup, or other area of the company as the pilot department? (Choose three.)

- ○ A. sufficient quantity of hardware that meets the minimum NetWare 4 migration and installation requirements
- ○ B. area of the network that can be relatively isolated from the rest of the network during pilot implementation
- ○ C. employees will not be affected by the pilot implementation of NetWare 4
- ○ D. enough employees to assist in the implementation and troubleshoot and solve problems as they arise

Answers

1. A
2. B
3. A
4. D
5. D
6. C
7. A C D
8. B
9. A D
10. A B D

Chapter 8

Following Up After Implementation

Novell has defined four phases in the NetWare 4 design and implementation process. Discussion of the first three phases—project approach, design, and implementation—account for the majority of this book, because they also account for the majority of the work associated with designing and implementing a NetWare 4 network.

The fourth phase of the design and implementation process—the manage and monitor phase—is the topic of this, the final chapter, which discusses the procedures defined for this phase: managing the NetWare 4 network, and monitoring the NetWare 4 network. A variety of tasks are associated with these two procedures. The ultimate purpose of the tasks, and thus of these procedures and this phase of the NetWare 4 network design and implementation process, is to ensure that the network as designed and implemented meets the needs of the users, fulfills the goals for which it was designed, and functions as efficiently as possible.

This chapter is designed to help you understand what managing and monitoring a NetWare 4 network involves. You will understand what tasks must be accomplished after network implementation to ensure that the NetWare 4 network provides everything network users need, including print services and security. You will also understand what tasks must be accomplished in order to determine whether the network is successfully fulfilling its goal.

After reading this chapter, you will understand how to do the following:

- Set up and monitor network print services
- Administer NDS security
- Monitor and maintain the NetWare 4 network

In short, this chapter shows you how to manage and monitor the NetWare 4 network successfully after its design and implementation has been completed.

Setting Up and Monitoring Network Print Services

Setting up and monitoring network print services may be required of network administrators immediately after the network is implemented, as well as on a continuing basis. Additional print services are often added to networks as they grow. New Printer, Print Queue, and Print Server objects can be added to accommodate network expansion or simply to ease the burden on existing network print services.

The following are the tasks that must be completed in order to set up and then monitor network printing services successfully:

- Planning NetWare 4 network printing
- Customizing NetWare 4 network printing
- Managing printing on the NetWare 4 network

- Monitoring network printing
- Troubleshooting network printing

This first section of this chapter discusses these five tasks.

Planning NetWare 4 Network Printing

Most NetWare 4 WANs are relatively complex networks, which often require complex printing environments. Setting up printing in a complex network generally means that several aspects of printing must be considered:

- Setting up, using, and maintaining multiple printers, print queues, and print servers
- Setting up, using, and maintaining a variety of print job configurations, and printer definitions
- Accommodating a variety of printer languages

To accommodate the quantity and variety of printing environment variables, NetWare 4.1 provides PSERVER.NLM, PSERVER.EXE, NPRINTER.NLM, and NPRINTER.EXE. The PSERVER NLM (NetWare Loadable Module) loads a print server onto a NetWare 4 file server. Each NetWare 4 print server can then control printing services for up to 256 network printers.

The NPRINTER NLM makes it possible for printers to be attached directly to NetWare 4 file servers. The NPRINTER NLM enables printers to be attached to any NetWare 4 file server. With NPRINTER, file servers that have a print server running on them (have PSERVER.NLM loaded), as well as file servers that do not have a print server running on them, can have attached printers.

The NPRINTER.EXE file is an executable program run on network workstations. NPRINTER makes it possible for printers that are attached to network workstations to be used as network printers. Because printers can be attached to regular NetWare 4 file servers, NetWare 4 file servers that also have a print server running on them, and regular network workstations, each NetWare 4 print server can accommodate as many as 256 network printers.

Planning network printing services can become quite complex. Extensive print services are often needed, however, on wide area networks. Such issues as how many print servers you will need and whether printers will be attached to file servers, print servers, or workstations—and, if so, to which ones—must be considered when planning network print services. In addition, you also need to determine how many print queues you will need and to which print servers you will assign those print queues. Finally, you need to determine where *direct-connect printers* (printers that can be connected directly to the network cable rather than to a server or workstation) will be attached to the network.

Providing the maximum printing throughput for the network is also an important planning and implementation issue. Options for increasing printing throughput include assigning multiple printers of the same type to a single print queue, providing print job configurations for network users, and providing for the use of printers that are not DOS-based, such as Apple or UNIX printers.

Assigning multiple printers of the same type to a single print queue enables all print jobs sent to that queue to be serviced by the next available printer. The printers must also be of the same type, such as all HPIII or all Apple printers, in order to use this approach, however.

Using various print job configurations helps provide efficient printing services to network users who are running applications that are not network-aware or which do not have a needed print driver. Print job configurations require the use of printer definition files, a large number of which are provided as part of the NetWare 4 networking software.

Providing printing services in a mixed printer-language environment—AppleTalk, UNIX, and so on—may require that you purchase separate software. You may also need to load additional NLMs on NetWare file servers and print servers to accommodate a mixed printing environment.

After planning what approaches you will take to network printing, you must then customize the network's printing environment.

Customizing Network Printing

Some of the default printing provided by NetWare 4 will be useful even on wide area networks. Some customization, however, will make network printing easier for users. You can choose what will be customized and then create special print jobs to implement your choices.

For example, you can choose always to have a banner page printed before each print job is released from the printer. In a network where printers are grouped and the first available printer is used to print a job request, a banner page makes it easier to separate one user's print job from another.

You can also create special print jobs that determine when a special form should be used with a particular print job. If the network uses printers with multiple paper trays, different trays can hold different types of forms. Custom print job configurations can be used to specify which paper tray should be chosen when printing a specific job. Choosing the right paper tray for the print job ensures that the job will be printed on the correct form. For example, you can specify one paper tray on a printer to print company payroll checks on preprinted check forms and another tray to print out the report associated with the check printing job.

In addition to customizing print jobs, NetWare 4 enables you to manage various aspects of print jobs. Print job management involves the management of network print queues, print servers, and printers. You can place holds on print jobs, reorder print jobs in print queues, or delete print jobs completely when they should not be printed or when they are causing problems on the network.

Once you have created custom configurations you can then use those configurations with various print jobs. To use custom print configurations, you use the `CAPTURE` or `NPRINT` *Job* option. This enables you to access a custom configuration when you send a print job to a printer.

To create customized printing configurations for your network's users, you can use the NetWare Administrator or PRINTCON utilities. When you create a custom printing configuration, you must create it in the container whose users need to access that configuration. Before creating the configuration, therefore, ensure that your context is set to the container in which the print job configuration is to be placed.

To create a print job configuration by using the NetWare Administrator utility, choose the NetWare Administrator icon. Next, if a browser window is not already open to display part of the directory tree, open a Browser window by choosing Browse from the Tools pull-down menu (see fig. 8.1).

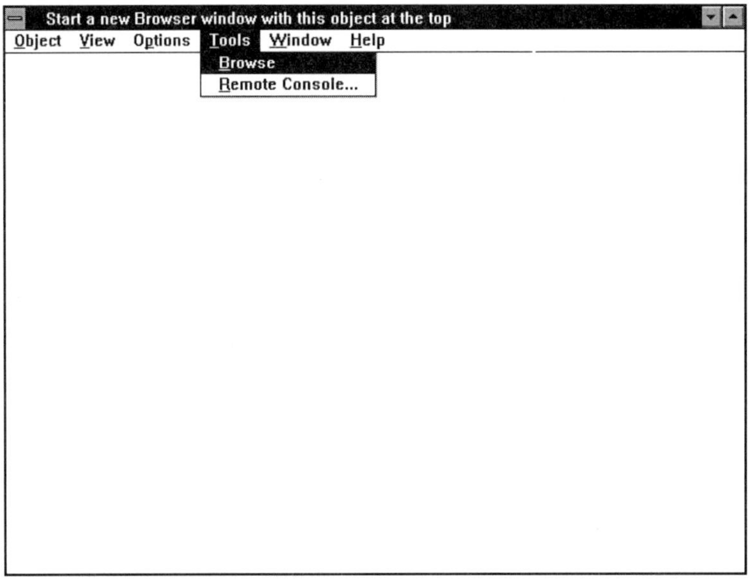

Figure 8.1
Browse option in Tools pull-down menu.

Then, expand the directory tree and change the context until you can select (highlight) the Organizational Unit where you want to place the print job configuration.

Because a print job configuration is a property of an Organizational Unit, with the Organizational Unit highlighted, choose Details from the Object pull-down menu. Next, choose the Print Job Configuration page button from the Organizational Unit object's list of page buttons displayed when the object's Identification page opens (see fig. 8.2).

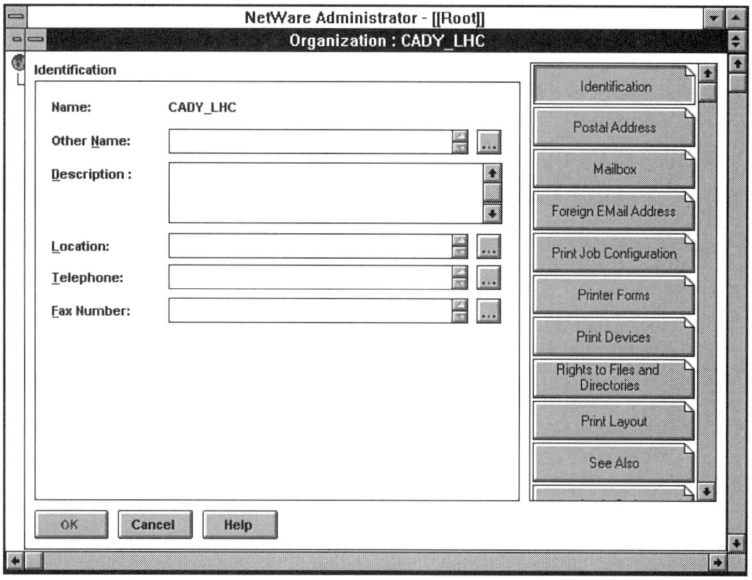

Figure 8.2

Organization Unit's identification page.

Choose the New button on the Print Job Configuration window to open the Print Job Configuration form. Next, fill in all appropriate fields on the form and choose OK to save the new configuration. Figure 8.3 shows a sample print job configuration form that has been filled in for printing Payroll checks.

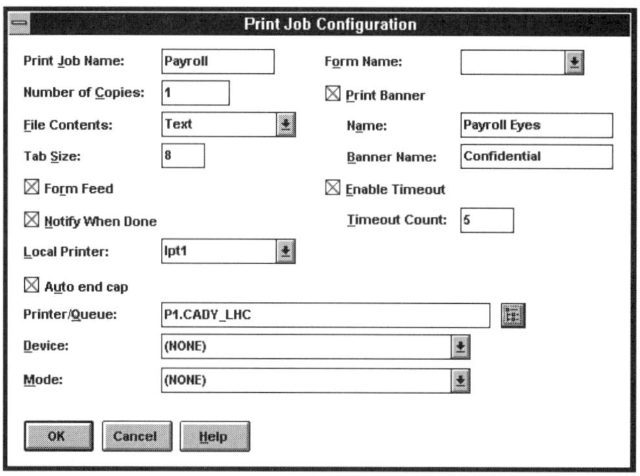

Figure 8.3

Print Job Configuration form.

When creating a print job configuration, remember that a name for the print job configuration (`Print Job Name`) and a printer or print queue object for the print job configuration to use (`Printer/Queue`) are required. Other fields can remain set to their default settings or can be modified as necessary.

The fields shown on the Print Job Configuration form, along with a brief description of the field's purpose are displayed in table 8.1.

Table 8.1
Fields Included on the Print Job Configuration Form

Name	*Purpose*
Print Job Name	Name to be used when choosing a print job
Form Name	Name of the form to be used when this print job configuration is used
Number of Copies	Number of copies to be printed when this print job configuration is used
Print Banner	Indicates whether a banner page should be printed before each print job
Name	Identifies on the banner page the user who sent the print job
Banner Name	Name of the print job
File Contents	Specifies whether the job is a Text job, wherein the tab commands are understood and their sizes can be set, or a byte stream job with no tabs
Tab Size	Specifies the number of spaces to be used between tab stops
Form Feed	Indicates whether the form should be ejected from the printer once the print job is complete
Enable Timeout	Specifies whether timeout should be enabled
Timeout Count	Specifies length of time to pass before the job is considered complete when the Enable Timeout option is set

Name	*Purpose*
Notify When Done	States whether the workstation from which the print job was sent should be notified that the job has been printed
Local Printer	Tells which printer port the printer is attached to
Auto end cap	Closes the print queue file after the printing of this job is complete
Printer/Queue	Indicates which printer or print queue this print job configuration should use
Device	Tells which print device is to be used with this configuration
Mode	Enables you to choose a print mode for the chosen print device

Customizing network printing also involves designating printer forms and then mounting those forms. In addition, customizing printing may require that you build or import printer definitions.

To designate printer forms you can use either the PRINTDEF utility, or the NetWare Administrator. To designate printer forms to be mounted or dismounted, use the Change forms as needed, Minimize form changes across queues, Minimize form changes within queues, and Service only mounted form service mode options.

To mount forms, first choose the Printer object from the display of directory tree objects. (To find the printer object you have to open a Browser window in the NetWare Administrator utility.) Once you choose the Printer object, choose Details from the Object pull-down menu. Next, choose the Identification page for the Printer object, then choose Mount Form. Finally, choose the form to be mounted.

To create a printer definition, choose the appropriate Organizational Unit in the NetWare Administrator utility. Next, open the Details window for the object, then choose the object's Print Devices page. Finally, choose the Create button, type in a name for this new printer definition, then choose OK (see fig. 8.4).

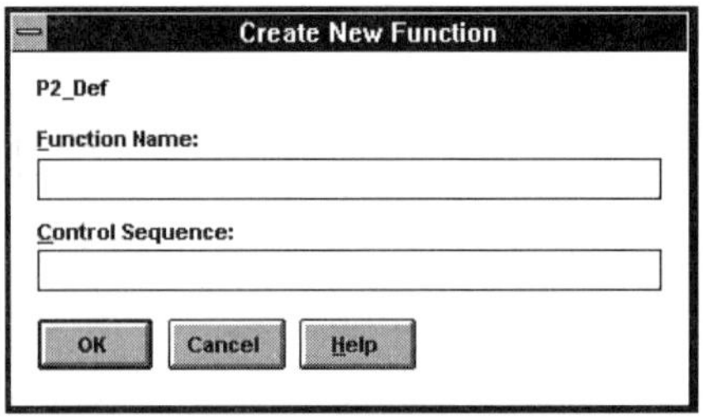

Figure 8.4
Create New Function dialog box.

After assigning a name to the printer definition, select the printer definition name you just created, choose Modify, then choose Create Function. You can now add any function calls specific to this printer to further customize the printer definition.

To import one or more printer definitions, select the appropriate Organizational Unit in the NetWare Administrator utility. Next, open the OU object's Details window and choose the Print Devices page button. Next, choose Import, then choose the printer definition to be imported.

Once you customize network printing, users can access and use the print job configurations you set up. To use a print job configuration, users can call the print job configuration by name from within the CAPTURE command. Users can also choose a device and mode from a list of available devices or modes.

Managing Printing on the NetWare 4 Network

Managing printing on the network requires that someone first be made responsible for managing network printing. On a small network with centralized administration, only one or two people may be responsible for managing network printing. Centralized printing management in a wide area network is almost never practical, however. The first step to managing printing in the WAN, therefore, is to assign users varying levels of responsibility for network printing management.

The majority of work associated with managing network printing relates to managing print jobs themselves. There are two utilities that can be used to manage print jobs. Those two utilities are PCONSOLE and NetWare Administrator. Once users have been assigned to manage network printing, they can be trained to use these utilities to perform their assigned tasks.

Assigning Responsibility for Network Printing Management

To decentralize the management of network printing, create different types of network users, then assign various printing management tasks to those users. By creating different types of users for printing management, you can assign different rights and responsibilities to those users.

The following is a list of different types of users and the functions each type is given the rights to perform by default:

- *Container Supervisor.* This user can create and delete Printer objects, Print Server objects, and Print Queue objects. This user can also change the print queue lists of users and operators, change print queue assignments, and change the Notify list. In addition, this user can monitor network print servers.
- *Members of the Printer Notify List.* Users who are included as members on the list of users to be notified when a printer has problems are automatically given the right to receive error messages from the specified printer.
- *Print Queue Operator.* These users can manage their own and other users' print jobs after they have been placed into a print queue. They can also change print queue operator flags.
- *Print Server Operator.* This user can change the assignment of print queues, modify the Notify list, change the status of a

printer, and bring a print server down by unloading the related print server files.

- *Print Queue User.* These users have rights only to their own jobs within a print queue. These users can submit print jobs to the specified print queue, modify parameters associated with their print jobs, and remove their own jobs from the print queue if the print jobs have not already been sent to a printer.
- *Print Server User.* This user can monitor network print servers, including receiving error messages from a printer.

Network print servers, print queues, and printers often require administrator intervention. In addition, multiple print servers, print queues, and printers exist on the network and are often geographically dispersed. Having a variety of users to assist with administering network printing services helps keep the print function up and running.

As the list details, print service users may have to perform a variety of tasks, which can be accomplished by using either the PCONSOLE or the NetWare Administrator utility.

Managing Print Jobs Using PCONSOLE

The PCONSOLE utility is provided to help you and other network printing management users accomplish a variety of print job management tasks. To use PCONSOLE, log in to the network, then type PCONSOLE, and press Enter. When the PCONSOLE Available Options menu opens, choose from the following menu items, depending on the task you want to accomplish:

- Print Queues
- Printers
- Print Servers

To manage print queues, printers, or print servers, choose the appropriate menu option from the Available Options menu.

For example, choose Print Queues from the Available Options menu to manage a specific print queue. Next, choose the print queue to be managed. Then, choose the appropriate option in order to perform the related management task (see fig. 8.5).

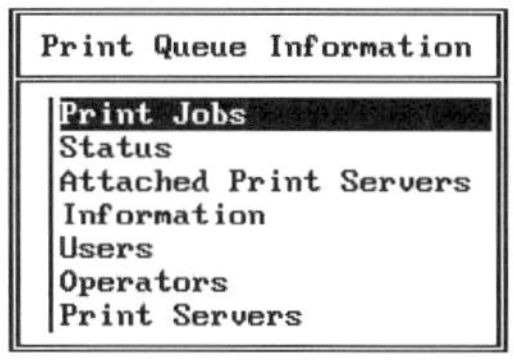

Figure 8.5
Print Queue Information menu.

From the Print Queue Information menu, you can choose any of the following options to perform the related print queue management task:

- Print Jobs — Add a print job to the print queue, cancel an existing print job, or change fields on a print job's information screen.
- Status — View information about the print queue.
- Attached Print Servers — See which print servers service this print.
- Information — View this print queue's Object ID, the name of the file server associated with this print queue, and the volume on which the queue is located.
- Users — Add or delete users who are authorized to place jobs into this print queue.
- Operators — Add or delete users from the list of authorized print queue operators.
- Print Servers — Add or delete print servers from the list of authorized print servers.

You can also choose from the following list of print server management tasks included on the Print Server Information menu (see fig. 8.6):

- Printers — Add, delete, rename, or modify a printer's configuration.
- Information and Status — Unload (down) the print server, or give it a different name.
- Users — Add users to or remove users from the list of users authorized to send print jobs to this print server.
- Operators — Add or delete User and other objects that can be assigned to manage this print server.
- Description — Create or edit the description of this print server.
- Password — Change the password associated with this print server.
- Audit — Set auditing for this print server, establish the maximum allowable size for the audit file, and view and delete the audit file.

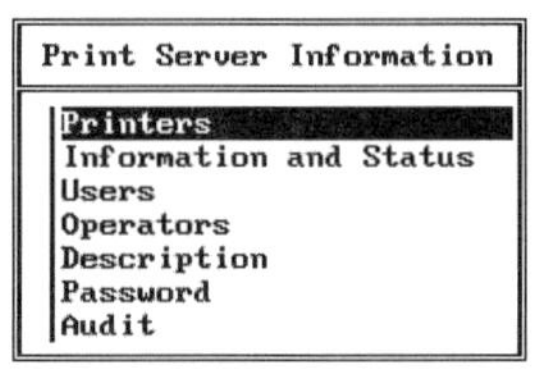

Figure 8.6
Print Server Information menu.

You can also modify printer information. To change information related to a network printer, first choose Printers from the Available Options menu, then choose a printer. After choosing a printer, you can modify information for that printer by changing any of the configuration fields associated with that printer.

For example, you can change the number of kilobytes of memory set aside to hold print jobs until the printer can service them (Buffer size in KB). You can also change the list of print queues assigned to this printer or the list of User and other objects to be notified when a problem with the printer exists (Notification).

Managing Print Jobs Using NetWare Administrator

If you prefer, you can use the NetWare Administrator utility to manage network print jobs. To start the NetWare Administrator utility, choose the NetWare Administrator icon. If a browser window is not already open to display part of the directory tree, open a Browser window by choosing Browse from the Tools pull-down menu. Then, expand the directory tree and change the context until you can select (highlight) the print object (Print server, Printer, or Print queue) that you want to manage from the NetWare Administrator. Next, choose Details from the Object pull-down menu and fill in or modify the fields on the form associated with the type of print object you have chosen to manage.

If you choose a Print Queue object to manage, you can view or modify the Print Queue object's identification, assignments, list of operators, list of authorized users, and current job list. If you choose a Print Server object to manage, you can view or modify the Print Server object's identification, assignments, users, operator, auditing log, and print layout. If you choose a Printer object to manage, you can view or modify the Printer object's identification, assignments, configuration, notification, features, see also, and printer status fields.

Monitoring Network Printing

To ensure the continued success of printing services, network administrators need to monitor overall network printing performance. In particular, network administrators need to monitor print queues and printers.

You can monitor print queues by using the PCONSOLE utility. To monitor print queues from PCONSOLE, change context to reflect the location of the print queue you want to monitor, run PCONSOLE, then choose Print Queues from PCONSOLE's Available Options menu. Next, choose the print queue you want to monitor from the Print Queues list, then choose Status from the Print Queue Information menu. Choosing the Status menu option opens the Print Queue Status screen from which you can view various items of information related to the print queue (see fig. 8.7).

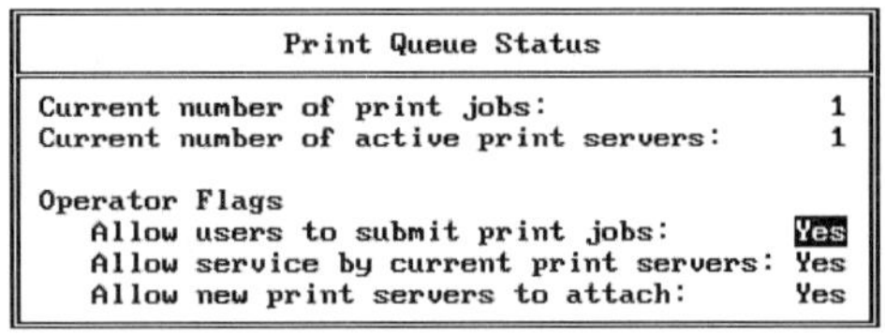

Figure 8.7
PCONSOLE Print Queue Status screen.

The PCONSOLE Print Queue Status screen shows you how many print jobs are currently waiting to be printed (Current number of print jobs). It also shows you how many print servers are actively assigned to this print queue (Current number of active print servers). In addition, it lets you modify three operator flags: Allow users to submit print jobs, Allow service by current print servers, and Allow new print servers to attach.

If you review this screen on a regular basis and track the number of jobs in the Current number of print jobs field, you can eventually estimate the average number of print jobs waiting to be sent to a printer. If this number is regularly high, it may be an indication that the print queue has too many users submitting jobs to it, or too few printers servicing it. It may also be an indicator of an insufficient number of print queues.

You can also monitor printers using the PCONSOLE utility by choosing Printers from the PCONSOLE Available Options menu, then choosing a printer from the list of Printers. You can then review several items of information that the Printer printer_name Configuration screen provides (see fig. 8.8).

Although not all the items of information displayed on the Printer printer_name Configuration screen contain information useful to monitoring network printers, some of the information may be particularly relevant. Each of the fields displayed on the printer's configuration screen is listed in table 8.2. In addition, a brief description is provided for each field, and where appropriate, how the information contained within those fields can be used to help you monitor and manage network printers.

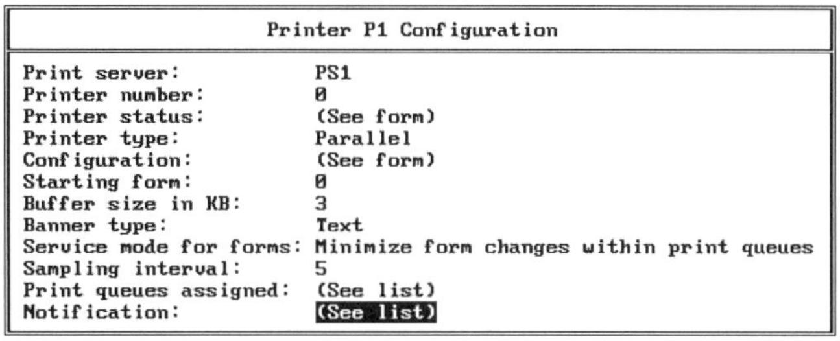

Figure 8.8
PCONSOLE Printer P1 Configuration screen.

Table 8.2
Printer Configuration Screen Information

Field Name	*Description/Use of Information*
Print server	Shows the name of the print server currently servicing this printer
Printer number	Gives the unique number assigned to this printer configuration
Printer status	Displays the status of the printer and its associated active print job; enables you to change the mode and form associated with the printer
Printer type	Displays and lets you change the type of printer (parallel, serial, and so forth); if the printer needs to be upgraded to a parallel from a serial printer, for example, you have to change this field
Configuration	Displays printer configuration information when this field is chosen, thus opening a separate form
Starting form	Specifies the number associated with the form assigned to the number to be used with the printer's current configuration
Buffer size in KB	Shows the amount of storage space this printer has available for storing print jobs waiting to be printed

continues

Table 8.2, Continued
Printer Configuration Screen Information

Field Name	*Description/Use of Information*
Banner type	Specifies whether the banner will be printed as a Text or PostScript print job
Service mode for forms	Specifies which print form is to be used with this print configuration and can be set so that form changes with print jobs can be minimized; if network printing from this printer seems to be slow, minimizing form changes can increase the speed of printing if the slowness is the result of print jobs that use a variety of print forms
Sampling interval	States the number of seconds the print server waits before checking the print queue for available print jobs; increasing or decreasing this time can help speed up or reduce congestion associated with printing jobs on this printer
Print queues assigned	Shows queues serviced by this printer; reducing the number of print queues servicing this printer also reduces the number of jobs it prints (this can be useful when attempting to relieve some of the workload on a very busy printer)
Notification	Displays a list of users and groups who are to be notified when a problem exists on the printer; although the problem may be as simple as the printer running out of paper, ensuring that someone is notified of the problem so that it can be quickly corrected and can help keep the printer up and running as long as possible

Use the printer configuration information to monitor network printers so that changes can be made when needed.

Troubleshooting Network Printing

The Notification field on the printer's configuration screen shows who will be notified when a printing problem occurs. When there is a problem more serious than the printer being out of paper, some troubleshooting may be needed in order to solve that problem. Troubleshooting of network printing can be done at three levels: physical, logical, and procedural.

Physical troubleshooting involves checking the actual printing hardware, and it is the most common reason for printing problems. Physical problems range from some simple problems, such as loose cables, paper jams, and empty paper trays, to less obvious and more difficult-to-locate problems, such as broken or damaged printer parts and malfunctioning interface boards.

Because some physical problems are easier to locate than others, one effective approach to troubleshooting physical problems is to look for the easiest possible problems first. If none of the simple problems (loose cable, printer turned off, paper jam, and so on) turn out to be the problem, begin looking for the more difficult problems (defective interface board, broken printer, and so on).

Assessing printer problems on the logical level requires that you look at the printing software and its associated configuration. More often than not, logical problems relate to incorrect object configuration, wrong network addresses, wrong form assignments, corrupted or incorrect print drivers, corrupted or incorrect communication software, and so on. As with physical problems, you should check the easiest potential problems first, then move on to check the more difficult potential problems. If you cannot determine what the software-related problem may be, you may be able to correct the problem by reinstalling the software and then reinitializing the printer.

Procedural level problems generally involve users themselves. Often, users send wrong commands or print jobs to the wrong printer. Problems of this type are best corrected (or avoided) by training network users, thus ensuring they understand how to use the printing services provided on the network properly. If educating all users is not practical or possible, you can at least make it less likely for users to repeat printing mistakes by customizing their environments. To customize their environments, you can place printing-related commands into their workstation configuration files, ensure printing objects are in the same container as the users' User objects, create Alias objects where appropriate, or place printing-related commands into container login scripts.

There are some common network printing problems that you may have to troubleshoot and resolve. For example, users may complain that their print jobs contain characters that were not in the document before they were printed. This usually means that the print job timeout value is set too short. Reset the timeout value to one that lengthens the number of seconds that must pass without print characters being received at the printer before the job is considered finished and the balance of the job in the print buffer is printed. You can set this value as high as 1,000 seconds.

If users complain that their print jobs never print out, the print job may be arriving at a context other than the user's default. To correct this problem, ensure that the user's `CAPTURE` or `NPRINT` commands use the full context.

When a printer continues to switch from online to offline, printer electrical interference may be the cause. Ensure that the printer is not located too close to any electrical source, such as an electric motor or a generator, or any strong radiation source, such as radar or microwave. If the printer cable is running next to a power cord designed to handle a heavy electrical load, the resulting effect may be interference with the printer's signal. The cure involves moving the printer away from the source of interference or moving the source of interference away from the printer.

If print jobs placed into print queues display errors, the problem may be a corrupted Print Queue or Print Server object. The solution is often merely to delete the print Queue or Print Server object and recreate it.

When print jobs seem to be printing in the wrong language or not printing at all, it may be the result of the print job being sent to a printer with a different printer language installed. The solution is to reroute the print job so that it arrives at the correct printer.

As with solving any problem, network-related or not, there are some basic steps that can be followed. There are six specific steps you can follow to help resolve NetWare 4 network printing problems:

1. Gather background information about the problem.
2. Investigate the problem.
3. Isolate the problem.
4. Repair the problem.
5. Return printing services to normal operation.
6. Document errors and malfunctions and their solutions.

Troubleshooting problems, resolving them to the best of your ability, and restoring network printing to its original or a better status is the responsibility of the network's administrators.

Administering NDS Security

NDS security has certain defaults established when the network is created. In addition to default security features, there are other NetWare 4 security features and issues with which you should be familiar if you are responsible for administering NDS security. This section discusses default security and other related NDS security issues.

NDS' Default Security

When you install NetWare 4, certain security defaults are placed in effect. For example, user network login and authentication is handled automatically by the workstation and NDS. When a user logs in, the workstation encrypts the password before it is broadcast to the file server where NDS authenticates the user. This verifies the user's User object login name and password and determines the user's rights on the network.

Another security feature implemented by default is *packet signature*. During the packet signature process, a session key is established once the workstation is logged in to the network. Each packet then received from the workstation is verified to determine that it contains the unique signature assigned to this workstation for this network session.

Both authentication and packet signature are part of the login security process. Login security is the first level of network security, and it is an automatic security process, although you can control the level of packet signature used on the network.

Object and Property Rights

Rights can also be used to protect the network and its resources. NetWare 4 has Object and Property rights in addition to the file system rights that NetWare 3 has.

Object rights are given to objects in the NDS database. Depending on the object rights assigned, a user may control one or more network objects. The following are available object rights:

- Supervisor — Provides unrestricted access to an object and all its properties.
- Browse — Enables users to see the object in the NDS tree structure.
- Create — Enables users to create other objects within the container object to which this object right applies.
- Delete — Enables users to delete the object for which this right was given.
- Rename — Enables users to change the object's name.

Property rights control what can be done to the properties associated with an object. Unlike object rights, which apply to the entire object, property rights can be assigned to all properties of an object or only to specific properties of the object. The following are the five property rights:

◆ Supervisor	Enables unrestricted access to all properties of the object.
◆ Compare	Enables users to compare the value of one property with that of another value, returning either a `True` or `False` response.
◆ Read	Enables the user who has this right to read the values of the object's properties. By default, a user who has the Read right also has the Compare property right, because it is a subset of the Read property right.
◆ Write	Enables the object granted this right to add, change, or delete values given to the properties for which this right is assigned.
◆ Add or Delete Self	Enables the trustee to add itself to or remove itself from a property whose value is a list of names, such as that found in a group membership or mailing list.

NDS security enables objects to receive object and property rights to other objects. NDS object and property rights are not the same as file rights, and granting object and property rights does not also grant file system rights, with one exception. That exception occurs when the Supervisor object right is granted to a server object.

By granting an object the Supervisor object right to a server object, you also grant the Supervisor file system right to the file system on that server. Thus, as a network administrator, you should occasionally verify that only those users who are supposed to have Supervisor rights to the file system have those rights, and that no user has been accidentally given file system rights as a result of having been given the Supervisor object right to a server object.

Be careful also about assigning the Write property right to the Access Control List (ACL) of an object. Users who have the Write property right to the ACL of objects have the capability of changing the rights associated with those objects. In addition, those users can rename or delete those objects. Having the Write property right to an object's ACL gives the user complete control over the object.

Managing and Monitoring Network Security

Other security issues can be managed and monitored. Some of these issues require user cooperation, and some are the responsibility of network administrators. The major user security issue involves the use of passwords on the network. Users must take responsibility for protecting their login passwords. Users must make certain no one can use their passwords to access the network.

Network administrators can help users take precautions to safeguard their passwords by setting security to require that all users meet the following requirements:

- Have passwords for their accounts
- Change their passwords after a given amount of time passes
- Have a minimum password length that makes it sufficiently difficult to guess a user's password
- Use passwords that are not easy to guess
- Remember their passwords rather than writing them down somewhere where they may be found
- Keep their passwords secret, never giving their passwords to anyone

Another security method that can be used to secure the network includes keeping the NetWare file servers protected from physical access. File servers should be placed in secure areas—in locked rooms if possible. Only those users with a need to have physical access to network file servers should be allowed to access them.

The following are additional security issues that you should consider when managing and monitoring network security:

- Creating workgroup managers to assist with administering the network
- Verifying effective rights for users to ensure that they have only the rights they were intended to have
- Modifying the IRF

Creating Workgroup Managers

A workgroup manager functions much like the network administrator, but is responsible for administering only a section of the NDS Tree. The workgroup manager is a user User object who is made a trustee of the container at the highest level of the tree for which the manager is responsible. Once you choose User objects to be workgroup managers and make them containers at the highest level, you then simply grant the Users the object rights needed to administer that section of the tree.

Verifying Effective Rights

To ensure that workgroup managers and other network users have only the rights they should have at any given location on the network, you should periodically verify effective rights for User and other objects on the network. To view effective rights for a network object, complete the following steps:

1. Change your context to the home container of the object whose rights you want to view.
2. Select the container object from the tree.
3. Choose Trustees of object from the Object pull-down menu to open the Trustees of object_name dialog box for the container.
4. Choose the Effective Rights button from the Trustees of object_name dialog box.
5. Choose the Browse button from the Effective Rights dialog box.

6. Change the context so that the object whose effective rights you want to view is displayed in the Objects area of the Select Object dialog box.
7. Select the object and choose OK.

You can now view the object's effective rights. The object's rights are all rights that are displayed but not grayed out.

Modifying the IRF

Just as file system rights flow down through the directory structure, NDS Object and Property rights flow down through the directory tree. When Object rights are granted to an object at one container, or when the All Property right is granted, these rights flow down the directory tree to other objects within the container, as well as to other subcontainers. Rights continue to flow down the directory tree until those rights are changed. You can change NDS rights by either assigning different rights or by modifying the IRF.

By default, the IRF allows all rights to flow down the NDS tree structure. To prevent rights from flowing to the object, you remove or block the right in the IRF by modifying the IRF.

To modify the IRF by using the NetWare Administrator utility, choose the object whose IRF you want to modify, then complete the following steps:

1. Open the Object pull-down menu.
2. Choose Trustees of this object.
3. Choose the Inherited Rights Filter button on the Trustees of object_name dialog box.
4. Modify property or object rights by marking or unmarking the box associated with each right (see fig. 8.9)

All modifications for the IRF will be effected for all users, including the ADMIN (if the Supervisor object right is blocked).

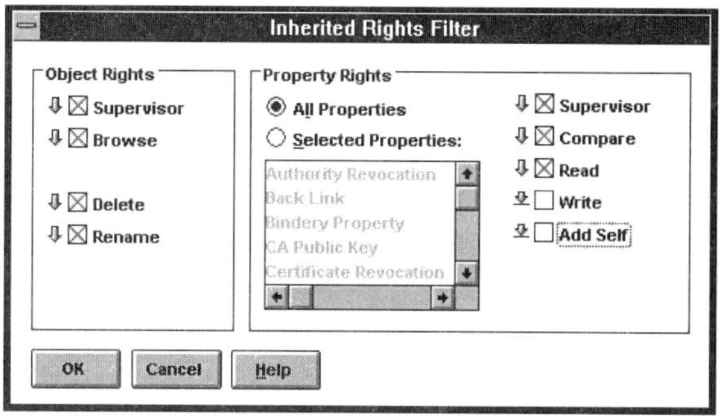

Figure 8.9

Inherited Rights Filter dialog box.

Monitoring and Maintaining the NetWare 4 Network

There are a variety of tasks associated with monitoring and maintaining the NetWare 4 network, the first of which is to establish guidelines for managing the network. The project team may set those guidelines as part of the design and implementation process. Establishing guidelines for monitoring and maintaining the network is not an official phase or procedure associated with the design and implementation process. The responsibility often falls, therefore, to the administrators who are responsible for the daily operations of the network.

Other tasks for which network administrators may be responsible as part of monitoring and maintaining the NetWare 4 network include the following:

- Verifying the viability of established guidelines
- Tracking and reporting on project results
- Anticipating and troubleshooting network problems
- Implementing recovery procedures
- Determining when to upgrade the network

Each of these six responsibilities is discussed here to help new and experienced NetWare 4 network administrators understand how to monitor and manage a NetWare 4 network.

Establishing Guidelines for Managing the Network

The first step to managing the NetWare 4 network once it has been successfully implemented is establishing some guidelines to help determine whether the network is functioning as intended. Although experienced NetWare 4 network administrators will generally be able to determine what must be done in order to keep the network functioning properly, a set of guidelines can be helpful to ensure that all responsible personnel understand how to monitor and maintain the network.

Network management guidelines may include a variety of tasks. Those tasks that relate directly to assessing the functionality of the NetWare 4 network can be generally grouped into two categories:

- Using NetWare 4 utilities to monitor the network
- Maintaining network integrity by using NDS utilities

There are three particular utilities that you can use to monitor the NetWare 4 network. Those utilities are DSTRACE, SERVMAN, and MONITOR. In addition to these three utilities, you can also use DSREPAIR and Partition Manager to maintain network integrity.

When you establish guidelines for managing and monitoring the network, you should consider how these and other utilities can best be used to accomplish your goal. The guidelines should then specify which utilities should be used and provide basic procedures for their use.

For example, your network management guidelines may specify that an SMS-compliant utility, such as Novell's SBACKUP, be used to conduct regular NDS backups to ensure continued network integrity. Your network management guidelines may further specify who will be responsible for using the SMS-compliant backup software and how frequently it is to be used. The guidelines may even specify when backups should be conducted.

Of course, in order to establish guidelines that specify the use of any particular utility or software product, you need to be familiar with that software or product. Therefore, you need to work with the product or at least review information related to that product or utility.

To monitor the NetWare 4 network, develop a basic understanding of the DSTRACE, SERVMAN, and MONITOR utilities. To maintain the network's integrity, use the Partition Manager and DSREPAIR NDS utilities. To help you understand these utilities and thus be better prepared to establish guidelines for and monitor and maintain the NetWare 4 network, each of these five utilities are briefly discussed here.

DSTRACE

NetWare 4's DSTRACE is a group of `SET` options that can be entered at the file server console. It is included in NetWare 4 to help you monitor a NetWare 4 file server for errors associated with NDS. It can also be used to monitor the status of NDS synchronization processes.

To use DSTRACE, you start DSTRACE on each file server on which you suspect NDS errors. To start DSTRACE, type `SET DSTRACE=ON` at the file server console and press Enter.

By using the `NDS TRACE TO FILE` parameter, you can capture the information generated by DSTRACE to a file, thus logging errors for later review. Other types of information that you can view by using DSTRACE include name resolution, synchronization processes, time stamp synchronization, auditing, partitioning, debugging, and a variety of other information.

SERVMAN

The SERVMAN utility can be used to perform the same functions as those performed by the SET command. In addition, SERVMAN performs some of the same functions as the MONITOR utility.

The SERVMAN utility provides basic file server information in its Server General Information area. Information provided in this area includes such items as the following:

- Length of time the file server has been up
- Percentage of time the microprocessor is used
- Microprocessor's speed
- Number of NLMs currently loaded
- Number of volumes currently mounted
- Number of active queues and logged-in users
- Number of name space NLMs currently loaded

The SERVMAN utility also has an Available Options menu from which you can make choices in order to set parameters for this file server (see fig. 8.10).

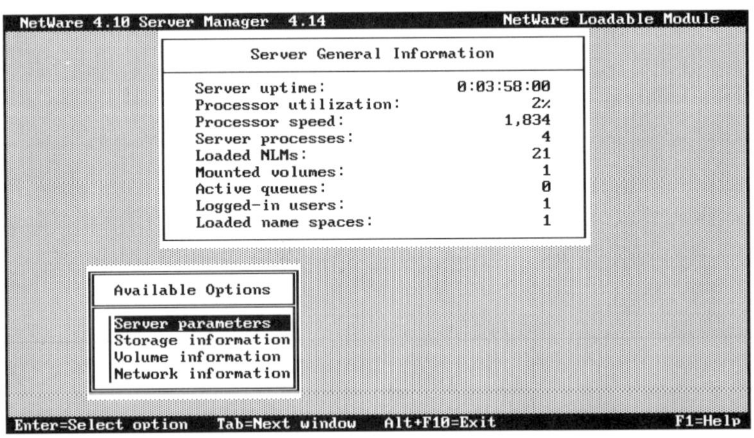

Figure 8.10
SERVMAN utility main screen.

You can choose the Server parameters option to see or change various operating system parameters. Changing parameters by using this method also places those changes into the related AUTOEXEC.NCF or STARTUP.NCF files. You can choose the Storage information option to view information on adapters, devices, and partitions. You can choose the Volume information option to view information about currently mounted volumes, or you can choose the Network information option to view other types of network information.

MONITOR

The MONITOR utility includes a General Information area just as the SERVMAN utility does. You can perform a variety of tasks using the MONITOR utility, including the following:

- Viewing file server statistics and activity
- Locking the file server console
- Viewing and analyzing file server RAM and microprocessor utilization
- Optimizing file server memory
- Viewing and managing the file server's hard disks

Partition Manager

You can use either the DOS-based PARTMGR utility or the Partition Manager option from the NetWare Administrator's Tools pull-down menu. Select the context from which to begin the partitioning operation, then start Partition Manager to open the Partition Manager window (see fig. 8.11).

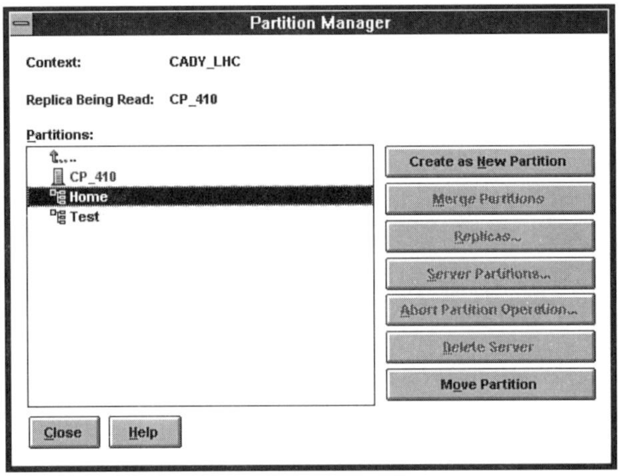

Figure 8.11
Partition Manager window.

When the Partition Manager window opens, you can choose to perform various partitioning and replication tasks, including the following:

- Creating new partitions
- Merging existing partitions
- Moving partitions
- Viewing replicas stored on file servers
- Adding replicas
- Deleting replicas
- Changing replica type
- Sending and receiving replica updates
- Deleting file servers no longer active on the network

Most of the required partitioning and replication should have been done as part of the design and implementation process. As time goes on, however, you should consider whether partitioning or replication changes should be made.

For example, if new file servers are added to the network, you may decide that a writable copy of one or more partitions should be placed on those file servers to reduce login time for network users. You use the Partition Manager to add replicas to the new file servers.

DSREPAIR

You use DSREPAIR to make corrections and repairs to the NDS database. Before running DSREPAIR, disable login from the file server console. Then load DSREPAIR at the file server console, and choose Unattended full repair from the Available options menu (see fig. 8.12).

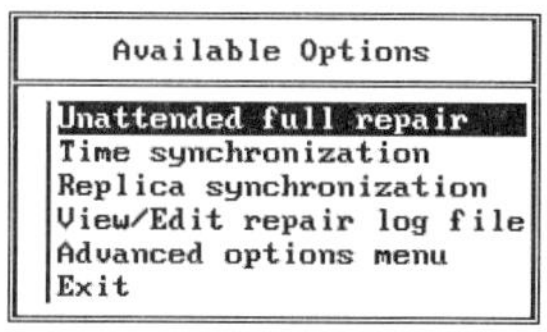

Figure 8.12
DSREPAIR Available Options menu.

The DSREPAIR utility goes through the database and locates and repairs errors wherever it finds them and as possible. You may have to run DSREPAIR two or three times to find and repair all NDS database errors.

Sometimes, even after having run the DSREPAIR utility multiple times, you may not be able to repair the database completely. At least, the utility may indicate that some errors still exist. If this is the case, consider waiting 24 hours to see whether NDS is able to synchronize and repair itself. Sometimes errors are just synchronization problems. This can be particularly true if the network is quite large.

Note

If you have recently made any network partition changes, do not run DSREPAIR until sufficient time has passed to enable any partition changes to be replicated fully across the network. Once you load the DSREPAIR NLM, the NDS database is locked and can be unlocked only by unloading (exiting) the DSREPAIR NLM.

If time does not seem to eliminate all errors in the NDS database, you can run DSREPAIR again. If you still cannot repair the database and it seems to be too corrupted, you may be able to delete the Master replica of the affected partition, modify a Read/Write replica to be the new Master replica, and solve the problem.

After running DSREPAIR, be sure to once again enable login from the file server console so that network users will be able to access the network.

The DSREPAIR, Partition Manager, MONITOR, SERVMAN, and other utilities discussed in this chapter are all tools provided with NetWare 4 to help you manage and monitor your network. As such, you should understand these tools so that you can establish guidelines for network administrators and other individuals who are responsible for the network based on using these tools. Once you establish guidelines for verifying the continued viability of the NetWare 4 network as designed, you can continue the fourth phase of the NetWare 4 network design and implementation process—managing and monitoring the network—the next task of which is to verify the viability of the guidelines you established for managing and monitoring the network.

Verifying the Viability of Established Guidelines

Once you are familiar with utilities you can use to monitor the network, and thus have also been able to establish guidelines for managing and monitoring the network, you need to determine whether those guidelines are successful. The success of the guidelines can be assessed by monitoring the network itself. If the network seems to be functioning smoothly, no major problems exist, network users can access the resources they need without undue problems, and security appears to be satisfactory, the guidelines you have established are probably also satisfactory.

Monitoring the network in order to verify the viability of established guidelines also means that you must maintain the network.

To monitor and maintain the network, you may choose to perform some or all of the following tasks:

- Compare object naming standard documents created during the network's design against object names currently used on the network. If you find objects whose names do not meet the guidelines established in the naming standards document, you should rename or remove those objects from the directory tree.
- Check the upper and lower layers of the directory tree to determine whether their current designs continue to meet the needs for which they were designed.
- Check different NDS objects on a routine basis to determine whether they are located in the most logical place in the tree structure (based on how users access those NDS objects and the resources they represent) and whether they are satisfactorily performing the function for which they were originally intended.
- Review network error logs to determine whether any errors are occurring repeatedly. If you find repetitive errors, attempt to determine whether these errors are the result of the network's design, evidence of a lack of user training, or a result of network growth or change. If possible, determine what modifications can be made to correct any design, training, or growth-related problems in order to reduce the number of or eliminate network errors.
- Analyze network storage use to determine whether storage capacity is sufficient. One way to ensure that the needs of network users are being met is by ensuring that sufficient storage space exists for each user on the network. Analyzing storage use means comparing current available storage space to the amount of storage space originally provided. It is one way to help prevent problems on the network before they occur.
- Track the use of bindery services. After the network is migrated, applications will eventually be upgraded and users

trained. The need for bindery services should almost go away on its own if applications are upgraded and users sufficiently trained. If you track the use of bindery services over a period of time, you will eventually be able to determine when bindery services are no longer needed and thus remove them from the network.

- Verify time synchronization functionality. Although the time synchronization strategy implemented for the NetWare 4 network should be satisfactory for some time to come, unexpected and extensive network growth can make the network's time synchronization strategy insufficient to meet the network's needs. Excessive network traffic may eventually result if the network outgrows its original time synchronization strategy. Periodically review network time synchronization to ensure that it is functioning as intended without generating an excessive amount of network traffic.
- Survey mobile users to determine whether the network's design successfully meets their needs. As the company continues to grow, markets expand, and mobile users travel more often and to more places, the strategy implemented for mobile users may become outdated. Although the methods for supporting mobile users are limited, growth may force you to revise the approach you took to deal with mobile users originally. Unless you periodically verify that mobile users are successful at using the network, their access problems may not be readily noticeable. Periodically assess the needs of the network's mobile users, and determine, if necessary, where changes in the network's design might be made in order to simplify network access for mobile users.
- Determine whether the design of the network correctly balances the workload among network administrators. Some administrators may be unfairly burdened due to excessive network growth in limited areas of the network. Problems of unbalanced workload may also indicate that the original approach to administration (centralized versus decentralized) is no longer working on the network. Checking the balance of administrative workload may help pinpoint areas where management modifications should be made.

- Review the current location and type of replicas. It is important to ensure that a sufficient number of replicas exists on the network in order to provide fault tolerance and easy network access. It is also important, however, to ensure that the replica strategy being used does not generate an excessive amount of network traffic or increase network costs beyond an acceptable limit. You may need to split or merge existing replicas to reduce network traffic, moderate network costs, and ease network access for users.
- Remove or add NetWare file servers or volumes to the network as needed. Changes of this type should reflect permanent network usage or company changes, an increased demand for network storage, or a modification in network management, such as decentralizing a fast-growing network that was originally designed to be administered from a central location.
- Verify that network communication across existing WAN links is still satisfactory and sufficiently designed to meet the network's needs.
- Monitoring SYS volume space. A sufficient amount of space on the network's various file server SYS volumes to accommodate the growth of the NDS database is important, because serious consequences can result from running out of room. For example, users may no longer be able to log in to the network if the SYS volume is full, because the login process requires space on the SYS volume in which temporary files related to the user login process can be stored.
- Ensure that the current design adequately handles various security issues. The network's present design should easily and successfully accommodate trustee assignments, object and property rights, inheritance, and effective rights.
- Determine the potential need for additional administrators to handle an expanding network directory tree. You can create subtle administrators to assist in managing and monitoring the network as discussed earlier in this chapter.

- Check the usage and effectiveness of special NDS objects. Special NDS objects are designed to help improve user accessibility. For example, Profile login scripts can be used to set up the environment for a given group of users, and Directory Map objects can be established to make it easy for users to locate and use applications on the network. Those objects that have been created to simplify access to and use of network resources should be eliminated or redirected if they no longer provide the service they were originally created to provide.
- Review the use of print queue, print server, and printer objects to ensure that these objects are properly located within the tree to simplify their access and use.
- Discuss auditing issues with the network auditor if either of you have any concerns related to the network. Monitoring network activity through the use of the audit function can help you gather the information you need in order to determine whether the network's design should be modified.
- Verify that workstation and file server backup and restore is adequate and relatively easy to use.
- Determine whether the current version of workstation networking software is adequate for users to access the needed resources, and plan to upgrade or replace it if it is not sufficient.
- Identify current network protocols and ensure that the network is adequately providing for and dealing with all protocols currently in use on the network.
- Review the success of other NetWare 4 features, such as block sub allocation, file compression, data migration, and internationalization. Ensure that they are currently meeting network users' needs. If they are not currently being used, determine whether one or more of these features should now be implemented.
- Check network optimization options, such as packet burst and LIP. Determine whether additional modification to these could enhance network performance.

- Monitor usage statistics by using utilities provided for that purpose, such as MONITOR and SERVMAN. In particular, check file server processor and memory usage. This information should help you determine whether file servers are placed in optimum locations within the directory tree structure or whether modifications to partitions or container objects could improve usage.

Use these guidelines to help you monitor the network, assess various network items and issues, and determine whether the guidelines that currently exist for managing and monitoring the network are successful. Once you assess the network and determine the viability of the network's manage and monitor guidelines, you can then move on to the next step—tracking and reporting on project results.

Tracking and Reporting on Project Results

When the project team first begins to design the NetWare 4 network, it has in mind the specific goal of developing a network that meets its user's needs. The project team collects a variety of documents and information to assess just what those needs are and to help it design the network. Now that the network has been running for a while, it is time to determine whether the network is successfully accomplishing its original goal.

To fulfill its intended goal, the network must be tracked. There are a variety of ways in which network activities can be tracked in order to determine what can be improved, what must be lived with for a while, and when it may be time to upgrade or replace the existing network.

Various logs, such as the file server error log, can be reviewed to determine the types of errors that are occurring and whether anything can be done to correct them on a permanent basis. Network auditing can also provide input. Audit reports can indicate what network resources are being used, how frequently, and by which network users.

Tracking information of this type can also help you determine whether you have sufficient licenses for all your network software. It can also help you determine whether applications are being used at all. This is particularly useful information if you are currently providing bindery services for an application. If that application is no longer being used or has been upgraded to be NetWare 4-compatible, you may determine it is time to reduce the number of containers where bindery services are set or to eliminate bindery services altogether.

If the company has a help desk or workstation troubleshooting personnel, they can be valuable sources of input. Asking to review their logs or talking with these individuals can help you assess where problems may still exist on the network and whether a more permanent fix for those problems can and should be found.

There is a variety of information available about and on the network. You need to determine what types of information are available, where they are located, and how you can get access to them. Then, you must review the information, decide what of it is relevant and what is not, and make network management or change decisions based on the result.

Anticipating and Troubleshooting Network Problems

Closely monitoring the NetWare 4 network and the activities that occur on it may also help you anticipate future network problems. For example, if you track application usage and note that at certain times of the day, week, month, and so forth, there are more users accessing an application than the company has licenses, future problems may exist. If the company is audited for license violations, and those violations were noted but not corrected, severe fines and penalties may result.

Finding potential problem areas before they become problems is an important approach to troubleshooting. Locating problems before as well as after they have surfaced helps keep the network running as smoothly and efficiently as possible.

Troubleshooting network problems once they surface is also a task of network monitoring. You need to be able to locate the source or cause of a network problem shortly after it becomes apparent. The sooner you develop an approach to solving any problems you discover, the less likelihood there is of a major problem, some of which may become quite costly to the company.

Implementing Recovery Procedures

When network problems are not caught in time, or unforeseen events occur that interrupt or bring down the network, a recovery process must be followed. Before a recovery process can be followed, however, some recovery procedures need to be defined.

For example, the network should have some type of backup procedure in place. The procedure should be well documented and diligently carried out. If that is the case, a major network loss can be replaced by restoring the most recent, usable backup.

Decisions such as what to do in the event of an earthquake, flood, fire, or other major disaster should be determined and included in recovery procedures. Smaller, less obvious issues should also be considered.

For example, if a trusted employee with extensive access to the network becomes sufficiently distressed to be destructive, some idea of how to handle the aftermath of this situation should be documented. Even if little can be done to salvage the situation, some process should have been defined.

You and your company put a tremendous number of hours and dollars into your network. Protecting it from disaster is an important part of the network administrator's responsibility. Planning recovery procedures to implement when the protection was not enough may fall to the project team as part of ensuring that the network continues to meet the needs of its users.

Determining When to Upgrade the Network

There may come a time when no amount of monitoring, troubleshooting, or recovery is sufficient. It may seem that no matter what you do, the network no longer meets the continuing needs of the users.

The problem may be as simple as the design having outgrown the network. It may be that technology has changed so significantly that you cannot do what you want to do with the existing network, but changing technologies may mean completely redesigning the network. A simple upgrade to the next version of NetWare may require that you revisit the original design of the network and consider major modifications.

Whatever it is that causes you to consider redoing the network, there may come a point in time when you simply must consider upgrading or replacing the current NetWare 4 network. The process you originally used to help you design and implement this NetWare 4 network will still be a valid one. Therefore, you can follow it to design and implement a better network that will continue to meet its user's needs for some time to come. Determining the need to redesign the network is the first step in starting the network design and implementation process again from the beginning.

Summary

As noted throughout this book, the manage and monitor phase of the Novell NetWare 4 network design and implementation process is the last phase. Its goal is to ensure that the NetWare 4 network is functioning as intended and to find areas where improvement can be successfully and cost-effectively implemented.

Eventually, the manage and monitor phase may lead you to begin the entire network design and implementation process again from the beginning. Until that time, however, continue to follow the guidelines that exist for managing and monitoring the network and its resources. Occasionally, verify that the guidelines that you are following are also still valid. Make it a habit to track network activity and to report on the results of the design and implementation of the network.

Whenever possible during the process of managing and monitoring the network, do your best to anticipate and troubleshoot network problems. If you have established an approach to take in order to recover from network problems, you should be able to continue with this NetWare 4 network for some time to come.

When the network no longer meets the needs of its users, despite your best efforts to keep it running smoothly and efficiently, continue to the last step in this network manage and monitor process—determining when it may be appropriate to upgrade or replace the existing network. When your review of network maintenance issues or the network's actual maintenance indicates that the network's design no longer fulfills its goals, or the cost of continued maintenance seems to be greater than the company wants to continue to spend, it may well be time to consider starting over.

As with any process that has proven itself over time, it will then be best to start the design process over with step one—analyzing the company's needs and current resources. This step should then be followed by starting the actual design and implementation of the company's network, and it will ultimately end with determining when it is time to replace the existing network.

If you and I are still around when the time comes, and we are still working with NetWare networks, we may find a sense of satisfaction (and job security) in knowing that the next improvement to a network is only as far away as the next, or rather the first, step in the Novell network design and implementation process.

Review Questions

1. You should consider spot checking various network resources to determine whether they are located in the most logical place within the directory tree. This process is part of the ____________ phase of network design and implementation.

   ○ A. Analysis

   ○ B. Design

   ○ C. Implementation

   ○ D. Maintenance

2. If you track the use of bindery services over a period of time, you may be able to determine ____________.

   ○ A. whether more file servers should be added

   ○ B. when to upgrade non-NetWare 4 file servers

   ○ C. whether additional partitions should be created

   ○ D. whether a WAN link should be added

3. If no serious security issues are noted when you review network security, it may indicate that ____________.

   ○ A. the network's design is adequate

   ○ B. security can be somewhat relaxed

   ○ C. the number of administrators is sufficient

   ○ D. network monitoring is no longer needed

4. Of the following, which one is *not* a network design and implementation maintenance task?

   ○ A. determining whether the current version of workstation network software is adequate

   ○ B. modifying IRFs to restrict user access to specific containers

○ C. deciding when existing partitions should be split or merged

○ D. identifying existing network protocols

5. Which *three* of the following are steps associated with the manage and monitor phase of the network design and implementation process?

○ A. establishing guidelines for managing the network and its resources

○ B. determining where network partitions and their replications should be placed

○ C. anticipating and troubleshooting various network problems

○ D. tracking and reporting on the results of the NetWare 4 Network design and implementation project

6. Of the following, which is *not* a utility provided for network printing?

○ A. PCONSOLE

○ B. PMANAGER

○ C. NPRINTER

○ D. PSERVER

7. To create customized printing configurations, which *two* utilities can you use?

○ A. NetWare Administrator

○ B. NPRINTER

○ C. PRINTCON

○ D. PSERVER

8. Both ___________ and ___________ are part of NDS login security.
   - ○ A. authentication
   - ○ B. large internet packets
   - ○ C. packet encryption
   - ○ D. packet signature
9. Which NetWare 4 utility can you use to help view NDS errors?
   - ○ A. SERVMAN
   - ○ B. DSTRACE
   - ○ C. MONITOR
   - ○ D. DSREPAIR
10. To make corrections to the NDS database when errors have occurred, you can run the ___________ utility at the file server.
    - ○ A. SERVMAN
    - ○ B. DSTRACE
    - ○ C. MONITOR
    - ○ D. DSREPAIR

Answers

1. D
2. B
3. A
4. B
5. A C D
6. B
7. A C
8. A D
9. B
10. D

Appendix A

Case Study Answers

This appendix contains answers to each of the case studies found in various chapters within this book. Most of these answers are suggested instead of dictated. If your answers vary from these answers, yours may still be correct. There are almost no absolute rules for NetWare 4 network design, but there are guidelines and recommendations.

Chapter 3: Johnson Shoes

If you were chosen as the consultant for Johnson Shoes, the information used to make the presentation to Mr. Johnson regarding the NetWare 4 design and implementation process should include the following:

- Project approach
  - Assemble project team
  - Determine project approach procedures
    - Gather related business information
    - Train project team
    - Determine design process scope
    - Do preliminary scheduling
- Design
  - Design directory tree
    - Create naming standards document
    - Design upper and lower layers of tree
    - Review tree design considerations
    - Revise directory tree (if needed)
    - Consider other design issues
  - Determine partition and replication strategy
    - Decide whether defaults are sufficient
    - Create partition plan (if needed)
    - Determine replica placement
  - Plan time synchronization strategy
    - Assess number of sites
    - Determine quantity of file servers
    - Plan time server strategy
    - Determine communications method
    - Create accessibility plan
      - Review user, application, and other resource needs
      - Create accessibility guidelines

Design accessibility strategies to implement guidelines

Implementation

Develop migration strategy

Create workstation migration strategy

Create file server migration strategy

Create applications migration strategy

Create implementation schedule

Identify tasks

Create schedules

Coordinate schedules with other groups (if needed)

Perform pilot implementation

Proceed with implementation

Manage and monitor

Manage NDS

Perform partition and replication operations as needed

Rename objects not meeting standards

Remove and reinstall NetWare 4 servers

Back up and restore NDS

Recover from server hardware failures

Troubleshoot client problems

Monitor NDS

Verify time synchronization

Monitor SYS volumes on file servers

Monitor file servers on the network

Monitor network partitions and replicas

Chapter 4: Apple Town

In the suggested answer, Figure A.1, note that no special organization has been made for future growth because the current structure will be adequate. One of the computers in the library and one in the town office will become file servers.

Figure A.1

Apple Town solution.

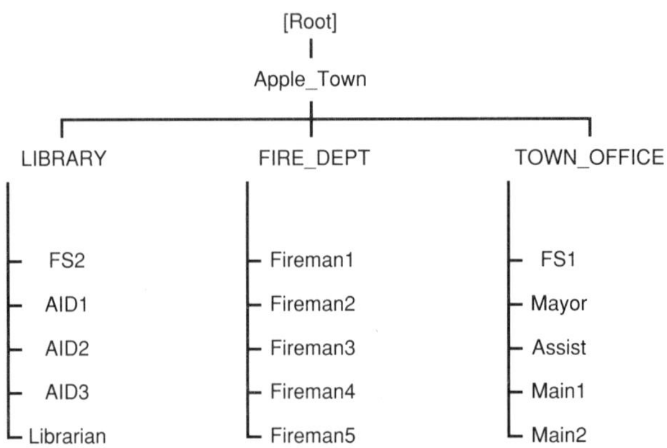

Chapter 5: Southtown Health Center

When comparing your task, note that your task list does not have to be exactly like the following one. Your task list should not, however, include tasks related to anything other than implementation. Because no network currently exists, migration, file server backup, and other related tasks do not have to be included in this list:

- Select and train the migration team.
- Decide what workstation configuration files need to be created or modified and what those files should contain.
- Choose a file server to use for testing because setting up a full testing lab is not possible. Install NetWare 4.1, then set up the

NDS directory tree as designed, including creating all container and leaf objects.

- Install the NetWare DOS Requester on the first workstation.
- Test the medical application and workstation communication software configurations against the NetWare 4.1 test server.
- Train the migration team.
- Train the individual who will be the network administrator.
- Install the NetWare DOS Requester on the six remaining workstations.
- Train users on using the new workstation software and accessing the NetWare 4 network.
- Install the second file server in the NDS directory tree.
- Determine, then document, how new user training and the addition of network workstations, file servers, and applications will be handled in the future.
- Review the complete workstation and file server migration process once network migration is complete, noting what went right and what went wrong, as well as what may be improved and how it might be improved the next time a network migration is done.
- Correct any problems or idiosyncrasies and train any remaining untrained users or administrators.
- Celebrate the successful implementation of the NetWare 4 network.

Chapter 6: The BJB Company

The single page-summary you present to the BJB Company's enterprise administrator may specify either of the following two options. If the network utilizes IPX, the first option may be the best choice.

Option 1

In the NET.CFG file on the user's laptop computer, place the `Set Name Context=` parameter to reflect a complete and typeful name for the user.

Next, create a Profile login script for mobile users that will include the following lines, assuming the network's directory structure is consistent across the network:

```
IF "%NETWORK_ADDRESS"="address"
THEN; MAP INS
S1:=server\SYS:PUBLIC;
MAP G:=server\SYS:home_directory\
%LOGIN_NAME; END
```

Repeat these lines in the Profile login script for each network address.

Option 2

Use a `SET NW_SITE=site` line in the AUTOEXEC.BAT file on the user's laptop. Then include the following in a login script:

```
IF <NW_SITE>=="site"
THEN BEGIN
       MAP ROOT M:=S4:=server\SYS:dir_path\app_file
       MAP ROOT W:=S16:=server\SYS:dir_path\app_file
END
EXIT
```

Use this alternative when the file system structure is the same throughout the network, replacing `server` with a file server name, `SYS:dir_path` with the volume and directory name where the application program is located, and `app_file` with the name of the executable program that runs the application that the mobile user needs to access. Repeat these lines for each application program that the mobile user needs to access.

Chapter 7: Xtra Company

Xtra Company File Server Migration Summary

Department	Server Name	OS	Configuration
Business	BUSI_001	3.11	80386, 16 MB RAM, 200 MB HD
	BUSI_002	3.11	80386, 16 MB RAM, 200 MB HD
	BUSI_003	3.11	80386, 16 MB RAM, 200 MB HD
	BUSI_004	3.11	80386, 16 MB RAM, 200 MB HD
	BUSI_005	3.11	80386, 16 MB RAM, 200 MB HD
Sales	BUSI_006	3.12	80486, 16 MB RAM, 200 MB HD
	BUSI_006	3.12	80486, 16 MB RAM, 200 MB HD
	BUSI_007	3.11	80386, 11 MB RAM, 120 MB HD
	BUSI_008	3.11	80386, 11 MB RAM, 120 MB HD
	BUSI_009	3.11	80386, 11 MB RAM, 120 MB HD
	BUSI_010	3.11	80386, 11 MB RAM, 120 MB HD
	BUSI_011	3.11	80386, 11 MB RAM, 120 MB HD
	BUSI_012	3.11	80386, 11 MB RAM, 120 MB HD
	BUSI_013	3.11	80386, 11 MB RAM, 120 MB HD
	BUSI_014	3.11	80386, 11 MB RAM, 120 MB HD
Training	BUSI_014	3.11	80386, 12 MB RAM, 80 MB HD
	BUSI_015	3.11	80386, 12 MB RAM, 80 MB HD
	BUSI_016	3.11	80386, 16 MB RAM, 200 MB HD
	BUSI_017	3.11	80386, 12 MB RAM, 80 MB HD
	BUSI_018	3.11	80386, 12 MB RAM, 80 MB HD
	BUSI_019	3.11	80386, 12 MB RAM, 80 MB HD
	BUSI_020	3.11	80386, 12 MB RAM, 80 MB HD
	BUSI_021	3.11	80386, 12 MB RAM, 80 MB HD

continues

Xtra Company File Server Migration Summary

Department	*Server Name*	*OS*	*Configuration*
	BUSI_022	3.11	80386, 12 MB RAM, 80 MB HD
	BUSI_023	3.11	80386, 12 MB RAM, 80 MB HD
	BUSI_024	3.11	80386, 12 MB RAM, 80 MB HD
	BUSI_025	3.11	80386, 12 MB RAM, 80 MB HD
	BUSI_026	3.11	80386, 12 MB RAM, 80 MB HD
	BUSI_027	3.11	80386, 12 MB RAM, 80 MB HD
	BUSI_028	3.11	80386, 12 MB RAM, 80 MB HD
	BUSI_029	3.11	80386, 12 MB RAM, 80 MB HD
	BUSI_030	3.11	80386, 12 MB RAM, 80 MB HD
	BUSI_031	3.11	80386, 12 MB RAM, 80 MB HD

Appendix B

B

Appendix Appendix Appendix Appendix Appendix

Networking Basics

In the early 1980s, the mainframe computer dominated business computing. Personal computers were mostly relegated to the lowly position of terminals, existing primarily to access the mainframe. Within 10 years, however, knowledgeable employees began to realize the power that desktop PCs placed at their fingertips.

These employees still needed access to the centralized databases, massive storage capabilities, printers, and business software that the mainframe provided, but they were no longer content to put up with waiting their turn in line for the mainframe to process their requests. Employees wanted faster turnaround, greater variety of business software, more processing power, and a sense of control over their work and working environment. Employees needed the capabilities that networking would soon provide them. Even though they may not have realized it at the time, employees needed networking technology. Companies such as Novell recognized that need and began developing and providing software that is today capable of connecting personal computers around the world.

Other companies, such as Microsoft, followed in the footsteps of people such as Henry Ford and turned toward developing software that would make personal computers user-friendly enough to help ensure that a personal computer could be placed on every desktop in every home. Companies such as Compaq, Hewlett-Packard, IBM, and others competed to make the size of personal computers more compact and the cost more affordable. The era of networked personal computers had begun.

Some people scoffed. Some people ran with the vision and helped shape and grow it. The government and industry sought to unify and standardize it. Businesses sought to make a profit from it. Organizations and people sought to benefit from it. Today, personal computers and networking have become a major factor in the everyday lives of many people. Even if you do not yet take full advantage of the capabilities, benefits, and resources that personal computers and networking place at your fingertips, you cannot ignore it for much longer. Therefore, it may be in your own best interest to at least seek to understand it.

Helping you understand networking is the function, topic, and purpose of this appendix, which seeks to perform this task by explaining the following topics of information related to networking:

- Networking concepts
- Characteristics of the physical transmission of information and data across a network
- Physical network configuration and methods of network access
- Network architecture
- Network operating systems

If you are a NetWare administrator, networking consultant, or other individual busily involved in personal computers and networking, you probably do not need to read this appendix. It is likely, however, that you will have to work with many people who do not understand even the most basic concept related to networking. It is primarily those people for whom this appendix was written. Please consider helping others understand networking by making it possible for them to read this appendix.

Networking Concepts

The term "networking" may be somewhat familiar to most people, although they may not be applying the term to personal computers. Most often, the term networking is taken to mean connecting with other people, either in a professional or personal way—or perhaps both. In the world of personal computers, networking means connecting people with other people and various resources through the use of personal computers.

Types of Networks

There are three types of networks; the primary difference between the three is the amount of physical area the network covers. The following are the three types of networks:

- Local Area Networks (LANs)
- Municipal Area Networks (MANs)
- Wide Area Networks (WANs)

A local area network is a network that covers a small geographic area, generally confined to a single building or small group of closely positioned buildings. Typical LANs can be found, for example, in small businesses, hospitals, and community colleges. Local area networks also generally use a single *transmission medium*, the method employed for communication, such as cables, radio waves, or satellite.

A municipal area network covers a larger geographic area than a LAN does, but it is generally still relatively confined. The area of confinement usually coincides with the boundaries of a city or township. Municipal area networks are most often found in local government, generally used to connect multiple city offices. A city with computers in the library, mayor's office, city offices, fire department, and other city buildings dispersed throughout the city, for example, would employ a municipal area network for their networking. Municipal area networks may take advantage of either a single transmission medium or a combination of transmission media.

A wide area network covers a larger geographic area, ranging from any size larger than a MAN to the entire globe. Wide area networks are also often called *enterprise networks* when the WAN includes a single global corporation, also known as an *enterprise*. Wide area networks generally require the use of a multiple transmission medium, often combining the use of a single medium for the local areas of the network with other media for connecting all the smaller networking areas.

Network Components

Besides some type of transmission medium by which individual computers are connected, there are other components that make up and further define a network:

- Personal computers
- Network communication hardware
- Software programs

Each of these components plays an important role in a successful network.

Personal Computers

Personal computers are the heart of networking. Without the capabilities that personal computers provide, no networking could exist. The personal computers themselves provide the one thing that makes networking substantially different from communal access to a mainframe computer—decentralized processing.

Decentralized processing means that each personal computer on the network can perform basic computer processing for itself. Each PC has the capability of performing the basic logic and mathematic functions that were originally handled by mainframes. That capability is given to the PC by a tiny unit within the computer known as the microprocessor.

The *microprocessor* is an electronic integrated circuit responsible for performing all the central processing functions of the PC. Those functions include tracking and performing instructions provided by various computer programs, controlling all components of the PC, and performing all logic and arithmetic tasks requested of it. The microprocessor that functions in combination to accomplish all these tasks is also referred to as the *Central Processing Unit (CPU)*.

The microprocessor is physically connected to a main circuit board in the PC through which all processing and control is conducted. The main circuit board, also commonly referred to as a *system board* or *mother board*, contains several components in addition to the CPU (see fig. B.1).

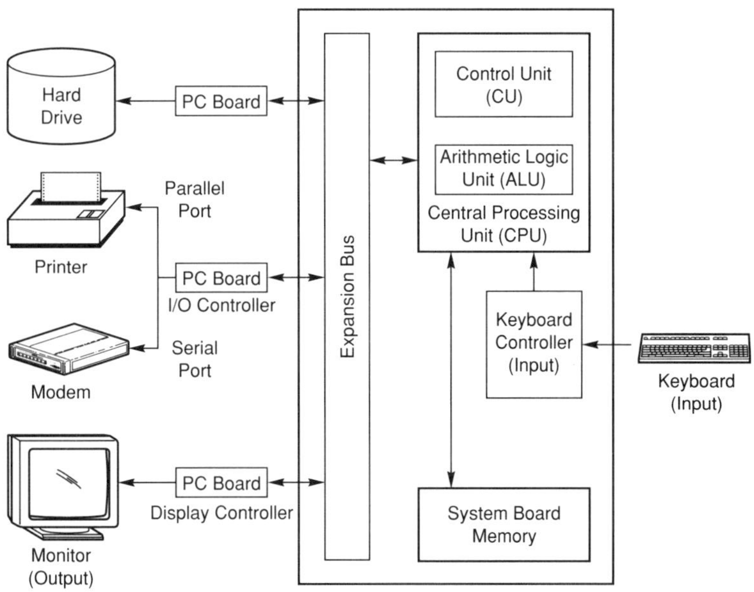

Figure B.1
System board components.

The following are additional components found on the system board:

- Keyboard controller
- Expansion bus
- Output ports
- Memory
- Storage device connections

The *keyboard controller* is responsible for ensuring that a computer user's input, as typed on the PC's keyboard, is ultimately transferred to the CPU. Transferring the user's keyboard input to the CPU makes it possible for the CPU to then process and fulfill the instructions or requests submitted by the user.

The *expansion bus* is a series of electronic connectors located on the system board. Various adapter cards can be connected to the expansion bus to ensure that each related piece of equipment (disk drives, monitor, and so forth) can communicate with the CPU.

The *output ports* are responsible for connecting the circuit board, and thus the CPU, to external devices such as printers and modems. Output ports are either serial or parallel in nature, and thus they enable communication between two devices to function in either one direction only, or in both directions.

The computer's *memory* consists of other electronic chips that can temporarily store data and program commands until such time as they can be accessed, used, and processed, or sent to more permanent storage by the CPU.

Storage devices are physical media, such as hard disks or floppy disks, where data and programs can be stored and from which they can later be retrieved. Storage is in the form of a magnetic code using only two states—on or off (positive or negative, respectively). Storage devices are primarily used for the long-term retention of information.

The microprocessor, contained on the CPU and through which all processing and control is conducted, is the heart of the PC. Other peripheral devices, such as the keyboard and monitor, constitute the balance of the physical components of the PC. In and of themselves, however, these physical components are little more than a collection of electronic equipment until you add specialized software programs to activate and control them. Just as the microprocessor is the heart of the PC, the software programs that activate and control it are the soul of the PC.

Some of the software programs that activate and control the PC are built into the electronic components themselves. When you turn on the PC and power is applied to those electronic components that store the activation software, the software takes over. It checks the internal functions of the PC itself, ensuring that each physical part of the PC is properly functioning and actively able to communicate with the other parts of the PC as designed. Once all physical parts of the PC are checked, activated, and verified for communication capability, control of the PC is turned over to the user and the operating system that controls it. This process is called *booting* the computer.

Network Communication Equipment

A PC is just a PC, however, and not part of a network until additional network communication equipment and software programs are added to it. The physical equipment that must be added to a PC in order to make it part of a network includes the following:

- A network board
- Cabling

A network board is an interface board that physically connects the PC to some type of transmission medium, such as a cable. The network board fits into a slot on the PC's system board, thus establishing an electronic connection between the CPU and the network board.

The transmission medium then connects the network board in one PC to the network board in another PC. The establishment of a connection of this nature between two or more PCs thus ensures that the PCs can communicate with each other.

There are many different types of network boards and many different types of transmission media. The different types of transmission media are discussed later in this appendix under the heading Physical Transmission Characteristics.

Software Programs

A physical connection between PCs is not sufficient to ensure communication, just as connecting all the equipment together through a system board inside the PC is not enough to ensure functionality. Software must be added to cause each connected PC to operate as part of a network. That software is referred to as the network's software components, of which there are two types:

- Workstation connection software
- Network operating system software

The workstation connection software consists of a series of programs that must be loaded into a PC's memory. Once loaded into memory, these programs turn a PC into a network workstation. A network *workstation* is a PC that is capable of communicating with other PCs and hardware devices on the network.

In NetWare 3.12 and later versions, the workstation software consists of four primary files and files that are associated with them. These are the four primary files:

- LSL.COM
- Network board driver
- IPXODI.COM
- NetWare DOS Requester

The *Link Support Layer (LSL)* file (LSL.COM) routes network information from various protocols to the network board driver and related communications software. Because it performs a switching function, the Link Support Layer is often called the switchboard.

Workstations accessing a NetWare 4 network must have the LSL.COM file loaded before the network board driver is loaded.

The network board driver software to be loaded on the workstation is the driver file that is compatible with the network board installed in your workstation. The purpose of the network board driver is to activate the network board, then control the actions of the board. The network board driver software functions as a go-between, ensuring successful communication between the workstation's software and the physical network hardware.

The communications protocol used by DOS workstations is a version of the NetWare IPX communications protocol, which is loaded when the IPXODI.COM file is run. The IPXODI.COM file provides communication based on the ODI specification, which ensures that multiple protocols can be used on the same cabling system and the same network board. You must load the communications protocol file after you load the network board file.

The NetWare DOS Requester is a series of *Virtual Loadable Modules (VLMs)*. The VLM files are loaded and controlled by the VLM manager, the VLM.EXE file. These files act as the connection point between the workstation's DOS operating system and DOS-based application files and the network.

Loading the NetWare DOS Requester makes it possible for DOS and DOS-based applications to communicate across the network and make requests for network services. In addition, the NetWare DOS Requester stores information related to the workstation's network connection. The stored information includes such things as drive mappings created from the workstation after the user has logged in to the network. When the user logs out of the network and breaks the logical network connection, the information stored by the DOS Requester is eliminated.

As with each of the other network connection files, the NetWare DOS Requester must be loaded on the workstation in the proper order. The VLM.EXE file must be run after the IPXODI.COM file is run.

Loading these files ensures communication between the PC and the network. These files make it possible for the PC to communicate with a variety of network hardware devices. Some of the devices with which the PC can communicate include file servers, printers, modems, FAX machines, and other electronic devices. You should already be familiar enough with printers, modems, and FAX machines not to require a description or additional information at this point, but you may not yet know what a file server is.

A *file server* is a PC with special software loaded into its memory. The special software is called the *Network Operating System (NOS).* One or more file servers connected with one or more workstations constitutes a network. Regardless of how many or how few workstations and file servers you have connected, the end result is still a network.

Many different companies provide PCs. Some of the more commonly recognized names—IBM, Compaq, and Hewlett-Packard—were previously mentioned. There are dozens of companies today that build and sell personal computers. You have a long list of companies from which you can purchase the PCs for your network. The same is true for the hardware associated with networking—network boards and transmission media.

A PC without networking software, however, is just a PC and not a network workstation or file server. Thus, in addition to purchasing PCs for workstations and file servers, and network boards and transmission media to establish a physical connection, you must also purchase networking software.

There are fewer companies that develop and sell networking software than there are companies who develop and sell PCs. Some of the companies that develop and sell networking software are IBM, Lantastic, Microsoft, and Novell. The industry leader is, by far, Novell, Incorporated, holding over 60 percent of the networking software market today.

As with the software that turns a PC into a usable piece of equipment, the networking software turns a collection of physically connected PCs into a usable network. The key lies in what that network is used for, however.

Networks can be used to accomplish a variety of tasks, which is the network user's and the network's responsibility. Providing the capability of accomplishing those tasks belongs solely to the network operating system, however. What the network operating system provides in the way of services to network users is called *network services*.

Network Services

Network *service providers* are computers or other devices that share their capabilities with other computers or entities on a network. The capabilities network service providers share are the network's services. There are four basic services that network service providers share:

- File
- Print
- Electronic mail (e-mail)
- Communication

Network file services include any function or service that can be provided to any data, program, graphic, or other type of file on the network. File services may include the short- and long-term storage of files. They may also include the retrieval of stored files. In addition, file services may include the *compression of files*—reduction in the amount of space the file requires for storage—as well as the *decompression of files*—restoration of the file to its original size and layout.

Other file services may include any or all of the following:

- Copying files
- Deleting files
- Transferring or moving files
- Salvaging or recovering deleted files
- Time and date stamping files
- Renaming files

Print services generally refer to the printing of a file on a printer, but they may also include printing of a file to another type of physical device, such as a plotter. Although the actual printing of the document is the ultimate outcome of print services, there are many printing service functions that occur but which are generally transparent to the network user who requests the print service.

For example, requesting the printing of a document from inside a network application program often requires that the document be redirected to a printer or print queue on the network from the workstation's printer port. In addition, transparent printing services may include the application of a configuration file to the file being printed in order to ensure that the file to be printed is handled correctly.

Electronic mail is the communication of written correspondence across the network from one user to another. The network provides an electronic mailbox for each network user. Users create mail, either while they are logged onto the network or as separate documents that can be attached to a quick mail message, and then they send the mail to the user's mailbox.

Communication services are those services that ensure that a communication can be sent from one network device and received by another network device. For example, communication may include the transmission of a file from a PC on one type of network to a PC on another, dissimilar type of network.

To ensure that communication across like and unlike networks is successful, the network operating system and workstation program files work together. These files were developed to follow a set of rules that govern just how communication is to take place between network devices. These rules or standards that enable two or more network devices to communicate successfully are called *protocols*.

Network Protocols

Many of the protocols themselves were developed to follow a standard or common approach to their design. The standard that many protocols have been modeled after is called the *Open Systems Interconnect (OSI) Reference Model*. The OSI Reference Model was developed by a group of individuals known as the *International Organization for Standardization (ISO)*.

The purpose of developing the OSI Reference Model was to give developers of network communication protocols a guideline to follow when developing communication protocols to be used for managing the exchange of information across a network. The OSI Reference Model, therefore, defines seven layers associated with the process of network communication. Each layer defines a standard for handling one aspect of network communication.

Many types of communication protocols exist. Most communication protocols have more than one layer associated with them. Thus, most communication protocols are modular in design, combining different modules to create the final communication protocol. A group of these modules together create the actual communication protocol. The final communication protocol is thus referred to as a protocol stack. A *protocol stack* is a set of protocols arranged in a hierarchical order, which, when implemented, are responsible for completing a communication process.

If two computers on a network, which are otherwise different types of computers, have the same protocol stack stored in their memories, they can successfully communicate with each other. These two types of computers can also successfully communicate with other computers on the network, if these other computers also have the same protocol stack stored in their memories. Because not all computers use the same protocol stack to communicate, however, a computer can have more than one protocol stack stored in its memory.

The workstation's communication software is then designed to determine which protocol stack was used to create a transmission that it has received from the network. Then it passes that communication to the appropriate protocol stack stored in its own workstation memory for further processing. The opposite process is followed when the workstation sends out a transmission. The workstation communication program that handles this process for workstations on a NetWare network is the LSL.COM file.

There are several types of protocols, four of which are commonly used on NetWare networks:

- IPX
- SPX
- Internet Protocols (TCP/IP)
- AppleTalk

One of the main differences between protocols is in how they handle the transmission of packets across the network. One difference in particular is the connectionless versus connection-oriented approach to packet delivery. *Connection-oriented delivery* verifies that packets sent out across the network to another connection were successfully delivered and verifies that packets received by the connection were received. *Connectionless delivery* does not verify the delivery or receipt of packets.

Some of the protocols use connectionless delivery, and others use connection-oriented delivery. Connectionless delivery of packets is less reliable, but faster, than connection-oriented delivery because it does not wait for a notice of receipt of the packet.

IPX is a connectionless protocol, and SPX is a connection-oriented protocol. TCP/IP is an internet protocol. It can be used to cross networks through bridges, routers, and so on. TCP/IP provides connection-oriented transport. IPX/SPX and TCP/IP are frequently used on DOS-based networks.

The AppleTalk protocol provides network communication and data transmission between file servers and clients in an AppleShare network.

There are many other protocols. The IPX/SPX, TCP/IP, and AppleShare protocols are commonly found on networks, particularly NetWare networks.

Physical Transmission Characteristics

There are two primary types of transmission media used by most networks, particularly the smaller local area networks. In wide area networks, you can be a little less concerned with the type of medium. In wide area networks, you are more likely to buy media services from companies that specialize in providing these types of services or to connect to an existing network, generally the Internet. You generally have to be concerned with the two types of transmission medium used on LANs:

- Cable
- Wireless

Regardless of the type of transmission medium you use, it is designed to accomplish one task—successfully transmit packets across the network. *Packets* are electronic messages to which headers have been attached in order to make it possible for the message to be sent from, received, and understood successfully by computers on the network.

Packets can contain anything from data to requests for network services. Packets can even contain a workstation's response to a request made of it by a file server or other workstation on the network.

When a user on a network workstation requests that a file be printed on a specific network printer, for example, that request is prepared as a packet and sent by the workstation through the network board and out to the transmission medium. The transmission medium then carries it to its destination where the packet is received, decoded to reveal the request for printing services, and then processed.

The sending of the packet to the transmission medium is handled based on the type of transmission medium being used on the network. Cable is the most common type of transmission medium found on LANs.

Cable Transmission Media

There are three types of cable medium: *coaxial, twisted-pair,* and *fiber optic*. Each of these types is discussed in the following sections.

Coaxial Cable

You are probably already familiar with coaxial cable as a transmission medium. Coaxial cable contains a central core that is usually made of solid copper wire. The central core is surrounded by a tubelike structure of braided wires, metallic foil, or a combination of the two, and is called the *outer conductor*. Around the outer conductor is an insulating layer that is enclosed in a plastic encasement called a *jacket* to protect the cable from damage (see fig. B.2).

Figure B.2

Coaxial cable.

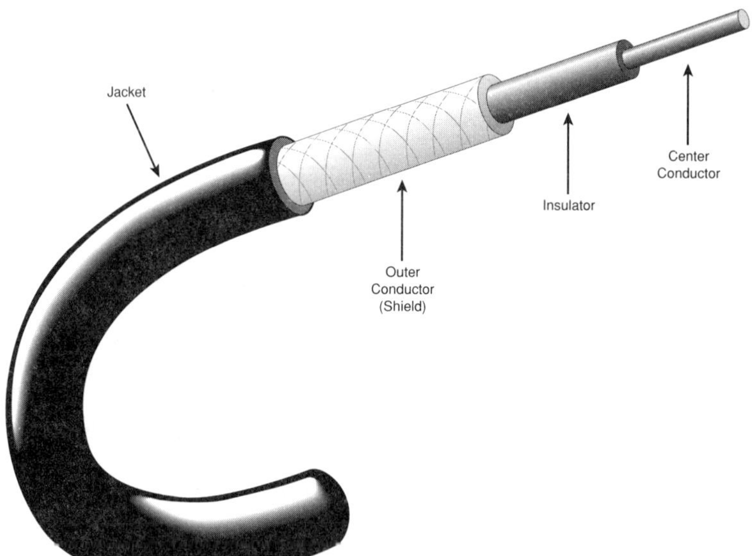

Coaxial cable is the type of cable used in homes to carry the local cable company's signal to your television set. Coaxial cables come in different types as well, defined for the amount of *impedance* (resistance in the cable as measured in ohms) that the cable carries.

For example, the type of coaxial cable used for carrying your television's cable signal is a 75-ohm, RG-59 cable. The type of coaxial cable used on a network with an Ethernet cabling system can be either a 50-ohm RG-58 cable, or a 50-ohm RG-8 or RG-11 cable. The RG-58 cable is used on networks running a thin Ethernet cabling system, and the other two are used on networks running a thick Ethernet cabling system. Arcnet cabling uses a 93-ohm, RG-62 cable.

Note The type of cabling system you use on your network is determined by the network boards you choose. Most Ethernet network boards enable you to use either thick Ethernet or thin Ethernet cabling. You must generally modify a setting on the board to choose one over the other, however.

Coaxial cable is also commonly used in LANs, because it is relatively durable and mostly affordable.

Twisted-Pair Cable

You may already be familiar with twisted-pair cabling as well. Twisted-pair cabling has been used in homes for many years to connect people by voice over the telephone. Because twisted-pair cabling is relatively low-cost and the easiest transmission medium to install, it is also one of the more frequently used transmission media.

There are two types of twisted-pair cable: *shielded* and *unshielded*. The difference is that shielded twisted-pair cable adds a layer of protection against interference in the form of a tube-like structure of braided wires, metallic foil, or a combination of the two that surrounds the insulated copper conductors. This structure is called a *shield*. To complete a shielded twisted-pair cable, a second set of twisted, insulated conductors are twisted around the first set, with the shield covering both pairs of cable and a jacket covering the shield (see fig. B.3).

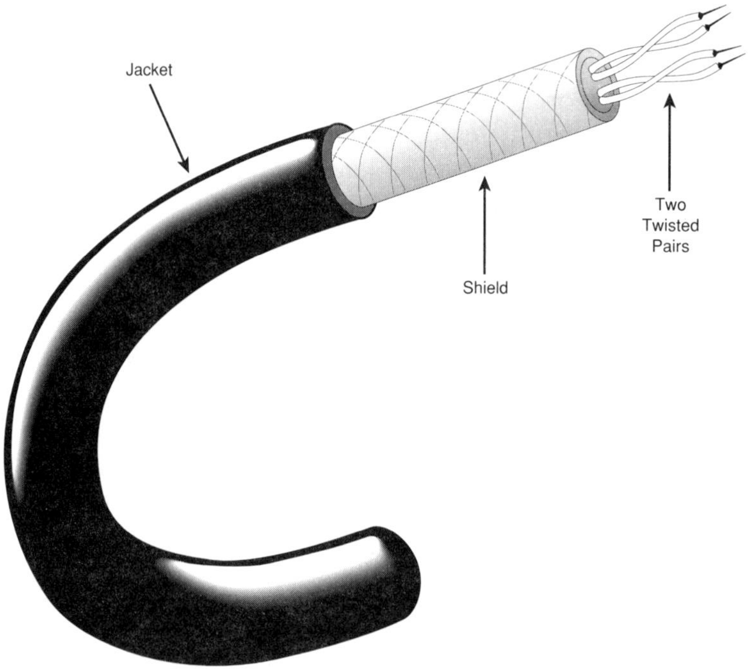

Figure B.3
Shielded twisted-pair cable.

The basic twisted-pair cable consists of two copper wires (conductors) that are covered with a jacket to form a coat of insulation. The two jacketed copper wires are then twisted around each other, much as you would twist a tie around a plastic trash bag. Next, the two pairs of twisted and jacketed copper wires are enclosed in a single cable. The unshielded twisted-pair cable does not include a shielding of braided wires, metallic foil, or a combination of the two (see fig. B.4).

Just as coaxial cable is named by its impedance as measured in ohms, twisted-pair cabling is named or categorized by its *grade*. Twisted-pair cable is available in five grades, also called *categories*, generally rated by the speed at which data can be transmitted across it.

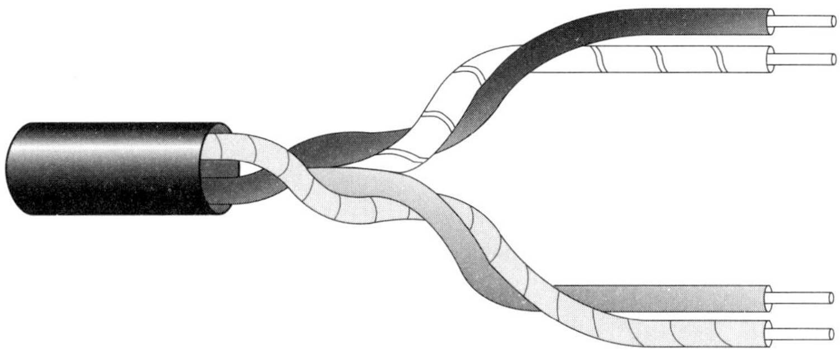

Figure B.4
Unshielded twisted-pair cable.

Categories 1 and 2 are used for voice transmission, being used originally as the standard for telephone systems. Categories 1 and 2 can handle data transmission, however, if the speed of that transmission does not exceed approximately 4 Mbps (megabytes per second).

Category 3 twisted-pair cables are used for data transmission, although this category is considered the lowest data grade transmission cable. This category of twisted-pair cable is designed to handle data transmission speeds of up to 16 Mbps.

Category 4 is a higher data grade cable. It is designed to handle data transmission speeds of up to 20 Mbps.

Category 5 twisted-pair cables are the highest category of data grade twisted-pair cable. Category 5 twisted-pair cable is designed to handle data transmission rates of up to 100 Mbps.

Fiber Optic Cables

Fiber optic cables consist of a core of multiple strands of extremely fine glass fibers, surrounded by a cladding and then by a plastic shield to protect the cladding and the glass fibers. The cladding functions somewhat like a reflector, reflecting any stray light signals back into the glass cables, thus ensuring the successful delivery of signals to their destination, without any signal loss (see fig. B.5).

Figure B.5
Fiber-optic cable.

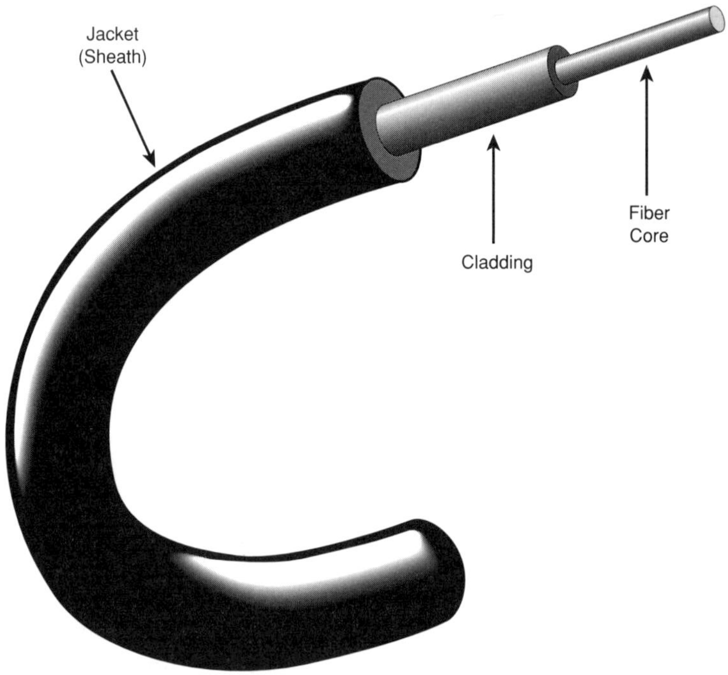

With fiber optic cables, the electric signal that goes to the cable must first be converted into a light signal and then back again into an electrical signal when the signal is delivered to its destination. Three characteristics affect the quality of fiber optic cables. Those characteristics are mode, core diameter, and cladding diameter.

The mode of a fiber optic cable defines the number of light paths the cable provides. Single mode cables provide only a single light path, and multiple mode cables provide multiple light paths. Multiple mode cables are generally of a lower quality than single mode cables. A typical use for a multiple mode cable is for a *Light Emitting Diode (LED)* such as that found on your watch. A typical use for a single mode cable is a laser.

The core diameter is the circumference of the cable. A fiber optic cable's circumference is so small that it must be measured in *microns* (millionths of a meter).

The diameter of the cladding around the fiber is another characteristic by which the quality of a fiber optic cable can be measured and thus defined. The cladding is also so small that it too must be measured in microns.

Typical fiber optic cable types include the 8.3 micron core/125 micron cladding/single-mode, the 62.5 micron core/125 micron cladding/multi-mode, the 50 micron core/125 micron cladding/multi-mode, and the 100 micron core/140 micron cladding/multi-mode cable.

Regardless of the type of cable chosen for the network—coaxial, twisted-pair, or fiber optic—the connectors used with those cables must match the type of cable exactly. This is particularly true with fiber optic cable because the fibers are so small that properly lining up the fibers becomes extremely important.

Wireless Transmission Media

There are also three common types of wireless transmission medium: *radio, microwave,* and *infrared.*

Radio

Radio transmission media include a specific range of the electromagnetic spectrum. That range is 10 KHz (kilohertz) to 1 GHz (gigahertz). Various frequencies are provided within this broad range. You are probably already familiar with some of these frequencies. They include the frequency bands known as shortwave, VHF (Very High Frequency), and UHF (Ultra High Frequency). Shortwave radios use the shortwave frequency, television and FM radios use VHF, and television uses UHF.

In order to use most of the VHF and UHF radio frequencies in the United States, you must contact the Federal Communications Committee (FCC) and have a special license for a particular frequency range within a specified geographic location assigned to you. There are some frequency ranges that are not licensed, however, and that can be used at will. The difficulty is that you may not have a clear communication channel in these frequencies because you are likely to be sharing it with such things as cordless telephones or remote control radio planes.

The type of radio transmission you choose to use can be determined at least in part by the type of antenna you must use, as well as the characteristics of the radio transmission itself. Most radio transmissions are line-of-site, thus restricting how far the transmission can be sent. Most radio transmission is limited to the horizon, or in the case of FM transmissions, a maximum of 100 miles, beyond which the signal cannot be received.

Microwave

Unlike radio signals that are restricted to line-of-site, microwave signals are restricted only by the availability of satellites and parabolic antennas, also known as satellite dishes. Satellites revolving around the earth at a distance of 22,300 miles receive microwave transmissions from a satellite dish on the ground and send them on to their destination—another satellite dish located elsewhere on the ground.

Because the satellites and parabolic antennas used to communicate with them are extremely expensive, the use of microwave as a transmission medium is also quite expensive. In addition, there is a time delay, also referred to as a *propagation delay*, associated with the use of microwaves. Because the signal has to travel 22,300 miles up to a microwave and then another 22,300 miles back down to a satellite dish, delays ranging from one-half of one second to five seconds are not uncommon. Despite these two drawbacks, however, satellite communication may be the only transmission medium available to you, particularly if you are using a mobile device, are located in a remote area, or are out at sea.

Infrared

You may also be familiar with infrared as a transmission medium. Infrared is used in your television and VCR remotes to control those devices. There are two types of infrared systems: point-to-point and broadcast.

Point-to-point infrared transmission media relay coded infrared signals from one device to another in a narrow, highly focused beam. To be successful, each device being used for infrared transmission must be carefully aligned. The signals are sent with high-powered laser devices and generally require that the receiving device is within the sending device's line of site. Point-to-point infrared transmission media can be used in many of the same situations where microwave transmission media may be used, but do not require a special license from the FCC.

Broadcast infrared transmission media do not use a highly focused narrow beam. Instead, they disperse a wide beam, the purpose of which is to make that transmission available to multiple receivers. Once a receiver picks up the transmission, it can then be sent to another receiver located where it can then send to all other receivers.

Besides the use of multiple receivers, broadcast infrared transmissions can be made without any specific receiver defined. To use this approach, sending and receiving devices must be located in the same building. Sending devices broadcast toward the ceiling of the building, which has been coated with a highly reflective material. The broadcast is then reflected back toward other devices that then receive the broadcast.

Although usable, infrared as a transmission medium is more expensive than cabling and less controllable. Thus, it is not one of the better transmission media for networking.

Network Topology and Access Control

Until now, this appendix has discussed networking and network devices in terms of using the network to transfer data and requests for services. The entire point of using a network is shared access to data and network resources. Shared access requires that some control over access to the network be exercised. Without some control over network access, packets would literally run into each other on the network. Those packets would be lost and not received; thus additional packets would be sent out to take their place. In a short period of time, no packet would be able to reach its destination anywhere on the network (a little like L.A. freeway traffic at 5:00 PM on Friday of a holiday weekend). Thus, access to the network must be controlled and organized to ensure that all workstations and file servers get their fair turn at using the network.

How network access is controlled depends on two primary issues: the network topology, and the access control method.

Network Topology

The network's topology is the physical configuration of network devices and the cabling system to which they are connected. Network topologies are named based on their shape. There are three common topologies used on most local area networks:

- Star
- Bus
- Ring

The star topology uses some type of central controller. Each network *node* (a connection point on the network to which a device such as a workstation or file server is attached) then connects directly to the central controller, which manages and controls all network communication (see fig. B.6).

In the star topology, in order for one workstation on the network to request a service of a file server, for example, the packets used to request and respond to the request for a service are both sent first to the controller, which then sends them back out to the appropriate network node.

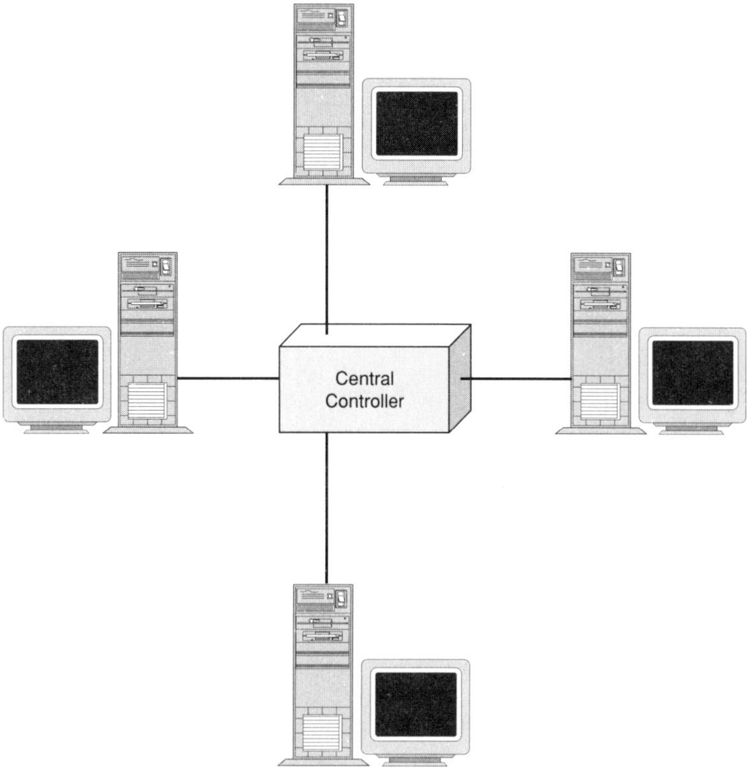

Figure B.6
Star topology.

The bus topology uses a common communication channel, to which all network nodes attach. A single coaxial cable may be used on the network (sometimes referred to as the network's backbone)—for example, as the common communication channel. The cable has a single origination point and a single end point. Throughout the network, different nodes use shorter cables to connect into the backbone, with one end of the shorter cable connected to the backbone and the other end connected to the device on the network node (see fig. B.7).

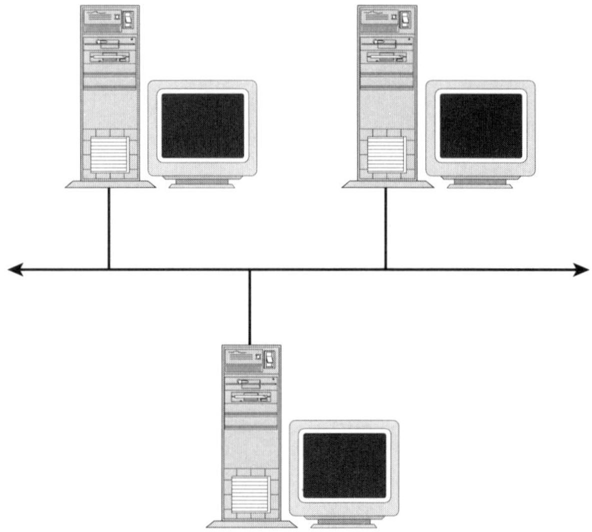

Figure B.7
Bus topology.

In the bus topology, devices send packets out to the network whenever necessary. Each packet contains an address that identifies which network node the packet is intended for (*destination address*). Each packet then visits each network node, where its destination address is checked. If the packet's destination address does not match that of the current network node's address, the packet is sent back out on the cable so that it can visit the next network node. This process is repeated until the packet reaches the network node whose address matches that shown in the packet's destination address.

The ring topology is one in which the cable has no single starting and ending point, but in which the cable forms a closed loop or ring. As with the bus topology, network devices connect to the ring through the use of shorter cables (sometimes referred to as *drop cables*), which connect at one end to the cable and at the other end to the device on the network node (see fig. B.8).

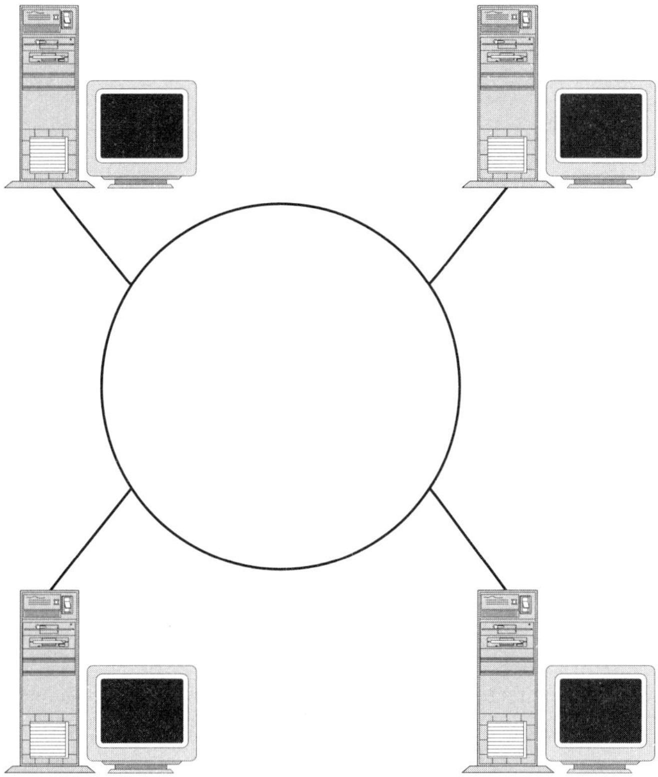

Figure B.8
Ring topology.

The ring topology is somewhat similar to the bus topology in that each node visited by a packet must determine whether the packet was intended for it. There is one major difference between the bus and ring topologies, however. The major difference is that after a network node on the ring topology receives the packet, if the node's address does not match the packet's destination address, the node returns the packet to the network at its original strength, acting as a repeater.

Although there are some variations to these three topologies, these are the three topologies commonly used on local area networks.

Access Control Methods

As mentioned previously, how network access is controlled depends on two primary issues. The second of those issues is the access control method. Access control methods are defined by where in the network the control of network access occurs. There are three access control methods:

- Random
- Distributed
- Centralized

The random method of access control enables any device connected to the network to access the network. The device simply checks to see whether access to the network is available, and when it is, sends the packet out across the network. This is the method of access control commonly used on networks that have a bus topology.

The distributed method of access control enables devices to access the network only when the device has permission to do so. Permission generally comes in the form of a ring; thus, this method is the one commonly used on networks that have a ring topology.

The centralized method of access control enables devices to access the network only when the central control device gives its permission. In this method, one device controls all transmission on the network. All devices on the network must have the central control device's permission to transmit. This is the method commonly used on networks that have a star topology.

Together, the network's topology and the method of access control used on the network help to define the network itself. They also help to define the type of network board and cabling you will use on the network. For example, networks with a bus topology use a random method to access the network. At the same time, they use a network board capable of dealing with random access, such as an Ethernet board. The use of an Ethernet board, which provides only coaxial cable connections, requires that either thin or thick coaxial cabling be used on the network. As you can see, the choices you make for one thing on the network, such as the layout of network cabling into a bus topology, can influence the decisions you make about other aspects of the network.

Network Architectures

Just as all of the pieces of a building—doorways, windows, roof shape, and so on—come together to define the architecture of that building, so too do the protocols, message formats, standards, and other pieces of a network come together to define the architecture of a network. Just as there can be many different building architectures, there also can be different network architectures.

The architecture of a network defines its overall plan. Unlike building construction, however, where the related hardware remains relatively unchanged during the construction of a building, the related hardware and software associated with a network can easily change during the development of a network. Network architectures are, therefore, more likely to change as their development progresses than building construction.

To help control some of that change, and ensure that the network meets the needs of the users for whom it was designed, some standards associated with network architecture have been developed. One example in particular includes the standards developed by the Institute of Electrical and Electronics Engineers (IEEE). The IEEE developed and proposed a set of standards that could be applied to networking software. Novell follows two of these proposed standards in its NetWare 3 and NetWare 4 operating system products: 802.3 and 802.2.

Because a variety of computer software manufacturers are active developers of network architectures, some of these companies have chosen to follow standards developed by the IEEE and others. By doing so, one manufacturer's software product can be compatible with that of another. If computer hardware manufacturers strive to develop networking equipment that fulfills the same standards as those being met by the software manufacturers, interconnectivity between hardware and software will exist. This benefits the manufacturers, because they are likely to sell more products when they have expanded their market by becoming compatible with other companies' products. This also benefits the users, because they can now mix and match hardware and software on their network.

To give companies something from which to work when designing the architecture of their networking products, the ISO has been instrumental in developing a standard from which companies could develop their own network architecture. The standard they developed has become known as the OSI model.

The OSI model defines seven layers. Each layer contains a set of functions with specific responsibilities. These are the seven layers:

- Application
- Presentation
- Session
- Transport
- Network
- Data Link
- Physical

The Application layer defines functions that handle the transmission of bit streams across a specific physical transmission medium. It is primarily concerned with the transfer of electrical signals between two computers.

The Presentation layer defines functions that handle how information is to be presented to network users. Its goal is to ensure that information presented to network users is done in a way that is meaningful to that user.

The Session layer defines functions that handle the dialog that occurs between users on the network. It also defines functions that deal with the organization and synchronization of user dialogs and data exchange, the most important aspect of which is controlling when users can send and receive across the network.

The Transport layer defines functions that regulate the level of quality of data transfer between two network nodes. Its main function is to choose the level of quality of communication and then ensure that level of quality is maintained.

The Network layer defines functions that route data from one network node to another. It provides functions related to establishing, maintaining, and ending the network connection between two users and for transferring data along that connection as long as it exists.

The Data Link layer defines functions that enable data transmission from one node to another to be reliable. In addition, this layer defines functions that shield the other layers of the OSI model from any concerns related to the physical transmission medium itself.

The Physical layer defines functions that are responsible for the transmission between network connections of electrical signals across a transmission medium.

Various networking software developers follow the OSI model in some way, although they rarely follow it exactly. For example, IBM has defined it as *Systems Network Architecture (SNA)*. SNA was designed primarily for use in a mainframe environment, however, rather than in a PC-based network. IBM's SNA architecture also uses seven layers, but it names and orders some of them differently than does the OSI model.

The fact that IBM's SNA architecture varies from that defined by the OSI model is perfectly acceptable. The OSI model is just that, a model to follow when building a networking architecture. It is not, however, cast in stone. The OSI model will not always fulfill a manufacturer's needs; thus it would be ridiculous to insist that the model be followed exactly. This is particularly true if the mode does not continue to provide the user with the best possible service on the network.

Network Operating Systems

Following standards to design a network operating system that is compatible with other PC products is an important step in developing a network operating system. This approach helps to ensure that all network users' needs are met; but users' needs vary, and thus so do the available network operating systems.

This book introduced you to one of Novell's operating systems—NetWare 4. Although Novell holds over 60 percent of the market share in networking software, it does it by selling different versions of its NetWare operating system. NetWare 3.12, a bindery-based network operating system, and NetWare 4, a hierarchical database network operating system, account for the market share, even though both operating systems serve a different group of users. Novell's two network operating systems implement standards defined in the IEEE 802.2 and 802.3 standards.

Other network operating systems, such as IBM's PC network, exist as well. IBM's PC network operating system implements standards defined in the IEEE 802.3 standards. Other network operating systems include Banyan Vines, Lantastics LAN Manager, and Microsoft's Workgroup for Windows.

There is no doubt that there is a variety of network operating systems available on the market, but all of those operating systems have one thing in common—providing shared access to resources for multiple users across a definable geographic boundary, even if that boundary encompasses the world.

Summary

Understanding how networking successfully provides communication among personal computers is much easier once you understand each of the individual aspects of networking, which make it all possible. To understand networking, therefore, you need to understand several basic networking concepts. You need to understand the three primary issues associated with networking in order to understand how networks function.

The first issue you need to understand is how PCs are designed and function and thus how they are physically connected together (network boards and cabling). Next, you need to know how the correct software loaded into memory on each workstation controls the communication between workstation and network. Finally, you need to understand how the network operating system provides network services.

In addition to understanding these three basic features of networks that enable the communication and sharing of resources, you also need to have a better understanding of related issues. The first of those related issues involves the characteristics of the physical transmission of information and data across a network.

The next issue to understand is the physical network configuration and methods used by devices connected to network nodes to access the network. Then you must also understand basic network architecture, because network access is affected by the network's architecture.

Finally, you need a basic understanding of some of the types of network operating systems. This enables you to see that there is more than one way to implement networking, even if Novell holds over 60 percent of the networking software market.

Understanding how networking functions, regardless of whose network operating system you are using, will help you better understand the benefits and uses of the network operating system you have chosen to use.

Appendix C

Introduction to NetWare Directory Services (NDS)

Versions of the NetWare operating system that were developed and sold before NetWare 4 stored network-related information—such as the users on the network, their password requirements, and even their passwords—in files, which together constitute the NetWare bindery. The NetWare bindery was a flat database; all information contained within the database had the same level or stature within the database. No items of information were subordinate to or superior to any other items of information.

In versions of NetWare before NetWare 4, the bindery is the one thing that all versions of NetWare had in common. In NetWare 4, there is no bindery. NetWare 4 does have a database, however. That database has a hierarchical structure, with subordinate and superior levels. This hierarchical database is called the NetWare directory tree.

The NetWare 4 database (directory tree) is part of the overall concept applied to networking with NetWare 4. This concept is referred to as NetWare Directory Services (NDS). After reading this appendix you should have a basic understanding of the following:

- NDS and the NetWare directory tree
- Objects within the directory tree
- Partitioning
- Replication
- Time synchronization

An understanding of these five topics as they relate to NetWare 4 will give you a good understanding of NetWare 4 itself.

Understanding NDS and the NetWare Directory Tree

NDS is a technology that provides global access to all resources on the network. It does not matter where the resources are physically located. A user on a workstation in Japan that is connected to the same NetWare directory tree as a printer in Canada, for example, can send a print job to the printer in Canada with almost no more effort than it would take to send that same print job to a printer physically located in the room next door.

Unlike NetWare 3.12 and earlier NetWare versions, users do not log in to a specific file server in a NetWare 4 network. Instead, users log in to the directory tree itself. Users still need access to the login directory and the files contained on a NetWare file server, but it does not matter which file server in the directory tree contains the login directory and files.

Note There is one exception to the requirement for logging in to the directory tree. The login files that are accessed in order to log a user into the network are stored on NetWare 4 file servers. The information about the user's object contained with a section (partition) of the NDS database, therefore, must also be stored on the file server that the user accesses for network login. (Partitions are discussed in detail later in this appendix.)

NetWare Directory Services, and thus the NetWare directory tree, is designed to meet international standards developed by the Institute of Electrical and Electronic Engineers (IEEE). These standards help ensure that a standard method of organizing information on a network that is accessed globally will be followed by companies developing networking technologies. This standard method of organization is a hierarchical arrangement, thus creating a structure with both subordinate and superior levels (see fig. C.1).

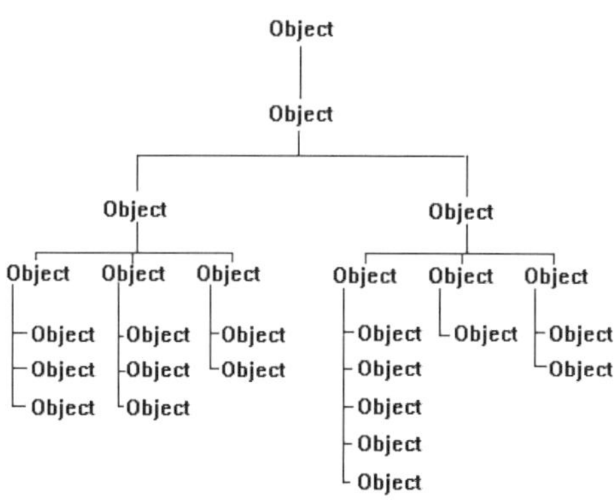

Figure C.1
Hierarchical nature of the NetWare directory tree.

This standard, which specifies, among other things, that objects within the tree are to be organized in a hierarchical arrangement, is known as the X.500 specification. In the X.500 specification, other additional requirements for designing global networks are also specified. Rules that define how a directory tree is to be constructed for a global network (*the directory schema*), for example, are also included in the X.500 specification.

The directory schema for NetWare 4 includes the following information:

- How additional information associated with an object in the directory tree can be specified. This information is called *attribute information*, and it specifies the constraints to be applied and the syntax that must be followed when defining what values can be associated with an object in the directory tree.
- How objects at lower levels of the directory tree receive rights to other objects in the directory tree. This flow of rights through the directory tree structure is called *inheritance*.
- How objects within the directory tree structure are to be named. These are known as the *naming rules* or conventions for directory tree objects.
- How the location of an object within the directory tree affects and thus determines the object's *subordination* to other objects within the directory tree.

Every item contained within the NetWare directory tree is called an *object*. You can get a better understanding of NDS and the directory tree by first understanding the objects that can be placed into the directory tree.

Understanding Objects in NDS

Objects can represent physical resources on a network, such as a printer or file server, or they can represent logical resources on a network, such as groups and computers.

There are three types of objects that the NDS database can contain:

- [Root]
- Container
- Leaf

Although there is only one [Root] object, there are different types of container and leaf objects. The [Root] object and container and leaf objects are discussed in the following sections.

The [Root] Object

The [Root] object is the top of the directory tree. Only one [Root] object can exist in a directory tree. The [Root] object is usually named for the company to which the directory tree belongs. The [Root] object is created at the time the first NetWare 4 file server is migrated or installed, and the directory tree is created. NDS creates the [Root] object. No network user can remove the [Root] object from the directory tree.

Container Objects

Container objects are any objects on the directory tree besides [Root] (although it technically is a container object because it contains all other directory tree objects) that contain or hold other objects. There are actually four types of container objects, although one of those objects (Locality) is not installed by default when you install NetWare 4 and create your directory tree:

- Country (C)
- Organization (O)
- Organizational Unit (OU)
- Locality (L)

Country objects are placed at the top of the directory tree, immediately below the [Root] object. This is the only location in the directory tree where a Country object can be placed. The Country object was developed to meet the X.500 specifications and to provide a container object that would enable you to divide your directory tree based on the country in which your network's physical and logical resources were located. Because using the Country object in the directory tree adds another level to the directory tree structure that users and NDS must then navigate, Novell does not recommend the use of a Country object unless a company has a real need to use it.

Organization objects are container objects that are designed primarily to help organize other objects within the directory tree and to simplify the assigning of rights to all other objects within the tree. The Organization object must be located directly below the [Root] object or directly below a Country or Locality object. An Organization object can never be placed below an Organizational Unit object. Every directory tree must have at least one Organization object.

The Organizational Unit object is also a container object designed to help you organize the directory tree, but primarily to organize leaf objects within the directory tree. The Organizational Unit objects can be located only below Organization objects, or other Organization Unit objects. (If it helps, think of Organizational Unit objects as being similar to directories and subdirectories such as you find in the directory structure on a DOS-based PC.) You can have multiple Organizational Unit objects in the directory tree.

The Locality object is used to designate where a section of the network physically resides and to organize other objects within that section of the network. Locality objects can be placed below the [Root] or below Country, Organization, or Organizational Unit objects. Locality objects are created at the time you install NetWare 4.

Leaf Objects

Leaf objects are any objects within the directory tree structure that cannot contain other object types, although they may have other objects associated with them. This description of a leaf object is sometimes confusing, but is best cleared up through the use of an example.

A Group object, for example, is a leaf object because you cannot position another object below it (subordinate an object to it) in the directory tree. The Group object is not responsible for or superior to any other object in the directory tree. Leaf objects are the lowest level in the directory tree. The Group object, as well as other leaf objects, cannot be used to organize any part of the directory tree.

A Group object can, however, have other objects associated with it. Most commonly, other objects associated with a Group object are User objects. User objects are generally associated with Group objects because this association is intended to combine two or more users on the network into a logical arrangement. That logical arrangement of User objects then makes it possible to give special consideration to more than one User object at a time. For example, by granting specific rights to a Group object, all User objects associated with that Group object also receive those rights.

There are 17 types of leaf objects that you can create, thus placing them into the NDS directory tree. Those 17 types of leaf objects are shown and described in table C.1.

Table C.1
NDS Directory Tree Leaf Objects

Leaf Object Name	*Description of Leaf Object*
AFP Server	File server running the AppleTalk Filing Protocol (AFP)
Alias	Pointer to a different object located elsewhere in the NDS tree

continues

Table C.1, Continued
NDS Directory Tree Leaf Objects

Leaf Object Name	*Description of Leaf Object*
Computer	Information about a network computer, such as its brand, serial number, and so on, but not an actual computer on the network
Directory Map	Similar to a mapped network drive; contains a path that points to a specific directory on a network volume
Distribution List	List of User and Group objects that can receive electronic mail
External Entity	Any non-NDS object that has been imported into the NDS database
Group	List of users who require the same rights assignment
Message Routing Group	Group of messaging servers with the capability of transfering messages among themselves
Messaging Server	Server residing on a NetWare 4 file server used to handle messaging between users and groups on the network
NetWare Server	NetWare 2.1*x*, 3.1*x*, or 4.*x* file server
Organizational Role	Job responsibility or position to which different users can be assigned in succession
Print Queue	Network print queue
Print Server	Network print server
Printer	Network printer
Profile	Common login script assigned to one or more network users requiring common access to network resources

Leaf Object Name	*Description of Leaf Object*
User	User with an assigned user name and associated Property and Object rights
Volume	Volume on a NetWare file server

Figure C.2 shows you what an NDS directory tree might look like if each type of container object and some leaf objects were included in the directory tree.

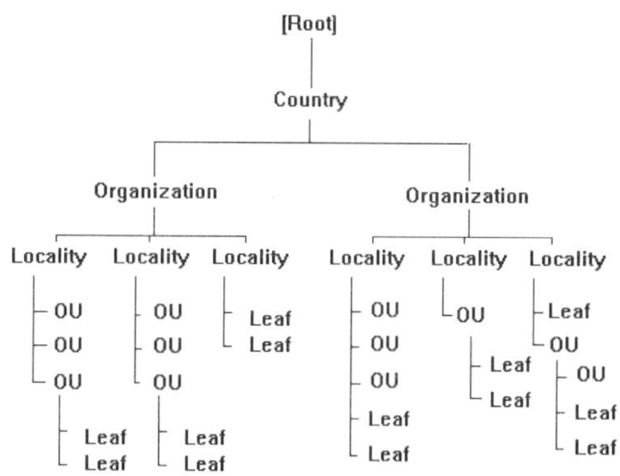

Figure C.2
Directory tree with all types of container objects.

Regardless of the size of your NDS tree, it can contain any or all of these types of objects. Regardless of the size of your directory tree, it must contain one or more partitions.

Understanding Partitioning

Directory tree objects are stored in the NDS database, but they are arranged in a logical hierarchical order within the directory tree. Sections of the directory tree can be designated by a process known as partitioning. Partitioning the directory tree enables you to divide the database into smaller units for storage on different NetWare 4 file servers. Partitioning the directory tree accomplishes two things in particular.

First, it makes it possible to store smaller portions of the database on file servers where access to those portions will most often be needed. Second, it provides fault tolerance for the network, preventing the loss of a single file server on the network from making the directory tree inaccessible.

A partition is a logical division of the NDS tree; a copy of that logical division must be placed on a NetWare 4 file server somewhere within the directory tree (see fig. C.3). That copy of the partition contains only information about the objects contained within that section of the NDS tree. No file system information or any of the directories or files the file system contains are included in the information that is stored about a partition.

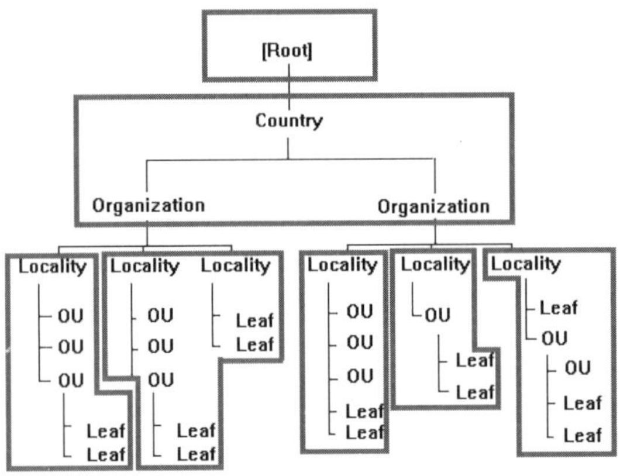

Figure C.3
Pictorial representation of directory tree partitioning.

Because a partition is a logical division of the NDS tree that must be stored on a NetWare 4 file server, and thus ensure network fault tolerance, more than one copy of a partition can and must exist on the network. Each copy of any given partition must be stored on a different file server. No NetWare 4 file server can store two copies of the same partition. Copies of directory tree partitions are called replicas.

Understanding Replication

In NDS, replication is the process as well as the result of making copies of partitions of the NDS database. There are three types of replicas:

- Master
- Read/Write
- Read Only

Note The list of all servers that have a replica of a specific partition is called the *replica ring*. It is maintained by each file server and can communicate with other servers in the ring. This communication ensures that changes made to the directory's partition strategy are updated to each replica located on all file servers included in the replica ring for that specific partition.

The Master replica is the first copy of a partition. It is created when a partition is created. There can only be one Master replica for each partition. The Master replica can be used by network users to log in to the network, as well as for splitting or merging network partitions. By default, the Master replica is stored on the same file server where the partition itself was created.

Read/Write replicas are copies of a partition that can be modified or, if necessary, used to replace the Master partition should it become corrupted. Read/Write replicas can be accessed for network login, but they cannot be used to merge or split a partition.

Read Only replicas are also copies of the partition. However, they cannot be used for anything other than searching, because they are not writable replicas as are the Master and Read/Write replicas. Because they are not writable replicas, Read Only replicas cannot be opened and written to during the login process. Because login requires this capability, it cannot use Read Only replicas to log a user into the directory tree.

Certain default configurations exist for replicas:

- The [Root] and first Organization are created as a sole partition and are automatically replicated to ensure that the first NetWare 4 file server created receives the Master copy of the replica.
- The second and third NetWare 4 file servers created on the network receive Read/Write replicas of the first partition.
- When a second partition is created, the file server on which it resides receives the Master replica of that partition. No other replicas are created by default. To have additional replicas of a second partition, they must be created by a network administrator or some other user who has rights to create replicas.

Replicas of the NDS database must be synchronized with each other so that all information about the database and its objects is the same for all replicas of each partition. Maintaining or synchronizing replicas is a process that NDS performs automatically in the background—thus not interfering with daily network operations.

The synchronization process occurs at regular intervals. By default, synchronization occurs at 10-second intervals. During synchronization, replica information is collected and sent out across the network to those file servers containing affected replicas.

Note One exception to this 10-second synchronization process is the change associated with user login. User login-related information is collected and sent out only every five minutes. Because user login information is temporary, lasting only as long as the user is logged in to the network, lengthening the time between synchronization for this type of network replica change is done to help reduce network traffic.

The synchronization of replicas is not the only synchronization that occurs on the network. Time is also synchronized.

Understanding Time Synchronization

Each object and transaction on the network is given a time and a date stamp. Time and date stamping is used to ensure that network transactions are processed in the order in which the administrator performed them.

All network services and NDS depend on network time synchronization. Each NetWare server, therefore, must be set up so that time synchronization can occur.

Network file servers can be either time providers or time users. Time providers fall into one of four categories:

- Primary time servers, which poll other time servers to determine the network time. Primary time servers can poll Reference time servers or other Primary time servers.
- Reference time servers, which also poll other time servers. Reference time servers must have at least one other server on the network that is a time provider.
- Single Reference time servers, which are the default type of time server used on a network. When a single time server exists, all other time servers must be secondary servers. The Single Reference time server obtains its time from either the computer's hardware clock or from an external source, then provides time to Secondary time servers and network clients, but never polls or negotiates network time.

- Secondary time servers, which synchronize with Reference time servers and accept as true whatever time the reference server tells them is the network time.

Time synchronization is accomplished through one of two methods: Service Advertising Protocol (SAP), which is the default method, or custom configuration. The SAP method is the easier of the two methods to implement because it does not have to be reconfigured for each server added to the network. The SAP method does, however, generate network traffic and, if the time synchronization has to occur across a WAN, the second method—custom configuration—is generally more appropriate.

The custom configuration method enables you to specify what type of time server each file server will be, and then specify which time server any of the other time servers must access in order to negotiate or poll for time. Custom configuration gives you complete control of time synchronization, thus enabling you to optimize network traffic and provide alternative time sources in the event of a failure. This method is time-consuming when it comes to planning, but relatively easy to maintain once the network is established.

Using custom configuration requires that you follow certain rules:

- Secondary servers cannot be synchronized with other secondary servers.
- Time sources should be limited to limit network traffic.
- Local time providers should be created whenever possible to avoid crossing the WAN to synchronize network time.

Figure C.4 shows a functional arrangement for time servers on a wide area network, which is used in place of the default of a sole Single Reference server and multiple secondary servers.

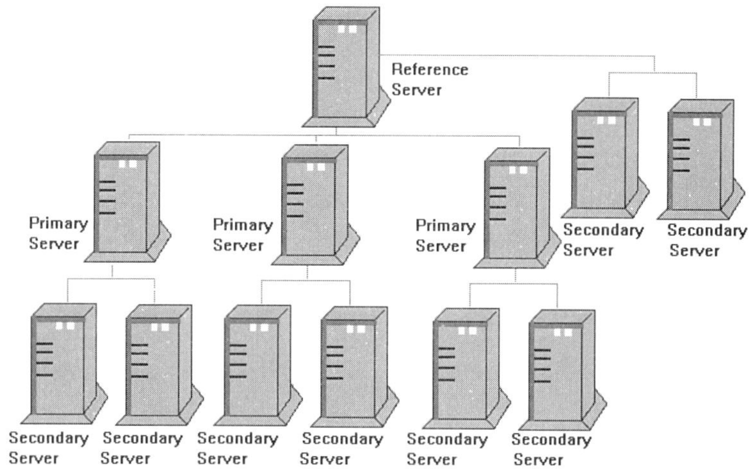

Figure C.4
Example of using a customized time server configuration.

Summary

NetWare Directory Services is the heart and soul of NetWare 4. NDS makes possible global network access and the sharing of network resources across geographic boundaries.

Because of NDS's extensive capabilities, it is also rather complex. Understanding NDS, therefore, can be a little difficult. If you understand the basic aspects of NDS—the NetWare directory tree, directory tree objects, partitioning, replication, and time synchronization—you will, however, have a pretty good grasp of NDS.

Bibliography

B

Bibliography Bibliography Bibliography Bibliography

Concepts: Novell NetWare 4. Provo: Novell, Inc., 1994.

Introduction to NetWare Directory Services. Provo: Novell, Inc., 1994.

NetWare Client for DOS and MS Windows User Guide. Provo: Novell, Inc., 1993-1994.

NetWare 4.1 Design and Implementation Instructor's Guide. Rev. 1.0. Provo: Novell, Inc., 1995.

Ayer, Steve, and Frank Patrinostro. *Documenting the Software Development Process*. New York: McGraw-Hill, Inc., 1992.

Cady, Dorothy, Drew Heywood, Debra Niedermiller-Chaffins, and Cheryl Wilhite. *Networking Technologies, Second Edition*. Indianapolis: New Riders Publishing, 1994.

Casady, Ph.D., Mona J., and Dorothy C. Sandburg. *Word/Information Processing: A System Approach*. Cincinnati: South-Western Publishing Co., 1985.

Cassel, Don. *The Structured Alternative: Program Design, Style, and Debugging*. Reston: Reston Publishing Co., Inc. A Prentice-Hall Company, 1983.

Collins, Garfield, and Gillian Blay. *Structured Systems Development Techniques: Strategic Planning to System Testing*. New York: John Wiley & Sons, 1982.

Davis, William S. *Computers and Business Information Processing*. Reading: Addison-Wesley Publishing Company, 1981.

Elliott, Orville C., and Robert S. Wasley. *Business Information Processing Systems*. Fourth edition. Homewood: Richard D. Irwin, Inc., 1975.

Hughes, Jeffrey F., and Blair W. Thomas. *QuickPath to NetWare 4.1 Networks*. Alameda: Sybex Inc., 1995.

Kuo, Peter, and Jim Henderson. *NDS Troubleshooting*. Indianapolis: New Riders Publishing, 1995.

Leathrum, J. F. *Foundations of Software Design*. Reston: Reston Publishing Co., Inc. A Prentice-Hall Company, 1983.

Mair, William C., Donald R. Wood, and Keagle W. Davis. *Computer Control & Audit*. Alamonte Springs: The Institute of Internal Auditors, Inc., 1978.

Martin, James, with Kathleen Kavanagh Chapman and The ARBEN Group, Inc. *Local Area Networks: Architectures and Implementations*. Englewood Cliffs: Prentice Hall, 1989.

Siyan, Karanjit. *NetWare 4 Update*. Indianapolis: New Riders Publishing, 1994.

Weiss, Alan. *Million Dollar Consulting: The Professional's Guide to Growing a Practice*. New York: McGraw-Hill, Inc., 1992.

Yourdon, Edward. *Managing the System Life Cycle*. New York: Yourdon Press, 1982.

Index

Index Index Index Index Index Index Index

A

B-C

D

E-F-G

H-I-J

L

M

N

O

P

Q-R

S

T

U

V

W

X

REGISTRATION CARD

NetWare 4 Network Design and Implementation

Name ______________________ Title ______________________

Company ______________________ Type of business ______________________

Address ______________________

City/State/ZIP ______________________

Have you used these types of books before? ☐ yes ☐ no

If yes, which ones? ______________________

____

How many computer books do you purchase each year? ☐ 1–5 ☐ 6 or more

How did you learn about this book? ______________________

Where did you purchase this book? ______________________

Which applications do you currently use? ______________________

____

Which computer magazines do you subscribe to? ______________________

____

What trade shows do you attend? ______________________

____

Comments: ______________________

____

____

Would you like to be placed on our preferred mailing list? ☐ yes ☐ no

☐ **I would like to see my name in print!** You may use my name and quote me in future New Riders products and promotions. My daytime phone number is: ______________________

New Riders Publishing 201 West 103rd Street ◆ Indianapolis, Indiana 46290 USA

Fax to **317-581-4670**

Fold Here

NO POSTAGE
NECESSARY
IF MAILED
IN THE
UNITED STATES

BUSINESS REPLY MAIL

FIRST-CLASS MAIL PERMIT NO. 9918 INDIANAPOLIS IN

POSTAGE WILL BE PAID BY THE ADDRESSEE

NEW RIDERS PUBLISHING
201 W 103RD ST
INDIANAPOLIS IN 46290-9058